Tortilleras

Hispanic and U.S. Latina Lesbian Expression

Tortilleras

Hispanic and U.S. Latina Lesbian Expression

EDITED BY

Lourdes Torres and
Inmaculada Pertusa

TEMPLE UNIVERSITY PRESS

PHILADELPHIA

Temple University Press, Philadelphia 19122
Copyright © 2003 by Temple University
All rights reserved
Published 2003

Printed in the United States of America

The paper used in this publication meets the requirements of the American National Standard for Information Sciences—Permanence of Paper for Printed Library Materials, ANSI Z39.48-1984.

Library of Congress Cataloging-in-Publication Data

Tortilleras : Hispanic and U.S. Latina lesbian expression / edited by Lourdes Torres and Inmaculada Pertusa.
    p. cm.
  Includes bibliographical references.
    ISBN 1-59213-006-2 (cloth : alk. paper) — ISBN 1-59213-007-0 (pbk. : alk. paper)
    1. Lesbians' writings, Spanish American—History and criticism.   2. Lesbians' writings, Spanish—History and criticism.   3. Lesbians' writings, American—History and criticism.   4. Spanish American literature—Women authors—History and criticism.   5. Spanish American literature—20th century—History and criticism.   6. American literature—Hispanic American authors—History and criticism.   7. Spanish literature—Women authors—History and criticism. 8. Hispanic American lesbians—Intellectual life.   9. Hispanic American women in literature.   10. Lesbians in literature.   I. Torres, Lourdes, 1959–   II. Pertusa, Inmaculada, 1963–

PQ7081.5 .T68 2003
860.9'9206643'098—dc21   2002073203

Excerpts of poetry by Luz María Umpierre (p. 50 herein) are reprinted from *The Margarita Poems* by permission of Luz María Umpierre.

Excerpts from "Milk of Amnesia" by Carmelita Tropicana (pp. 150–56 herein), originally published in *Latinas on Stage* (Berkeley: Third Woman Press, 1999), copyright © 1995, are reprinted by permission of Third Woman Press.

Excerpts from "Toma de nombre/Talking of Name" by Miriam Bornstein-Gómez (p. 199 herein) are reprinted by permission of Miriam Bornstein-Gómez.

Excerpts from Cherríe Moraga, *Loving in the War Years: Lo que nunca pasó por sus labios* (Boston: South End Press, 1983) (p. 203 herein) are reprinted by permission of South End Press and Cherríe Moraga.

Excerpts (pp. 204–7 herein) from *Borderlands/La Frontera: The New Mestiza*. Copyright © 1987, 1999 by Gloria Anzaldúa. Reprinted by permission of Aunt Lute Books.

Excerpts (p. 264 herein) from "The Marimacha's Tale" by Gloria Anzaldúa are reprinted by permission of the author.

2 4 6 8 9 7 5 3 1

Contents

Part III: Sites of Resistance

Part IV: Racialized Lesbianisms

Acknowledgments

Lourdes Torres thanks Ann Russo, Sherry Velasco, and Alba Jo Torres for their feedback and support throughout the completion of this project. Many thanks also to Robyn Epstein for her efficient editorial help and for taking Alba Jo out on walks.

Inma Pertusa thanks Melissa Stewart for her unconditional support and unrequested patience. She was there every time.

Lourdes Torres

Introduction

Radical new Latina lesbian representations emerged in the 1980s with the rise of a Third World women's movement and the publication of texts such as *This Bridge Called My Back, Loving in the War Years, Borderlands/La Frontera: The New Mestiza,* and *Compañeras: Latina Lesbians.*[1] Until that time, depictions of Latinas in both mainstream Anglo and Latino/a popular culture were limited primarily to a constant rehashing of trite, outdated, heterobiased roles. This new body of work boldly challenged the virtual absence of Latina lesbian representations and created an impetus for the emergence of Latina lesbian political, creative, and scholarly works in various genres.

These new, specifically lesbian representations created a space not only for Latina lesbians, but also for Latino gay men, as well as for progressive Latina women who had felt ignored and underrepresented in both mainstream and Latino popular culture. Interestingly, this is one of the rare instances in which lesbians rather than gay men were the first to achieve public visibility in a cultural context. While Latina lesbians do not identify themselves exclusively on the basis of sexuality, choosing rather to foreground the multiple dimensions of their racial, class, and sexual experience, their relatively open, lesbian visibility positions them in sharp contrast to lesbians in Spain and Latin America, who for the most part have not assumed a highly visible public presence.

Historically, lesbianism in Latin America and Spain has emerged in a veiled or ambiguous manner in political, cultural, and literary life. However, transgressive female sexuality seems always to have existed, as is evident in the number of conference papers, articles, and books that now explore female same-sex desire in a variety of historical and social contexts in Europe and Latin America. For example, there has been a recent proliferation of studies of female sexuality in early modern Spain, an era when one might not expect to find much evidence of female same-sex desire, especially given that some recent critics argue that lesbianism as an identity category did not exist before the nineteenth century. A new generation of readers armed with novel and traditional critical tools is discovering evidence of female homoeroticism in sixteenth- and seventeenth-century Spanish legal, medical, literary, political, and religious discourses.[2] In fact, in an overview of non-heterosexual desire in this time period, the historian Louis Compton remarks that Golden Age Spaniards were specialists on lesbianism.[3]

Perhaps what began as the questioning of transgressive gender categories in scholarly research has led to the exploration of transgressive desire in seemly improbable places and time periods. Likewise, in the Latin American context we have witnessed contentious debates over the sexuality of two Latin American icons from different time periods: the colonial Mexican Sor Juana Inés de la Cruz and the Chilean Nobel Prize-winner Gabriela Mistral. These stimulating controversies have opened the door to lesbian readings of canonical and non-canonical texts in the past decades, as gay and lesbian Hispanists have attempted to overcome the "homosexual panic" of earlier critics and begun to explore transgressive sexuality in a variety of sites.[4]

By the end of the twentieth century, a previously silenced subject, lesbian and gay Hispanic writing, came out of the closet. With collections such as *Entiendes: Queer Readings, Hispanic Writings* (1995), *Hispanisms and Homosexualities* (1998), *Queer Iberia: Crossing Cultures, Crossing Sexualities* (1999), *Reading and Writing the Ambiente: Queer Sexualities in Latino, Latin American, and Spanish Culture* (2000), *and Lesbianism and Homosexuality in Spanish Golden Age Literature and Society* (2000),[5] the study of queer writing by "Hispanic" writers from Europe to Latin America and the United States emerged as a field (described by Silvia Molloy as "homosexual Hispanisms") worthy of serious scholarly attention.[6] Given the tradition of heterobiased conservatism prevalent in Hispanic studies, these anthologies are particularly groundbreaking. Although the broad category of homosexual Hispanisms includes lesbian studies, most anthologies in fact tend to focus the majority of their essays on male homosexualities; as a result, about one-quarter of the articles in the collections mentioned feature female same-sex desire, and even fewer study Latina lesbians. Ironically, one of the most balanced anthologies, *Lesbianism and Homosexuality in Spanish Golden Age Literature and Society,* studies transgressive sexuality during the early modern period, when lesbian desire was believed to be invisible and, for some, nonexistent or even anachronistic.

The imbalance is not limited to these anthologies. It is found in most collections that deal with homosexuality in Spain and Latin America. For example, the source book *Spanish Writers on Gay and Lesbian Themes* contains entries about sixty writers who are either identified as homosexual or write on homosexual themes.[7] Of these, only thirteen refer to writers who address lesbian themes. One explanation frequently offered for this inequity is the lack of both lesbian writing and critical work on literary representations of female same-sex desire. In his introduction to *Spanish Writers on Gay and Lesbian Themes,* for example, Daniel Eisenberg provides a historical overview of homosexuality in Spain from prehistory to the present that dedicates only four paragraphs in twenty pages to lesbian writing in Spain. He explains that "female homosexuality is largely exempt, and thus little is known about it."[8] Similarly, in David Foster's *Gay and Lesbian Themes in Latin American Writing,* only five of thirty-five novels examined address lesbian themes.[9] Foster laments this imbalance and suggests that "lesbian interests have yet to be as consistently thematized as male homosexual ones have."[10]

Unfortunately, even in contexts in which lesbian writing is available and in which studies on lesbian same-sex desire are in circulation, anthologies that present critical essays on lesbian and homosexual men's writing still tend to privilege male homosexuality. For example, unlike the peninsular and Latin American case, U.S. Latina lesbians in the past two decades have been much more visible and have published more extensively than Latino gay writers in both creative and critical venues. However, in the one Latino/a gay and lesbian collection now available, *Chicano/Latino Homoerotic Identities,* only six of the sixteen critical studies deal with lesbian sexualities.[11] Such a pattern of marginalization within this emerging field needs to be examined. We might bear in mind that the study of homosexualities in Spanish, Latin American, and Latino/a literatures is a new intervention, and that many of the initial studies in this exciting field focus on same-sex desire in canonized works. Because women, particularly lesbians, are so poorly represented in the literary canon, it is not surprising that scholarly studies of their work have not been at the foreground of this nascent field.

Although the recent anthologies strive to be inclusive, their generalized introductions to gay and lesbian history or studies tend to refer almost exclusively to male homosexualities. Because of the relative scarcity of texts documenting lesbian history, women tend to be rendered invisible or marginalized in works that seek to represent both gay male and lesbian writing. *Tortilleras: Hispanic and U.S. Latina Lesbian Expression,* the first anthology to focus exclusively on queer readings of Spanish, Latin American, and U.S. Latina lesbian literature and culture, begins to address the notable underrepresentation and marginalization of lesbians. A separate study examining lesbians in Hispanic literature is perhaps a necessary step, given that lesbian cultural history in many significant ways has evolved differently from that of male homosexuals and cannot always be collapsed under the same rubric. Because men's and women's experiences are structurally different in all societies, and political and cultural contexts shape and condition sexuality in particular ways for men and women, conflating lesbian and gay homosexualities can be problematic. Subsuming the study of lesbians under a general homosexual umbrella often erases the gender hierarchy and gender ideologies inherent in most societies and thus renders lesbians less visible.

It is certainly true that, given the historical tendency to focus on men's sexuality, studies of women's same-sex desire are less available; consequently, there is a tendency to conflate the male homosexual and lesbian practices and histories. However, by positing analogous practices or meanings for male and female same-sex desire, well-intentioned studies run the risk of undertheorizing and underanalyzing lesbian identities and practices. Although there may be good reasons for presenting a unified trajectory of lesbian and gay histories, at this juncture, as more and more studies focusing on women become available, insights can be gained by separating the histories and focusing exclusively on female same-sex desire. *Tortilleras: Hispanic and U.S. Latina Lesbian Expression* thus brings to the forefront essays on Spanish, Latin American, and Latina lesbianisms in the spirit of encouraging more studies in this area.

Another problem emerges, however, when one assumes that lesbian practices are the same, or have the same meaning, in all historical, political, and geographic contexts. As Evelyn Blackwood and Saskia Wieringa document in their collection *Female Desires: Same-Sex Relations and Transgender Practices across Cultures,* sexual acts, patterns of behavior, and the meanings attributed to these vary according to historical moment and sociocultural context.[12] In this collection, it is not surprising to see that, in sites where dictatorships and right-wing governments rule, possibilities for lesbian expression may be limited, and expressions of same-sex desire may take a different form than in places where such expression entails less risk. Latina lesbians in the context of the United States have been able to express same-sex desire more openly than lesbians living in some Latin American counties, where openly gay and lesbian people are routinely subjected to state and police violence.

Lesbianisms thus merit their own investigation in each sociocultural context. Yet this still raises a question about including in one collection studies of female same-sex desire in Spanish, Latin American, and U.S. Latina contexts. The field of Hispanism pertains to those communities with a cultural connection to Spain, as well as to the study of Spanish-speaking peoples and to those who share a Spanish-speaking heritage. As Sylvia Molloy and Robert McKee Irwin remind us, for some the groups encompassed by this term share some basic cultural values and practices, whereas for others "Hispanism" refers to an imagined community that spans centuries and nations and is nothing more than a convenient organizing construct.[13] In fact, even within these general geographic and national categories there is little sense of uniformity. The multiple subcultures in Spain (Catalan, Basque, and Castilian, for example) and the United States (Puerto Rican, Chicana, Cuban, and so forth), as well as the nationalistic and indigenous divisions in Latin America, create anything but a unified lesbian "Hispanic" identity. In any case, one thing that clearly links Spain to Latin America and Latino/a communities is a history of colonization. In the present context, it is worthwhile to ask whether this link or any other connections can be established among Spanish, Latin American, and Latina lesbianisms or the representation of female same-sex desire in the literary arts in these three broad contexts.

Especially in the cases of Spain and Latin America, investigations of female homoeroticism have been marginalized and obscured. In this volume, Sherry Velasco shows that the legislation of lesbianism in early modern Spain resulted in a tendency to ignore or minimize the criminal transgression of sexual love between women because such love was not interpreted as threatening to normative heteropatriarchal order. However, contemporary critics have been slow to consider the study of same-sex desire in the early modern period because of the assumption that lesbian identity is a nineteenth-century phenomenon. While some scholars reject use of the term "lesbian" (as an identity category) for pre–nineteenth-century women-loving women, Velasco argues that this term is not anachronistic, because there is evidence that this and other phrases denoting same-sex desire between women were already in circulation during the early modern period. Moreover, most concepts and terms have changed meaning over time, but selectively avoiding the term "lesbian" in discussions of same-sex desire before the nineteenth century excludes lesbianism from certain considerations. The history of female homoeroticism is still being written, and regardless of the terms used, lesbian desire has a unique history that requires further investigation. Literary studies of lesbianism in contemporary Spanish literature seek to uncover an often veiled or ambiguous representation of female same-sex desire (see especially the chapters by Wilfredo Hernández, Inmaculada Pertusa, Gema Pérez-Sánchez, and Nancy Vosburg in this volume). For example, Hernández traces the similarities and evolution of the image of the lesbian in contemporary Spanish literature and relates the changing treatment of lesbianism to the gradual liberalization from the era of Francisco Franco's dictatorship to the emergence of democratic reforms in Spain following his death in 1975. He demonstrates that, during the era of government censorship, writers had to use coded references and ambiguity to represent lesbianism. Hernández argues that, although the early works of writers such as Teresa Barbero and Ana María Matute may seem muted by today's standards, they represent a challenge to existing Spanish mores and laws against homosexuality, given the social and political climate of the time in which they were written.

Likewise, the relative dearth of studies of female same-sex desire in Latin America can be attributed in part to the heteropatriarchal regimes that make explicit explorations of lesbianism a life-risking venture for writers. As Norma Mogrovejo and others document, Latin American lesbian activists began organizing an autonomous lesbian movement in the 1980s after attempts to work with other potential allies proved untenable.[14] Although they had worked for decades within the male-dominated gay and lesbian movement and within the mainly heterosexual and heterosexist feminist program, they became frustrated with sexism in the gay movement and with lesbophobia in the feminist movement. It has been much more difficult for lesbians to organize and conduct meetings like the series of Latin American and Caribbean feminist meetings that have taken place. Internal conflicts account for some of the difficulties in organizing, but the deadly repression and violence with which lesbians are often threatened presents a greater obstacle. Critical treatment of lesbian topics will also be slow to emerge in a context in which academic feminism is underdeveloped, as Amy Kaminsky points out, because scholars do not want to be marked as lesbian.[15] Thus, it is not surprising to find that most writers who address female same-sex desire do so in a veiled form or from an exiled position. Writers who dare to deal with lesbianism in their home country often suffer persecution and abuse.

As I noted earlier, the situation of Latinas in the United States is very different from the situation of those in Spain and Latin America. In the Latino/a case, discussions of homosexuality were initiated not by Latino gay men but by Latina lesbian political and creative writers. In the 1980s, discussions and publications centering on Latina lesbianisms emerged. This body of work not only boldly challenged the virtual absence of Latina lesbian representations; it also created an impetus for the proliferation of Latina lesbian creative works in many genres, including film (*Carmelita Tropicana: Your Kunst Is Your Waffen* and *Brincando el charco: Portrait of a Puerto Rican*[16]); comedy (Monica Palacios, Marga Gomez[17]); journal publications (*Esto No Tiene Nombre,*

Conmoción[18]); and literary fiction (Terri de la Peña, Emma Pérez, Alicia Gaspar de Alba, and Achy Obejas[19]). These new and specifically lesbian representations made possible innovative readings of gay and lesbian Latina and Latino identity that had been absent from the political and literary Latino/a world.

There are historical and situational differences in the genealogy of Spanish, Latin American, and Latina lesbianisms, but there is also a common struggle for representation and legitimacy in the sociocultural and literary worlds. "Tortilleras" in the title of this anthology is one of the many names used for lesbians in Hispanic and Latina contexts. Others include "jota," "loca," "pata," "marimacho," "culera," "lambiscona," and "pajuelona." Although these words are often used in derogatory ways, Hispanic and Latina lesbians have reappropriated many of them as affirming identity markers. This ongoing project of redefining and reconfiguring same-sex desire has myriad historical and cultural variations that encompass questions of gender, nationality, race, ethnicity, and class, making it impossible to posit a singular Hispanic or Latina lesbian. The essays in this anthology investigate the creation, maintenance and contradictions of lesbian space(s) and lesbian identities in a range of Hispanic and Lesbian texts and performances. The book is divided into four parts, each of which focuses on central issues of Hispanic and Latina lesbian reality: Coming Out/Covering Up, (Re)presenting Lesbian Desire, Sites of Resistance, and Racialized Lesbianisms.

The essays in Part I: Coming Out/Covering Up engage the complications and intricacies involved in the coming-out process for Hispanic and Latina lesbian women and for literary expressions of lesbianism. They explore some of the factors that shape the revelations and limitations possible in various historical, political, and cultural contexts. It was not until the 1990s that a Spanish writer (Andrea Luca) publicly discussed her lesbianism.[20] Prior to this, lesbian writing in Spain was ambiguously represented. In his chapter "From the Margins to the Mainstream: Lesbian Characters in Spanish Fiction (1964–79)," Wilfredo Hernández explores the effects of political and social repression on Catalan authors writing on lesbian themes or presenting women-loving women characters during two decades of extreme censorship. Hernández offers a specific lesbian trajectory for lesbian writers in a particular historical site, positing a genealogy of representations of same-sex desire in five novels by Catalan writers published in the 1960s and '70s in Spain. He argues that similar images, location, motives, and outcomes in the writing of Ana María Matute, Teresa Barbero, Ana María Moix, and Esther Tusquets point to an indigenous lesbian tradition in Spanish letters, and that later novels by Tusquets, Moix, and Luis Goytisolo differ from earlier representations in their more explicit treatment of lesbian sexuality. Despite this movement toward a more open articulation of lesbianism, Hernández concludes that in the end an autonomous lesbian subject does not surface in any of the five novels discussed.

The ambiguous and coded coming-out process through which lesbianism emerges in Spanish literature is also taken up by Inmaculada Pertusa in "Carme Riera: (Un)covering the Lesbian Subject or Simulation of a Coming Out?" which discusses the con-traditions inherent in the coming-out process through an analysis of two of Carme Riera's short stories. Reading Riera's stories through the lens of Eve Kosofsky Sedgwick's proposal concerning the epistemology of the closet, Pertusa shows how, in "Te dejo, amor, en prenda la mar" and "Pongo por testigo a las gaviotas," the coming-out process signals a covering up as well as a revealing. Gestures of disclosure by the stories' protagonists reveal that the act of coming out simultaneously enacts a making visible and a reproduction of closed spaces. While Riera opens a discourse on lesbians and thus renders them visible in Spanish letters, Pertusa argues, the stories ultimately emphasize through narrative strategies such as ambiguity, silence, and denial the double act of (re)vealing and veiling, of simultaneously coming out and covering up. Interestingly, a recent text on lesbianism in Spain in the 1990s by Olga Viñuales argues that female desire remains muted even within the visible lesbian movement where lesbians, although they may be out, are reluctant to identify specifically as lesbians publicly.[21] The women interviewed preferred vague identity markers such as "tener pluma," "entender," and "mas que amigas" to less ambiguous terms such as "lesbiana." Viñuales argues that lesbians' fear of being treated as a homogeneous group, one that conforms to social stereotypes of the masculine dyke, continues to make difficult any public discussion of the subject of lesbian identity.[22]

The coming-out process is no less fraught with contradictions and uncertainties in Latin America. Given that region's political reality, with its dynamic mix of Catholicism, heterobiased traditions, and authoritarian regimes, Norma Mogrovejo describes the writing of the history of the lesbian movement as much more than a historical, anthropological, or sociopolitical task. She refers to it primarily as an archaeological task that relies on oral histories and the reconstruction of personal archives that are always in danger of being destroyed or disappearing.[23] Lawrence La Fountain-Stokes explores coming-out dynamics in a Caribbean context in his chapter, "Tomboy Tantrums and Queer Infatuations: Reading Lesbianism in Magali García Ramis's *Felices días, tío Sergio.*" If representations of male homosexuality have been scant in Puerto Rican letters, lesbianism and lesbian desire have been all but invisible. La Fountain-Stokes proposes that lesbianism is in fact present but coded in Puerto Rican literature and that only a queer reading will unveil the taboo subject. In the novel *Felices días, tío Sergio,* La Fountain-Stokes argues, lesbianism is insinuated through the depiction of a young girl's marginality and oddness. The "lector entendido" reads Lidia's lesbianism in her rebelliousness and in the anxiety provoked at home by her refusal to adopt "appropriate" gender behavior. Lidia is linked to her homosexual uncle because of their gender nonconformity and similar nationalistic sympathies; in the middle-class Puerto Rican society of the 1950s, such an affinity, like gender (in)difference, was read as aberrant. Thus, La Fountain-Stokes argues that, rather than an explicit presence of lesbianism, Magali García Ramis's novel contains an exchange between lesbian and male homosexuality.

The last chapter in Part I engages aspects of coming out in the work of the Chicana novelist Terri de la Peña. Of the authors analyzed in this section, de la Peña is the one whose writing most clearly articulates an out, openly lesbian identity. This is not surprising, given that her work has evolved in the U.S. context, where lesbians in the past decades have established a more visible presence, as shown by the growth of a specifically American genre of coming-out stories in lesbian fiction. In "Coming-Out Stories and the Politics of Identity in the Narrative of Terri de la Peña," Salvador Fernández traces the creation of Chicana lesbian space in autobiographical and fictional writing and discusses the articulation of a new Latina lesbian voice by employing Emma Pérez's theoretical musings on constructing "un sito y lengua" for silenced Chicanas. Fernández identifies de la Peña's *Margins* as the first Latina lesbian coming-out novel, locating it within the tradition of the work of Cherríe Moraga and Gloria Anzaldúa and crediting de la Peña's intervention for its nuanced exploration of Chicana lesbian sexuality and erotic discourse in fiction. Fernández also documents how de la Peña's work challenges the hegemonic discourse of the Anglo mainstream, as well as of Anglo feminist and lesbian literary traditions. The work creates a "sitio y lengua" for the representation of Latina lesbian subjectivity. All of the essays in Part I underscore the idea that, although similar difficulties are encountered in the coming-out process in the Spanish, Latin American, and Latina context, this process of revelation is also marked by specific historical and situational particularities.

Part II: (Re)presenting Lesbian Desire takes up the question of how Hispanic and Latina lesbian desire is represented in literature, theater, and film. The essays in this part interrogate diverse strategies that enunciate lesbian desire in a variety of Hispanic and Latina contexts. Given that external and internal oppression problematize an open expression of lesbian identity, the articulation of same-sex desire will sometimes be located in unexpected places. The first two chapters in Part II explore diverse aspects of silence and desire in two of Ana María Moix's most powerful texts. In an elegant reading of Moix's "Las virtudes peligrosas," Nancy Vosburg demonstrates how the text de-centers "women's silence" in symbolic discourse, foregrounds the power of the silent gaze, and characterizes the failure of patriarchal force to control women's sexuality. Her essay, "Silent Pleasures and Pleasures of Silence: Ana María Moix's 'Las virtudes peligrosas,'" asks whether the text about two women who engage in a life-long, silent, scopophilic relationship should be read primarily in terms of narcissistic pleasure or lesbian desire. Vosburg embraces a lesbian reading that is characterized by ambiguity, the deferral of desire, delayed revealing of narrative voice, and many layerings of silence. Critiquing other readings of "Las virtudes peligrosas" that silence lesbian desire, Vosburg maps a lesbian reading that finds the reader, like the story's narrator, engaged in a voyeuristic process, attempting to unveil the ambiguities of the text. Employing Moix's own theory of the erotic, which "is a question of communicating as much as possible by silencing as much as possible," Vosburg locates the text's erotic nature in the deferral of desire and the staging of appearances as disappearances.

Gema Pérez-Sánchez also problematizes issues of authorial and critical silence in her chapter, "Reading, Writing, and the Love that Dares Not Speak Its Name: Eloquent Silences in Ana María Moix's *Julia*." She explores the layers of silence(s) in the 1968 Spanish novel *Julia* and in the critical responses it has generated. Because the novel was published under Franco's dictatorship, astute readers must read between the lines, via the novel's gaps and silences, to flesh out a narrative of lesbian desire. By playing on the said and the unsaid, Pérez-Sánchez deconstructs how Moix deploys a veiled lesbian narrative that, in a context of censorship and repression, is "understood" only by a "lector entendido" who can recognize queer codes and the re-semanticization of silence(s). Pérez-Sánchez deciphers the encoded meanings of silence(s) that pervade the text and, like Vosburg, argues that previous readings of the novel perpetuate the censorship of the forbidden topic of lesbianism. While Pérez-Sánchez demonstrates that the narrative's silences ultimately are an unsuccessful feminist strategy for the novel's young narrator, she argues nevertheless that Moix successfully dramatizes the dangers of silence as a feminist strategy for heterosexual and lesbian women. Thus, these two essays consider the benefits and dangers of silence as a vehicle for the expression of lesbian desire and feminist politics.

Because works that theorize lesbian desire in Spanish, Latin American, and Latina contexts are scarce, European and North American models of reading and analysis frequently are transposed and grafted onto these texts. Janis Breckenridge breaks a different type of silence as she seeks to expand the paradigms now available for conceptualizing attraction between women. In "Outside the Castle Walls: Beyond Lesbian Counterplotting in Cristina Peri Rossi's *Desastres íntimos*," she undertakes a lesbian reading of two short stories in the 1997 collection by Uruguay's Cristina Peri Rossi. Although Peri Rossi's texts for the most part are not overtly marked as lesbian, she often encodes her work by using a male narrative voice that identifies the female body as its object of desire. Breckenridge builds on Terry Castle's proposition that, in lesbian fiction, a subverted triangulation allows for female bonding by positioning men between women. According to Castle, this "counterplotting" leads to both a disruption of heterosexual relationships and a realignment of canonical narrative codes. Breckenridge analyzes two of Peri Rossi's short stories, "La semilla" and "El testigo," as examples of lesbian counterplotting that pre-empt male homosocial bonding and thus create a space for the surfacing of lesbian desire. Thus, Breckenridge goes beyond Castle's paradigm for lesbian narratives, which is found to be too rigid and limiting to account for desire as represented in Peri Rossi's work, as well as in other recent lesbian texts.

Regina Buccola is interested in theorizing ways to both represent women as desiring subjects and articulate women's experience of sexual abuse in women's theater. In her chapter, "'He Made Me a Hole!' Gender Bending, Sexual Desire, and the Representation of Sexual Violence," Buccola develops an analysis of Cherríe Moraga's *Giving Up the Ghost* that embodies a troubling intersection of lesbian sexual desire and abuse. Although elements of the play lend themselves to heterosexual readings, Buccola argues, feminist performance strategies subvert the male gaze. One such strategy involves disrupting linear temporality, while another addresses the fracturing of the subject, since Corky and Marisa are presented together on the stage at different moments of development. An interactive performance strategy that engages the spectator as a participant in the theatrical performance also provides a disruption of the male gaze and enacts the possibility for a powerful subject position for female characters and audience participants. All of the essays in Part II suggest that lesbian desire is represented and embodied in Spanish, Latin American, and Latina texts in ways that involve a rereading of silence and a disruption of familiar paradigms.

Although the patterns and practices of female same-sex desire are clearly mediated by the customs, traditions, and laws that exist in any sociocultural context, Hispanic and Latina lesbians have enacted creative tactics to defy the forces that seek to make them invisible. Part III: Sites of Resistance examines strategies of resistance and rebellion enacted by Hispanic and Latina lesbians. The studies in this part consider a range of tactics deployed in lesbian texts as successful or not-so-successful means of articulating a lesbian presence. In "*Bomberas* on Stage: Carmelita Tropicana Speaking in Tongues against History, Madness, Fate, and the State," Karina Cespedes explores the weapons used by Alina Troyano to create a space for Cuban American lesbianism in her performance piece *Milk of Amnesia.* By using tools such as campy choteo, drag, and CUMAAs (Collective Unconscious Memory Appropriation Attacks), Cespedes dissects how Carmelita Tropicana, a transplanted Cuban, attempts to negotiate the meanings of *cubanidad* offered to her from both the reactionary right and the idealistic left. According to Cespedes, *Milk of Amnesia* deconstructs these idealized visions and in the process, through the use of Latina lesbian camp and humor, posits a new queer *cubanidad.* A trip back to Cuba is narrated through the voices of both Alina Troyana and her creation, Carmelita Tropicana; this parallel journey allows for a multiplicity of viewpoints, from the logical to the schizophrenic. The piece challenges sexist, racist, and homophobic constructions of *cubanidad* and provides a site of resistance previously unarticulated for the Cuban American lesbian.

Because of the power of heteronormative patriarchy, the tools used to resist its grip are often subtle but no less effective. María Claudia André considers some of the methods used to resist the recent readings of Sor Juana Inés de la Cruz's conjectured lesbianism. In "Empowering the Feminine/Feminist/Lesbian Subject through the Lens: The Representation of Women in María Luisa Bemberg's 'Yo, la peor de todas,'" André traces Bemberg's feminist filmic discourse, specifically as it is exemplified in her historical film *Yo, la peor de todas,* which is based on Octavio Paz's biographical work of the seventeenth-century Mexican nun. André discusses how Bemberg represents the relationship between Sor Juana (renowned as Latin America's first feminist) and the Spanish vicereine who befriends and protects her. Despite Paz's suppression of the possibility of Sor Juana's lesbianism, André reads the film as a study of the intellectual, emotional, and erotic relationship that ensues between these women, who, although they are from very different worlds, are similarly subjected to gender restrictions in their respective spheres of the convent and the court. André argues that duality or doubleness between the two women is enacted throughout *Yo, la peor de todas,* and ambiguous erotic discourse pervades the film. As viewers enter the closed worlds of the two women, they become accomplices in a voyeuristic act and must decode the nature of the erotic relationship. The differences between the sacred and the profane, as well as between eroticism and spirituality, are blurred in the film. André contends that, because lesbianism is still perceived as a threat, feminist cultural workers such as Bemberg must subvert mainstream heterosexual discourse via strategies of ambiguity and multiplicity to challenge heteronormativity and create a new language of representation.

Another way to resist patriarchy is by destabilizing the notion that the family unit is conceivable only through the heterosexual union of a man and a woman. Sara Cooper considers a radical departure from this normalized ideal in "The Lesbian Family in Cristina Peri Rossi's 'The Witness': A Study in Utopia and Infiltration." Cooper underscores that, in addition to the invisibility of lesbians in Latin American letters, there is a lack of narratives on Latin American lesbian or homosexual family structures. Departing from insights offered by family studies theory, Cooper explores the concept of the gay family in a Latin American cultural context. As with coming-out stories that play a vital part in making visible gay and lesbian stories, lesbian family stories play a similarly important cultural role. In Rossi's "El testigo," two lesbian women and the son of one of the women set up what initially seems to be a utopic alternative family unit. Cooper finds a tension between the presentation and possibility of an ideal lesbian family and the reality of patriarchal violence. She argues that, although the story culminates in a horrific and fantastically violent episode, the narrative is revolutionary for representing an overtly lesbian family in Latin American.

In the final chapter in Part III, Elisa A. Garza considers how Chicanas are reshaping the narrative form itself as an act of resistance that mirrors and reflects their lesbian lives. In "Chicana Lesbianism and the Multi-Genre Text," she examines how Chicana lesbians refuse to silence any part of themselves in their literary work. This essay explores the meaning of the multi-genred text in the writing of Cherríe Moraga and Gloria Anzaldúa—specifically, the breaking out of traditional genre boundaries by these Latina lesbian authors. Garza places the work of Moraga and Anzaldúa in the transgressive tradition of ethnic women's writing that often departs from canonized literary tradition and is realized in nontraditional texts such as cookbooks and journal entries. Garza argues that writing in multiple genres involves a rejection of fragmentation and of the silencing of contradictions in narrative voice. Such writing rejects the dichotomy of public and private, community and individual, and is articulated from a racial, cultural, sexual, and academic space. Garza documents how Anzaldúa and Moraga traverse geographical, cultural, and literary borders and how the shifting of genres mirrors the resistance of multiple oppressions. The essays in Part III, then, explore the myriad tactics Latin American and Latina lesbians deploy to resist, rebel, and create new possibilities for their lives and their writing.

While all of the essays in the anthology investigate questions of lesbianism and identity, the chapters in Part IV: Racialized Lesbianisms deal explicitly with the intersections of race, ethnicity, class, and sexuality in the lives of women. In the 1980s and '90s, women of color developed critiques of political movements against racism, sexism, classism, and homophobia founded on issues or strategies that isolate any one of these factors as singularly important.[24] Monocausal or additive models of oppression have been replaced by theories that explore the intersectionality of oppressions. Such approaches foreground the necessity of considering not only gender when discussing women's condition but also its interconnection with discrimination based on race, ethnicity, sexuality, and class. These models, which consider the simultaneity of oppressions, create a space to examine how diverse oppressions intersect, feed, and reinforce one another. The studies in Part IV underscore the centrality of intersectionality, regardless of period or geographic location. In her study "Interracial Lesbian Erotics in Early Modern Spain: Catalina de Erauso and Elena/o de Céspedes," Sherry Velasco traces the history of two transgendered individuals in seventeenth-century Spain. Although Erauso and Céspedes both lived as men and desired women, they received very different treatment from royal, religious, and legal authorities when their anatomical status was investigated. Céspedes, a mulatta claiming hermaphroditism, received punishment; the aristocratic Basque lieutenant nun Erauso, by contrast, was rewarded by church and crown. This, Velasco argues, exposes the genealogies of race, class, and ethnicity that account for the divergent trajectories of these two women-loving transgendered historical figures.

The other chapters in Part IV consider issues of intersectionality in the context of Latinas in the United States. All three studies articulate how the complexities of race, class, and sexuality play out in the Latina communities. In "Violence, Desire, and Transformative Remembering in Emma Pérez's *Gulf Dreams*," Lourdes Torres analyzes how race and ethnicity are intimately related to questions of desire, power, and violence in her reading of Emma Pérez's *Gulf Dreams.* This novel chronicles the obsessive love of two Chicanas, whose twenty-year relationship is marked by repression, manipulation, and emotional and physical violence. Departing from a framework grounded in the intersectionality of oppressions, Torres suggests that early experiences of molestation and of racial, class, and sexual discrimination condition the development of sexual desire. The protagonists, who have been victimized by childhood sexual assault, seem destined to model their perpetrators and engage in a cycle of seduction and abuse in their relationships with men and other women. Torres claims that memory serves as a central strategy to explore the complexities of Latina lesbian violence and desire. Pérez enacts what bell hooks refers to as "a politicization of memory that distinguishes nostalgia, that longing for something to be as it once was, a kind of useless act, from that remembering that serves to illuminate and transform the present."[25]

The politics of race within Latino/a communities has been a thorny issue that too often has been marked by denial or lack of sustained discussion. Although the racial system imposed on Latinos in the United States may be different from the categorizations that originate in our home countries, native hierarchies do exist and are transposed to the already highly racialized U.S. context. The often painful repercussions of refusing to confront racial hierarchies and difference within Latino communities and families has been a frequent subject of literary works;[26] it has also been the subject of scholarly attention within Latino/a studies.[27] Interestingly, while Cherríe Moraga's work has received much critical attention, issues of race—and, in particular, "blackness"—in her work have largely escaped critical attention. Christina Sharpe's "Learning to Live without Black Familia: Cherríe Moraga's Nationalist Articulations" analyzes borders in Moraga's work as sites where racial differences are interrogated and simultaneously enforced and erased. In her reading of Moraga's work, from *This Bridge Called My Back* to *Loving in the War Years* and *The Last Generation*, Sharpe finds that Moraga not only rejects but also reproduces repressive borders.[28] She traces in Moraga's work a shift from the development of a third-world feminist movement, a movement premised on the centrality of coalition building, to a more limited Chicano nationalist project. Sharpe argues that the recuperation of Chicano nationalism is ultimately accomplished through an exorcism of "blackness."

In "Shameless Histories: Chicana Lesbian Fictions Talking Race/Talking Sex," Catrióna Rueda Esquibel explores how Chicana lesbian writers are creating their own histories, as they have been written out of Chicano heterosexual and white lesbian accounts. Rather than being completely rejected, oppressive and exclusionary heterosexual Latino and white lesbian cultural forms are appropriated and reconfigured to represent a specifically Latina lesbian history. Drawing on three aspects of Chicano/a and lesbian popular culture—the corrido, pulp fiction, and oral history—Rueda Esquibel documents how a racialized Chicana existence is created in three Chicana lesbian short stories. Although these racialized Chicana lesbian representations are "fictions," they serve to validate a Chicana lesbian history that is erased in other literary and scholarly genres. The stories that Rueda Esquibel analyzes are steeped in working-class Southwestern Chicana rural realities; they elucidate how the love of Chicana lesbians is conditioned by their gender, racial, and class positions. Rueda Esquibel's work explores a strategy used by Chicana writers that consists of the re-appropriation and transformation of heterosexual Latino and white lesbian cultural forms. Rueda Esquibel demonstrates how Chicana writers use this strategy of "queering" Chicano heterosexual cultural codes and racializing white lesbian cultural forms to write themselves into history.

The Spanish, Latin American, and Latina lesbian texts analyzed in this volume share a number of concerns, such as an exploration of the coming-out process, the challenge of expressing lesbian desire within the context of heteropatriarchy, the exploration of sites of resistance, and the articulation of the self within the intersectionality of race, ethnicity, class, and sexuality. They are all related in one way or another to the power of naming that, in this instance, involves making female same-sex desire visible. However, the range of texts analyzed in this anthology interrupts an inclination to configure a monolithic Hispanic or Latina lesbianism. Similarly, the analyses used demonstrate a diversity of queer readings and literary perspectives that open, rather than limit, lesbian readings. Although the anthology clearly does not offer an exhaustive treatment of Spanish, Latin American, and Latina lesbianisms, it continues the task of revealing how Hispanic and Latina lesbian practices and identities are defined, negotiated, and projected across a range of historical moments and cultural and literary spaces. As Spanish, Latin American, and Latina lesbian creative works become more available, and as new readings of contemporary, modern, and premodern texts that feature female homoeroticism are undertaken, the emerging field of homosexual Hispanisms promises to be as rich with readings of female same-sex desire as it is with readings of gay male homosexualities.

Notes

1. Cherríe Moraga and Gloria Anzaldúa, eds., *This Bridge Called My Back: Writings by Radical Women of Color* (Watertown, Mass.: Persephone Press, 1981); Cherríe Moraga, *Loving in the War Years: Lo que nunca pasó por sus labios* (Boston: South End Press, 1983); Gloria Anzaldúa, *Borderlands/La Frontera: The New Mestiza* (San Francisco: Aunt Lute Books, 1987); Juanita Ramos, ed., *Compañeras: Latina Lesbians* (New York: Latina Lesbian History Project, 1987).

2. See Sherry Velasco, *The Lieutenant Nun: Transgenderism, Lesbian Desire and Catalina de Erauso* (Austin: University of Texas Press, 2000), esp. chap. 2, which provides an overview of studies of lesbianism in the early modern period.

3. See Louis Compton, "The Myth of Lesbian Impunity: Capital Laws from 1270 to 1791," in "Special Issue: Historical Perspectives on Homosexuality," ed. Salvatore J. Licata and Robert P. Peterson, *Journal of Homosexuality* 6, nos. 1–2 (1980–81): 11–25.

4. This body of research has also given rise to contemporary explorations of lesbianism in a variety of cultural forms. For example, Pedro Almodóvar's 1982 film *Entre Tinieblas* explores the fascinating relationship between lesbian desire and mysticism in a post–Franco Spanish convent, and Luisa Bemberg's 1989 film *Yo, la peor de todas* presents a modern reading of the relationship between Sor Juana Inés de la Cruz and Vicereine Maria Luisa Manrique de Lara y Gonzaga in colonial Mexico.

5. Emile L. Bergmann and Paul Julian Smith, eds., *¿Entiendes? Queer Readings, Hispanic Writings* (Durham, N.C.: Duke University Press, 1995); Sylvia Molloy and Robert Mckee Irwin, eds., *Hispanisms and Homosexualities* (Durham, N.C.: Duke University Press, 1998); Josiah Blackmore and Gregory S. Hutcheson, eds., *Queer Iberia: Crossing Cultures, Crossing Sexualities* (Durham, N.C.: Duke University Press, 1999); Susana Chávez-Silverman and Librada Hernández, eds., *Reading and Writing the Ambiente: Queer Sexualities in Latino, Latin American, and Spanish Culture* (Madison: University of Wisconsin Press, 2000); María José Delgado and Alain Saint-saens, eds., *Lesbianism and Homosexuality in Spanish Golden Age Literature and Society* (New Orleans: University Press of the South, 2000).

6. Other important works include Daniel Balderston and Donna J. Guy, eds., *Sex and Sexuality in Latin America* (New York: New York University Press, 1997); David William Foster and Roberto Reis, eds., *Bodies and Biases: Sexualities in Hispanic Cultures and Literatures* (Minneapolis: University of Minnesota Press, 1996); Elena M. Martínez, *Lesbian Voices from Latin America* (New York: Garland Publishing, 1996); Juanita Ramos, ed., *Compañeras: Latina Lesbians* (New York: Routledge, 1994); Carla Trujillo, ed., *Chicana Lesbians: The Girls Our Mothers Warned Us About* (Berkeley: Third Woman Press, 1991).

7. David William Foster, ed., *Spanish Writers on Gay and Lesbian Themes* (Westport, Conn.: Greenwood Press, 1999).

8. Ibid., 17–18.

9. David William Foster, ed. *Gay and Lesbian Themes in Latin American Writing* (Austin: University of Texas Press, 1991.

10. Ibid., 3.

11. David William Foster, ed. *Chicano/Latino Homoerotic Identities* (New York: Garland Publishing, 1999).

12. Evelyn Blackwood and Saskia Wieringa, eds., *Female Desires: Same-Sex Relations and Transgender Practices across Cultures* (New York: Columbia University Press, 1999).

13. Sylvia Molloy and Robert Mckee Irwin, "Introduction," in *Hispanisms and Homosexualities*, ix–xvi.

14. See Norma Mogrovejo, *Un amor que se atrevió a decir su nombre* (México, D.F.: Plaza y Valdés, 2000), and Juanita Díaz-Cotto, "Lesbian-American Activism and Latin American Feminist Encuentros," in *Sexual Identities, Queer Politics*, ed. Mark Blasius (Princeton, N.J.: Princeton University Press, 2001), 73–96.

15. Amy Kaminsky, *Reading the Body Politic: Feminist Criticism and Latin American Women Writers* (Minneapolis: University of Minnesota Press, 1993), xiv.

16. *Brincando el charco: Portrait of a Puerto Rican*, dir. Frances Negrón Muntaner (Women Making Movies, 1994); *Carmelita Tropicana: Your Kunst Is Your Waffen*, dir. Ela Troyana (Women Making Movies, 1994).

17. Monica Palacios and Marga Gomez are Latina lesbian comedians and performance artists. Among Palacios's work are the performance pieces *Confessions, Greetings from a Queer Señorita,* and *Latina Lezbo Comic.* Gomez's performance pieces are *Memory Tricks, Marga Gomez Is Pretty Witty and Gay,* and *A Line around the Block.*

18. *Esto no tiene nombre,* later issued as *Conmoción,* was published from 1990 to 1996 in Miami. The journal was produced by an editorial collective headed by Tatiana de la Tierra.

19. Works of fiction by Latina lesbians include Terri de la Peña's three novels, *Margins* (Seattle: Seal, 1991), *Latin Satins* (Seattle: Seal, 1994), and *Faults* (Los Angeles: Alyson Books, 1994). See also Emma Pérez, *Gulf Dreams* (Berkeley, Calif.: Third Woman Press, 1996); Achy Obejas, *We Came All the Way from Cuba So You Could Dress Like This* (Pittsburgh: Cleis, 1994), and *Memory Mambo* (Pittsburgh: Cleis, 1996); Alicia Gaspar de Alba, *The Mystery of Survival and Other Stories* (Tempe, Ariz.: Bilingual Press, 1993), and idem, *Sor Juana's Second Dream* (Albuquerque: University of New Mexico Press, 1999).

20. See the introduction to Foster, *Spanish Writers*, 19.

21. See Olga Viñuales, *Identidades lésbicas* (Barcelona: ediciones bellaterra, 2000).

22. Ibid., 94.

23. Norma Mogrovejo, "Sexual Preference, the Ugly Duckling of Feminist Demands: The Lesbian Movement in Mexico," in Blackwood and Wieringa, eds., *Female Desires,* 308.

24. See Lourdes Torres's chapter in this volume for a discussion of this work.

25. bell hooks, *Yearning: Race, Gender and Cultural Politics* (Boston: South End Press, 1990), 147.

26. See, for example, Piri Thomas, *Down These Mean Streets* (New York: Knopf, 1967); Richard Rodríguez, *Hunger of Memory* (Boston: David R. Godine, 1982); and Junot Diaz, *Drown* (New York: Riverhead Books, 1996).

27. See Clara E. Rodríguez, *Changing Race* (New York: New York University Press, 2000); Roberto P. Rodríguez-Morazzani, "Beyond the Rainbow: Mapping the Discourse on Puerto Ricans and 'Race,'" in *The Latino Studies Reader,* ed. Antonia Darder and Rodolfo D. Torres (Oxford: Blackwell, 1998), 143–62; Angel R. Oquendo, "Re-imagining the Latino/a Race," in *The Latino/a Condition: A Critical Reader,* ed. Richard Delgado and Jean Stefancic (New York: New York University Press, 1998); Linda Martin Alcoff, "Is Latina/o Identity a Racial Identity?" in *Hispanics/Latinos in the United States: Ethnicity Race, and Rights,* ed. Jorge J. E. Gracia and Pablo De Greiff (New York: Routledge, 2000), 23–44.

28. Cherríe Moraga, *The Last Generation* (Boston: South End Press, 1993).

Part I

Coming Out/
Covering Up

Wilfredo Hernández

1   From the Margins to the Mainstream:
     Lesbian Characters in Spanish
     Fiction (1964–79)

This essay analyzes the representation of lesbians in twentieth-century Spanish fiction, focusing on five novels in which homosexual women are either main or secondary characters. Lesbian characters are scarce in Spanish fiction written in the first half of the twentieth century; therefore, the works explored in this study were published in the two decades between 1964 and 1979. Undoubtedly, the late appearance of homosexuals in Spanish literature is a result of Francoist censorship and repression of gays and lesbians, as well as of contemporary perceptions reflecting both religious and scientific prejudices.

The first two novels in Spanish literature to include lesbian characters appeared during the 1960s. In the first, *Los soldados lloran de noche* (The soldiers cry at night, 1964), by Ana María Matute, a same-sex encounter is mentioned as an influential incident in the life of a young female character.[1] In the second, *El último verano en el espejo* (Last summer in the mirror, 1967), by Teresa Barbero, several lesbians are referred to, and one of them becomes an important person in the life story of the main character, also a young woman.[2] The two novels are key because they contain the very first lesbian images produced in modern Spanish fiction. However, the differences in the treatment of the subject by Matute and Barbero are striking. After 1970, those images are revisited and reshaped by the new writers as a consequence of the active participation of homosexuals in the political arena and the emergence of a new conceptual framework produced by the international gay liberation movements of the late 1960s and early 1970s.

I suggest that the link between the Spanish gay movement and literary expression is the most important reason for the changes that occur in lesbian images. Indeed, *Julia*, a 1970 novel by the gay female writer Ana María Moix, shows a different perspective of the lesbian experience.[3] Moix includes a main character, a young lesbian named

Julia, whose sentimental life becomes the main focus of the book. Narrated immediately after a failed attempt to commit suicide, the depiction of the main character's fight against heterosexism and homophobia, although markedly tragic, is complex and psychologically authentic.

After Francisco Franco's death and the subsequent arrival of democracy in the mid-1970s, legal and social conditions changed in Spain. The last works analyzed in this paper are two novels from this period: Esther Tusquets's *El mismo mar de todos los veranos* (The same sea every summer, 1978),[4] and Luis Goytisolo's *La cólera de Aquiles* (Achilles' cholera, 1979).[5] We will see that in less than two decades, the representation of lesbian characters changes visibly. In the earlier novels, lesbian characters are members of marginal groups; at the end of the period, however, lesbians make up part of the middle and upper classes. All five novels considered in this chapter were written by Catalan writers, four of them women. I propose that these works establish an indigenous tradition that should be taken into account when analyzing other pieces of Spanish contemporary gay literature produced in the same period or later.

The Lesbian Subject in Fiction Published under the Francoist Regime (1964–70)

According to María D. Costa, the pioneer work depicting lesbian characters was written by Ana María Matute, whose fiction also includes gay men as characters.[6] In *The Soldiers Cry at Night*, one of the main characters, Marta, recalls her life before the civil war (1936–39). Her mother, Elena, had a sentimental relationship with Raúl while she was living with a woman, Dionisia. As Janet Pérez shows, the lesbian relationship is not clearly defined.[7] Dionisia is depicted through a set of innuendos that suggest that she possesses a deviant personality: "En tiempos, Dionisia fue camarera de barco, y hacía la ruta de Shangai a Marsella. Trataba en todo. Drogas, contrabando."[8] Traits such as these would have signaled to the contemporary reader that Dionisia was neither a "decent" nor a heterosexual woman. This type of codification or innuendo was the only means available to the writer to escape the censor's vigilance regarding sexual representation. This textual strategy, which was also a social strategy, took place in a very specific context in which "decent" women did not work outside the home, except in jobs stereotyped as belonging to their sex. Dionisia's working on a liner is not exactly a "decent" feminine job because it means being far away from masculine control. Moreover, Dionisia's route is a very well-known drug route of the time.[9]

During the time to which the narrator refers, Martha's mother and Dionisia manage a bar and trade drugs. The involvement of these women in illicit activities is clear. Also, they share a house and business—that is, they live together without the sanction of a legal bond (they are not legally related). Two conclusions are to be drawn by the reader: First, these women are "indecent"; second, they are a butch-and-femme couple. The former—Elena's mother—is a bisexual whose female companion, Dionisia, accepts the idea of her having a male lover. After Marta turns eighteen, Dionisia tries to seduce her: " 'Es verdad, no eres ninguna niña, tienes mucha razón. No debe[n] hacer esto contigo, Martita, pobrecita mía'. Ella no se atrevió a moverse. Dionisia seguía acariciándole las piernas: 'Eres preciosa, Marta, si pudieras vestirte y arreglarte como las demás'."[10] To avoid Dionisia's sexual advances, Marta decides to leave home and become the mistress of her mother's male lover, Raúl. Sexualities, both bisexual and homosexual, are depicted as something despicable in this novel. Indeed, bisexuality and homosexuality are shown as being pathologically and morally deviant.

The second novel that includes a lesbian character is Barbero's *Last Summer in the Mirror*. The main character, Marta, is a young married woman in her late twenties who is going through a difficult pregnancy and is unsure about continuing her marriage. Fusing the past with the present, Marta tells the story of her life. One of the key periods of narration is the time she spent in a private religious secondary school. One of her classmates, a wealthy Barcelona native named Elena, is the leader of a group of students who engage in sexual activities with one another: "En la soledad de la antecapilla, con aquel fuerte olor a incienso y cera derretida, las palabras de Clarita parecían venir de ultratumba: 'Son mujeres malas, ¿sabes? Se cierran en los wateres de dos en dos . . . y se desnudan."[11] *Last Summer* contains two important elements signaling the development of an indigenous Spanish tradition of lesbian fiction. First, there is the repetition of some of the names of Matute's characters (such as Marta and Elena) within a middle- and upper-class context; and second, Barbero repeats Matute's initial motif of portraying a female character recalling her life. But while Matute prefers that the lesbian character be secondary, Barbero chooses to include her as a protagonist.

In Barbero's book, there are several pertinent novelties. First, the word "lesbian" is used for the first time as a way to depict a female character. A second innovation is found in the way in which she widens the representation of lesbian sexuality. In contrast to Matute, Barbero quite openly depicts sexuality. For instance, Marta's first sexual experience is with Elena, who invites her to spend Christmas in Barcelona at her parents' house. "Cuando nos llamaron para cenar estábamos muy excitadas. Después, en el dormitorio, al apagar la luz, Elena dijo: '¿Quieres que vaya un ratito a tu cama? Así podemos hablar mejor, ¿quieres?' La sentí deslizarse entre mis sábanas. Me asusté mucho cuando ella dijo: '¿Sabes lo qué hacen los novios cuando están a solas?' "[12] Sexual activity among the students is quite common in the religious school. Of greater interest, however, is that most of the female characters to whom the narrator refers also have heterosexual sex later in their lives. However, not all of them feel comfortable with having a same-sex companion at the same time that they are involved with someone of the opposite sex. Nevertheless, when Elena marries, she continues to have female sexual partners: "Elena tenía amigos con los que iba a bailar y se besaba, y una amiga pelirroja, con aire varonil, que no la dejaba ni a sol ni a sombra y que parecía estar siempre de mal humor. 'Es lesbiana' nos explicó Clara una noche 'y está enamorada de Elena como una loca. Elena tiene algo que atrae a las lesbianas.' "[13]

By remembering the past, Marta seems to realize that she is not at all happy with her present situation. The key to this feeling is the link she finds between her memory of the first time she ever had sexual intercourse—with Elena—and her present feelings: "Elena había trastornado mi vida. De día todo hubiera sido igual, de no ser por aquella mala conciencia que me acusaba como un dedo amenazador."[14] She thinks about leaving her husband and moving to Argentina. Of particular interest, however, is that the man with whom she is planning to go is Elena's husband, Pablo. A character previously mentioned, Clara, a former classmate of Elena and Marta, tells the latter that the truth is that Elena is still in love with her.[15] In the end, Elena makes a proposal to Marta: "¿Sabes lo que deberíamos hacer? Deja a Angel y entre las dos cogemos un apartamento. . . . Tú lo que necesitas es independizarte de una puñetera vez. . . . Además, ¡qué caray!, me gusta estar contigo; me gusta hablar contigo, hacerte confidencias."[16] Elena's proposal is the first step toward reaching the topos Matute introduces—that is, two women, economically independent, living together. But Marta does not accept. Instead, she continues to live with her husband and suffers a miscarriage.

Differences between present and past styles of narration in these two novels deserve comment. In Matute's case, the character-narrator explicitly recognizes that it is only after Dionisia's advances that she decides to leave home, to avoid lesbian sex and to become Raúl's mistress. In this respect, Barbero is ambiguous. It could be argued that Marta does not resolve the conflict that arises from the realization that she is not content leading a heterosexual life. Her rejection of both Pablo's and Elena's proposals seem to indicate her confusion about her true feelings about her sexual orientation. Besides, economic restrictions make it more difficult to go beyond Martha's available options. Elena, by contrast, enjoys an economic situation that allows her to do whatever she wants, be it traveling to New York or maintaining her independence from her husband. Hypothetically, if social conditions were different, Barbero's novel could be one about lesbian development. As Bonnie Zimmerman writes, "The lesbian novel of development thus generally focuses on the heroine's adolescence, much like the traditional bildungsroman. Her growth from adolescence into adulthood is an educational process often set in a girl's school or college, where the protagonist's general education is inextricably linked to the discovery of love and sensuality."[17] However, there is no such development in this novel, or in the next novel of lesbian representation we will consider.

In 1970, Ana María Moix published *Julia*, the story of a twenty-year-old college student of the same name. Julia, who is also a native of Barcelona, is in love with her literature professor, Eve. Unable to enter into a romantic relationship with her professor because of numerous threats from her family, Julia decides to commit suicide. The novel deals with her thoughts after realizing that she has failed at taking her own life. Quite similar to *Last Summer* in its use of literary techniques, though more refined in its mastery, this novel includes numerous memories of the character's childhood and adolescence. As a teenager, Julia is sent to her grandparents' home, where she meets aunt Elena. Julia falls in love for the first time: "Añoraba el cuerpo de tía Elena tendido al lado del suyo, y la piel fina, suave, los largos cabellos negros que ella acariciaba una y otra vez hasta quedarse dormida."[18] However, her aunt does not understand her niece's affection in the same way; she was in love with a townsman. After a long stay, the teenager returns to Barcelona: "Por las noches, en la cama, le resultaba imposible no pensar en tía Elena. Echaba de menos el cuerpo tendido junto al suyo y sus caricias. Se abrazaba a la almohada, cerraba los ojos e imaginaba que tía Elena estaba allí, a su lado."[19]

Julia refuses to pay attention to personal appearance, which in her society means being less feminine. Female heterosexual orientation requires that women care about clothing. Julia's mother is extremely concerned that her only female child (Julia has two brothers, one of whom is depicted as a young queer) does not worry about such things: "Se quejaba en cambio de que Julia jamás tuviera iniciativa para comprarse un vestido, o unos zapatos, arreglarse el pelo o cualquier cosa que Mamá calificaba como pruebas de feminidad. Cuando Julia le pedía algo, algún objeto de lucimiento personal o decorativo, Mamá se alegraba y lo adquiría sin regateos. Una chica debe ser coqueta y presumida, de lo contrario parece un hombre."[20] Such a conclusion is supported by Carmen Martín Gaite's research on social habits during the Francoist period. According to Martín Gaite, "De las chicas poco sociables o disciplentes, que no se ponían a dar saltos de alegría cuando las invitaban a un 'guateque', descuidaban su arreglo personal y se aburrían hablando de novios y de trapos se decía que eran 'raras, que tenían un carácter raro.' "[21]

Julia falls in love again as a teenager, this time with her school principal, Señorita Mabel, whose feelings seem to correspond to those of the student. After one of Julia's brothers passes away, the principal approaches Julia to let her know that she cares. For Julia, such a moment becomes very important in clarifying the kind of affection she wants from the principal: "Julia, a menudo, sentía deseos de que la directora fuera más cariñosa con ella, que la estrechara entre sus brazos, como el primer día de clase después de la muerte de Rafael."[22] What is important in the present is that the character, a twenty-year-old college student, continues to be dependent on her parents, who control her in such a way that she is not able to make any decision of her own without her mother's approval. The novel suggests that Julia does not have many ways to assume her sexual orientation, and that the only solutions are to live as a heterosexual or to be in the closet. This is particularly ironic because Julia's brother is able to live a more or less openly gay life.

Moix continues this apparent tradition by using both the motif of a female narrator recalling her life and a set of characters' names previously used by Matute and Barbero. She also situates the story in the same location, Barcelona. Moix, however, adds several important new elements. First, she creates a main character who does not give up in her fight to live openly as a homosexual. Second, where Barbero introduces the wealthy Catalan Elena as a secondary character, Moix gives her upper-class character a leading role. Third, Moix depicts members of specific professions traditionally regarded as those in which gay people are found (writers, artists, actors, etc.). The preferred Spanish lesbian image in the next decades after Moix's work was published would be the city-dwelling, college-educated, wealthy woman. As noted earlier, the first images, contained in Matute's work, were of marginal women. In Barbero's novel, there was a gradual change to the middle class. With Moix, there is a movement to the top of the social spectrum.

Censorship, Literature, and the Homosexual Experience

The three novels discussed thus far were published under Francoist censorship, which was established legally in 1938 with the passage of the Press Law.[23] The censorship office was divided into three sections: books; theater and movies; and information and "censorship." The pertinent section here, books, was directed by Juan Beneyto Pérez, a prestigious professor at the time who surrounded himself with other well-known professors and writers.[24] The Nobel Prize winner Camilo José Cela was among them for a while.[25] One of the first cases studied by Manuel Abellán in his groundbreaking book is that of Jardiel Poncela, whose novel *Amor se escribe sin hache* (Love is spelled without "h") was read by the censor in 1939. Once the book was submitted, the censor could edit it; if changes were numerous, the writer was asked to make them. This happened to Poncela's next novel submitted for approval, *¿Hubo una vez once mil vírgenes?* (But were there ever eleven thousand virgins?). A cursory look at the corrections made by the censor are revealing. "My first lover" was changed to "my first husband"; "being aroused" was changed to "be enjoying"; "bed" was changed to "bedroom."[26] Not all books submitted were allowed to be published.[27]

The 1938 law was in force until 1966, when a new Press Law was enacted. The new law was active for ten years, until it was repealed in 1976. This time, writers were asked to submit manuscripts voluntarily. However, a book could not be published without approval from the censor's office. Both laws contained numerous restrictions on what was possible to publish. Political and moral limitations formed the core of Francoist censorship. Moral limitations were defined as a search for decency, "understood as a banning of press freedom when the book contained an attempt against prudery and public decency. Any writing dealing with abortion, homosexuality, and divorce was particularly prohibited."[28] During Franco's dictatorship, homosexuality was treated like a sin, following a tradition that goes back to medieval times. According to Raymond Carr and Juan Pablo Fusi, "Church influence on the censor's office made any attack on Catholic morals or any touch of eroticism non-publishable."[29] The Press Law also banned the publication of works by foreign authors dealing with suspect themes, as well as works by or about known homosexual writers. For example, a study by the critic Germán Gullón on the gay poet Luis Cernuda was prohibited because its subject was an author who was a homosexual (*uranista*), besides being a communist.[30]

Homosexuality was not banned only from books. It was also censored in real life. Moreover, as of 1933, when the Law of Vagrants was enacted, homosexuality became a crime. An excerpt from an official report included as a footnote in Carmen Martín Gaite's *Usos amorosos* reads: "La plaga de invertidos que, sin recato alguno, se muestra con frecuencia en todos los lugares, es el capítulo más vergonzoso de la ciudad."[31] The report explicitly states that the homosexuals referred to are men (*invertidos*). Because there is no study that deals with the subject of homosexuality under Franco's regime, it is difficult to know the extent to which the legal prohibitions affected homosexual behavior. Also, the differences in the lives of male and female homosexuals remain unknown. What the report makes clear, however, is that groups of male homosexuals were not deterred from expressing themselves in ways that the report's writers found scandalous. Taking police repression into account, one can assume that behavior regarded as scandalous did not include actual sexual practice but, instead, focused on demeanor, clothing, and public behavior regarded as inappropriate but not illegal. Later, we will see how behavior suspected of being homosexual was considered a crime.

From the three novels under study, and from Martín Gaite's depiction of private customs during this period, it is possible to draw preliminary conclusions about lesbian behavior under the Francoist regime. First, as Martín Gaite puts it, "Restringir y racionar siguieron siendo vocablos clave, admoniciones agazapadas en la trastienda de todas las conductas."[32] Second, social behavior was highly homogeneous: The rule was to act like everybody else.[33] In a society where difference and dissidence are not accepted, lesbians have to adopt many of the traits of heterosexual women. In Matute's novel, it is evident that motherhood was a requirement to be considered "normal." If not, as in the case of Dionisia (a representation of the mannish lesbian), lesbians were treated with social contempt. Bisexuality became one of the means used to escape the accusation of practicing an illegal act. It is necessary to find out what changes the censor ordered in Matute's first manuscript to comprehend why, in this definitive text, the lesbian relationship is so strangely depicted. Matute's troubles with censorship were continuous. Her novel *In this Land*, published in 1955, came out after two years of work and "tricks" with the editor.[34] The writer had to delete, and sometimes change the whole text, including the title. "When the first edition sold out, I did not allow it to be reprinted. I will never permit it, because for me it was a shameful halt."[35]

Matute's experience provides a strong example of the limitations writers faced when deciding to create fiction that dealt with homosexuality. Therefore, when studying other literary texts from this period, one has to bear in mind that the text being read was subject to changes aimed at complying with the demands of the censor. As mentioned earlier, the relationship between Elena's mother and Dionisia is not clearly stated in Matute's *Los soldados*. However, the mere fact that these two women share a house and business and live together without a legal bond allows us to interpret the relationship as homosexual.[36] A reader in the 1960s would have reached this conclusion from the numerous clues Matute gives in the book.

Barbero's *El último verano* was published after the passage of the Press Law of 1966. As noted earlier, it was in this book that the word "lesbian" appeared for the first time to describe a homosexual female character. But it is not only the use of this word that makes Barbero's text noteworthy. The novel also describes lesbian sexuality openly and, most important, depicts lesbian characters in a novel fashion. Martha Vicinus finds that "in the 1950s both the general public and lesbians themselves privileged the predictable figure of the mannish lesbian."[37] This image, which to a certain extent is Dionisia's, fades away in Barbero's novel. All of the lesbian characters there, particularly the ones who receive the most attention, are closer to Elena's mother—

that is, Matute's other lesbian character. Most of them are married with children and have female lovers. Only one is said to be "mannish."

In 1970, the Spanish government proposed a new law, the Danger and Social Reha-bilitation Law, according to which "conduct even suggestive of a homosexual nature was deemed legally suspect."[38] The bill passed, and following a modification to the law a year later, it was enacted. The law indicated that homosexuals would be sent for sexual rehabilitation in specific facilities: "A further modification on 1 June 1971 made specific provision for the internment of homosexuals in a 'rehabilitation cen-tre' at Huelva, thus reverting almost to the same degree of severity of the previous law (which had, since 1954, specified labour camps)."[39] Homosexual activist groups protested, and the change was removed. One of the groups leading the campaign was the Catalan Gay Liberation Front.[40] It was during this time that Moix's *Julia* came out. The novel enhances Barbero's contributions in such a way that, after Moix's book, one can assert that Spanish literature reached a maturity sufficient to permit the explo-ration of a subject previously considered too taboo to be dealt with. I argue that *Julia* points to the existence of a deep-rooted dissidence toward the law and the general perception of homosexuality.

It is no coincidence that *Julia*'s author is Catalan and a lesbian, and that her brother, Terenci Moix, also a writer, was openly homosexual when the new law was proposed. It is not my purpose here to analyze the differences in the representation of mascu-line and feminine homosexuality under the Francoist regime. Suffice it to say that the reader should be aware that, in *Julia*, Moix creates a gay male character who seems to be modeled after her own brother. The characters' lives, at home and outside, are completely different. For example, while her brother has no restrictions against going out whenever he wishes, Julia is restrained. Further, Julia's brother is loved by their mother because he cares about dressing up, while Julia is criticized by her mother and grandmother for not acting accordingly. Julia is a lesbian who knows she is homo-sexual and does not believe she is wrong. Also, she is a college student and able to understand that heterosexual life does not fit her desires and needs. Throughout the book, the character rejects her family's pressure to conform to compulsory hetero-sexuality and attempts to live her own life. However, family and legal restrictions make achieving her goal difficult.

But if the main character's quest in Moix's fiction is a failure, it seems to me that the failure is not a definitive one. Julia is twenty years old; she is a college student; and she lives in Barcelona. This last element is crucial because it was mainly in the Catalan and Basque cities where homosexual activist groups were strong in the mid-1970s. After they succeeded in getting the change to the 1970s law repealed, gay-rights groups continued a very active campaign. Evidence for these groups' philos-ophy can be found in a manifesto published in 1977 by the Catalan Gay Liberation Front. "The manifesto is noteworthy," Stephan Likosky writes, "because the desig-nation 'gay' is defined in it not as a positive rescription of the negatively constituted essence of homosexuality but as a move away from the essentialist categories homo-sexual/heterosexual, masculine/feminine, and even male/female."[41]

Lesbian Characters in Post–Francoist Fiction

On 16 November 1976, democracy was reestablished in Spain with the passage of the Law of Political Reform. From a literary viewpoint, this date is crucial because it removed book censorship as a powerful force that writers had to face.[42] In Spain, the emergence of democracy brought freedom and signaled the removal of laws repressing homosexuality. The next two novels with which this essay deals were published under these new circumstances.

The Same Sea Every Summer was the Catalan publisher–writer Esther Tusquets's first novel. In it, a Renaissance literature professor falls in love with one of her students, Clara. The novel tells the story of how the romantic relationship develops. Its narrator, a fifty-year-old married and wealthy Catalan professor is unhappy with family life: Her husband, a successful movie director, is a womanizer who is interested in younger women; her mother and daughter are distant and focused on traveling and work, respectively. The narrator meets Clara, thanks to a lesbian friend, Maite, and they soon become lovers. Their relationship takes place mainly in the professor's beach house. It lasts for about a month until the narrator–protagonist meets with her husband and reconciles. This event marks the end of the relationship with Clara, who decides to quit school and return to Colombia, her native country. The narrator continues living as an unhappy lesbian married to a womanizer who does not love her.

Stylistically, Tusquets's work is characterized by its dense poetic prose. References to classical, Renaissance, and children's literature abound. The discourse requires that the reader be able to decode numerous references, particularly mythological ones. However, when the narrator describes sexual scenes, the poetic language is transparent: "Y mi mano va abriendo suavemente el estrecho camino entre su carne y mi carne, entre nuestros dos vientres confundidos, hasta llegar al húmedo pozo entre las piernas."[43] Descriptions such as this these are numerous; they are also among the first lesbian sex depicted realistically—and beautifully—in Spanish fiction.

Tusquets's novel contains additional innovations. First, the narrator is a mature woman who has no trouble making love to another woman. She acknowledges that the relationship with Clara was one of the best experiences of her life: "Ni ella ni yo sabíamos que pudiera existir tan siquiera un amor vacío de programas y de metas, . . . tan tierno y torpe y delicioso y sabio como el de dos adolescentes que llevaran siglos ocupados en un amor que no conoce paroxismos ni desfallecimientos."[44] The creation of such a character is remarkable not only in the context of the works studied here. A quick glance at literary tradition finds rich depictions of love between young heterosexual partners or between older men and younger female characters; Tusquets subverts this heterosexual tradition.

Although innovations are present in Tusquets's novel, it still does not include the newer strategy of having the main character divorce and live with a new lover. Instead of a permanent companion, she seems to be looking for a mere affair. The Clara character, however, is a prototype of the new generation of lesbians, eager to explore the possibility of living with the other woman. She proposes "un futuro que puede situarse en los suburbios de Marsella como en las selvas colombianas, y que a veces parece desarrollarse en París o en Nueva York o en la misma Barcelona, pero en el que estamos invariablemente juntas, siempre amándonos y convirtiendo este amor en mágica palanca que pueda transformar el mundo."[45] The narrator—a wealthy, wise, and well-read professor—rejects the offer so she can continue to be the woman whom her husband and other family members expect her to be. The main character refuses the real possibility of carrying on a lesbian relationship, with all the personal and public implications it involves.

The title of Tusquets's novel, *El mismo mar de todos los veranos*, refers explicitly to the title of Barbero's novel *El último verano en el espejo*. Its content provides internal similarities. The stories, for instance, take place during the same season; there are identically named characters (Clara); and both refer to Barcelona. These elements allow me to posit a continuous, autonomous tradition of lesbian fiction developed and carried out by female Catalan novelists writing in Spanish. In Tusquets's work, upperclass characters continue to be the main focus of narration. The novel also shows a predilection for specific professional groups, such as writers, artists, and intellectuals, and it includes a new age group originally introduced by Moix: college students. These findings are similar to those discussed by Esther Newton, who studied the professional make-up of a homosexual neigborhood in New York in the 1960s: "Some had inherited wealth, while many were businesswomen or professionals in such fields as publicity, media, and theater, including some famous names like Cheryl Crawford, founder of the Group Theater and Actor's Studio, and writers Carson McCullers, Patricia Highsmith, and Janet Flanner, and her companion, Natalia Murray."[46]

The Catalan writer Luis Goytisolo published *Achilles' Cholera* in 1979. The novel tells the story of Matilde Moret, a writer in her fifties who is married but has a female lover. At the story's opening, Matilde is spending summer vacation at her beach house with her young lover, Camila. The latter has been seeing a gigolo named Roberto. When Matilde finds out about the affair, she manipulates both Camila and the gigolo to catch them together.

Goytisolo's language is transparent in a way that Tusquet's is not: "Hablaba y hablaba mientras yo la desnudaba despacio y con cuidado, gozando de la afloración paulatina de aquel cuerpo dilatado por el amor, todo él abriéndose como unos grandes labios."[47] Still, several similarities can be found between the two works. First, in both, the narrator is also the main character; second, both depict relationships between two women from different age groups; and third, power relations between the two characters are extreme. Indeed, in Goytisolo's book this last element has been enhanced in such a way that it can be said that the main character controls her lover's life at various levels, mainly for economic reasons.

During the narration, Matilde finds a copy of a novella titled *El edicto de Milán* (The Milan edict), which was published in 1963 as a private edition to avoid official censorship. This novella-within-a-novel occupies three chapters of *Achilles' Cholera*'s nine—that is, about 100 of the 325 pages of the original Spanish edition. The novella (and the novel itself) deals with women's lives under the Francoist regime. *The Milan Edict*'s main character, Lucía, is a young Catalan woman studying fine arts in Paris during the 1960s. Lucía's Parisian stay abounds in sexual experimentation, including both bisexual and homosexual activity. According to Matilde, the novella could not have been published except as a private edition. The depiction of sexuality and political opposition to Franco are the two reasons Matilde offers for not trying to publish the book commercially. Actually, social and sexual customs would have prevented the book from receiving the censor's approval. Lucía ends a relationship with a boyfriend, returns to Barcelona, and marries a wealthy Catalan named Javier.

When Matilde finishes reading *The Milan Edict*, she states it was written over a one-month period in the middle of a marriage crisis. The reader should note that *Achilles' Cholera* also starts during the summer and in the middle of a crisis—this time, between Matilde and her permanent female lover. This is one of the many novelties of this book. Matilde makes reference to childhood, adolescent, and adulthood events. A recurrent theme in these memories is one of sexuality and social convention: "Yo, por ejemplo, si me casé fue sólo para huir del medio familiar, para disponer de mí misma con mayor independencia."[48]

As I mentioned earlier, under Francoism most lesbian women had only two ways to escape discrimination: by having bisexual relationships or through motherhood. In *Achilles' Cholera*, the main character marries a wealthy man, rejects motherhood, and is able to pursue homosexuality. In doing so in the way depicted in the book, Matilde becomes an unusual literary example of a middle-aged woman looking for affection. Nevertheless, Matilde's manipulation of Camila is morally despicable: "La natural supeditación de una sierva, lo que ella es respecto a mí en lo que a supeditación económica se refiere, ni más ni menos que una sierva, viviendo como vive a mi costa."[49] To a certain extent, both characters are presented as engaged in an economic transaction. On the one hand, Camila is depicted as a young bisexual who does not hesitate to sell herself to a lesbian customer; on the other hand, Matilde is someone who uses her economic power to buy sex and affection.

An Autonomous Tradition

The development of Spanish lesbian fiction began in the 1960s with the pioneering work of Matute, who is now a member of the Royal Academy of Language. The late appearance of the lesbian subject in Spain is a direct consequence of the political and religious repression exercised during the Francoist regime. Book censorship made it extremely difficult for writers to deal openly with sexuality. As a consequence, sexual minorities could not be depicted, except in the ways ordered by the state and the Catholic church. Matute's *Soldiers Cry at Night* depicts the homosexual female subject in this way, and the topic is included as a minor incident within the narrative. Yet despite the restrictions, Matute was able to present two different images of lesbians: a mannish woman and a femme. Lesbians appear as outcasts and immoral beings.

Indeed, homosexual women are equated with criminals and are believed to have perverse personalities. The story is located in rural Catalonia; the homosexual characters come from lowerclass and marginal origins, and they are situated in marginal social contexts.

After the passage of the Press Law of 1966, book censorship continued to be enforced. However, Barbero proves that changes, even if they are minor ones, are possible and have important literary implications. Although it was published less than three years after *Soldiers Cry at Night*, Barbero's *Last Summer* depicts the lesbian subject under a new light. In addition to its avant-garde use of the word "lesbian" to refer to homosexual women, *Last Summer* includes new elements that widen the configuration of gay women in the 1960s: Lesbians receive more attention, with one becoming a principal character in the fictional work; homosexuality is depicted as common behavior in religious private schools for girls; the main lesbian character is wealthy and married, though she continues to have homosexual sex. Further, women's sexuality is presented openly on several occasions. The novel's main character recalls her past and does not seem to realize—or does not want to accept—that she may be a lesbian. This conclusion is supported by the fact that the depiction of heterosexuality is problematic, leading one to think that the character is going through a process of questioning her sexual orientation. Barbero uses Matute's characters' names and sets the story in Madrid and Barcelona. In this 1967 novel, lesbian characters stop being configured as marginal outcasts. After *Last Summer*, lesbian subjects will commonly be represented as middle- and upper-class individuals, among them writers, actors, and artists.

The third novel analyzed, Moix's *Julia*, was the first work to present a young lesbian refusing heterosexism and fighting against homophobia. *Julia* deals with the struggles of growing up as a lesbian in a society in which homosexuality is repressed and gay people are hated. With Moix's contribution to contemporary Spanish literature, the subject reaches a level that makes possible a more profound exploration of the realities of homosexual life. Expression of homosexual anguish and of unsatisfied sexuality abound in *Julia*, making the text essential for studying lesbian self-representation in this national literature. The main character is a young college student and a native of Barcelona, where she grows up in a wealthy family. The book is pioneering in its depiction of lesbian love among different age and social groups. It includes a new model of lesbian identity that surpasses the one depicted in previous books—that is, closeted homosexuality. Heterosexual marriage and motherhood are rejected as appropriate ways to assume a different sexual identity. The appearance of this important novel suggests deep-rooted opposition within the gay community toward contemporary perceptions and repression of homosexuality. This high level of group consciousness in the Spanish urban gay community is shown vis-à-vis the public protests against repressive anti-homosexual legislation that took place at the beginning of the 1970s, when numerous gay organizations were formed in the Catalan and Basque regions.

After 1976, Spain entered a period marked by political change. Laws repressing homosexuality and censorship were modified, and books on homosexual matters and by homosexual authors were permitted. The two novels discussed from this time were published in 1978 and 1979. In addition to being the only ones in the study that were not subjected to censorship, both novels share characteristics in the ways they depict lesbian relationships, which are different from the depictions in the books written in the 1960s. Tusquets presents as a main character a wealthy Catalan professor who is having an affair with one of her female students. The main character is married and has a grown-up daughter. Tusquets's character is unable to assume homosexuality openly. Goytisolo's main character, by contrast—a writer named Matilde Moret who is also a wealthy resident of Barcelona—is able to sustain a stable relationship with her lover, Camila. However, power relations between the characters are unequal. Moret uses money to control her partner's behavior. Even when Tusquets and Goytisolo continue to depict female homosexuality within the same social framework used by Moix, they do not deepen the subject. To a certain extent, both novels revisit Barbero's idea behind the Elena character in *Last Summer:* a wealthy Catalan who marries and continues to have homosexual sex. What is really new in Tusquets's and Goytisolo's novels is that both writers display the subject with a different focus that openly treats lesbian sexuality.[50]

By focusing on five novels that depict lesbianism, I have attempted to prove that the five writers work within an independent literary framework. Initial images seem to be revisited and changed according to each writer's needs and the time when she or he was working. By using a set of identical names, common literary motives, the same story location, and even the same season of the year, this group of Catalan novelists started and developed an autonomous Spanish lesbian tradition that has come to include other writers, such as Carme Riera and Ana Rossetti. Further, the lesbian tradition discussed here seems to be different from that found in studies of men's homosexual writing.[51] A larger study comparing the representation of gay and lesbian characters in Spanish literature, as well as specific studies of the homosexual experience under Francoism, is needed to gain a better understanding of a minority group marginalized until very recently.

Notes

1. Ana María Matute, *Los mercaderes. Los soldados lloran de noche* (Barcelona: Ediciones Destino, 1964).

2. Teresa Barbero, *El último verano en el espejo* (Barcelona: Ediciones Destino, 1967).

3. Ana María Moix, *Julia* (Barcelona: Seix Barral, 1970).

4. Esther Tusquets, *El mismo mar de todos los veranos* (Barcelona: Editorial Lumen, 1978).

5. Luis Goytisolo, *La cólera de Aquiles* (Barcelona: Seix Barral, 1979).

6. María D. Costa, "Spanish Literature," in *The Gay and Lesbian Literary Heritage,* ed. Claude Summers (New York: Henry Holt, 1995).

7. Janet Pérez, *Contemporary Women Writers of Spain* (Boston: Twayne Publishers, 1988), 134.

8. "In the past Dionisia had worked as a ship stewardess doing the Shangai–Marseille route. She was involved with every thing: drugs, smuggling": Matute, *Los soldados.* This and all

subsequent translations from Spanish, including literary and nonliterary works, are mine. I thank Barbara Riess and Thomas Harrington for proofreading and editing this essay. Miguel Gomes and Monserrat Ferrés also provided valuable insights and encouragement on a previous version of this essay.

9. Jorge Salessi, *Médicos maleantes maricas. Higiene, criminología y homosexualidad en la construcción de la nación Argentina (Buenos Aires: 1871–1914)* (Rosario, Argentina: Beatriz Viterlo, 1995), 202–204.

10. "'You are right, you are not a child any more. They should not do this to you, Martita, poor thing.' Marta did not dare move. Dionisia continued caressing her legs. 'You are beautiful, if you were only allowed to dress up like the other girls your age'": Matute, *Los soldados*, 110.

11. "In the solitude of the chapel, with a very strong smell of incense and melted wax, Clarita's voice seemed to come from beyond the grave: 'They are bad girls, you know? They lock themselves in the bathrooms in pairs, and then undress'": Barbero, *El último verano*, 67.

12. "When we were called to have dinner, we were aroused. Later, in the bedroom, when Elena turned the light off, she asked me if I wanted her to come into my bed for a little while. 'That way we can talk much better; you want to?' Suddenly I felt her slip between my sheets. I got very nervous when she asked me, 'Do you know what lovers do when they are alone?'": ibid., 79–80.

13. "Elena had friends she would go dancing with, and whom she kissed; one of her friends, a redheaded girl with a masculine demeanor, does not leave her alone for a minute; she always seems to be in a bad mood. 'She is a lesbian,' Clara explained to us one evening. 'She is in love with Elena. Elena has something that attracts lesbians'": ibid., 227.

14. "Elena had disturbed my life. During the day, everything could have been normal if it wasn't for that conscience that accused me much like a threatening pointed finger": ibid., 83.

15. Ibid., 242.

16. "Do you know what we should do? Leave Angel, then you and I rent an apartment together. . . . What you need is to be independent. . . . What's more, damn it, I like to be with you, I like talking with you, confiding in you": ibid., 248.

17. Bonnie Zimmerman, "Exiting from Patriarchy: The Lesbian Novel of Development," in *The Voyages in Fictions of Female Development*, ed. Elizabeth Abel (Hanover, N.H.: University of New England Press, 1983), 247.

18. "She missed her aunt's body close to hers; she missed her delicate, soft skin, as well as her long hair that she used to caress time and again before falling asleep": ibid., 108–109.

19. "At night, in bed, she found it impossible not to think about aunt Elena. She missed her body lying by her own and her caresses. She hugged the pillow, closed her eyes, and imagined aunt Elena there, close to her": ibid., 130.

20. "[Mother] complained that Julia never took the initiative to buy a dress or some shoes for herself, that she never did her hair or anything of the like that she considered a demonstration of her femininity. When Julia asked for something, any sort of decorative personal item, she eagerly bought it for her without question. According to her, a girl should be coquettish and vain; the contrary, is man-like": ibid., 145.

21. "Girls who were not very friendly, who refused to go to a party, did not care for their personal appearance, and got bored talking of boyfriends and of fashionable clothes, were said to be 'weird'; they had a very strange behavior": Carmen Martín Gaite, *Usos amorosos de la postguerra española* (Barcelona: Anagrama, 1987), 38.

22. "Often she would prefer that the principal be more affectionate toward her, that she hold her like the day after Rafael's death": Moix, *Julia*, 157.

23. Books that were not published under Francoism are numerous. See, for example, Luis Cernuda, *La realidad y el deseo* (Madrid: FCE España, 1996); Jaime Gil de Biedma, *Antología poética* (Madrid: Alianza Editorial, 1981); and Jesús Fernández Santos, *Extramuros* (Barcelona: Argos Vergara, 1978). Fernández Santos's book deals with same-sex representation, but not in a contemporary setting.

24. Manuel L. Abellán, *Censura y creación literaria en España (1939–1976)* (Barcelona: Ediciones Península, 1980), 22.

25. Raymond Carr and Juan Pablo Fusi, *Spain: Dictatorship to Democracy* (London: George Allen and Unwin, 1997), 115, and Abellán, *Censura*, 69.

26. Abellán, *Censura*, 70.

27. Among the foreign homosexual authors who were banned from publication were André Gide, E. M. Forster, and Constantin Cavafis. For a detailed list, see Abellán, *Censura*.

28. Ibid., 87–88.

29. Carr and Fusi, *Spain*, 113.

30. Abellán, *Censura*, 162. On this subject, see Armand De Fluvia, *Aspectos jurídico-legales de la homosexualidad* (Barcelona: Instituto Lambda, 1986); Ricardo Llamas, *Teoría torcida: prejuicios y discursos en torno a la homosexualidad* (Madrid: Siglo XXI, 1998); Manuel Soriano Gil, *Homosexualidad y represión* (Madrid: Zero, 1978).

31. "The numerous gangs of flamboyant queers found everywhere is the most shameful aspect of the city": Martín Gaite, *Usos amorosos*, 105.

32. "Restriction and moderation were key words, the hidden admonitions in everybody's behavior": ibid., 14.

33. Ibid., 38.

34. Abellán, *Censura*, 78.

35. Ibid.

36. Elena Martínez interprets a relationship in this way when analyzing the poetry of Magaly Alabau. See Elena Martínez, *Lesbian Voices from Latin America* (New York: Garland Publishing, 1996), 40–41.

37. Martha Vicinus, "'They Wonder to Which Sex I Belong': The Historical Roots of the Modern Lesbian Identity," in *The Lesbian and Gay Studies Reader*, eds. Henry Abelove, Michéle Aina Barale, and David M. Halperin (New York: Routledge, 1993), 446.

38. Robert R. Ellis, *The Hispanic Homograph: Gay Self-Representation in Contemporary Spanish Autobiography* (Urbana: University of Illinois Press, 1997), 116.

39. Chris Perriam, *Desire and Dissent: An Introduction to Luis Antonio de Villena* (Washington, D.C.: Berg, 1995), 18.

40. Stephan Likosky, ed., *Coming Out: An Anthology of International Gay and Lesbian Writings* (New York: Pantheon Books, 1992), 204–208.

41. Ibid., 17.

42. José B. Monleón, *Del Franquismo a la postmodernidad* (Madrid: Ediciones Akal, 1995), 5.

43. "My hand softly opens the narrow path between her skin and mine, between our confused bellies, until it gets to the moist well between her legs": Tusquets, *El mismo mar*, 155.

44. "Neither she nor I knew that a love empty of schedules and goals could exist . . . so affectionate and clumsy and delicious and wise as that of two teenagers who spent centuries busy loving each other, a love that knows little of paroxysms and of dying": ibid., 181.

45. "A future that can be located in Marseilles, the Colombian jungles, Paris, New York, or even here, in Barcelona, but in which we are always together, without an end, always loving each other and making from this love a magical lever able to change the world": ibid., 185.

46. Esther Newton, "Just One of the Boys: Lesbians in Cherry Grove, 1960–1988," in Abelove et al., *Lesbian and Gay Studies Reader*, 529.

47. "She didn't stopped talking even when I was taking her clothing off. I was doing it slowly and carefully, enjoying the slow appearance of a body which I had previously possessed, opening itself up like big lips": Goytisolo, *La cólera de Aquiles*, 77.

48. "If I, for example, got married it was just because it was the only means to leave my parents' home and have more freedom": ibid., 161.

49. "She depends on me like a servant. An economic dependence which is natural, taking into account that I am the one in power, have the money she needs and I give to her": ibid., 25.

50. For more on recent lesbian representation in Spanish fiction, see Brad Epps, "Virtual Sexuality: Lesbianism, Loss, and Deliverance in Carme Riera's 'Te deix, amor, la mar com a penyora,'" in *¿Entiendes? Queer Readings, Hispanic Writings,* ed. Emilie Bergmann and Paul Julian Smith (Durham, N.C.: Duke University Press, 1995), 317–45; Xosé Buxán Bran, ed. *Conciencia de un singular deseo. Estudios lesbianos y gays en el Estado español* (Barcelona: Leartes, 1997); and Carmen de Urioste, "Las novelas de Lucía Etxebarria como proyección de sexualidades disidentes en la España democrática," *Revista de Estudios Hispánicos* 34, no. 1 (2000): 123–37.

51. See Angel Sahurquillo, *Federico García Lorca y la cultura de la homosexualidad* (Edsbruk, Sweden: Akademitryck, 1986); and Perriam, *Desire and Dissent*.

Inmaculada Pertusa

---

2   Carme Riera:
(Un)covering the Lesbian Subject
or Simulation of Coming Out?

> *Coming out: it can bring about the revelation of a powerful unknowing as*
> *unknowing, not as a vacuum or as the blank it can pretend to be but as a*
> *weighty and occupied and consequential epistemological space.*
> *—Eve Kosofsky Sedgwick*

Carme Riera published "Te deix, amor, la mar com a penyora" (I leave you the sea, my love) in 1975 and "Jo pos per testimoni les gavines" (I call as a witness the seagulls) in 1977.[1] Although they form integral parts of her first two collections of short stories, these stories were not translated into Spanish until 1991.[2] In fact, both volumes of her stories were limited to readers of Catalan for those fourteen years. Yet, according to Luisa Cotoner, Riera forms part of the "generación del boom de la literatura catalana escrita por mujeres, junto con Montserrat Roig, María Antonia Oliver, Isabel Clara Simó, Helena Valentí, entre otras."[3]

Taking advantage of the new liberty granted by Spain's constitutional monarchy, Riera addressed the still controversial theme of lesbian love, describing a love relationship between an adolescent girl and a mature woman.[4] In "I Leave You the Sea, My Love," Marina, who is about to give birth to her first child and fears she may die, writes a letter to María, a high-school teacher with whom she once had a love affair.[5] She recounts the details of their relationship and attempts to explain the reasons for their breakup. "I Call as a Witness the Seagulls," published two years later, is María's response to Marina's letter.[6] María confirms the emotional liaison with her student but denies that their relationship ever resulted in physical contact. Riera thus presents a woman as another woman's object of desire, offering the possibility that, as Teresa de Lauretis explains, "in the very act of assuming and speaking from the position of subject, a woman could concurrently recognize women as subjects and as objects of female desire."[7] Riera did not use the lesbian theme merely as "a defense of free love";

she employed the option of lesbianism to show that a woman can be both the subject and the object of love.[8]

In an interview with Neus Aguado, Riera explained that, athough "I Leave You the Sea" is a defense of free love, it also shows that "la libertad de uno acaba donde empieza la libertad del otro, que estamos siempre en función del otro, pero si este otro acepta, cada uno sabe con las posibilidades que cuenta. Me pareció bien darle una normalidad a este tema, que por otra parte desde el punto de vista de la realidad no lo tenía."[9] When asked in an interview with Geraldine Nichols why she made lesbianism the theme of these short stories, Riera explained that she made the choice when she realized that "había otros seres distintos a los heterosexuales,"[10] and that she was interested in presenting the homosexual woman's story. Riera recalled that she "[s]e empez[ó] a interesar por Safo de Lesbos como poeta, lo cual [l]a llevó a observar este aspecto y a considerar que la gran aportación de Safo era precisamente elevar a la categoría de objeto del deseo a otra mujer por una mujer; que la mujer fuera a la vez sujeto y objeto del deseo en relación a su propio sexo."[11] This statement strongly suggests that one can correctly argue that Riera used the theme of lesbian relationships not as just another manifestation of sexuality but, rather, as a medium in which to give women a subjectivity denied in the traditional definition of "woman."

Marilyn Frye clearly explains the significance of the lesbian relationship's bearing on womanhood when she writes:

> If the lesbian sees the woman, the woman may see the lesbian seeing her. With this, there is a flowering of possibilities. The woman, feeling herself seen, may learn that she can be seen; she may also be able to know that a woman can see, that is, can author perception. With this, there enters for the woman the logical possibility of assuming her authority as a perceiver and of shifting her own attention.[12]

Riera's two protagonists, María and Marina, express the mutual discovery of their desire through the medium of vision. María's gaze initiates the courtship, the game of seduction, when from the theater box "ésta miraba de reojo"[13] at Marina. Marina learns to see the world around her through María's eyes in the first act of identification with her. She says, "Mis ojos, que eran los tuyos, porque yo contemplaba el mundo a través de tu mirada, captaron matices, colores, formas, detalles, que a ti te parecían nuevos y sorprendentes,"[14] and she see herself looking at María's nude body, able to "saciar [su]s ojos mirándola tanto tiempo como quisiera,"[15] and finally able to see herself looking at herself "in the mirror" of María's body.

It is along the lines of Riera's attempt to create a space for feminine self-representation that writers such as Susan Wolfe and Julia Penelope identify the efforts of feminist criticism in general, as well as what they call "lesbian cultural criticism," to deny the notion that women can be seen only in relation to men, that they can be defined only in terms of male discourse.[16] According to Wolfe and Penelope, the greater literary visibility of lesbian relationships and experiences has increased the opportunity for relationships between women. It has reduced the power of masculine connotations and masculine representation of feminine inner space.

We must not forget, however, that the lesbian experience is characterized by a high degree of invisibility, not only socially and culturally, but also on the personal level. Wolfe and Penelope say that "most lesbians spend portions of our lives invisible to ourselves as well as to others," their invisibility being "part of the social construction of a lesbian identity."[17] This invisibility is real; it is not merely rhetorical. It is the product of dynamics related to coming out of the closet. Invisibility is the silence imposed on the lesbian who instinctively rejects identities imposed on her by everyone and everything in her life. This silence is intended to destroy a lesbian's sense of self and leads to the formation of the "space of the closet"—a space that will be impossible to overcome or eliminate because it is part of the construction of a lesbian identity.

Eve Kosofsky Sedgwick, although more interested in male than in female homosexual discourse, has described the "closet" dynamic precisely, including the contradictions that surround it.[18] Along with Michel Foucault, Sedgwick recognizes 1870 as the birth year of the term "homosexual," when it was defined by the legal, medical, and pedagogical discourses of the day.[19] These three areas of study shaped the debate over homosexuality and provided lasting conclusions. They made it possible to see the individual not only in terms of a biological gender assigned at birth, but also from the perspective of sexual behavior imposed by the medical, moral, and legal norms of conduct of the moment. They made clear that the formation of sexual identity is based on two absolute binaries: masculine–feminine, on one hand, and heterosexual–homosexual, on the other.

It was also toward the end of the nineteenth century that Western culture, spurred by scientific debates about sexuality, established a much more direct relationship between the construction of individual identity and the definition of human sexuality. Observing the current polemic regarding the establishment of a satisfactory definition of the binomial heterosexual–homosexual, Sedgwick argues that the space of "the closet" is the product of contradictions in this "crisis of definition." The origin of this modern crisis is found in the contradictions created both by the universalist and minoritizing conceptions of sexual identity and by the paradigms of transitivity through which a concept of gender is granted to homosexuality. In the universalist conception, homosexuality is considered a result of the situation of individuals who desire sexual relationships with the same sex. They are at the margins of the gender; they are neither men nor women. In the minoritizing view, homosexuality is seen as an example of what gender is par excellence. In a society that attempts to separate these concepts by approving heterosexual and disapproving homosexual behavior, a "crisis of definition" develops. A categorical definition of these terms refuses to recognize that the two concepts are superimposed, making it impossible to do without either of them.[20]

Foucault notes that, toward the end of the nineteenth century, knowledge and sex are synonymous and inseparable terms, in which "to know" implies sexual knowledge and "not to know" sexual ignorance. This sexual ignorance, produced in a conscious and willful manner as a result of the dynamic of "knowing" and, at the same time "hiding," which characterizes modern societies, led to the development of the "sexual secret." From that moment on, details of individual sexual practices circulated exclusively within the boundaries of a "secret," their revelation being possible only under the jurisdiction of one of the three dominant discourses: medical, legal, and religious. These discourses guaranteed control over the revelation of sexual knowledge and the effect that such a revelation could have, thus creating at the same time a secret space that one could not leave without their consent: the space of the closet. As Sedgwick explains:

> A lot of the energy of attention and demarcation that has swirled around issues of homosexuality since the end of the nineteenth century, in Europe and the United States, has been impelled by the distinctively indicative relation of homosexuality to wider mappings of secrecy and disclosure, and of the private and the public, that were and are critically problematical for the gender, sexual, and economic structures of the heterosexist culture at large.[21]

In this model, the figure of "the closet" is not only seen as a consequence of the crisis of defining heterosexuality and homosexuality. It also appears to reproduce the same contradictions between the desire for knowledge and the persisting ignorance that keeps it active. Coming out of "the closet" is based on the same necessity to know (to reveal and to conceal) that created the "crisis of definition." They are both produced by the dynamic of both keeping a secret and promising to reveal it.

If we accept Sedgwick's proposal that "closet relationships" (the known and the unknown, the explicit and implicit with regard to the homosexual–heterosexual definition) have the latent ability to bring forward hidden discourses and, at the same time, cover other discourse,[22] then "I Leave You the Sea" and "I Call as a Witness" can be seen as an attempt to come out of a closed space formed by the secret that envelops the love relationship of the protagonists. It describes the coming out of a silence imposed on the lesbian subject, on María and on Marina, by a system of cultural and social norms: Spain of the 1960s and 1970s. Cotoner has in fact concluded that the significance of the stories in the two volumes lies in

> la capacidad de transfiguración que tiene su lenguaje y la facilidad con que sumerge al lector en un mundo *sensible y enfermizo*, en el ámbito de los *deseos difícilmente materializables*, de intranquilizadoras sospechas de que la belleza existe, más allá de nuestros propios límites, pero cuya consecución acarrea un *riesgo definitivo*.[23]

Cotoner's comment shows her own prejudices about the nature of Marina and María's relationship; she considers it part of a "sensitive and sickly world." Yet it does point to the difficulty the protagonists confront in their coming out of silence, in coming out of the closet in which they have been enclosed. This difficulty is clearly transmitted in the strategies employed by the narrators. If we read both stories as examples of the dynamics of coming out of the closet, we should see that "coming out" is in fact a new covering up. I propose here to interpret the act of (un)covering (which is repeated on many levels in the narratives) as a reflection of the state of being inside and outside the closet at the same time. Revelation supposes two contradictory and simultaneous acts: While it places a woman "outside" a space that limits and oppresses, making the lesbian subject visible, it simultaneously places her "inside" another space that imposes another form of silence.

One of the concerns of current lesbian theory is to establish the meaning of the lesbian subject's "coming out" of a private space, the closet. The exit from this closet is a problematic process and presents the difficulty that, even if it is the entrance into a new space, it does not mean that the new space is any less limiting. As Judith Butler states:

> Conventionally, one comes out of the closet: . . . so we are out of the closet, but into what?, what new unbounded spatiality? The room, the den, the attic, the basement, the house, the bar, the university, some new enclosure whose door, like Kafka's door, produces the expectation of a fresh air and a light of illumination that never arrives? . . . For being "out" always depends to some extent on being "in"; it gains its meaning only within that polarity. Hence, being "out" must produce the closet again and again in order to maintain itself as "out."[24]

The effort of coming out does not necessarily correspond to the disappearance of the space that has been abandoned, because the idea of inside and outside can be perceived only as an opposition of two mutually contradictory terms. Because being outside something implies the existence of an inside space, the exit from the closet obliges the individual to enter a space with new limits that will, in turn, reproduce new forms and feelings of control.

In Riera's two stories, the closed physical spaces are continuations of the secret space in which both protagonists were locked "por culpa del escándalo público," and the threats "en nombre de la moral y de las buenas costumbres."[25] They enter these new spaces during the very process of coming out, exchanging one silent space for another that is no less oppressive. In the first lines of "I Leave You the Sea," Marina says that she is writing beside a window that does not offer a view of the ocean. The beginning of her coming out of the closet acknowledges that she is occupying another closed space, one that limits visibility to a highly significant element: the ocean. This is the same ocean that once witnessed the love between the two women and that, in Cotoner's words, "se configura . . . como emblema del amor desafiante y de lo inasequible, per se, del deseo."[26]

Marina observes that she felt the need to come out of the silence concerning her feelings for María while in the basement of a prison, visiting a friend detained for participating in a student protest. "Él estaba preso y yo libre,"[27] says Marina, expressing her feelings of guilt that it was not she who was enclosed in this physical space. She confesses that after she visited the prison, she wrote María a letter without daring to address it to her, because she already "insistía en olvidar[s]e de [s]u nombre y de [s]us señas."[28] Marina's initial attempt to come out of the closet, by writing the letter, came at a moment in which she knew a false state of freedom: freedom from prison, freedom from María. Marina's feeling of guilt for not being incarcerated with her friend, along with the fact that she found herself needing to write a confession that ended up torn into a thousand pieces, demonstrates her internal struggle. Although writing the letter let her come out of the space of repression and shame, it also forced her to confront potential censorship and social rejection, which she had never before faced. Not having a secured space in which to retreat, her fear of being marginalized proved stronger than her desire to uncover the truth.

When Marina writes the new letter that reveals once again the nature of her relationship with María, she does so in the safety provided by the closed space of marriage and pregnancy. Eight years after her physical relationship with María it is possible for her to uncover something that now will not place her in the group of the silenced. At this time, she has adapted her life to the heterosexual standards that once forced her to live in the closet. Marina's first act of coming out is not this letter to María, however; it is her confession to her husband, Toni, "sin omitir ningún detalle,"[29] of everything that happened between them. She does not receive the personal recognition from Toni that she seeks from María; she receives only confirmation of her belonging to the accepted space of heterosexuals. Now she is looking for personal recognition.

Marina's apparent coming out makes María's even more difficult, because, as Sedgwick says, "to come out does not end anyone's relation to the closet, including turbulently the closet of the other."[30] María performs a first act of coming out by confirming part of the relationship she experienced with Marina, but in fact she does so from the "cuatro paredes asépticas"[31] of a hospital, an institutionalized space where she secludes herself voluntarily and where she will return so as to "dejar de escribir" in order to "desaparecer, volver a palidecer en la oscuridad,"[32] in silence. Marina's letter threatens the safety María has found in the space of remembrance, where she watches over Marina's memory day and night, by forcing her to come out of that space to respond to the letter and the clarity of the facts. María makes an effort to come out of the silence, "para que nunca más nadie escriba ningún otro comentario, ni diga que me conoció a mí,"[33] and then to recuperate the stability of her space, to return with the friends who "esperan siempre, que jamás [le] hacen preguntas, que no buscan razones."[34] Fortunately, her friends respect the silence that has been broken by Marina's coming out of the closet, the silence that she can never fully restore.

María and Marina demonstrate that the process of coming out of the closet is related to the binary figure "inside–outside." On the one hand, outside implies making visible those negative concepts of the subject that caused the appearance of the closet in the first place. On the other hand, by accessing language and breaking her silence, outside offers the lesbian subject the possibility of being a visible part of the culture that had condemned her to invisibility. Sedgwick explains that the difficulty with coming out is establishing a gay identity within a society that represses it, by that very act forcing it to exist:

> In many, if not most, relationships, coming out is a matter of crystallizing intuitions or convictions that had been in the air for a while already and have already established their own power-circuits of silent contempt, silent blackmail, silent glamorization, silent complicity.[35]

Coming out implies reaching beyond the purely personal by forcing one to confront a power system that, through its control over the expression of desire and its institutionalization of sexual relationships, imposes a separation into categories: heterosexual relationships as the legitimate form of sexual desire in the dominant discourse and homosexual relationships as the "deviant" form of that discourse.

One way to come out of the closet is to uncover that which was hidden, to reveal the secret, to speak about what one would rather ignore, to make evident the existence of that which is denied. The secret relationship between María and Marina could have been revealed only through letters, as, according to María, both had tacitly prohibited the other from pronouncing the words orally. However, the use of the epistolary form helps achieve the desired effect on the addressee. As Riera said in the interview with Aguado:

> La carta no es más que un diálogo aplazado en el que tú no te sometes a las preguntas, al interrogatorio del otro, como ocurre en un diálogo directo. Cuando se escribe una carta se intenta explicar el punto de vista personal y se intenta convencer, de la mejor manera posible, al destinatario, que siempre es el lector.[36]

Both Marina and María comment on the existence of a love that passes beyond gender limits and, in so doing, beyond conventional morality. Marina breaks the tacit silence they had agreed to maintain by expressing in detail her feelings for and behavior with María. Even she keeps María's identity hidden until the end, protecting her by not referring to the gender of her lover. The personal recognition that she is looking for from María expands to include a recognition or pardon that she hopes to receive from other readers of her confession.

The concealment of María's sex until the end is a very important element in the story, and it reflects the ambiguity that characterizes much of Riera's writing. It is not until the end that we realize María's story is about two women, not about a man and a woman. In the Catalan version, Riera is able to maintain this ambiguity because of the language's pronoun "nosaltres," used in place of the gender-specific "nosotros" and "nosotras" of Spanish. Also, the use of the name María helps cover the relationship. Written Marìa, it is a man's name; written María it is that of a woman. Riera chose not to accent the name in the Catalan version to reach the maximum ambiguity possible. Having studied the strategies of writing employed by various writers to escape gender, to transcend it, to deny it, to represent it in excess, "to break the agreed upon relation of the reference to the signified, of the flesh to the language," de Lauretis has observed a resistance to represent sexual subjects. She says that "a way of escaping gender is to so disguise erotic and sexual experience as to suppress any representation of its specificity."[37] Marina escapes the domination of gender by hiding the gender identity of her lover. This cover-up provokes a rupture of the reader's universe of expectations, because, from the beginning, the reader thinks that he or she is reading about a love story between a man and a woman.

However, even though "I Leave You the Sea" takes the form of a letter to María, written in a moment of sudden sincerity and with a "mezcla de confidencia y confesión"[38] because of a need to make visible that which has been hidden for eight years, Marina does not really know who will read it. She hopes it will be María, but in the letter itself she considers the possibility that it might not be, saying, "No sé si las cir-cunstancias te harán conocer este escrito, ni si lo entenderás en el caso de que Toni te lo mande."[39] By offering María, or who ever reads the letter, the possibility of not understanding it, she retreats from her revealing act and permits a new cover to obscure the significance that she wanted to give the letter and her relationship with María.

María, like Marina, uses a letter to liberate herself from the oppression of silence, to recount her version of the events and her feelings for her old lover. But she also hides herself with an illegible concluding signature. While Marina resists revealing the generic identity of her lover, María resists revealing her own identity, creating for herself a new closed space—that of anonymity—in which she will be able to continue to be invisible. Both women find ways to hide their secret, and only the sea and sea-gulls know the silence they have failed to break.

Marina's and María's letters, composed by a gifted woman writer, prove that com-ing out of the closet is the expression of a need to be recognized by others in order to recognize oneself. It is a process of seeking recognition, of acquiring an identity oth-erwise denied to a lesbian. As Barbara Smith says, "Unlike many other oppressed groups, homosexuals are not a group whose identity is clear from birth. Through the process of coming out, a person might indeed acquire this identity at any point in life."[40] The fact that encounters between Marina and María always occurred in closed and hidden places (a dark theater box, solitary walkways, the cabin of a boat, the inte-rior of a car) contributes to Marina's need for María's explicit recognition of what the two women experienced together. It is a need that at times manifests itself in a cer-tain tone of reproach when referring to the fact that they themselves were reluctant to give a name to their relationship. In her recollection of moments spent with María, Marina repeatedly refers to the "amor del que jamás habla[ban] por aquel entonces,"[41] a love that both women disguised as friendship, just as Marina says when referring to "ese amor, que llamábamos amistad."[42]

In this letter-writing game, María recognizes her love for Marina without coming to accept herself as lesbian subject. Although she does accept certain similarities between Marina's story and her own experience, she denies other parts of the story and even suggests the possibility that the fictitious author, Carme Riera, overheard the story somewhere and put it together as she pleased. In the letter directed to Carme Riera that precedes her own story, María comments: "No sé quién pudo contarle, con minuciosidad de miniaturista, unos hechos desmenuzando los sentimientos con tanta precisión, al tiempo que escamoteaba otros tergiversando el final."[43] When speaking about her "version of the facts," María denies that the feelings between the two women could have materialized as Marina recalled them in her letter because, "justo en el momento de iniciar el juego ... [a]zorada y estremecida, sali[ó] del camarote dejando su cuerpo de adolescente perfectamente cubierto por una sábana."[44] María covers up Marina's coming out of the closet by denying the response Marina hoped to receive from her. She does acknowledge her desire for another woman when she confesses having rejected Marina "con reconvenciones morales al uso, en las que

[ella] tampoco creía, mientras [se] negaba por dentro a la fortísima llamada del deseo, mientras esquivaba el ansia inmediata de abandonar[s]e a ella, de sumergir[s]e en el deseo de su piel,"[45] yet she still hides Marina's attempt to come out.

Beginning with the first lines of "I Leave You the Sea," one sees Marina's attempt to escape the closed space of the secret in which she has been locked for eight years. In a letter disguised as a confession, she explains for the first time the "real nature" of her relationship with María, certain that Marina will be able, also for the first time, to recognize her lesbian identity. But the revelation of the feelings she experienced with María, of the circumstances that surrounded the failed love story, is not enough to allow Marina to come completely out of the closet. In each act of revelation a new act of covering lies hidden that places Marina in new closed spaces from which she will do nothing to free herself. The refusal on Marina's part to reveal the name of her lover, her insistence on placing herself in enclosures that will protect her from the accusing eye of society, and her doubts about finding an adequate addressee demonstrate her fear of coming completely out of the closet and accepting her lesbian experiences as part of her identity.

With her response in "I Call as a Witness," María recognizes her lesbian identity by accepting Marina's story, but she, too, is unable to come completely out of the closet. From a hospital she admits that she has allowed social pressures and her own fears to rob her of happiness and believes it is too late to abandon the silence that interrupted her relationship with Marina in the first place. The revelations that María makes about her own feelings and her situation remain covered when she refuses to offer her name openly, using age as an excuse. Safeguarded by anonymity, just as being married and having a baby make Marina feel safe, María gives her version of the facts not so much so that what happened will be known but, rather, so that there will be certainty about what did not happen. Although she felt a physical attraction for Marina, she emphasizes that she never consummated her desires for her. The very act of coming out of the closet by admitting her desires is countered by her emphatic assurance that "nothing happened" between them.

The two acts of (un)covering in these stories clearly demonstrate that the process of coming out of the closet involves a new covering up. They confirm Diane Fuss's argument that "most of us [gay and lesbians] are both inside and outside at the same time."[46] The acts of uncovering and covering up, of being both inside and outside, result from society's imposition of negative images on the lesbian subject. In the end, she often opts for invisibility, for keeping her identity secret.

Notes

Epigraph: Eve Kosofsky Sedgwick, *Epistemology of the Closet* (Berkeley: University of California Press, 1990), 77.

1. Carme Riera, "Te deix, amor, la mar com a penyora," in *Te deix, amor, la mar com a penyora* (Barcelona: Laia, 1975); idem, *Jo pos per testimoni les gavines* (Barcelona: Laia, 1977).

2. A Spanish translation that differed markedly from the original story appeared in 1980 under the title "Te entrego, amor, la mar, como ofrenda." Luisa Cotoner's translation did not appear until 1991. It was done with Riera's approval and followed the original Catalan very closely: See Luisa Cotoner, "Introduction," in *Te dejo la mar*, trans. Luisa Cotoner (Madrid: Espasa Calpe, 1991), 11–34.

3. "The boom generation of Catalan literature written by women, together with Montserrat Roig, María Antonia Oliver, Isabel Clara Simó, and Helena Valentí, among others": Cotoner, "Introduction," 19. This and all subsequent English translations are mine. Cotoner does not mention among those "others" Esther Tusquets, who published the first volume of her trilogy, *El mismo mar de todos los veranos* (The same sea every summer) (Barcelona: Editorial Lumen, 1980) in 1978; the second, *El amor es un juego solitario* (Love is a solitary game) (Barcelona: Editorial Lumen, 1980) in 1979; and the third, *Varada tras el último naufragio* (Beachhead after the last shipwreck) (Barcelona: Editorial Lumen, 1985) in 1980. All three volumes were in Spanish, making Tusquets well known earlier than Riera. The fact that Tusquets did not publish in Catalan is not, in my opinion, sufficient reason to exclude her from the category of the "boom generation." Her trilogy is an important expression of the lesbian voice in both Catalan and Spanish, and her name should appear at the top of Cotoner's list. Tusquets's trilogy, together with the two stories by Riera discussed here, initiated a Spanish lesbian literary movement that brought Spanish women's fiction to prominence in the world of feminist experiences.

4. In 1978, Spain adopted a new constitution that declared all people equal and prohibited discrimination against any individual for reasons of "birth, race, religion, opinion, or any other personal or social condition or circumstance" (Art. 15). This guarantee led to the appearance of numerous new newspapers, to the publication of many books heretofore censored, and to the establishment of an Institute of Women's Studies. It is not an overstatement to say that it opened the way for the birth of the Spanish feminist movement.

5. Carme Riera, "Te dejo, amor, en prenda la mar," in Cotoner, trans., *Te dejo la mar*. Subsequent references are cited as "I Leave You the Sea."

6. Idem, "Pongo por testigo a las gaviotas," in ibid. Subsequent references are cited as "I Call as a Witness."

7. Teresa de Lauretis, "Sexual Indifference and Lesbian Representation," in *The Lesbian and Gay Studies Reader*, ed. Henry Abelove, Michéle Aina Barale, and David M. Halperin (New York: Routledge, 1993), 142.

8. This came at a time when, as Luce Irigaray explained in 1975, "the feminine occurs only within models and laws devised by male subjects. Which implies that there are not really two sexes, but only one. A single practice and representation of the sexual": Luce Irigaray, *This Sex Which Is Not One*, trans. Catherine Porter (Ithaca, N.Y.: Cornell University Press, 1985), 86.

9. "One's freedom ends where someone else's begins, that we always affect others, but if the other is in agreement, each one knows what possibilities may abound. It seemed good to me that a normality had been given to this topic, which, from the point of view of reality, it did not have before": Neus Aguado, "Epístola de mar y de sol. Entrevista con Carme Riera," *Quimera* 105 (1991): 34.

10. "There were beings other than heterosexuals": Geraldine C. Nichols, *Escribir espacio propio: Laforet, Matute, Moix, Tusquets, Riera y Roig por sí mismas* (Minneapolis: Institute for the Study of Ideologies and Literatures, 1989), 208.

11. "Began to get interested in Sappho of Lesbos as a poet, which made her look at this aspect and consider that Sappho's great contribution was precisely to elevate a woman to the cate-

gory from object of desire by another woman; that the woman was at one and the same time subject and object of desire in relation to her own gender": ibid.

12. Marilyn Frye, *The Politics of Reality: Essays in Feminist Theory* (New York: Crossing Press, 1983), 172.

13. "She look[ed] with a side glance": Riera, "Te dejo, amor," 55.

14. "My eyes, which were yours, because I contemplated the world through your vision, picked up nuances, colors, forms, details, that to you seemed new and surprising": ibid.

15. "to satiate [her] eyes looking at her as long as she wanted to": ibid.

16. Susan J. Wolfe and Julia Penelope, eds., *Sexual Practice, Textual Theory: Lesbian Cultural Criticism* (Cambridge: Blackwell, 1993), 3.

17. Ibid., 23.

18. Sedgwick, *Epistemology.*

19. Michel Foucault saw 1870, the year Westphal's article regarding "the opposing sexual sensations" was published, as highly symbolic. In that article, Westphal insisted that "homosexuality" no longer be identified as the practice of sodomy but assigned to a psychological, psychiatric, and medical category: Michel Foucault, *La historia de la sexualidad. Volumen 1. La Voluntad de Saber* (Madrid: Siglo Veintiuno de España Editores, 1985], 56.

20. Sedgwick, *Epistemology*, 11.

21. Ibid., 71.

22. Ibid., 3.

23. "The capacity of transfiguration that their language has and the facility with which the reader is submerged into a *sensitive and sickly world*, into a climate of *desires difficult to realize,* of disturbing suspicions that beauty exists beyond our own limits, but whose attainment carries a *definite risk*": Cotoner, *Te dejo la mar,* 14; emphasis added.

24. Judith Butler, "Imitation and Gender Insubordination," in Abelove et al., *Lesbian and Gay Studies Reader,* 309.

25. "Because of public scandal" and "in the name of morality and good conduct": Riera, "Te dejo, amor," 56–57.

26. "Shapes itself . . . as an emblem of defiant love and of desire which is, per se unattainable": ibid., 33.

27. "He was imprisoned, and I was free": ibid., 65.

28. "Insisted on forgetting [her] name and [her] address": ibid.

29. "Without omitting any details": ibid., 68.

30. Sedgwick, *Epistemology,* 54.

31. "Four sterile walls": Riera, "Pongo por testigo," 132.

32. "Abandon writing" and "disappear, grow pale again in the darkness": ibid., 131.

33. "So that no one ever again writes another commentary nor says that she has known me": ibid., 131.

34. "Always wait, who never ask questions, who don't look for explanations": ibid., 132.

35. Sedgwick, *Epistemology,* 53.

36. "The letter is nothing more than a postponed dialogue in which you don't submit yourself to questions, to the other's interrogation, as happens in direct dialogue. When one writes a letter, he or she attempts to explain his or her personal point of view and tries to convince, in the best way possible, the addressee, who is always the reader": Aguado, "Entrevista," 36.

37. De Lauretis, "Sexual Indifference," 145.

38. "Mixture of confidence and confession": Riera, "Te dejo, amor," 64.

39. "I don't know if circumstances will allow you to read this writing, nor if you will understand it if Toni sends it to you": ibid., 68.

40. Barbara Smith, "Homophobia: Why Bring It Up?" in Abelove et al., *Lesbian and Gay Studies Reader,* 100.

41. "Love of which [they] never spoke at that time": Riera, "Te dejo, amor," 56.

42. "That love, which we called friendship": ibid., 56.

43. "I don't know who could have told you, with the minute detail of a miniaturist, some of the facts, scrutinizing the feelings with such precision, while at the same time eliminating others and distorting the ending": Riera, "Pongo por testigo," 130.

44. "Exactly at the moment of initiating the game . . . she [María] ran out of the ship's cabin bewildered and trembling, leaving [Marina's] perfect adolescent body covered with a sheet": ibid., 136.

45. "With moral conventionalities, ones [she] didn't believe in, either, while inside denying her own very strong call of desire, while dodging the immediate longing to abandon herself in her, to submerge herself in the desire of her skin": ibid., 135.

46. Diane Fuss, ed., *Inside/Out: Lesbian Theories, Gay Theories* (New York: Routledge, 1991), 123.

Lawrence La Fountain-Stokes

3   Tomboy Tantrums and Queer
     Infatuations: Reading Lesbianism
     in Magali García Ramis's
     Felices días, tío Sergio

The history of lesbianism and of lesbian representation in Puerto Rican and Nuyorican literature is a work in progress that remains mostly unwritten to this day.[1] It is possible, by consulting diverse sources, to begin to assemble an archaeology of sorts, which can also include several moments of notorious female gender insubordination; this project is bound to have gaping holes without further historiographic and archival investigation. Where to start? Should this lesbian edifice begin with the nineteenth-century poet and independence leader Lola Rodríguez de Tió, as Daniel Torres has suggested?[2] Should it include the militant anarchist, feminist, and free-love advocate Luisa Capetillo, who was an avowed homophobe yet was among the first women in Puerto Rico to dress in (and be arrested for wearing) what were then considered men's garments?[3] Who were the first Puerto Rican lesbians to leave their cultural mark?

In a provocative and crucial article titled "Nationalism, Male Anxiety, and the Lesbian Body in Puerto Rican Narrative," Agnes I. Lugo-Ortiz has identified Emilio Díaz Varcárcel's short story "El asedio" (The siege, 1958) as perhaps the earliest open thematization of a lesbian character in Puerto Rican letters.[4] Díaz Varcárcel's portrayal of a "mannish lesbian" is anything but positive. Quite to the contrary: It insists on her "unnaturalness" as a detrimental influence on the nation or "patria" (fatherland). Lugo-Ortiz convincingly argues that this story is emblematic of the general (misogynist, homosocial) politics of mid-twentieth-century Puerto Rican male writers, exemplified best by the figure of René Marqués.

Other early and somewhat controversial representations of lesbianism have occurred on the Puerto Rican stage. According to Juan González-Bonilla, the play *Doce paredes negras* (Twelve black walls), which was presented by Producciones Candilejas in the

Sylvia Rexach Theatre in 1973 with the grande dames of Puerto Rican theater Esther Sandoval and Myrna Vázquez, and later restaged with Lydia Echevarría and Alba Nydia Díaz, was the first theatrical representation of lesbianism in Puerto Rico.[5] This play was followed by *Flor de presidio* (Prison flower) in 1989,[6] about lesbianism in Puerto Rican prisons; the production broke ticket-sale records when it was presented and was declared one of the biggest happenings of the 1980s.[7]

Although there are important poetical manifestations of lesbian desire in Puerto Rico in the 1980s, most visibly in Nemir Matos Cintrón's and Luz María Umpierre's books, and in the 1990s with Aixa Ardín, Mariposa, and Lilliana Ramos Collado, there is still a considerable absence of textual representation of lesbians in the narrative of all but the most recent decade, particularly by self-identified Puerto Rican lesbian authors.[8] The essays and poems of the numerous Puerto Rican women included in the 1987 anthology *Compañeras: Latina Lesbians*, edited by Juanita Díaz-Cotto (but published under the pseudonym Juanita Ramos), are a fundamental contribution. Janis Astor del Valle, Rosario Ferré, Erika López, Nicholasa Mohr, Mayra Montero, Frances Negrón-Muntaner, and Mayra Santos Febres come to mind as some of the few well-known Puerto Rican lesbian and non-lesbian women authors (and filmmakers) who have openly dealt with lesbian or female bisexual issues in their creative work.[9] Finally, the remarkable portrayal of Antonio Martorell's lesbian aunt, Consuelo Cardona, in his autobiography *La piel de la memoria* (The skin of memory),[10] has completely been ignored by all of the critics who have reviewed his work; it is worthy of further sustained attention.[11]

These are only the openly visible traces of the edifice. Yet, one is led to ask, is this really all there is? Or have we purposefully or unconsciously ignored earlier "seminal" texts under our very own eyes? Has this silence been the necessary condition for production or survival in a country where there is still rampant discrimination against lesbians?[12] Does it reflect a real lack of interest in the question of lesbian experience? Or has it been the silence of bourgeois complacency with dominant norms?

In an important article written around 1987 and titled "Lesbian Tantalizing in Carmen Lugo Filippi's 'Milagros, Calle Mercurio,'"[13] Luz María Umpierre complains about this situation and recounts how she, as a "Lesbian" reader (or, to follow her graphesis, a "Lesbian, reading"), has been willing and, in fact, has actively engaged in the process of reading lesbian desire in Puerto Rican texts that are not clearly identified as such.[14] Although I do not share her essentialist positioning (that to read *as* a lesbian one must *be* a lesbian), I am in full agreement with her contention that apparently non-lesbian texts can often hold, within their folds, profoundly homoerotic lesbian and gay stories that are apparent to a sympathetic reader. This has, in fact, been one of the greatest contributions of queer theory and of the new critical reading strategies that have accompanied the development of this academic field.

Umpierre's article focuses on her rather different reading of a story by Carmen Lugo Filippi from that proposed by Magali García Ramis in an article ironically entitled "Para que un día Luz María pueda comprar los zapatos que le dé la gana" (So that one day Luz María can buy whatever shoes she wants).[15] García Ramis's reading of Lugo Filippi's story does not bring up any of the lesbian undertones that are so obvious to Umpierre; quite the contrary. Understandably, Umpierre wonders why and how such different readings are possible; what is at stake; what would lead the two readers to have such a divergent interpretation of the same text. Umpierre concludes that both readings are facilitated by a very concrete textual strategy engaged in by Lugo Filippi, who caters to a more conservative audience through the specific indeterminacy of plot development and narrative voice while simultaneously (surreptitiously?) presenting a story of female, lesbian, desire.

It is extremely interesting (and fortunate) for me that Umpierre's reading diverges from that of none other than García Ramis, for the main argument of this article will be precisely that García Ramis's novel *Felices días, tío Sergio* (Happy days, uncle Sergio), published in 1986, provokes or allows a very similar ambiguous (lesbian) reading.[16] I believe that *Felices días, tío Sergio* should be central to the constitution of a lesbian Puerto Rican canon. This is not as simple a proposition as it might seem, for I will have to read "between the lines" and rescue a lesbian story where most readers and critics have not seen one.[17] In this novel, I will argue, there is an exchange between lesbianism and male homosexuality that readers for the most part have either not noticed or have been unwilling to discuss.

The subject of male homosexuality in García Ramis's novel has been amply remarked on by critics, mostly as it concerns the character in the novel's title, uncle Sergio.[18] Yet this novel is not simply about the uncle's homosexuality, as I will attempt to show. Although only indirectly hinted at, male homosexuality is, along with Puerto Rican nationalism, the "safe" marginalized Other against which a never openly acknowledged lesbian (or proto-lesbian) identity is constructed.[19] The novel itself certainly does not explicitly propose lesbianism as an explanation for the character Lidia's marginality, which it rather insistently associates with the frustrations of childhood in a patriarchal environment in which particular gender norms are obsessively imposed on young subjects by adults.

Felices días engages in what can be called lesbian "tantalizing" (to use Umpierre's term), an insinuation that should not be taken lightly or, worse, dismissed as insignificant by any careful reader of the work. With the exception of Luis Felipe Díaz, however, no critic has suggested that Lidia, the protagonist and narrator, be read as a lesbian or proto-lesbian character. Díaz does not employ the word "lesbian" itself but, rather, suggests that Lidia's sexual identity is similar to that of her uncle Sergio.[20] Further, and contrary to the general critical trend, he asserts that the novel elicits an informed response from readers who are in tune with the novel's lesbian subtext—that readers will understand that the links and parallels between Lidia and her uncle are not limited to the political sphere (since both are or end up being nationalists) or to that of sex/gender oppression (since both women and male homosexuals are in subordinate positions) but in fact extend to a commonality in sexuality, of nonheterosexual orientation, in which Lidia is lesbian and uncle Sergio is gay.[21]

In my reading, I will follow Díaz's initiative and proceed to tease out a lesbian Lidia. I will, as Frances Negrón-Muntaner has suggested in her interview with García

Ramis, give weight to the erotic potential of the protagonist's attraction to Sophia Loren and will discuss the accusations made against her of being masculine (or "marimacha") in the context of constructs of monstrosity and of the "mannish les- bian," two central tropes of the twentieth-century lesbian imaginary. I will also, fol- lowing Judith Halberstam, read the tomboyish behavior of the protagonist as a prom- ising sign of lesbianism.

Tomboys, Gender Noncompliance, and the Formation of a "Mannish" Female Subject

> *—Yo no soy un perro—contesté—yo no soy un perro, yo no soy "Fido lárgate" ni "Lidia afuera."*
> *—Hazme el favor de dejar las malascrianzas—Mami me gritó.*
> *Salí, obedecí refunfuñando y con ganas de gritar.*[22]

> *They would like*
> *to put the tick and flea collar*
> *around her neck and*
> *take her for walks on sunny afternoons*
> *in order to say to the neighbors:*
> *"We have domesticated this unruly woman."*[23]

If, as Judith Butler has proposed, gender categories are established in daily life through the performance of a series of acts which have received particular significations,[24] the violation of these norms will serve to differentiate the subject and place her at odds with the dominant values of her society. Under our patriarchal system, as Umpierre reminds us, "unruly" women (that is, those who do not comply with the prescrip- tions for adequate behavior) represent a threat to the established order, and the dom- inant system will attempt to control and neutralize such individuals in order to pro- tect and maintain its power in place. Ironically, in *Felices días*, it is a group of women composed of Lidia's aunts and her mother who have all received higher education and have professional employment, who insist on "taming" the young female pro- tagonist, on doing everything possible to "break her in." As several critics have observed, these women reproduce and maintain the dominant values of patriarchal society (or what can be called, following Lacan, the "Symbolic Order") even while they themselves apparently operate somewhat outside of those very same norms.

One way to understand this dichotomy is by focusing on Lidia's initial status as a prepubescent child in the process of maturation. The novel chronicles her entry into adolescence and adulthood. As Judith Halberstam points out:

Female adolescence represents the crisis of coming of age as a girl in a male-dominated society. If adolescence for boys represents a rite of passage (much celebrated in Western literature in the form of the bildungsroman) and an ascension to some version (however attenuated) of social power, for girls adolescence is a lesson in restraint, punishment, and repression. It is in the context of female adolescence that the tomboy instincts of millions of girls are remodeled into compliant forms of femininity.[25]

And what does Lidia do that provokes such anxiety and anguish in her household? She constantly refuses to accept the adults' authority without question, and she visibly expresses her rage, something that is considered an exclusively male prerogative. As her mother tells her:

> Tú tienes que corregir ese genio, ¿sabes? en eso saliste a tu padre, pero en un hombre pasa, en una mujer sólo lleva a la vulgaridad, a la parejería. Tienes que aprender a controlarte. Cuando uno se pone furioso, secreta una sustancia que se llama adrenalina y uno se va poniendo peor. Por eso hay que rezar para que Dios le dé a uno humildad, y uno pueda controlarse y no ser parejero, ¿entiendes?[26]

In this case, gender differences are given a biological origin: the secretion of hormones, specifically adrenaline.[27] This contrast or division in what is appropriate for men and for women—that is, the double standard—that the mother enforces irritates Lidia to no end.

Of course, it is interesting to observe that Lidia's rebelliousness merely emulates the position of other women in her household, particularly that of her mother and grandmother, who in fact is compared to an Amazon, a member of a tribe of female warriors traditionally seen as symbols of lesbianism (or, at the very least, as powerful and independent women).[28] There are two significant instances in which the mother's unusual or unpredictable relationship vis-à-vis standard codes of femininity is mentioned. The first occurs in the novel's very first paragraph, when the narrator describes how the mother stood on one foot on the beach, the other leg folded like a bird's, while the children imitated her and the adults criticized her behavior.[29] The other has to do with the mother's strict belief in the need for emotional distancing, manifested in her admonitions against crying and feeling sad: "a ella le encantaba dar discursitos sobre el sentirse triste o ser llorón."[30] It is not surprising that a woman widowed young, as she was, and left with two children to raise would have such a philosophy. This maternal coldness and distance, however, coincide with a classic scenario for lesbian childhood, as in the case of Radclyffe Hall's Stephen Gordon, the protagonist of *The Well of Loneliness*, an all-time example of tomboyism (tomboyism, interestingly enough, cannot be adequately translated into Spanish).

Lidia's "disrespect" toward her elders is not the only element that marks her as different. It is merely the one that is most remarked on in the text. Lidia exhibits a whole series of behaviors that conform to those of a tomboy, and these go completely unnoticed by the narrative voice; they are naturalized, and their possible subversiveness is masked under the guise of normalcy. These activities include being obsessed with climbing trees and digging holes; requesting a Davy Crockett hat for Christmas from the Sears catalog; and always playing with two boys while having no female friends her own age.[31] What is noticeable is how Lidia conceptualizes her state of non-femininity as one of savagery, the only state that seems available as an option for resistance. This is particularly visible when the children play "Tarzan": If Lidia wants to climb trees, she has to be Cheetah, the monkey; if she is Jane, she will be relegated to taking care of "Boy" (her cousin Quique) on the ground. There are additional repeated and insistent mentions in the book of Lidia as "idiot" and "not civilized," as when her brother states that she likes Fauvist painters "porque ella es una salvaje."[32]

In her conceptualization of tomboyism, Halberstam has observed that at least two different dominant models are in place. Under the first, tomboys are seen as embodying some positive aspects such as independence and adventurousness that are typically associated with boys. It is expected that these traits will subside as girls mature or that they will not interfere with girls' incorporation into traditional female adult roles. This tomboyish behavior is not perceived as a threat to heterosexuality. A more challenging type of tomboy behavior, Halberstam contends, occurs when a girl refuses to wear girl's clothes, identifies as a boy, and attempts to extend this and other kinds of subversive behaviors well into adolescence and adulthood. This type of tomboy, which Halberstam identifies as masculine, poses a serious challenge to heterosexual norms, as it can signify adult lesbianism or even a transgender or transsexual orientation.

Lidia's "unladylike" aggressiveness and non-feminine behavior culminate in an episode in which she decides to defend her older brother against the aggression of a group of schoolboys who go around violently "initiating" all of the "weaker" male students. This episode will not only gain Lidia severe punishment from her family (not being allowed to go on a family outing to the countryside); it will also bring about the first and only explicit textual mention of her potential lesbianism. Before the actual fight, Lidia anticipates her behavior and offers the following assessment of her personality:

> Yo, que era viciosa y mala, ahora iba a ser además asesina, porque yo sabía que los iba a asesinar, fríamente, con un pañuelo de seda como los estranguladores de Bombay.[33]

The protagonist will not reach these extremes, inspired as they are by the comic books and popular fiction she and the other boys read and with which they identify. The physical altercation between the protagonist and the adolescent boys results instead in the following verbal exchange:

> —Idiota—me gritó—¡marimacha!
> —Pato, patito, pato, patuleco—le canté y tiré una piedra, también llena de lodo que le dio en el codo a Juan Rafael y yo sé que le dolió.[34]

Although one can argue that "marimacha" does not explicitly mean "lesbian" but, rather, is a signifier for masculine women (or literally, a "macho" María), I would insist on reading the term in relationship to the scenario the novel sets up.[35] The young protagonist's reaction to the verbal insult against her confirms the term's derogatory use in opposition to male homosexuality, as signaled by the term "pato" (which translates literally as "duck" but is closer in meaning to faggot, queer, or fairy) and its derivatives, which she employs.[36] Lidia's use of the term "pato," consonant with traditional practice, activates the word to challenge the boy's masculinity (in this case, for being a brute in his attack on her brother and of herself, a girl) but not in actual reference to a homosexual act or identity, because fighting is not usually constitutive of being homosexual, at least as the category is usually defined. She thus ripostes with the word as an insult and threat.[37]

The applicability of the term "marimacha" to herself, however, is consonant with the term's definition; the word sticks because, as we have seen, all of her previous actions in her home indicate the same.[38] In fact, her subsequent action (throwing a stone) confirms her "male"-like aggressive behavior, the very same behavior that has garnered her the epithet. The bully Juan Rafael merely names what all readers have been made aware of by the protagonist and her family: There is no doubt that Lidia is a bona fide "marimacha"—that is, that she violates her society's norms of femininity. The novelty of the text will be to present this in a positive light, contrary to dominant values. It proposes the *marimacha* as an authentic figure of resistance and female emancipation.

The other model that deserves mention in this context is that of the lesbian as monstrous, an idea most developed by postmodern theorists of lesbianism.[39] As we have seen, the novel repeatedly presents Lidia as "savage," which is only a step away from the totally feared monster of nightmares and horror stories, the abject figure of social exclusion.

Monstrous Nationalists, Monstrous Sexual Other(s)

Up to this point, we have emphasized how the construction of Lidia as a tomboy—and, at times, a masculinized or monstrous character—sets her apart, makes her a center of disruption. In this section, I will extend the space of "difference" constructed in the novel to encompass two additional crucial spheres: the space of gender/sexual transgression (including both male homosexuality and female nonnormative heterosexuality) and that of nationalist politics. Lidia's character forms part of this more complex grid, which both hides and demands her potential lesbianism.

The emphasis on gender disruption with which the novel opens ("no es que mi mamá no fuera femenina") is continued throughout the text by Lidia and other characters.[40] The first significant mention of a different type of marginality corresponds to the family's treatment of Margara, a next-door neighbor whose father is a nationalist: "nos habían explicado que la Margara era una mujer callejera, mala; y entendíamos sin entender que hacía cosas que uno no se podía ni imaginar."[41] The children's fascination with Margara is coupled with repulsion and disgust. In one incident, after they call to her and she comes close to them, the children run to the bathroom and wash, to make sure that they have not been "contaminated" by her proximity. Margara will soon be joined in the position of "other" by the figure of the uncle, who, along with Lidia, will form the novel's central triad of marginality. Toward the end of the novel, Margara will be replaced by Micaela, the maid with whom the uncle has unsuccessfully attempted sexual intercourse. Margara's similarity to the uncle is not only based on sexual nonnormativity; it is also, and quite significantly, grounded in their nationalist political orientation.

In García Ramis's novel, uncle Sergio is presented as a mirror of the protagonist's aspirations for a fulfilled identity. This mirroring recalls, of course, the plenitude Lacan describes for the child inserted in the realm of the imaginary, who cannot distinguish her body from that of her mother, who sees these bodies as extensions of each other. Lidia's relationship with her own mother is somewhat lacking in affect, given the mother's general seriousness. Her aunts and grandmother seem to have the same dry nature. Lidia will obtain emotional fulfillment through her relationship to her uncle, whose homosexuality is hinted at directly and indirectly throughout the book. In this sense, his figure comes to substitute for the mother's as a primary relationship, disrupting the models presented in feminist discourses, in which the mother becomes the epitome of female solidarity or a metaphor of all female desire. Lidia's identification, instead—as in Stephen Gordon's case—is with the father figure, except here that figure is a flawed, homosexual one.[42]

Felices días is saturated with discourses of male homosexuality, which make it particularly easy to infer the uncle's unspoken identity early on. His very first description, remitting to popular notions of the homosexual as feminized male, hints at this: He is described as having almost feminine eyelashes, "sus ojos enormes, de pestañas largas casi de mujer."[43] Lidia, by constrast, is described in masculinized terms. Even when Sergio's sexual orientation is not discussed, there are ample comments about his unmasculine behavior, such as his crying; there is open acknowledgment of gender insubordination, if not of sexual misconduct. Our suspicions are nearly confirmed (and certainly stoked, if not validated) when, at the end of the novel, Lidia comments: "Según nos fuimos enterando, él fue un paria, un inconforme y, probablemente un homosexual."[44] Yet, one may wonder, why is this insistence on the uncertainty of his status as a homosexual accompanied by a clear affirmation of his status as a social pariah and nonconformist?

Needless to say, male homosexuality is presented throughout the novel as a huge aberration, something completely against the values of middle-class Puerto Rican society and comparable only to the shock produced by extramarital female sexuality, such as that of Margara, who is to have a child out of wedlock.[45]

Although the uncle's homosexuality is never openly discussed, his political orientation is often the source of great debate. Nationalism in the novel is as monstrous as sexual "aberration." It should not be forgotten that the novel is set during the 1950s, one of the worst periods in Puerto Rican history in terms of the repression levied against nationalists and marking the beginning of the Cold War. Dislike of "independentistas" is manifested in the novel by the family's general contempt for all nationalists but also, and perhaps most dramatically, by the way in which the term "nationalist" is employed to describe totally unrelated kinds of conduct. "Nationalist" becomes synonymous with homelessness, madness, and unkemptness.

The process of Lidia's social and intellectual maturation depicted in the novel culminates in her embrace of politics similar to her uncle's. Traditionally, critics have also
noted that Lidia's identification as a liberated woman who does not submit to general social impositions regarding female identity also parallels her uncle's noncon-
forming position. This is correct in a sense, yet it is incomplete, for Lidia replicates
not only "gender" emancipation but also, I would argue, his "sexual" liberation. This
claim is difficult to make, given that the uncle never discusses his sexuality openly.
Neither does Lidia, except to enumerate her failures. The similarity between the two
characters can be inferred with some certainty from the construction of desire made
explicit in the book. To this I will dedicate the next section. But first, I will clarify the
apparent confusion of Lidia's sexual attraction to her uncle.

The biggest objection to a lesbian interpretation of García Ramis's novel could stem
from Lidia's uncontrolled declaration of sexual and emotional love for her uncle, feelings that go beyond traditional familiar affect and border on the domain of incest.[46]
I would caution, however, against taking the protagonist's expressed feelings as the
definitive interpretation of the nature of their relationship. First, the uncle's masculinity is questioned from the very first moment he appears. And most significant,
toward the end of the novel, Lidia's dream of total identification with her uncle is
irrevocably shattered by the sight of his engaging in (unsuccessful) heterosexual intercourse with the maid Micaela—a failed Freudian primal scene—and by the uncle's
departure from Puerto Rico and subsequent death.

As Luis Felipe Díaz has observed, Lidia is aware of her uncle's heterosexual dys-
function.[47] She has spied his frustrated sexual encounter; she has overheard Micaela
say that his impotence is a recurring phenomenon.[48] That is, Lidia knows that her
uncle is more than just a pariah or a marginal figure. He is a failed model of dominant heterosexual masculinity, a failure that is often read in Caribbean society as
equivalent to homosexuality. These differences are precisely what attract her to him,
what allow for links of solidarity; what make him safe.[49] Let us not forget her earlier
affirmation, in which she states that she is one of his kind, even though the meaning
of this statement is left ambiguous: "los niños desde pequeños saben, intuyen, se
reconocen en los prohibidos, *si está dentro de ellos ser así cuando grandes*";[50] "Yo, en liga
entonces y quizá para siempre con los parias, los distintos, ¿con el Tío Sergio? ¿Le
habría pasado algo así a él?"[51] To what precisely does Lidia refer when she states "ser
así cuando grandes" (be like that when we grow up)? How is it that she becomes one
of the pariahs, or the "different ones"?

Under Freud's conceptualization of family romance, the child will fantasize about
the creation of an alternative genealogy in which the negative actions of the parents are countered by idealized substitutes. Lidia, orphaned in early childhood by
the death of her father, displaces her feelings for men (or paternal figures) to her
uncle, the sole adult who consistently reaches out to the children in a nonhier-
archical way. Lidia's apparent love obsession with this figure should not be read
straightforwardly, much as the text seeks to propose. It is much more productive to
understand the obsession of a (proto) lesbian (or bisexual) subject for a homosexual

man as a displacement of psychic energies, a displacement that will be replaced by books and art when the uncle leaves.

At the end of the novel, the adult Lidia/narrator will articulate her debt to her uncle regarding her acquisition of a national identification as a proud Puerto Rican. Yet this still leaves the question of sexuality up in the air. Lidia's mentioning her failed or unsatisfactory relationships with men is particularly telling of the elisions, silences, and incongruities of the narration. She goes out with men but gets nothing out of it except disillusionment. She expresses her frustration as being based on not having the correct object of affection. The novel (problematically) suggests that the real object is the uncle:

> Un día, en una fiesta, me dejé besar por un muchacho, Juan Miguel. Me dejé besar porque todo el mundo lo hacía ... Cuando llegué a casa con dos cuba libres tomados a escondidas y con mi boca llena de besos que no eran los que yo quería, empecé a llorar. A llorar por ti y por mí y por todo lo que no había querido saber nunca. Me dio entonces por ser ridícula.[52]

Whose kisses did she really want? What is it that she "no había querido saber nunca" (had never wanted to know)? Her affective (sexual) identity is resolved (if that is the appropriate term) or played out only in the realm of fantasy, within grasp of that which is unspoken in the novel but suggested by Lidia's longing.

Scenarios of (Perverse) Desire: Cinema, the Formation of Fantasy, and the Specter of Exile

One of the crucial details for an elaboration of Lidia as lesbian is her fantasies in which she is rescued by Sophia Loren and whisked away to Italy:

> Cuando me di cuenta de que ya no saldría bien en las clases nunca, de que no tenía amigos en esta escuela, de que Andrés, Quique y yo ya no jugaríamos más por la casa, de que la vida era más sola y terrible de lo que había imaginado, de que me estaba poniendo gorda y fea, feísima, decidí que no quería seguir viviendo en esta isla, y comencé a esperar que Sophia Loren viniera a buscarme para llevarme a vivir a Italia.[53]

This fantasy is significant for two reasons. First, it expresses the protagonist's longing for an object of desire that is unobtainable in her present situation; and second, the desire to leave Puerto Rico, which echoes the children's initial "alejarnos para siempre de la vida que llevábamos,"[54] closely parallels the exile of marginal figures (that is, nationalists and homosexuals) of which uncle Sergio is part, and which is a general constitutive trait of how homosexuality (as well as any other threatening sexuality) is commonly dealt with by Puerto Rican society.[55]

Since its inception, literature about the Puerto Rican diaspora has dealt with migration as a "safety valve" for sexual nonconformity.[56] In *Felices días*, this is established early when the family's adults discuss a similar case in which a homosexual man was sent to the United States by his parents, as far from Puerto Rico as possible:

—¡QUÉ BARBARIDAD!

—¡Qué barbaridad, tan guapo!—decía Nati.

—Sí, hombre, pato, le salió pato ese muchacho a la pobre Tati Almeyda. Ajá, pero ya lo mandó para Estados Unidos, allá lejos, a California que dicen que allá es que los están mandando a todos.[57]

It is no surprise that Lidia dreams about leaving, about being (even if only at an unconscious level) just like uncle Sergio and Tati Almeyda's son. And she plans on doing this with the help of Sophia Loren.

Feminist film critics have dedicated extensive effort to understanding the processes of women's film spectatorship—that is, what happens when a "woman" sees a movie. According to one controversial view, proposed by Laura Mulvey in the 1980s, the codes of dominant Hollywood film create products that privilege the male gaze; Mulvey goes so far as to argue that films allow only this particular gaze and that all spectators thus see as men.[58] To obtain viewing pleasure, women must thus adopt a masculine stance, buying (even if only unconsciously) into patriarchal, sexist views. More recently, scholars such as Teresa de Lauretis have criticized feminist film critics' elision of lesbian desire and subjectivity and challenged the notion that the gaze is necessarily masculine.[59]

The issue of female spectatorial pleasure is particularly relevant in the case of Lidia. As de Lauretis argues, following Jean Laplanche and Jean-Baptiste Pontalis's re-elaboration of psychoanalytic thought, "fantasy" is an integral component of desire, and cinema is one of the main mechanisms or technologies that allow for its formation. In the case of *Felices días*, it seems likely that the heterosexual attractions that Lidia professes throughout the novel may be misguided psychic displacements, unconscious desires to conform, perhaps even a ruse (not only to the reader but even to herself). It is in her relationship to cinema that a more convincing, believable desire appears. In this case, fantasy seems a more liberating but also a more accurate reflection of feelings and emotions than her apparently straightforwardly expressed attractions to men. In a remarkably forthright passage, Lidia comments:

> Mi infatuación con Sophia comenzó con la película *Boy on a Dolphin*, la cual vi once veces. Que esa mujer de pueblo pudiera casarse con el americano guapo arqueólogo y se quisieran . . . eso, más que nada en el mundo, me causaba un temblar que no podía explicar. Yo soñaba que Sophia estaría casada con el mismo Alan Ladd o con Yul Brynner, y con ellos me iría a vivir.[60]

Among other remarkable things, it is interesting to point out that Lidia's crush is on an actress; that she experiences repetitive-compulsive behavior (seeing what is now considered a rather minor movie eleven times); that she dreams of re-establishing a family romance; and that the male actors are totally interchangeable.[61] Curiously, there is no indication in the novel as to her own family's reaction to her obsession. Although one could argue that Lidia's interest is in the fantasy of heterosexual coupling (Sophia and an interchangeable man), I would insist that it is the relationship between Sophia and Lidia that takes center stage in the protagonist's psychic sphere.

Later in the novel, Lidia comments further on her obsession, shifting location from Italy to New York (and thus, while not acknowledging it, imitating her uncle in yet one more way):

> Yo sabía que un día encontraría [a Sophia Loren], cuando ya ella estuviera vieja y nadie le buscara, yo le invitaría a pasar un tiempo en mi penthouse neoyorquino porque yo pensaba ser a veces una "career girl", que era algo soberbio aunque yo no podía definir bien de qué se trataba, y todas las "career girls" tenían apartamentos de lujo en Nueva York, y Sophia me visitaría y juntas tendríamos reminiscencias de cómo nos criamos cada cual y nos maravillaríamos de haber nacido ambas un 20 de septiembre, y yo tendría dinero para convidarla a ella y a Carlo Ponti y a sus dos nenes a una elegante cena en Nueva York.[62]

The wonderful ambiguity of what a "career girl" is is extremely revealing of Lidia's longing for independence, autonomy, and, I would argue, female-centered sexuality. Notice that, while Sophia Loren's heterosexuality is highlighted, there is no mention of Lidia's having a partner. Lidia suggests that there is something out there that she cannot define but that she wants. I propose that that is lesbianism.

While interviewing García Ramis, Frances Negrón-Muntaner asked the writer why there were no strong, independent, female role models for Lidia—and for other young female protagonists in her stories. Commenting on this last passage, Negrón-Muntaner observed that Sophia Loren is not allowed to stand on her own but is always presented with men:

> En la novela y en algunos relatos, estas niñas generalmente encuentran la voz más progresista en un personaje masculino. Existe muy poca validación de otras mujeres y de otras niñas. Lidia por ejemplo, no tiene amigas. En el pasaje donde ella describe sus deseos de vivir con Sofía Loren, lo cual tiene un contenido erótico, ella habla de incluir a Carlo Ponti y los niños, no a Sofía Loren nada más. ¿Por qué no se validan los espacios de solidaridad entre mujeres y/o modelos progresistas de personajes femeninos?[63]

García Ramis responded by commenting on her professional attachment to male figures:

> En mi vida, de joven adulta, prácticamente la mayoría de las personas que me ayudaron a crecer fueron varones. En el trabajo, tiendo a hacer más amistad con los hombres que con las mujeres. Cuando comencé la vida profesional, las mujeres me parecían tontas. Entonces los modelos que yo tenía para romper estructuras eran varones. Yo podía entender de adulta que mis tías, al ser profesionales que trabajaban, rompían unos modelos. Sin embargo, creo que la mayoría de las personas quienes me sembraron ideas y me hicieron pensar y dudar fueron varones. Aunque no era exclusivo . . . Yo tuve amigas que fueron bien influyentes en mí.[64]

This response may clarify García Ramis's motivation, but it does not help to explain the nature of Lidia's attraction to Sophia Loren.

Yet there is an answer to Negrón-Muntaner's question—one that involves triangular configurations of desire. Lesbian feminist critics such as Terry Castle and Marilyn Farwell have paid a great deal of attention to Eve Kosofsky Sedgwick's analysis of eighteenth-century English novels and to her claims that, in novels with plot structures that focus on two male characters and a female, the men use the woman as a means for their own homosocial (and occasionally homoerotic or homosexual) relationship—or, following Levi-Strauss and Gayle Rubin, as an object of exchange.[65] In these novels, the woman is thus at times nothing more than a token. For the men, the distinction between homosocial and homoerotic exchange can sometimes be blurry; the novels are ultimately about them and about the deep emotions they share.

If Sedgwick has advanced René Girard's formulations of triangular character relationships, she has done so, according to feminist critics, by totally neglecting the issue of female desire and, most troubling, of lesbian experience.[66] Although Farwell critiques Castle's approach of simply substituting the male dyad in the triangle with a female dyad, I believe that this approach is particularly useful in our case. There are a number of triangular configurations in *Felices días*. They include: 1) Lidia—her mother—uncle Sergio (an Oedipal trio in which bonding with the male attempts to recuperate a link with displaced femininity); 2) Lidia—Margara/Micaela—uncle Sergio (a failed family romance); and 3) Lidia—Sophia Loren—an interchangeable man (in which the male figure acts as a "safety" or approximation of "normalcy").

I propose that Lidia be read as a woman who has not reached self-identification as a lesbian but whose acts (a mimicry of standard masculine behaviors) and passions (specifically the frustrated relationship with men—both Sergio and Juan Miguel—and her phantasmic attraction to Sophia Loren) suggest this. Lidia's reconciliation with her uncle after his death leaves her affective identity unresolved. It is only in fantasy that we are given deep insight into her psyche.

The critic Iván Silén has found fault with García Ramis for not allowing the novel's incest story to flesh out and find a satisfactory resolution. He accuses her of being too faithful to her bourgeois class background to present a truly scandalous text.[67] I likewise believe that the author failed to explore and develop the lesbian subtext that is so strong in the novel and that, as we have seen, begs for clarification.[68] Like Umpierre reading Carmen Lugo Filippi's text, I have felt strongly "tantalized" by a narrative that insistently refuses to mention lesbianism yet is rife with details, scenarios, emotions, and clues.

The portrayal of Lidia as a tomboy with a cold and distant mother, which in turn allows for intimations of female masculinity and monstrousness, coupled with the undeniable cinematographic fantasies of a lesbian relationship, lead me to favor strongly a lesbian reading of *Felices días*. This was, in fact, my experience when I taught this book recently in a Queer Caribbean Culture class at Rutgers University. Some of the students suggested, unprompted, that lesbianism was a strong underlying theme in the book. All of this doubt and confusion would undeniably be clarified if only García Ramis herself, who repeatedly has stated that the novel is based on her own life, would share a little more about her personal experience in this respect. For now, let us be "tantalized" and plow ahead in the construction of a corpus (or dare I say, a canon) of Puerto Rican lesbian cultural productions, a project that is in well-advanced stages and continues to grow every day. It is a project that, in my estimation, can include both open and explicitly lesbian texts, as well as others that require a more active or sympathetic reading: the reading of a queer, like a queer, or in search of queer meaning.

Notes

1. The term "Nuyorican" refers to New York-centered Puerto Rican cultures and identities produced by immigrant, diasporic communities; the term became popular starting in the 1970s. Other, more recent terms that have been proposed for this cultural production include "Diaspo-Rican" (see Juan Flores, *From Bomba to Hip-Hop: Puerto Rican Culture and Latin Identity* [New York: Columbia University Press, 2000]) and "Boricua" (see Lisa Sánchez González, *Boricua Literature: A Literary History of the Puerto Rican Diaspora* [New York: New York University Press, 2001]).

2. Daniel Torres comments in a very brief article in *Centro Journal* on "the lesbian overtones" of Lola Rodríguez de Tió, "who like George Sand used to dress as a man": Daniel Torres, "An AIDS Narrative," *Centro Journal* 6, no. 1–2 (1994): 179. Carlos Rodríguez Matos has also attempted to register the earliest homoerotic contributions to Puerto Rican literature: Carlos Rodríguez-Matos, "Actos de amor: Introducción al estudio de la poesía puertorriqueña homosexual y lesbiana / Actos of Love," trans. William Mena, *Desde este lado* 1, no. 2 (Fall 1990): 21–33.

3. See Luisa Capetillo, *Amor y anarquía: los escritos de Luisa Capetillo,* ed. Julio Ramos (Río Piedras: Ediciones Huracán, 1992); Norma Valle Ferrer, *Luisa Capetillo: historia de una mujer proscrita* (Río Piedras: Editorial Cultural, 1990).

4. Agnes I. Lugo-Ortiz, "Nationalism, Male Anxiety, and the Lesbian Body in Puerto Rican Narrative," in *Hispanisms and Homosexualities,* eds. Sylvia Molloy and Robert McKee Irwin (Durham, N.C.: Duke University Press: 1998), 76–100. Emilio Díaz Varcárcel, "El asedio," in *El asedio y otros cuentos* (México, D.F.: Arrecife, 1958), 11–28.

5. See Juan González, *Doce paredes negras* (Río Piedras: Editorial Cultural, 1974). For a critical review, see Roberto Ramos-Perea, "Estudio preliminar de la obra dramática de Juan González-Bonilla," in Juan González-Bonilla, *Lo que no se habla: teatro puertorriqueño* (San Juan: Ediciones Gallo Galante, 1997), 25–42.

6. Juan González-Bonilla, "Flor de presidio," in González-Bonilla, *Lo que no se habla,* 45–76.

7. Juan González-Bonilla to Lawrence La Fountain-Stokes, personal communication, August 1977, San Juan. See Lawrence La Fountain, "Los muchachos del combo," *Claridad,* 15–21 August 1997, 28. For reproductions of yellow-journalism articles on lesbian crimes in Puerto Rico, see José Ramón del Puente, *El homosexualismo en Puerto Rico: ¿crimen, pecado, o enfermedad?* (Río Piedras: n.p., 1986). Lía Fiol Matta's unpublished master's thesis is an excellent study of lesbianism on the island: Lía Fiol Matta, "Análisis sobre el control de la sexualidad de la mujer: Estudio del lesbianismo en Puerto Rico" (master's thesis, Universidad de Puerto Rico, Río Piedras, 1986).

8. See Nemir Matos Cintrón, *A través del aire y del fuego pero no del cristal* (Río Piedras: Atabex, 1981), and idem, *Las mujeres no hablan así* (Río Piedras: Atabex, 1981). Both are illustrated by Yolanda V. Fundora. See also her contributions to *Compañeras: Latina Lesbians,* ed. Juanita Ramos (Juanita Díaz-Cotto) (New York: Routledge, 1994); Luz María Umpierre, *The Margarita Poems* (Bloomington, Ind.: Third Woman Press, 1987); Aixa Ardín, *Batiborrillo* (San Juan: Calzado Ajeno Editoras, 1998); Lilliana Ramos Collado, *Reróticas* (San Juan: Libros Nómadas, 1998).

Mariposa (María Fernández) is a Bronx-born Puerto Rican performance poet who is most famous for her bisexually inspired poem "Pussyology." She was recently featured in the documentary *Americanos,* produced by Edward James Olmos, which notably elided the issue of her sexuality in favor of her insights on being a "Diasporican" and of African heritage.

9. Janis Astor del Valle, "Fuschia," in *Intimate Acts: Eight Contemporary Lesbian Plays,* ed. Nancy Dean and M. G. Soares (New York: Brito and Lair, 1997), 85–110; idem, "I'll Be Home para la Navidad," in *Torch to the Heart: Anthology of Lesbian Art and Drama,* ed. Sue McConnell-Celi (Red Bank, N.J.: Lavender Crystal, 1994), 97–113; idem, "Transplantations: Straight and Other Jackets Para Mí," in *Action: The Nuyorican Poets Cafe Theater Festival,* ed. Miguel Algarín and Lois Griffith (New York: Simon and Schuster, 1997), 373–93; idem, "Where the Señoritas Are," in McConnell-Celi, *Torch to the Heart,* 82–96. Erika López, *Flaming Iguanas: An Illustrated All-Girl Road Novel Thing* (New York: Scribner, 1998); idem, *Lap Dancing for Mommy: Tender Stories of Disgust, Blame and Inspiration* (Seattle: Seal Press, 1997); idem, *They Call Me Mad Dog! A Story for Bitter, Lonely People* (New York: Simon and Schuster, 1998). Nicholasa Mohr, "The Perfect Little Flower Girl," in *Nueva York* (Houston: Arte Público Press, 1977). Frances Negrón-Muntaner, *Brincando el charco: Portrait of a Puerto Rican,* film (1994). Mayra Santos Febres, "Pez de vidrio" and "Espejo con salmuera," in *Pez de vidrio* (Río Piedras: Huracán, 1996); idem, *Anamú y manigua* (Río Piedras: La Iguana Dorada, 1991). Other Puerto Rican lesbian writers include Brenda Cotto, the poet Samantha Martínez, and Iris Zavala. I limit myself here to literary writings and film; a more comprehensive analysis would have to include performers such as Lucecita Benítez and Sophie, who have large lesbian followings. It is also important to mention that non–Puerto Rican lesbian authors have created Puerto Rican lesbian characters in their work: see Achy Obejas, *Memory Mambo* (Pittsburgh: Cleis Press, 1996), and Mariana Romo Carmona, *Living at Night* (Duluth, Minn.: Spinsters Ink, 1997).

10. Antonio Martorell, *La piel de la memoria* (Trujillo Alto, P.R.: Ediciones Envergadura, 1991).

11. See Efraín Barradas, "Las palabras de las cosas: En torno a 'La piel de la memoria' de Antonio Martorell," *Claridad,* 31 January–6 February 1992, 19–21; Rubén Ríos Avila, "La letra que mata y vivifica" (unpublished article in the author's possession); and Carmen Dolores Trelles, "La piel de la memoria de Antonio Martorell," *Hómines* 19, nos. 2–20, no. 1 (February–December 1996): 406–407. These critics have also neglected to comment on Martorell's flirting with male homosexuality and gender insubordination, a subject that I address elsewhere: see Lawrence La Fountain-Stokes, "Memorias sensuales: La piel de la escritura de Antonio Martorell," paper presented at the Sixth Columbia/New York University Graduate Conference on Spanish and Portuguese Literatures, New York, March 1997.

12. It should be clear, of course, that an author need not be a lesbian to write about lesbianism, yet the threat of being identified as such has most likely limited the number of (female) artists who are willing to do so. The same mechanism of fear about accusations of lesbianism has historically influenced women's identifications as feminist.

13. Luz María Umpierre, "Lesbian Tantalizing in Carmen Lugo Filippi's 'Milagros, Calle Mercurio,'" in *¿Entiendes? Queer Readings, Hispanic Writings,* ed. Emilie Bergmann and Paul Julian Smith (Durham, N.C.: Duke University Press, 1995), 306–14.

14. I capitalize the word "Lesbian" here in accordance with Umpierre's (essentialist) usage.

15. García Ramis says that "Luz María," or something like that, is the name of a young and attractive, yet unmarried, woman she once met at an artisans' fair, who motivated her to write the article "una muchacha cuyo nombre, como de costumbre, no puedo recordar, pero que de seguro se llama Luz María o Virgen Luz o algo de eso que alumbra y es puro como debemos de ser las mujeres" (a young woman whose name I cannot remember, as usual, but who for

sure was called Luz María or Virgin Luz or something like that, which illuminates, and is pure, just like us women are supposed to be): Magali García Ramis, "Para que un día Luz María pueda comprarse los zapatos que le dé la gana," *Caribán* 1, no. 3–4 (May–December 1985): 6, 30–31. (This and all additional translations are mine.) As such, there is no stated, direct link to Luz María Umpierre except for the generalizations made about such a name. It is nevertheless uncanny that this textual debate occurred, particularly given a notorious exchange between Sandra María Esteves and Umpierre about the name "María Cristina." In yet another bizarre twist, the "obsession" that García Ramis developed for her muse "Luz María" is remarkably similar to that which Umpierre sees between Marina and Milagros in Lugo Filippi's story. I would read García Ramis's article as the story of an undeclared attraction.

16. Magali García Ramis, *Felices días, tío Sergio* (San Juan: Editorial Cultural, 1986).

17. Mary Jane Treacy is an example of a critic whose comments are to this effect. Commenting on uncle Sergio, she writes, "The homosexual is not just situated at the margin: he (García Ramis does not explore what position the lesbian might have) opens up rigidly protected categories and thereby serves as a catalyst for change on many levels": Mary Jane Treacy, "García Ramis, Magali," in *Latin American Writers on Gay and Lesbian Themes*, ed. David William Foster (Westport, Conn.: Greenwood Press, 1995), 172; emphasis added.

18. See Eliseo R. Colón Zayas, "Felices días, Tío Sergio," *La torre (nueva época)* 1, no. 1 (1987): 165–70; Luis Felipe Díaz, "Ideología y sexualidad en *Felices días, tío Sergio* de Magali García Ramis," *Revista de Estudios Hispánicos* (Río Piedras) 21 (1994): 325–41; Margarite Fernández Olmos, "Growing up puertorriqueña: El *Bildungsroman* feminista en las novelas de Nicholasa Mohr y Magali García Ramis," in *Sobre la literatura puertorriqueña de aquí y de allá: Aproximaciones feministas* (Santo Domingo: Alfa and Omega, 1989); Juan G. Gelpí, *Literatura y paternalismo en Puerto Rico* (San Juan: Universidad de Puerto Rico, 1993), and "René Marqués y Magali García Ramis: Dos acercamientos a la novela de aprendizaje," *Revista de Estudios Hispánicos* (Río Piedras) 17–18 (1990–91): 353–68; Ivette López, "Minute and Fragrant Memories: *Happy Days, Uncle Sergio* by Magali García Ramis," in *Splintering Darkness: Latin American Women Writers in Search of Themselves*, ed. Lucia Guerra Cunningham (Pittsburg: Latin American Literary Revue Press, 1990), 111–22.

19. It is interesting that, although there is almost unanimous consensus about the uncle's homosexuality (or bisexuality, as García Ramis reminds us in an interview), knowledge of this still requires some interpretive skill on the reader's part. Alvin Joaquín Figueroa comments, "La homosexualidad del tío Sergio no se da de una forma directa y le toca al lector conjeturar: el adverbio que utiliza Lidia, 'probablemente', la 'impotencia' sexual con Micaela, las cartas y su llanto después de la conversación telefónica con su amigo de Nueva York. De este modo intuimos que el personaje lucha también por otorgarle un espacio a su identidad" (Uncle Sergio's homosexuality does not appear in a direct fashion, and the reader has to conjecture: the adverb that Lidia uses, "probably," the sexual "impotence" with Micaela, the letters and his tears after his phone conversation with his friend in New York. In this way, we intuit that the character also struggles to create a space for his identity): Alvin Joaquín Figueroa, "Feminismo, homosexualidad e identidad política: El lenguaje del otro en *Felices días, tío Sergio*," *La Torre* 5, no. 20 (1991): 504. I would argue that Lidia's lesbianism, correspondingly, "does not appear in a direct fashion and the reader has to conjecture." This also seems to be what Luis Felipe Díaz suggests in his article "Ideología y sexualidad en *Felices días*."

20. "Conviene destacar aquí, no obstante, cómo, pese a esta toma de conciencia, resulta muy peculiar el que la niña ya adulta tampoco haga referencia a su identidad sexual, y ello a pesar de que podríamos sospechar que esa identidad es parecida a la del tío" (It should be noted,

however, how, in spite of this process of consciousness-raising, it is striking that the adult girl also does not make reference to her sexual identity, even when we could suspect that that identity is similar to her uncle's): Luis Felipe Díaz, "Ideología y sexualidad en *Felices días*," 333.

21. "Al parecer la hablante espera, en este aspecto, la complicidad de un lector capaz de reconocer que su liberación, además de política, ha sido profundamente sexual (en ello estriba la razón de ser de la novela, en el fondo preocupada por la ineludible relación entre política y sexualidad, entre mente y cuerpo, tal y como la entiende la postmodernidad). Bien podemos decir que domina finalmente en el discurso de la novela, la subversión desde el clandestinaje de la consciencia, desde la complicidad que ofrece el irónico silencio. Y ello tal vez debido a que la autora del discurso novelesco, al igual que el tío Sergio y la protagonista, se encuentran aún en un contexto represivo que no tolera discursos auténticos y abiertos, por lo que recurre a un distanciamiento irónico que pretende pasar casi desapercibido y que es poco delatador" (Apparently, the speaker expects, in this respect, the complicity of a reader who is able to understand that her liberation, in addition to political, has been profoundly sexual [this is essentially the novel's motivation, which is basically worried about the inevitable relationship between politics and sexuality, mind and body, such as it is understood by postmodernity]. Ultimately, we can well argue that what dominates the discourse of the novel is subversion from the clandestine position of conscience, from the complicity that ironic silence offers. And this is due, perhaps, to the fact that the author of the novel's discourse, just like Uncle Sergio and the protagonist, are still in a repressive context that does not allow authentic and free discourses, which is why she recurs to an ironic distancing that pretends to barely be acknowledged and which is barely revealing): ibid., 333–34.

22. "'I'm not a dog,' I answered, 'I'm not "Fido, go" or "Lidia, out!"' 'Please stop misbehaving,' my mother shouted. I went outside, grumbling and wanting to scream": García Ramis, *Felices días*, 53. For a different translation, consult Magali García Ramis, *Happy Days, Uncle Sergio*, trans. Carmen C. Esteves (Fredonia, N.Y.: White Pine Press, 1995).

23. Umpierre, *Margarita Poems*, 21.

24. Judith Butler, *Gender Trouble: Feminism and the Subversion of Identity* (New York: Routledge, 1990).

25. Judith Halberstam, "Oh Bondage Up Yours! Female Masculinity and the Tomboy," in *Sissies and Tomboys: Gender Nonconformity and Homosexual Childhood*, ed. Matthew Rottnek (New York: New York University Press, 1999), 156.

26. "You have to improve that temper of yours, you know? You are just like your father, but in a man it's acceptable. In a woman it only leads to vulgarity. You have to learn to control yourself. When you get angry, you secrete a substance called adrenaline, and that makes it worse. That is why you have to pray so that God will give you humility and you can control yourself and not be an embarrassment, do you understand?": García Ramis, *Felices días*, 53.

27. See Halberstam, "Oh Bondage Up Yours!" 165, for a discussion of gender and sexual dysphoria brought about by "imbalances" of the hormones androgen and cortisol.

28. "Decían que era una gran amazona, que corría a caballo como nadie, y que le gustaba mucho bailar" (They used to say that she was a great Amazon, that she rode horses like no one else, and that she really loved to dance): García Ramis, *Felices días*, 75.

29. "No era que mi mamá no fuera femenina, sino que le gustaba pararse como las garzas. . . . Mami se paraba en un solo pie, con el otro puesto en la rodilla del que la sostenía, y nosotros dos imitándola . . . retábamos al mundo, al buen gusto y a la familia" (It's not that my mother wasn't feminine, but rather that she liked to stand like the cranes. Mommy would stand on a single foot, with the other resting on the knee of the leg that sustained her, while

both of us imitated her . . . and challenged the world, good taste, and our family): ibid., 1. The aunts' behavior is described as follows: "Mis tías Elena y Sara F. le pedían que no se parara así, que no se veía bien, que no era femenino" (My aunts Elena and Sara F. would ask her not to stand like that, that it was unsightly, that it was not feminine): ibid., 2. The children's biggest desire is to grow up and move away, so as to be free from this constant nagging. "Si algo ansiábamos mi hermano y yo era poder responder a los regaños y consejos, acabar de ser grandes y alejarnos para siempre de la vida que llevábamos" (If my brother and I desired any-thing, it was to be able to respond to the chastisement and advice, to finally grow up and dis-tance ourselves forever from the life that we led): ibid., 2. This desire to leave is, of course, reflected in the uncle's exile in New York and in Lidia's desire to leave for Italy and New York with Sophia Loren.

30. "She loved to give little speeches about feeling sad or being a crybaby": ibid., 16. This aversion to "emotionalism" is also indicated in one of the novel's epigraphs, in which "Boab-dil el chico" is told by his mother to not cry about "lo que no supiste defender como hombre" (that which you did not know how to defend like a man), an expression the children heard repeatedly: ibid., 1.

31. When Frances Negrón-Muntaner asked García Ramis about her girl-protagonist's appar-ent lack of same-age girlfriends, the author responded that she had a large number of male friends herself and that at times she even preferred the company of men, because women seemed "silly" to her: Frances Negrón-Muntaner, "Magali García Ramis," *Hispamérica* 22, no. 64–65 (1993): 89–104.

32. "because she was a savage": García Ramis, *Felices días*, 20.

33. "I, who was vicious and bad, was now going to also be an assassin, because I knew that I would assassinate them, coldbloodedly with a silk scarf, like the Bombay stranglers": ibid., 94.

34. "'Idiot,' he called me, 'marimacha!' 'Queer, faggot, queer, fairy!' I replied and threw a stone full of mud that hit Juan Rafael on the elbow, which I know hurt": ibid., 95. I have not translated "pato" (duck) literally; instead, I have used terms that convey similar meanings and associations.

35. According to María Moliner's *Diccionario del uso del español* (Madrid: Editorial Gredos, 1979), "marimacho," which is identified as a "vulgar" term, means: "mujer de aspecto y modales masculinos" (a woman of masculine appearance and manners). The dictionary lim-its its definition of "lesbiano, -a" (lesbian) to "lesbio, -a: de la isla de Lesbos" (from the island of Lesbos).

36. At another moment in the novel, the children spend substantial time defining "pato" and explaining what it means. This is a valuable moment in the clarification of popular (mis)under-standings of sexuality and sexual identities in Puerto Rico.

37. "Lo de patos [lo dije] porque sabía que ese era el peor insulto que uno podía dar" (I men-tioned the patos thing because I knew that was the worst insult that one could make): García Ramis, *Felices días*, 95.

38. One possible translation for "marimacha" is "tomboy," but the English-language term lacks the severely critical charge that the Spanish words entails.

39. I am thinking of Teresa de Lauretis's elaboration of the subject in *The Practice of Love: Les-bian Sexualities and Perverse Desire* (Bloomington: Indiana University Press, 1976), as well as Monique Wittig's 1973 classic, *The Lesbian Body*, trans. David Le Vay (New York: Avon Books, 1976). Giannina Braschi's novel *Yo-Yo Boing* (Pittsburgh: Latin American Literary Review Press, 1998) offers a fascinating example of a New York Puerto Rican homage to Wittig, specifically through her representation of the monstrous deconstruction of the body into constitutive frag-

ments and the engagement with scatological organic processes of decomposition. Braschi also engages issues of lesbianism, homosexuality, and transvestism in her earlier work, *The Empire of Dreams*, trans. Tesss O'Dwyer (New Haven, Conn.: Yale University Press, 1994).

40. "It's not that my mother wasn't feminine": García Ramis, *Felices días*, 1.

41. "They had explained to us that Margara was a bad, streetwise woman, and we knew without understanding that she did things that one could not even imagine": ibid., 13. Although there is no indication that Margara is actually a prostitute—her main "crime" seems to be to have had sexual intercourse out of wedlock—it is valuable to compare her, as a literary character, to other notable "bad" women of Puerto Rican letters. Interesting examples include Juanita in René Marqués's *La carreta* (Río Piedras: Editorial Cultural, 1963) and Gurdelia Grifitos in Luis Rafael Sánchez's short story "Tiene la noche una raíz," in *En cuerpo de camisa* (Río Piedras: Editorial Antillana, 1971). "Bad" women are represented cinematographically in Luis Molina's *La guagua aérea*, film (1993). Oscar Lewis also emphasizes female prostitutes in his study of Puerto Rican lower classes, *La vida: A Puerto Rican Family in the Culture of Poverty—San Juan and New York* (New York: Random House, 1966). Contemporary writers such as Rosario Ferré, Manuel Ramos Otero, and Ana Lydia Vega have done much to disentangle the associations of female sexuality with moral perdition. See María M. Solá, "Angel, arpía, animal fierno y tierno: Mujer, sociedad y literatura en Puerto Rico," in *La mujer en Puerto Rico*, ed. Yamila Azize Vargas (Río Piedras: Huracán, 1987), 193–228.

42. For an elaboration of mother–daughter bonds, see de Lauretis, *Practice of Love*, 163–90.

43. "His large eyes with long, almost woman-like eyelashes": García Ramis, *Felices días*, 7. Popular nineteenth-century sexological reductionism posited homosexuality as gender inversion, as in Ulricks's famous pronouncement that male homosexuality was nothing more than an "anima muliebris in corpore virile inclusa." For more on Ulricks, see Kaja Silverman, *Male Subjectivity at the Margins* (New York: Routledge, 1992).

44. "As we went on to learn, he was a pariah, a nonconformist, and probably a homosexual": García Ramis, *Felices días*, 155.

45. Numerous discussions of homosexuality throughout the novel include one about "[el] muchacho [de] la pobre Tati Almeyda" (poor Tati Almeyda's son), who was sent to California; "que dicen que allá es que los están mandando a todos" (that's where they say they are sending all of them). This is followed by a discussion among the children of what "pato" means: ibid., 31, 32–33.

46. She also mentions other relationships, such as that with Manuel (ibid., 71), but does not go into detail. Of course, I should mention that one possible method of "mediating" Lidia's sexuality is to insist not on a "lesbian" identity but on a "bisexual" one—one that can account for the attraction to both men and women. On Lidia's love for her uncle as the novel's central structuring device, see Aurea María Sotomayor, "Si un nombre convoca un mundo . . . *Felices días, tío Sergio* en la narrativa puertorriqueña contemporánea," *Revista Iberoamericana* 59, no. 162–63 (1993): 317–27.

47. Luis Felipe Díaz, "Ideología y sexualidad en *Felices días*," 325–41.

48. "Le oí decir a ella: 'No importa, eso no es nada, aunque te pase a menudo, algún día se te quitará, voy a subir ahora no sea que venga alguien y me busque'" (I heard her say: "It doesn't matter, it's nothing, even if it happens to you often, one day it won't happen any more. Let me go upstairs before someone comes looking for me": García Ramis, *Felices días*, 132).

49. In her otherwise insightful analysis of the novel, Sotomayor fails to account for how the uncle's homosexuality affects Lidia's desire. (The critic in fact never discusses the uncle's homosexuality.)

50. "From the time they are young, children know, intuit, recognize themselves in prohibited people if it is within them to be like that when they grow up": García Ramis, *Felices días*, 80; emphasis added.

51. "I, in league then and perhaps forever with pariahs, different ones, with Uncle Sergio? Had something similar happened to him?": ibid., 90.

52. "One day, at a party, I allowed myself to be kissed by a guy, Juan Miguel. I let myself be kissed because everyone did so. When I got home after secretly drinking two Cuba Libres, and with my mouth full of kisses that were not the ones I wanted, I started to cry. To cry for you and me and for everything that I had never wanted to know. I then started to be ridiculous": ibid., 144–45.

53. "When I realized that I would never do well in my classes, that I had no friends in this school, that Andrés, Quique, and I would never play again in the house, that life was lonelier and more terrible than I had ever imagined, that I was getting fat and ugly, extremely ugly, I decided that I did not want to keep on living on this island, and I started to wait for Sophia Loren to come pick me up and take me to live in Italy": ibid., 119.

54. "Distance ourselves forever from the life that we led": ibid., 2.

55. Forced exile of middle-class homosexuals is not unique to Puerto Rico. For a similar case in Brazil, see Silviano Santiago's wonderful novel *Stella Manhattan,* trans. George Yúdice (Durham, N.C.: Duke University Press, 1994). For an example of a young woman's forced migration from Puerto Rico because of her relationship with a married male relative, see Pedro Juan Soto's short story "La cautiva," in *Spiks* (México, D.F.: Los Presentes, 1956). Sylvia Molloy's novel *En breve cárcel* (Barcelona: Seix Barral, 1981) is an example of lesbian migration as survival strategy.

56. Note Carlos Gil's analysis of the episode in which Bernardo Vega throws his watch overboard when he arrives to New York so he will not be confused with "effeminate" men: Carlos Gil, *El orden del tiempo: Ensayos sobre el robo del presente en la utopía puertorriqueña* (San Juan: Editorial Postdata, 1998).

57. "'HOW HORRIBLE!' 'What a shame, so handsome,' Nati said. 'Yes, indeed, a pato, poor Tati Almeyda's son turned out to be a pato. Aha, but she already sent him to the United States, you know, far away, to California. That's where they say that they're sending all of them'": García Ramis, *Felices días,* 31.

58. Laura Mulvey, "Visual Pleasure and Narrative Cinema," *Screen* 16, no. 3 (Fall 1975); idem, *Visual and Other Pleasures* (Bloomington: University of Indiana Press, 1989).

59. De Lauretis, *Practice of Love.*

60. "My infatuation with Sophia began with the film *Boy on a Dolphin,* which I saw eleven times. That this townwoman could marry the handsome American archaeologist and that they could love each other . . . that, more than anything in the world, made me tremble in a fashion I could not explain. I would dream that Sophia would be married even to Alan Ladd or Yul Brynner, and I would go to live with them": García Ramis, *Felices días,* 119.

61. An indication of *Boy on a Dolphin*'s status as a minor film is that it is not even available on video. Apparently, Sophia Loren was considerably taller than Alan Ladd, and the film crew had to dig holes in the sand so he would not be dwarfed by her. For more details about the film, see Tony Crawley, *The Films of Sophia Loren* (Secaucus, N.J.: Citadel Press, 1976), 81–84, and Alan Levy, *Forever Sophia* (New York: St. Martin's Press, 1979).

62. "I knew that one day I would find [Sophia Loren], when she was already old and nobody looked for her. Then, I would invite her to spend some time in my New York penthouse, because sometimes I thought about being a 'career girl,' which was something presumptuous,

although I couldn't really tell what it was. All 'career girls' had luxury apartments in New York. Sophia would visit me, and we would reminisce together about how each of us had grown up, and we would marvel at both having been born on 20 September, and I would have money to invite her and Carlo Ponti and her two sons to an elegant dinner in New York": García Ramis, *Felices días*, 144.

63. "In the novel and in some short stories, these girls usually find the most progressive voice in a male character. There is very little validation from other women and other girls. Lidia, for example, doesn't have female friends. In the passage where she describes her desire to live with Sophia Loren, which has erotic content, she talks about including Carlo Ponti and the children, not Sophia by herself. Why aren't spaces of solidarity among women or progressive models for female characters validated?": Negrón-Muntaner, "Magali García Ramis," 89–104.

64. "In my life, as a young adult, most of the people who helped me to grow up were men. At work, I usually make better friendships with men than with women. When I began my professional life, women seemed foolish to me. The models that I had at that time to break structures were men. As an adult, I was able to understand that my aunts, by being professionals who worked, broke models. However, I think that most of the people who planted ideas in me and who made me think and doubt were men. Although this was not exclusive . . . I had female friends who influenced me greatly: ibid, 100; ellipsis in the original.

65. See Marilyn R. Farwell, *Heterosexual Plots and Lesbian Narratives* (New York: New York University Press, 1996), 41–42, 59–60. Gayle Rubin's groundbreaking "The Traffic in Women: Notes on the 'Political Economy' of Sex" (in *Toward an Anthropology of Women*, ed. Rayn Reiter [New York: Monthly Review Press, 1975], 157–210) is a fundamental feminist reinterpretation. For a Puerto Rican take, see Agnes Ortiz-Lugo, "Sobre el tráfico simbólico de mujeres: Homosocialidad, identidad nacional y modernidad literaria en Puerto Rico (Apuntes para una relectura de *El puertorriqueño dócil* de René Marqués), *Revista de crítica literaria latinoamericana* 23, no. 45 (1997): 261–78.

66. See de Lauretis, *Practice of Love*, for a scathing review of Sedgwick's work.

67. Iván Silén, "Del hacer como el ser de la novela puertorriqueña: Sobre *Maldito amor* y *Felices días, Tío Sergio*," *Caribán* 2, no 1–2 (January–August 1987): 16, 28.

68. In her interview with Negrón-Muntaner, García Ramis directly confronted the issue of why she did not develop an incest story line. "Yo creo que la única decisión absolutamente política y no literaria que yo he hecho en mi vida fue la de no dejar que Sergio se acostara con Lidia. Me pareció que no era justo con un personaje que es tan moral a su manera y que lo que quiere es ayudar a la gente a crecer. Desde mi punto de vista yo detesto, y me parecen completamente injustas, las relaciones de adultos con niños sean o no homosexuales o heterosexuales" (I think that the only absolutely political and not literary decision I have made in my life was to not allow Sergio to go to bed with Lidia. It seemed to me that it was not fair for a character who was so moral in his own way and who really wanted to help people to grow. From my point of view, I hate and find completely unfair relationships between adults and children, be they homosexual or heterosexual": Negrón-Muntaner, "Magali García Ramis," 101.

Salvador C. Fernández

4 Coming-Out Stories and the Politics of Identity in the Narrative of Terri de la Peña

In her book *Getting Specific: Postmodern Lesbian Politics*, Shane Phelan develops a theory of lesbian identities based on the politics of postmodernism.[1] For Phelan, a cultural lesbian identity evolves from the continuous change and evolution of public discourses that deal with the representation of specific communities. At the literary level, the emergence of new discourses manifests the multiplicity and diversity of aesthetic representations that postmodernism embraces. More specifically, the discursive practices of these communities construct narrative strategies that question and challenge the cultural hegemony of metanarratives of Western civilization.[2]

Thus, the dominance of cultural metanarratives, which are generally written by men, is challenged by one of the topoi that lesbian narratives treat: representing the process or moment of coming out. Phelan defines coming out as an open admission of being a lesbian or a process of discovery that traces the history of the characters' latent lesbianism. The lesbian writer portrays the nonconformity of her characters in this process of coming out to highlight the sexist societal standards of femininity; this, in turn, provides an analysis and demystification of the heterosexual order(s).

The focus on the representation of local communities in a postmodern politics of identity also signifies the recognition of multiple lesbian spaces and narratives, which marks the role that diverse communities play in society. One such literary space is that occupied by Chicana lesbian literature, which began with the publication of Cherríe Moraga and Gloria Anzaldúa's pioneer anthology, *This Bridge Called My Back: Writings by Radical Women of Color*.[3] Several years later, Anzaldúa accented the historical position and significance of the Chicana lesbian space in her pivotal text *Borderlands/La Frontera: The New Mestiza*.[4] These two works not only opened the doors to Chicana lesbian writers; they also advocated a theory of a Chicana lesbian identity based on a literary concept of multiple identities and split subjectivities. Moreover, this theory of identity challenged the cultural hegemony of Anglo-American feminist critics who traditionally were not concerned with the formation of the Chicana community.

Recently, the importance of the Chicana lesbian space has been recapitulated in *Chicana Lesbians: The Girls Our Mothers Warned Us About,* edited by Carla Trujillo, an anthology of poetic works and essays that focus on the cultural politics of Chicana lesbian identity.[5] The anthology contains two essays that are essential to understanding the construction of Chicana lesbian identity. The first, written by Emma Pérez, is "Sexuality and Discourse: Notes from a Chicana Survivor." Pérez establishes that Chicana lesbian works emerge from *un sitio y una lengua* (a space and a language) that reject the colonial ideology, the byproducts of colonialism, capitalist patriarchy, sexism, racism, and homophobia.[6]

While Pérez delineates the uniqueness of the space and languages of the Chicana lesbian experience, Carla Trujillo, in her essay "Chicana Lesbians: Fear and Loathing in the Chicano Community," focuses on the sociopolitical issues Chicana lesbians confront within their own communities.[7] For Trujillo, sexuality is the most important sociocultural element that a Chicana lesbian faces. Trujillo's validation of Chicana lesbian sexuality and these women's identity defies the negative belief that characterizes them as *vendidas* or *malinchistas.*

Trujillo also strives to identify the problems that Chicana lesbians encounter when they come out. This process, she says, is a major source of pain for Chicana lesbians because they fear rejection from both their families and their tight-knit communities. Thus, the Chicana lesbians' works often represent coming out as an agonizing process in which the characters feel alienated. The alienation of these characters indicates the ambivalent sociocultural context in which they live. The characters that Chicana lesbian writers create fight to free themselves from patriarchal control and sexual repression; at the same time, however, both the Chicano community and the dominant community adhere strongly to the traditional heterosexual order(s). Therefore, Trujillo says, Chicana lesbians must create or modify *la familia, la religión,* and *la comunidad.*

One of the new Chicana voices concerned with the politics of Chicana lesbian identity is Terri de la Peña. Educated at a parochial school in Santa Monica and at Santa Monica Community College, de la Peña is a self-taught writer. She began to write fiction as an adolescent, although her first publication did not appear until her fortieth birthday, in 1988.[8]

De la Peña's narratives focus on the myriad cultural and social issues that Chicana lesbians face. Among them are coming out, a search for identity, the raising of class and gender consciousness, a sense of historical awareness, internal and external racism, and homophobia. De la Peña has published three novels: *Margins, Latin Satins,* and *Faults.*[9] She also has published numerous short stories in Chicana/o and lesbian literary anthologies and has a forthcoming collection of short stories titled *Territories.*[10] Her writings continue and develop literary traditions and thematics treated by earlier Chicana lesbian writers such as Anzaldúa and Moraga.

In this study, I will analyze two early texts written by de la Peña—the autobiographical essay "Good-bye Ricky Ricardo, Hello Lesbianism" and her first novel,

Margins–to examine her representation of the Chicana lesbian space.[11] "Good-bye Ricky Ricardo, Hello Lesbianism" is a coming-out narrative that analyzes de la Peña's personal experiences and her search for her identity as a Chicana and a lesbian. One of the crucial issues that she examines is her feeling of distinctness from the sexual identity that both the Anglo-American and Chicana cultures assign to her gender, a difference that she has felt since childhood. This sense of being other, different, is born most significantly out of her physical and emotional reactions to her relatives. "When confronted with aunts and uncles intent on *besitos y abrazos*," De la Peña writes, "I would grow rigid, unable to respond. But I had no trouble expressing affection towards my younger sisters and little girl friends."[12] De la Peña also refers to the television program *I Love Lucy* to illustrate her childhood feelings of sexual difference. She recounts that, as a child, she played the role of Ricky because she "had the privilege of kissing 'Lucy,' as enacted by Frances, a hazel-eyed, auburn-haired beauty whose familial roots originated in Jalisco."[13] Through these autobiographical episodes, de la Peña not only traces her feelings of sexual difference. She also narrates difficult yet significant moments that help her to realize her latent lesbianism, which is eventually resolved by her coming out.

Although many of de la Peña's references to *I Love Lucy* episodes provide comic relief for the everyday and personal issues that the characters face, de la Peña's narration of her denial of latent lesbianism and sexual distinctness is simultaneously a recounting of painful personal experiences endured within a closed and repressive social space. This denial often takes the form of self-hatred. For example, the author's feelings of sexual distinctness are ascribed to her physical appearance. "At first," she says, "I attributed it to being skinny, wearing glasses, and having buck teeth and, later acne."[14] Later, as a high-school student, when her lesbian feelings become stronger and more intense, she begins to feel detached from her classmates, family members, and even herself. In fact, she explains, "I remained a gangly beanpole, with minuscule breasts, no hips, toothpick legs, and a melancholy face oozing with acne. My romantic Ricky Ricardo image had been rudely replaced by the repulsive female stranger in my mirror."[15] De la Peña's rejection of her body and her physical appearance is a common literary trope found in coming-out narratives in order to accentuate the physical, personal, and social struggles of a subject, who is exploring and discovering a new physical space. Moreover, as a literary trope, the rejection of the body represents the author's search for a center and a space that has been taken away by the hegemonic cultural parameters.

Rejection of her body is a primary trope de la Peña uses to characterize her search for identity and her coming-out experience as agonizing. The death of her maternal grandmother, an experience that significantly affected her childhood and left "a huge void in my life," also changed her social behavior. De la Peña narrates that, at eleven years old, she decided to reform: "I had to pull myself together and quit thinking about kissing girls."[16] In addition to repressing her lesbian feelings, she also becomes ultra-religious and seeks social comfort in the Catholic church. She begins to attend mass every day and starts to confess her lesbian sins of flesh to her priest. It is ironic that, for de la Peña, confessions in the Catholic church provide a safe and secure space to express lesbian identity. In essence, she deconstructs and subverts two closed, patriarchal and homophobic spaces—the Catholic church and, within it, the even more repressive confessional.

Even as de la Peña appropriates the act of confession to find a social and cultural space for her pre-lesbianhood life, her interactions and contact with her extended family negatively affect her life. For example, at the same time that she falls in love with a former classmate, a member of her family unknowingly marries a gay man. This unexpected turn of events causes homosexuality to become "a whispered topic" in the family, and she poignantly says: "My family's absolute rejection of the gay man unnerved me. What would happen if they discovered I loved my girl friend?"[17] Indeed, de la Peña tellingly reveals the particularly painful dilemma faced by Chicana/ Latina lesbians: assertion of self, of her identity, as "different" means total rejection, and subsequently exile from the center of the community, the family.

This tragic and sad family episode intensifies de la Peña's personal evolution in two ways. It creates a desire to inform herself about the issues that she faces as a lesbian, and it begins a cultural and historical search to define her Chicana identity. She begins to research and read studies on homosexuality. Not surprisingly, she does not find a solution to her emotional and physical pain in the studies that she reads. In fact, the studies, published in the mid-1960s, primarily framed homosexuality psychologically in terms of deviance and presented negative attitudes about the subject. Moreover, she finds few studies of lesbianism in her research. It is not until later, in the late 1970s or early 1980s, that she "discovers" the Sisterhood Bookstore near the Westwood campus of the University of California, Los Angeles (UCLA), where she comes across literature and studies that validate her identity as a lesbian. At the same time, to fulfill her desire to explore her identity as a lesbian intellectually, she begins to write a novel centered on the life of two Chicano brothers, one gay and another straight. She says that writing became a way to develop her "own thoughts and feelings on homosexuality."[18]

De la Peña's final stage of coming out, a period of self-discovery, begins with a search for her historical roots, exemplified by a trip to Mexico City and her work at the UCLA Chicano Studies Center. At the center she faces two different social issues: sexism and classism. The Chicanos at the center make a class distinction between Chicanos from East Los Angeles and Chicanos from West Los Angeles. She is identified as a "westside Chicana," one who is "'too white" to have credibility with the [Chicano] Movement."[19] Her rejection by the center's Chicanos leads her to look for a personal and social space in the women's movement. Her identification with the women's movement and the feminist literature that she devours at the Sisterhood Bookstore serve as the catalyst for coming out to herself as a lesbian. This personal coming out occurs in 1978, when she is thirty-one years old.

De la Peña's autobiographical essay serves as more than a coming-out text. Because it recounts several events that reappear in her other works, it also functions as an intertextual reference for her novels and short stories. One example is the story of her first date with Rose, a Polish American woman, who also comes from a working-class background. Rose appears as a character in two short stories, "Sequences" and "Beyond El Camino Real."[20] Both stories narrate the relationship between Monica Tovar and Jozie Krozinski as a way to describe the formation of Tovar's consciousness both as a woman who loves women and as a Chicana. According to Alicia Gaspar de Alba, this type of cross-cultural relationship is charged with particular significance because it "reveals the internal conflicts of a café-con-leche relationship" between the colonizer and the colonized.[21] Thus, the author's sexual evolution brings with it a cultural and political challenge: What does it mean to be a Chicana lesbian?

This simultaneous questioning serves as a direct thematic link between "Good-bye Ricky Ricardo, Hello Lesbianism" and de la Peña's other narratives. For example, the representation of the social discrimination that Chicanas and lesbians face establishes a thematic bridge between the autobiographical coming-out essay and de la Peña's second novel, *Latin Satins.* One of the central episodes in *Latin Satins* focuses on the social experiences of two children, Yolanda and Angelita, who at an early age experience racial discrimination both in and outside of their own cultures. Another significant topic that links her coming-out narrative and the novel is de la Peña's critique of homophobic prejudices directed at lesbians. This is exemplified when Jessica Tamayo, the novel's protagonist, suffers discrimination at the day-care center where she works when two upper-class Anglo mothers try to get her fired because she is a lesbian. Significantly, the exploration of these diverse types of discrimination within the Chicano community distinguishes de la Peña from other Chicana/o writers who treat this theme.[22]

Although "Good-bye Ricky Ricardo, Hello Lesbianism" is a very significant text for the author on a personal level, I feel that her most important literary work is her first novel, *Margins.* The first coming-out novel in Chicana literature, *Margins* narrates the sexual coming out of Verónica Meléndez, a Chicana graduate student and writer. Verónica's increasing awareness of her cultural and sexual identity parallels her physical rehabilitation after a car accident in which her first lover, Joanna Núñez, dies. Verónica's physical pain reflects her psychological anguish and the social problems she encounters when she identifies herself as a Chicana lesbian. Her emotional recovery begins when she writes a collection of short stories as a class assignment. Thus, the process of writing serves as a therapeutic device that eases both her physical and her emotional suffering.[23]

Margins is divided structurally into three intertwined sections. The first narrates the initial meeting and subsequent intimate relationship between Verónica and her next lover, Siena Benedetti. The description of Verónica's affair with Siena is characterized by an erotic discourse with sexual imagery that exalts the representation of the female body. In one of the most erotic passages in the novel, the narrator explicitly recounts an encounter between the two women:

> Soon her mouth was where her fingers had been. Siena had a cidery fragrance, a musky taste. Veronica reveled in her. She was relentless, licking, sucking, her mouth and tongue

indefatigable. Siena opened her thighs wider, and Veronica swept her tongue repeatedly along her clitoris, liking the way the pink nub rose to greet her. It glistened with moisture, and as she sucked harder, Siena came with a breathless cry.[24]

De la Peña's representation of lesbian eroticism is both a literary and sociocultural act of transgression. Moreover, the description of carnal pleasures, such as masturbation, orgasms, and sexual fantasy, symbolize a further narrative shift: from a male-dominated to a female-centered erotic discourse. Thus, the lesbian erotic discourse used by de la Peña deconstructs the hermetic space that characterizes Mexican/Chicano society in a number of ways.

In her study *Women Singing in the Snow: A Cultural Analysis of Chicana Literature,* Tey Diana Rebolledo interprets the thematics of this type of erotic discourse as a sign of empowering the body, one's sexuality, and self-writing.[25] For Rebolledo, these writers and their characters represent *las mujeres andariegas, atravesadas, y de fuerza* (restless, wayward, and strong women). Moreover, according to Rebolledo, lesbian Chicana writers are at the forefront of sexual politics because these *mujeres escandalosas* (scandalous women) represent an oppressed and marginalized subjectivity.

As stated earlier, the relationship between Verónica and Siena represents the first phase in the protagonist's physical and psychological rehabilitation. Dreams and flashbacks throughout this section simultaneously reconstruct Verónica's prior partnership with Joanna: "She wanted to empty her mind of distractions, but writing about Joanna recreated haunting images of those smooth hands caressing, sepia eyes beckoning. Veronica had never loved anyone else and she craved Joanna still."[26] Thus, these dreams function as a narrative strategy that traces Veronica's repressed lesbian manifestations in order to reconstruct the protagonist's coming-out.

The second section of *Margins* narrates the ensuing relationship that Verónica has with René Talamantes, a Tejana lesbian and film student at UCLA. Verónica's relationship with this woman permits de la Peña to highlight cultural and social differences within the Chicano community. For instance, René and her mother, Guadalupe, are less assimilated than Verónica and her family. This difference in acculturation is symbolized by objects found in the Talamantes' home: the serape on the sofa, the Spanish newspaper they read, and the votive candles lit in homage to El Santo Niño de Atocha and the Virgin of Guadalupe. Languages spoken at home also illustrate the difference: René's family speaks more Spanish; Veronica's, more English. Finally, from the beginning, René expresses deep pride in her cultural and sexual identity, a feeling Verónica does not voice until the end of the novel.

An excerpt from this section of *Margins* appeared in the collection *Lesbian Bedtime Stories* under the title "Tortilleras."[27] Although the term "tortillera" has negative connotations in the Chicano community, it is appropriated in the collection's title as a culturally and emotionally charged term to identify Chicana lesbians. Simply said, a term that was originally meant to hurt, to insult and belittle Chicana lesbians, is reappropriated. In *Margins,* the new meaning of the term is associated with René, who is an archetype of the Chicana tortillera. Verónica describes her this way:

René seems secure with her identity, whether anyone likes it or not. Some guys in the audience tonight were downright hostile, but she handled them. . . . René's out to her parents; they are divorced. She's a working-class kid, the first college graduate in her family. She won a film award at the University of Texas before winding up here. She has lots of guts—and talent.[28]

De la Peña's René character represents the formation of a new literary archetype, one that is also developed by other Chicana lesbian writers. That is, Rene's characterization is not only positive and assertive. It also exemplifies Rebolledo's characterization of these Chicana women as *mujeres de fuerza*.

The third section of *Margins* recounts Veronica's coming out as a lesbian, represented by her increasingly open relationship with René. The process of disclosure begins when Verónica's nephew Phil, who is staying with her, sees Verónica and Siena in an intimate moment and runs out into the street, where he is hit by a car. The episode affects Verónica deeply, and her dreams are filled with violent images, such as Joanna's dead body lying beside her. Phil's accident intensifies Verónica's personal crises and eventually leads her to disclose her sexual orientation to her family. This coming out signifies both personal and social freedom. As a closeted Chicana lesbian, Verónica had experienced loneliness and isolation in her closeknit, although sometimes suffocating, Chicano family.

In addition, Verónica's coming out allows de la Peña to criticize the repressive sociocultural institutions and ideologies that strongly influence the Chicano community (for example, the Roman Catholic church and Chicanismo). Although Verónica is the product of a hybrid culture and acknowledges the diverse influences that have formed her identity, she also rejects the oppressive ideological elements that characterize certain sociocultural institutions. For instance, Verónica's struggles with public and private spaces serve as a stage for de la Peña to attack the sexism inherent in the Chicano community and its rejection of its homosexual population. Thus, Verónica's resolution of her difficulties serves as a novelistic answer to those within the Mexican/Chicano community who feel that gays and lesbians taint a family's honor, attack the moral values of society, or hinder the Chicano community's social status.

Interestingly, Verónica's acceptance of herself, and her acceptance by her family, symbolize the solidarity of Chicana motherhood and sisterhood. This unity is portrayed when the mothers, Guadalupe Talamantes and Sara Meléndez, sing the popular folksong "De colores" in their daughters' presence. As Pérez has noted, a Chicana lesbian writer comes from *un sitio y una lengua*. In this case, this truth is presented through the use of a popular song that promotes harmony among peoples of different colors. Singing is an oral tradition, a "language" and "dialect" that calls attention to the bond between Spanish-speaking mothers and their children. It is also a linguistic point of intersection and union within the Chicano community, the "place" where de la Peña belongs. Finally, "De colores" is a political song sung by the farmers and followers of the United Farm Workers; thus, its use signfies the collective empowerment of Chicanas that de la Peña advocates throughout all of her narratives. Songs such as

"De colores" and "Cielito lindo" acquire political meaning and represent a form of counterdiscourse that challenges society's traditional cultural values.

Indeed, de la Peña's use of popular discourse as a narrative strategy to challenge the sociocultural hegemony of metanarratives also appears as a thematic structure in *Latin Satins*. The novel narrates the experiences of four Chicana singers, the Latin Satins, who satirize "golden oldies" songs to empower Chicana lesbians. The main character is their songwriter, Jessica Tamayo, a child-care worker. Jessica also performs in a lesbian chorus and writes music reviews for a lesbian magazine.

The Latin Satins advocate social change and celebrate their cultural heritage through their music. The lyrics of their ballads, included in the narrative itself, highlight the internal and external social problems faced by the Chicano community. Written in Spanish and English, the songs reflect contemporary social concerns such as racism, homophobia, and misrepresentation of Chicanos/as and Latinos/as by the mass media, themes that de la Peña treats in the novel. De la Peña localizes the identity of the protagonist by identifying her native state, her political status, the color of her skin, and her language. That is, using Pérez's terms, de la Peña defines Jessica Tamayo physically, geographically, and linguistically.

In conclusion, de la Peña's works are concerned with social and cultural problems that Chicanas face within the Chicano community, as well as in Anglo society. Her narratives, works that come from the margin, depict the survival of internal and external oppression typical of a patriarchal system. Nevertheless, her writing resonates with Chicana/o, feminist, and lesbian literary traditions that challenge hegemonic discursive practices. De la Peña's recounting of the process of coming out, her incorporation of erotic discourse, and her representation of discrimination that Chicana lesbians suffer within their own community, as well as in the dominant Anglo community, symbolize the *nueva conciencia* of many Chicana lesbians who are sociopolitically aware and sexually liberated. These narratives represent a postmodern Chicana lesbian space, which presents an alternative view to the representation of women in patristic metanarratives. De la Peña's narratives, therefore, belong to the lesbian and feminist literary traditions represented by Anzaldúa and Moraga, as well as those of Adrienne Rich.[29] Most significantly, her creation of this sociocultural space is a significant step that shows how empowered Chicanas can create their own *sitio y lengua*.

Notes

1. Shane Phelan, *Getting Specific: Postmodern Lesbian Politics* (Minneapolis: University of Minnesota Press, 1994). There is a current of lesbian criticism that departs from poststructuralist and postmodernist theories. An excellent example is Sally Munt, *New Lesbian Criticism: Literary and Cultural Readings* (New York: Columbia University Press, 1992). See also "Special Issue: Theorizing Lesbian Experience," *Signs: Journal of Women in Culture and Society* (Summer 1993).

2. This is a reference to Jean-Francois Lyotard, *The Postmodern Condition: A Report on Knowledge*, trans. Geoff Bennington and Brian Massumi (Minneapolis: University of Minnesota Press,

1988). Phelan sees the lesbian narrative as an example of the postmodern condition characterized by the end of metanarratives.

3. Cherríe Moraga and Gloria Anzaldúa, eds., *This Bridge Called My Back: Writings by Radical Women of Color* (Watertown, Mass.: Persephone Press, 1981).

4. Gloria Anzaldúa, *Borderlands/La Frontera: The New Mestiza* (San Francisco: Aunt Lute Books, 1987). For a study of these works, see Norma Alarcón, "The Theoretical Subject(s) of *This Bridge Called My Back* and Anglo-American Feminism," in *Criticisms in the Borderlands: Studies in Chicano Literature, Culture, and Ideology,* ed. Héctor Calderón and José David Saldívar (Durham, N.C.: Duke University Press, 1991); and Sonia Saldívar-Hull, "Feminism on the Border: From Gender Politics to Geopolitics" in Calderón and Saldívar, *Criticism in the Borderlands.*

5. Carla Trujillo, ed., *Chicana Lesbians: The Girls Our Mothers Warned Us About* (Berkeley, Calif.: Third Woman Press, 1991). For a review of this anthology and other works that deal with Chicana lesbians, see Alicia Gaspar de Alba, "Tortillerismo: Work by Chicana Lesbians" in *Signs* 18, no. 4 (1993).

6. Emma Pérez, "Sexuality and Discourse: Notes from a Chicana Survivor," in Trujillo, ed., *Chicana Lesbians.* See also the excellent study by Aida Hurtado, "Sitios y lenguas: Chicanas Theorize Feminism," *Hypatia* 13, no. 2 (1998), and Carla Trujillo, ed., *Living Chicana Theory* (Berkeley, Calif.: Third Woman Press, 1998).

7. Carla Trujillo, "Chicana Lesbians: Fear and Loathing in the Chicano Community," in idem, *Chicana Lesbians.*

8. For an introduction to her work and an extensive list of her publications, see Salvador C. Fernández, "Terri de la Peña," in *Dictionary of Literary Biography,* vol. 209, ed. Francisco A. Lomelí and Carl R. Shirley (London: Bruccolli Clark Layman Book, 1999).

9. Terri de la Peña, *Margins* (Seattle: Seal Press, 1992); idem, *Latin Satins* (Seattle: Seal Press, 1994); idem, *Faults* (Hollywood: Alyson Publications, 1999). *Margins* was published in Germany under the title *Chicana Blues* (Berlin: Krug and Schadenberg, 1994). In addition to these novels, de la Peña, with Cynthia Chin-Lee, published the children's book *A Is for the Americas* (New York: Orchard Books, 1999).

10. De la Peña's works have been reviewed in Rose Cosme, "One Chicana Lesbiana's View of *Margins,*" *Esto no tiene nombre* (Spring 1993); Mary Ann Daly, "A Study in Character: Terri de la Peña's Latina Lesbians Light Up the Page," *Lambda Book Report* (July–August 1992); Donají, "A Closer Look at Terri de la Peña," *Esto no tiene nombre* (Spring 1993); Ellie Hernández, "A Blind Sided View of *Margins,*" *Esto no tiene nombre* (Spring 1993); Camille D. Loya, "Terri de la Peña," in *Contemporary Lesbian Writers of the United States: A Bio-Bibliographical Critical Sourcebook,* ed. Sandra Pollack and Denise D. Knight (Westport, Conn.: Greenwood Press, 1993); and Teresa Ortega, "Sex and Salsa—*Latin Satins* by Terri de la Peña," *Lambda Book Report* (May 1995).

11. Terri de la Peña, "Good-bye Ricky Ricardo, Hello Lesbianism," in *The Coming Out Stories,* ed. Julia Penelope and Susan Wolfe (Freedom, Calif.: Crossing Press, 1989).

12. Ibid., 224.

13. Ibid.

14. Ibid.

15. Ibid., 225.

16. Ibid.

17. Ibid., 226.

18. Ibid.

19. Ibid., 227.

20. Terri de la Peña, "Sequences," in *Finding the Lesbians: Personal Accounts from around the World*, ed. Julia Penelope and Sara Valentine (Freedom, Calif.: Crossing Press, 1990); idem, "Beyond El Camino Real," in Trujillo, *Chicana Lesbians*.

21. Alicia Gaspar de Alba, "Tortillerismo: Work by Chicana Lesbians,"in *Signs* 18, no. 4 (1993).

22. De la Peña also emphasizes the negative impact that AIDS has had on the Chicano community. One of de la Peña's short stories, "Frankie," in *Blood Whispers*, ed. Terry Wolverton (Los Angeles: Silverton, 1991)—which recounts the life of the narrator's childhood friend who dies of AIDS—best exemplifies the impact of this disease on the Chicano community. The emergence of AIDS as a literary theme can also be seen in the works of such young Chicano/a writers as Rubén Martínez and Luis Alfaro.

23. For a study of *Margins,* see Catrióna Rueda Esquibel, "Memories of Girlhood: Chicana Lesbian Fictions," *Signs* 23, no. 3 (1998).

24. De la Peña, *Margins,* 55.

25. For further discussion, see Tey Diana Rebolledo, "Mujeres Andariegas: Good Girls and Bad," in idem, *Women Singing in the Snow: A Cultural Analysis of Chicana Literature* (Tucson: University of Arizona Press, 1995).

26. De la Peña, *Margins,* 22.

27. Terri de la Peña, "Tortilleras," in *Lesbian Bedtime Stories,* ed. Terry Woodrow (Little River, Calif.: Tough Dove Books, 1989).

28. De la Peña, *Margins,* 106.

29. In *Women Singing in the Snow,* Rebolledo indicates that the reinterpretation of cultural paradigms into Chicana lesbian topographies has served to create new myths. We see this act of creation with Mónica Palacios' reinvention of La Llorona in "La Llorona Loca: The Other Side"; Anzaldúa's creation of a lesbian Chicana mythos in "La historia de una marimacho"; and Ana Castillo's notion of *la macha* in "La Macha: Toward a Beautiful Whole Self," all in Trujillo, *Chicana Lesbians,* 49–51, 64–68, 24–48, respectively.

Part II

(Re)presenting
Lesbian Desire

Nancy Vosburg

---

5   Silent Pleasures and the Pleasure
of Silence: Ana María Moix's
"Las virtudes peligrosas"

> *But let us not take the role of Revolutionary either, whether male or*
> *female: let us on the contrary refuse all roles to summon this "truth"*
> *situated outside time, a truth that is neither true nor false, that cannot*
> *be fitted in to the order of speech and social symbolism, that is an echo of*
> *our* jouissance, *of our mad words, of our pregnancies. But how can we*
> *do this? By listening; by recognizing the unspoken in all discourse, how-*
> *ever Revolutionary, by emphasizing at each point whatever remains*
> *unsatisfied, repressed, new, eccentric, incomprehensible, that which*
> *disturbs the mutual understanding of the established powers.*
>   —*Julia Kristeva*

Unfulfilled Promises?

Judging from the relatively scant criticism on the works of Ana María Moix, and the nature of that criticism, it would appear that for many Moix has yet to "deliver" on the promise implicit in Josep María Castellet's inclusion of her in his 1970 *Nueve novísimos poetas españoles*.[1] Moix's early poetry, short stories, and novels, innovative in both form and content, were followed by a twelve-year period of virtual silence.[2] When she returned to the literary terrain in 1985 with her collection of five short stories, *Las virtudes peligrosas* (*Dangerous Virtues*, 1997),[3] some critics found her still struggling with the demon that had obsessed her in her early works—"the problematic relationship of the female subject to language."[4] It is a theme that indeed can be traced throughout the collection. Yet the title story of the collection, with its aura of an unresolved enigma, offers itself to other readings that decenter the predicament of women's silence in symbolic discourse.

A Tale of Silent Pleasures

The narrative is addressed to Alice, a character whose relationship to the other characters is revealed slowly. She is instructed at the beginning of the tale to "rewind the reel" of memory, to "view" once again images from an earlier time period that she has repressed or forgotten. The film that she is instructed to "re-view," guided by the voiceover narrative of Rudolph, another character whose identity is only slowly revealed, deals with the enigmatic relationship between Rudolph's mother and another woman—two women of extraordinary beauty who never speak to each other, never embrace, yet maintain an intense and enduring relationship through their mutual gaze. Their gaze, which "seems to convey meaning through its very silence,"[5] and the pleasure they derive from gazing incite an uncontrolled fury in Rudolph's father, a brilliant military strategist:

> Vestidas ambas con trajes del mismo color, caminaban despacio, separadas por la calzada, sin hablarse, pero envueltas en una dicha y en una seguridad que las aislaba del resto de los humanos y, por supuesto, de él. Gozaban.

> Wearing dresses of the same color, both walked slowly, separated by the road, not speaking to each other, but wrapped in a happiness and security that separated them from all other human beings and, of course, from him. They took pleasure in this.[6]

During the many years he spends spying on them in a vain attempt to decode the meaning of their gaze, the general gradually descends into madness and, finally, suicide. As old age and wrinkles befall them, the two women, both supposedly "blind," cease to engage in their specular activity. Rudolph's mother, now widowed, withdraws into her bedroom, surrounded by silence and draped mirrors. She employs Alice as a reader, as does another old woman. The two women lovingly adorn Alice with remarkably similar pins and ribbons that each in turn removes, making of Alice the site of their union.

As I read of their silent pleasure, I, too, take pleasure in the power of their gaze, reveling in the enigmatic bond their gaze has silently forged and the general's inability to penetrate it. My pleasure is heightened by the deferral of knowledge—is this a story of a narcissistic recognition and celebration of their mutual beauty, as is suggested in a fictional text that Rudolph's mother asks Alice to read to her?

> Muere joven quien posee el don de la belleza si bello desea morir. Los otros la poseerán en él, que se debatirá en un mundo de formas inferiores poseyéndose sólo a sí mismo o, lo que es peor, a su igual si lo hallase en su camino. Triste destino, entonces, el de ambos; pues tras el exultante período de exaltación de la belleza de uno reflejada en la belleza del otro, espejo mútuo de dones y de gracias, condenados a no separarse jamás, esta misma indisolubilidad les condena a reprocharse mutuamente, más tarde, el deterioro labrado en ellos por los años, la enfermedad, la vejez y la muerte por el mero hecho de mostrarse uno al otro, o lo que es lo mismo, de contemplarse. Unicamente los iguales que dejan de existir para el mundo de las formas corruptibles en plena posesión de la belleza, antes de

que los inicios de la decrepitud hagan mella en ellos, permanecerán eternamente bellos, en el inmutable espejo que cada uno de ellos fue para con el otro.

He who possesses the gift of beauty dies young, if he wishes to die beautiful. Others will possess that beauty in him, but he will struggle in a world of inferior forms, possessing only himself or, even worse, his equal, should he find him in his path. Then both suffer a sad fate, that of never separating, for after the exultant period of elation, when the beauty of one is reflected in the beauty of the other—reciprocal mirrors of charm and grace—then this very indissolubility condemns them eventually to reproach each other for the deterioration wrought in them by the years—sickness, old age, and death—simply because they display themselves to each other, or, what amounts to the same thing, contemplate each other. Only equals who cease to exist for the world of corruptible forms at the moment when they enjoy full possession of their beauty, before the onset of decrepitude has damaged them, will remain eternally beautiful in the immutable mirror that each has been for the other.[7]

Or is this a tale of lesbian desire, of a subversive female response to the compulsory matrix of heterosexuality, masked by the fictional intertext and shadowing the tale? Their silent gestures, which have replaced the gaze in old age, suggest that this bond is something more than narcissistic recognition—that it is, indeed, a lesbian desire, that desire condemned, due to social, cultural, and personal limitations, as Rosalía Cornejo-Parriego succinctly asserts: "al ámbito de lo innombrable e innominado."[8] Sexuality does seem to be masquerading here; its presence is silently inscribed on Alice's—the reader's—body.

In this tale of silent pleasures, other silences abound. Identities are veiled, relationships silenced. It is not until the final pages, for example, that the identity of the narrator is revealed. Rudolph has been present, but only in the third person. We are told of his apparently unwitting role in bringing about his father's madness, for it was he who, as a young aspiring artist, painted the portraits of the two women that now hang in his mother's bedroom, capturing in concrete, eternal form their extraordinary bond:

Desde ambos lienzos se miraban fijamente estableciendo una corriente que lo sacudía a él desde el cerebro a la punta de los pies. Se contemplaban creando un mundo sólo habitado por ellas y por ellas regido, como hacían desde sus respectivos palcos de la ópera, durante sus paseos por el parque, por las calles o por el campo al amanecer, como lograban hacer incluso durante las noches de tormenta y luna llena, una semidesnuda en la terraza, la otra cabalgando por los bosques. No, Alice, el general no podía soportar la *presencia* de aquellas miradas en su propia casa, aquellas miradas fijadas en los lienzos por su propio hijo, hechas realidad bajo el techo de su propio hogar de donde, implacables, lo expulsaban.

From both canvases they stared at each other, generating a current that shook him from his head to the tip of his toes. They contemplated each other, creating a world inhabited by them alone and ruled by them alone, as they did from their respective boxes at the opera, during their strolls through the park, the streets, or in the country at dawn, as they managed to do even during stormy nights in full moon, one half-naked on the roof terrace, the other riding through the woods. No, Alice, the general could not bear the *presence* of those stares in his own house, those gazes captured on the canvases by his own son; they had become a reality under the roof of his own home from which, implacably, they expelled him.[9]

The silencing of narrative identity, the uncertainty, the ambiguity transform the reader, this reader, into a voyeur, who, much like Rudolph and his father, watches and waits for the revelation. My pleasure is heightened through the veiling of identity, through deferral of that knowledge, a deferral that allows me (like the general, like Rudolph) to project my own fantasies of sensuality onto the text. Yet when Rudolph's identity is unveiled, it reveals yet another layer of desire in the text, for beyond the passionate bond between the two women captured on the canvases, the painted images focus and express another, latent passion, an Oedipal desire that has also been stalking the text. In subsequent readings, I now focus on this Oedipal desire, myself stalking its contours. And I recognize that, more than a tale of the women's silent pleasures and desire, this is also a story of men's desires and madness.[10]

Herself Beheld—The Female Gaze

Gazing, spying, reviewing the images of memory, projecting the image onto the cinematic screen, capturing on canvas the look, draping the mirrors—the text immerses me in signs of specular activity and its differing degrees of power. As a woman, the reciprocal female gaze entices me; "its power renders irrelevant the proprietary male gaze,"[11] it confirms feminine subjectivity by resisting the Sartrean objectification of the other.[12] I feel complicit in the female gaze, silently watching as the general descends into madness and suicide. Wanting to see, he sees without wanting:

> lleno de espanto, dominado por un pánico en aumento por momentos, veía como su hijo plasmaba increíble e insólitamente la mirada de su madre, aquella mirada, precisamente aquélla, la que él, el general, temía y sabía su verdugo.

> full of horror, overcome by a panic that increased by the minute, he saw how his son captured—incredibly, remarkably—his mother's gaze, that gaze, the very one, the one that he, the general, feared and knew as his executioner.[13]

Yet like Rudolph, perhaps like Alice, I see, but I do not see. The image of the horrified general adds fuel to my own imaginations, my own desire (the desire to make this gaze erotic rather than narcissistic, much as the general must have done in his own wild imaginings). My inflamed desire inscribes itself on the text, it supplants the unseen, unspoken, textual image. Spying through the window of language, I wait for the revelation, the confirmation, that is sure to be my reward. Yet when my gazing fails to reward me, I am not deterred. I return again to gaze through the textual window, knowing that my pleasure has simply been deferred, and in that deferral, my desire has been enhanced.

The Pleasure of the Text

As I read others who have read Moix, however, my pleasure momentarily wanes. Their readings emphasize women's problematic relationship to language;[14] the ultimate power of the male gaze, because the narrative control is patriarchal;[15] the "entrapment" of women's sexuality in male-dominated discourse;[16] the lack of viability of the "unnamable desire" given its spatial and discursive marginality.[17] Their readings suggest that I have been taken in by the artifice and point to my own complicity in the silencing of women. I turn, or re-turn, after many years, to Roland Barthes: "Text of pleasure: the text that contents, fills, grants euphoria; the text that comes from culture and does not break with it, is linked to a *comfortable* practice of reading."[18] Is my pleasure then linked to this *comfortable*, because traditional, literary convention—the male domination of language, of the narrative and its female protagonists?

No, I don't think so. I *choose* to focus on presence rather than absence, in the text, for it is what is present that plunges the general into madness. I am intrigued by the staging of the women's desire, its quality of performance and masquerade. The site of the general's first knowledge (and ours) of their bond is the opera, where he sees (panoptically) them gazing at each other, rather than at the performance, through their opera glasses. They are the spectacle, performing not just for each other but also for the general (and for Rudolph, for Alice, for us). I turn to Emma Wilson, who speaks in *Sexuality and Masquerade*, of sexuality as masquerade, "a performance which is viewed and received by an other. In those instants when the meaning of performance is veiled, when the viewer is uncertain or deluded and transparency denied, then pleasure is heightened, desire ensured."[19] Like the general, like Rudolph, and like Alice, I am the spectator of this performance, whose uncertain meaning awakens desire. But while the general's desire (to know, to control, to assert his authority and patriarchal privilege) leads only to madness, his uncertainty devolving into incomprehension and humiliation, I am teased/pleased by the perversity—by the frustration of the general's desire. Barthes: "The text is (should be) that uninhibited person who shows his behind to the *Political Father*."[20]

Textual/Sexual Pleasure

This text of (un)fulfilled(?) desire seduces me, it pleases and pleasures me. Linda Gould Levine has asserted that "there is no eroticism—neither sexual nor textual—in Moix's world."[21] Yet I find that "Las virtudes peligrosas" is a highly erotic text, one that resonates with Moix's own description of what constitutes "erotic literature":

> El poder del lenguaje erótico cuando permanece en el límite de lo "indecible" y aguanta, impertérrito, en ese mágico umbral sin traspasarlo, es inmenso. Se trata de no traspasar ese umbral de lo indecible pero dejando que el lector entrevea sin, en realidad, ver absolutamente nada.[22]

Glimpsing, but not seeing. Barthes: "It is intermittence, as psychoanalysis has so rightly stated, which is erotic: the intermittence of skin flashing between two articles of clothing (trousers and sweater), between two edges (the open-necked shirt, the glove and the sleeve); it is this flash itself that seduces, or rather: the staging of an appearance-as-disappearance."[23]

Moix on eroticism:

> Es un engaño magistral: el lector, que no ha visto, tiene la sensación de que no ha visto porque la supuesta y ansiada visión lo ha cegado y sustituye, en su crédulo sensibilidad, la visión por algo más valioso que la visión en sí misma y que es el deslumbramiento que producía esa posible visión.[24]

In this staging of appearance as disappearance, the role of the imagination is reinforced; the text is transformed into "un juego compartido entre autor y lector, con reglas claras de interpretación; cuanto más se aleja el lector de la 'realidad concreta,' más intensos son los efectos suscitadores de la sensualidad y el deseo que se perciben."[25]

A Chronicle of Madness

Just as the general succumbs to suicidal madness, after years of futile spying, so his son, in his own desire to piece together and decipher the text of the two women, to understand their silent bond, also teeters on the edge of madness. Prohibited by his father from pursuing a promising artistic career, and far from engaging in scientific research in a remote place in North Africa, as his mother has told Alice, Rudolph has been lurking in his former studio, hiding from Alice while he spies on both her and his mother. Alice, on whose silent body the women have inscribed their wordless love, now becomes the canvas onto which Rudolph projects his own desire (to comprehend, to control). His textual desire mirrors and replicates his father's sexual desire. It is a desire that is Oedipal, a desire "to denude, to know, to learn the origin and the end," which, as Barthes reminds us, is "what the pleasure of the text is not."[26]

Rudolph's gesture of dominance and possession, his narrative, merely masks his inability to know or comprehend his mother. Her tale of silent pleasure is to him a text of bliss: "The text that imposes a state of loss, the text that discomforts, unsettles the reader's historical, cultural, psychological assumptions, the consistency of his tastes, values, memories, brings to a crisis his relation with language."[27] Yet this text of bliss eludes him (Lacan: "bliss is forbidden to the speaker, as such";[28] LeClaire: "Whoever speaks, by speaking denies bliss."[29]) Rudolph, a logophile like his father, on whose diaries he builds his narrative, is denied access to his mother's bliss. Part of my pleasure, I must recognize, lies paradoxically in Rudolph's speech. I revel in the male discomfort and failure to control, either physically or linguistically, female sexuality. Female self-representation in symbolic discourse is seemingly absent in this tale, but Moix suggests, through her narrative artifice, that phallologocentrism itself may well be a site of loss and madness.

Alice in Rudolph's Hands

"No, Alice, si recapacitas y tu memoria obra con rectitud, aceptarás la verdad: nunca viste los ojos de la anciana señora" ("No, Alice, if you think about it and you are honest about what you remember, you will admit the truth: you never did see the elderly woman's eyes").[30] Thus begins, somewhat unpleasantly, our tale of pleasure. The name "Alice" evokes Lewis Carroll's exploration of the "wonderland" of the unconscious, a mysterious landscape shaped by games (croquet, chess). The reference is seductive; I am primed to look for further analogies (a condemnation of Victorian moralism? a fairy-tale universe shaped by some implicit game? an oscillation between language and silence?). Rudolph's condescending instructions initially construct an image of a passive and naive interlocutor, upon whom he inscribes his tale. Yet as his narrative progresses, Alice acquires new contours; we glimpse that, like Carroll's Alice, she is propelled by a curiosity, an inquisitiveness, that moves her beyond her role of naive and passive reader:

> Te atreviste a entrar, a escondidas y sin permiso, en estancias carentes de acceso para ti. Pero no falsees, ahora, capaz tu mente de mayor y más profunda reflexión, las intenciones inductoras de tu curiosidad. No, Alice, no finjas ahora, poseedora de datos más o menos ordenados, adjudicarte retrospectivamente, en el pasado, una suspicacia que te faltaba ni te veas entrar en las habitaciones prohibidas en busca de pruebas capaces de desenmascarar a la anciana señora.

> Secretly and without permission, you dared to enter rooms to which you were not allowed access. Don't misrepresent the reasons for your curiosity now, because your mind is capable of greater and deeper reflection. No, Alice, now that you are in possession of information that is arranged, more or less, in some order, do not pretend retrospectively that you had, in the past, a suspicion you did not have; do not pretend you entered the forbidden rooms in search of proof that would unmask the elderly woman.[31]

Unmask, mask, masquerade, sexuality as masquerade. As Alice probes the mysteries that surround her—the painted faces populating the widow's room, the footsteps coming from the invalid's room as Alice climbs the stairs, the general's inexplicable "unhappy end," Rudolph's whereabouts and ultimate destiny—Rudolph waits and watches, spying on her much as the general spied on the two women. Finally, ironically, it is through Alice's "gaze" that Rudolph believes he has found the key to understanding what eluded his father:

> O, ¿cuántas veces, Alice, te hizo leer (al hacerlo, ¿fue casual tu gesto, para mi revelador?: alzaste la mirada hacia las gafas oscuras de la anciana y, acto seguido, la clavaste en los retratos de las dos mujeres que, al contemplarse, se poseen, triunfales, para siempre) aquel pasaje perteneciente a una novela romántica, donde uno de los personajes, tras arrebatarle la muerte a su amada en sus propios brazos, deseó cegarse a sí mismo para que fuera la imagen de la amada la última que viera y guardaran sus ojos?

> As you read, Alice, you raised your eyes toward the elderly woman's dark glasses, and immediately afterwards, you stared at the portraits of the two women who, as they

contemplate each other, possess each other triumphantly, forever—was that gesture acci-
dental, although a revelation to me? Or how many times did she make you read that passage from a romantic novel, in which one of the characters, after death has snatched away
his beloved from his very arms, wanted to blind himself so that the image of his beloved
would be the last thing he would see and his eyes retain?[32]

Subtly, ironically, Moix again endows the female gaze, this time Alice's silent gesture,
with the power to convey meaning, even as Rudolph, deluded, persists in claiming
that power through his narrative control.

The Pleasure of Silence

Returning to Moix's "Erotismo y literatura," I read: "se trata de comunicar lo máximo, esa experiencia límite que es la erótica, callando también el máximo posible."[33]
Moix elaborates in her story a desire born in and borne by the silent mutual gaze, a
desire—indeed unspoken; perhaps unspeakable—that becomes wordlessly inscribed
on the body of the reader. Perched on that "magical threshold of the unspeakable,"
"Las virtudes peligrosas" delights this reader not only through its multiple layering
of desire, but also through the very silencing of those desires, which shadow the text
without ever coming into full view. "Vision" and "blindness," appearance as disappearance, knowing and not knowing, madness masquerading as discourse, meaning
conveyed through silence—these are the pleasures of the text. Moix "disturbs the
mutual understanding of the established powers" (see epigraph), and by listening,
by valuing the unspoken in her discourse, we find the echo of our own *jouissance*.

Notes

Epigraph: Toril Moi, ed., *The Kristeva Reader* (New York: Columbia University Press, 1986), 156.

1. Josep María Castellet, *Nueve novísimos poetas españoles* (Barcelona: Barral, 1970).

2. At the time of Castellet's writing, Moix was just beginning to appear on the literary scene.
Her early works include *Baladas del Dulce Jim* (Barcelona: Ediciones Saturno, 1969), *Call Me Stone*
(n.p.: Esplugues del Llobregat, 1969), *Julia* (Barcelona: Seix Barral, 1969), *Ese chico pelirrojo a quien
veo cada día* (Barcelona: Editorial Lumen, 1971), *No time for flowers y otras historias* (Barcelona:
Editorial Lumen, 1971), and *Walter, ¿por qué te fuiste?* (Barcelona: Barral Editores, 1973). See Margaret E. W. Jones, "Ana María Moix: Literary Structures and the Enigmatic Nature of Reality,"
Journal of Spanish Studies: Twentieth Century 4 (1976): 105–16, for an overview of these early
works.

3. Ana María Moix, *Las virtudes peligrosas* (Barcelona: Plaza y Janés, 1985); idem, *Dangerous
Virtues*, trans. Margaret E. W. Jones (Lincoln: University of Nebraska Press, 1997).

4. Andrew Bush, "Ana María Moix's Silent Calling," in *Women Writers of Contemporary Spain,*
ed. Joan L. Brown (Newark: University of Delaware Press, 1991), 150. Early responses to Moix's
1985 collection tended to focus on the masculine narrative control in the story "Las virtudes
peligrosas," in *Las virtudes peligrosas.*

5. Margaret E. W. Jones, "Translator's Afterword," in Moix, *Dangerous Virtues*, 147.

6. Moix, *Las virtudes peligrosas*, 27; idem, *Dangerous Virtues*, 16.

7. Moix, *Las virtudes peligrosas*, 15; idem, *Dangerous Virtues*, 7–8.

8. "To the sphere of the unnamable and unnamed": Rosalía Cornejo-Parriego, "Desde el innominado deseo: Transgresión y marginalidad de la mirada en 'Las virtudes peligrosas' de Ana María Moix," *Anales de la literatura española contemporanea* 23, no. 1–2 (1998): 609. When I originally drafted this article in 1997, Cornejo-Parriego's excellent article on lesbian desire in "Las virtudes peligrosas" had not yet been published. Although her article raises interesting questions about the (im)possibility of constructing an exclusively homosexual space and language within a heterosexual and heterosexist ideology, it ignores the erotic potential of Moix's text, particularly for the lesbian reader.

9. Moix, *Las virtudes peligrosas*, 35; idem, *Dangerous Virtues*, 23.

10. María Dolores Costa reads Moix's story as "an inquiry into the totalizing efforts of male-centered readings and writings": María Dolores Costa, "'Las virtudes peligrosas': The Story of Men Reading Women Reading Women," *Letras peninsulares* 8, no.1 (Spring 1995): 96.

11. Jones, "Afterword," 147.

12. See Sartre's chapter on his existentialist interpretation of "le regard," in *Being and Nothingness: An Essay on Phenomenological Ontology*, trans. Hazel E. Barnes (New York: Philosophical Library, 1956). Joyce Tolliver's article, "'Otro modo de ver:' The Gaze in *La última niebla*," *Revista canadiense de estudios hispánicos* 17 (Fall 1992): 105–21, was particularly helpful to me in sorting through the Sartrean, Lacanian, and Foucauldian constructions of the gaze and the possibility of imagining a non-phallic mutual erotic gaze.

13. Moix, *Las virtudes peligrosas*, 30; idem, *Dangerous Virtues*, 23.

14. Bush, "Ana María Moix's Silent Calling," 150.

15. Jones, "Afterword," 148.

16. Linda Gould Levine, "'Behind the Enemy Lines': Strategies for Interpreting *Las virtudes peligrosas* of Ana María Moix," in *Nuevos y novísimos*, ed. Ricardo Landeira and Luis T. González-del-Valle (Boulder, Colo.: Society of Spanish and Spanish-American Studies, 1987), 99.

17. Cornejo-Parriego, "Desde el innominado deseo," 616.

18. Roland Barthes, *The Pleasure of the Text*, trans. Richard Miller (New York: Hill and Wang, 1975), 14; emphasis added.

19. Emma Wilson, *Sexuality and Masquerade* (London: Dedalus, 1996), 9.

20. Barthes, *Pleasure of the Text*, 53.

21. Levine, "'Behind the Enemy Lines,'" 101.

22. "The power of erotic language when it remains on the magical threshold of the 'unspeakable' and, undaunted, manages to stay there without stepping through, is immense. It is a question of not crossing over the threshold of the unspeakable, yet letting the reader glimpse without, in reality, seeing anything": Ana María Moix, "Erotismo y literatura," in *Discurso erótico y discurso transgresor en la cultura peninsula*, comp. Myriam Díaz-Diocaretz and Iris M. Zavala (Madrid: Tuero, 1992), 207. All translations from this essay are mine.

23. Barthes, *Pleasure of the Text*, 10.

24. "It is a masterly deception: The reader, who has not seen, has the sensation that he has not seen because the ostensible and coveted vision has blinded him and substitutes, in his credulous sensibility, the vision for something more powerful than the vision itself: the bewilderment that produced that possible vision": Moix, "Erotismo," 207.

25. "A *game shared* between author and reader, with clear rules of interpretation; the more distanced the reader becomes from the 'concrete reality,' the more intense are the perceived

effects that provoke sensuality and desire": Myriam Díaz-Diocaretz, "El misterio entre el comunicar y el no querer o no poder decir," in Díaz-Diocaretz and Zavala, *Discurso erótico*, 8.

26. Barthes, *Pleasure of the Text*, 10.

27. Ibid., 14

28. Ibid., 21.

29. Ibid.

30. Moix, *Las virtudes peligrosas*, 9; idem, *Dangerous Virtues*, 3.

31. Moix, *Las virtudes peligrosas*, 37; idem, *Dangerous Virtues*, 25.

32. Moix, *Las virtudes peligrosas*, 43; idem, *Dangerous Virtues*, 29.

33. "In that border experience we call the erotic, it is a question of communicating as much as possible by silencing as much as possible": Moix, "Erotismo," 207.

Gema Pérez-Sánchez

6 Reading, Writing, and the Love
That Dares Not Speak Its Name:
Eloquent Silences in
Ana María Moix's *Julia*

One of the most intriguing contemporary Spanish writers, Ana María Moix (b. Barcelona, 1947), first became known as part of a group of promising young poets whose works the critic Josep María Castellet selected to represent the state of contemporary poetry in his influential 1970 collection *Nueve novísimos poetas españoles*.[1] She was the only woman and the youngest poet in the collection and soon proved to be a prolific writer of fiction, as well. By 1973, at age twenty-six, Moix had already published three books of poetry, a book of short stories, two novels, and a book of journalistic interviews with important cultural figures of her time.[2] After these publications had confirmed her as a talented writer and had won her critical acclaim, Moix fell into an inexplicable period of silence as a poet and a writer of fiction for adults until 1985, when she published another collection of short stories.[3]

In uncanny parallel with her real-life publication impasse, silence constitutes one of the most recurrent themes in Moix's fiction.[4] Accordingly, this essay develops a reading of silence(s) in Moix's first novel, *Julia*, a book published under the close scrutiny of Francoist censorship. I seek both to unravel the complex web of silences in and around Moix's novel and to qualify those silences, some of which represent real lapses into voicelessness, and some of which speak out eloquently, but only to attuned listeners. In *Julia*, Moix effectively exploits a paradox: Through the eponymous protagonist's failure to communicate, Moix negates silence as a viable feminist political strategy because it leads women into a deadly impasse. Yet in publishing her novel during the last decade of Franco's regime, Moix—as a lesbian writer—deploys silence in such a way as to create a complicit, active relationship between a *lector entendido* and the text.

In my use of the term *"entendido,"* I invoke two of its possible meanings in Spanish. On the one hand, Moix's novel calls for a *"lector entendido"* who is a wise, careful reader who does not stop at a cursory reading of *Julia*. On the other hand, and more important, the book requires a *lector entendido* in the queer-coded sense of the word: a reader who is "family," who is queer, one who can understand (*entender*) Moix's queer writing between the lines. Through his or her knowledgeable interaction with Moix's text, the *lector entendido* cannot fail to recognize that the theme of the novel is, ironically, a type of love that dares not speak its name. Ultimately, in eliciting the cooperation of this *lector entendido, Julia* involves him or her in an exploration of the relations among pedagogy, shame, and queer subjectivity.[5]

The actual narrative time of the novel encompasses a sleepless night during which Julia, at age twenty, is haunted by a whirlwind of tormented memories from her childhood and adolescence. These memories carry her from her childhood to her present traumatic psychological stagnation. Through the apparently chaotic narrative—which effectively illustrates the jarred remembrances of the protagonist—Moix takes the reader through the main events and relationships in Julia's life. These include Julia's relationship to her family members: the progressive deterioration of her love for her mother, the death of her beloved brother Rafael, her conflictive rapport with her older brother Ernesto, the contempt toward her father, her loathing of her conservative maternal grandmother, and her adoration of her anarchist paternal grandfather.

The reader also confronts a number of events in Julia's life that are barely sketched out and are left to the imagination to complete. The taboo nature of these events accounts for their schematic presentations: Some are unspeakable traumas (child molestation and possible rape), and others are unthinkable in a heterosexist society (lesbianism and male homosexuality). Although some discomforting facts in Julia's past are clearly stated,[6] the most important and traumatic events in the story—sexual abuse and disavowed lesbianism—remain implicit and are left for a careful reader to construct and to understand by reading between the lines.[7] This obscuring, as we will see, works as an encrypted signal that attracts the attention of the *lector entendido* but eludes the *no entendido*.

The verb *entender* (to understand) has traditionally been employed in the Spanish gay male world as a safe code word for finding out the orientation of a potential sexual partner, especially by way of the question *"¿Entiendes?"* (Do you understand?).[8] Today, Spanish lesbians and gays also use *entender* as a general way to signify "being queer," while some heterosexuals who are familiar with queer culture deploy the term to refer to non-heterosexuals. Óscar Guasch justly reclaims the term as a culturally specific conceptual category through which to theorize sexual relationships between men in the Spanish context. By using *entender,* Guasch hopes to escape the colonizing effect of "un modelo gay hegemónico de origen netamente anglosajón, que genera un discurso incapaz de reconocer los matices y adaptaciones interculturales" of same-sex relationships.[9]

Following Guasch, I use *entendido* to signify "cualquier persona capaz de relacionarse sexualmente con personas de su mismo género, y ello al margen de la frecuencia e intensidad con que tales relaciones tengan lugar."[10] However, I also apply the adjective to a particular reader who *understands* how a *"texto entendido"* such as Moix's should be read. In other words, and as Pierre Bourdieu emphasizes, to understand in this reading context "also means to understand without having to be told, to read between the lines, by re-enacting in the mode of practice (in most cases unconsciously) the linguistic associations and substitutions initially set up by the producer."[11] The *lector entendido* that Moix's text calls forth can be understood further as a special case of Wolfgang Iser's "implied reader": She or he will be not only an active reader whose convergence with the text will bring "the literary work into existence."[12] He or she more specifically will be a reader attuned to a desire carefully muted behind the revealing silences of the text.[13]

The condition of silence (that is, the absence of voice) can result from potentially conflicting scenarios in terms of a subject's agency. One may be silent out of choice, but more often than not one is forced into silence. Oppressed peoples are very familiar with the state of being silenced, of not being able or allowed to speak out about their experiences and having others (the oppressors) speak for them. Certainly, a number of queer activists disavow silence as a useful weapon against oppression. The AIDS Coalition to Unleash Power (ACT UP) is the U.S. group responsible for launching the most famous slogan to date regarding the silence of minorities: "SILENCE = DEATH."[14] No matter how effective this slogan has been in bringing AIDS and the marginalized lives of lesbians and gay men to the attention of the public, however, it is important to remember that speaking out is a strategy that not all oppressed groups can afford. Under certain historical and cultural circumstances, some people may in fact find such a strategy detrimental.[15] As is widely known, during Franco's regime in Spain, intellectuals and artists often had to conceal their opinions and outwardly conform to (or, at least, not speak against) the official political and moral doctrines of the regime. Under such oppressive conditions, a message such as "SILENCE = DEATH" would have been reversed into "Speaking Out = Death"—or, at least, "Speaking out = (Self)Censorship."[16]

For any writer who lives under an oppressive regime with strict censorship laws, the mere act of writing about imposed silence means breaking that silence. Women writing under a fascist dictatorship face a further oppression: that of a sexist system that operates under strict gender expectations.[17] Doubly silenced because of their gender and because of their profession, with no acceptable space from which to "talk back" or to talk at all, how might women writers manipulate silence—the oppressor's tool—to their own benefit? In *Talking Back: Toward a Latin American Feminist Literary Criticism*, Debra Castillo offers an answer to the paradox of how to speak out while simultaneously remaining silent. She describes helpful "strategies of a feminist literary practice in the Latin American context," among which is the "tactical deployment" of silence.[18]

Before Castillo lays out what she understands to be the subversive deployment of silence by women writers, she explains the relationship between being forced into silence and choosing silence in order to survive: "One reaction to the pressures of the dominant social force is silence. Initially, however, silence is not a response but a condition imposed from outside: silencing, rather than silence freely chosen."[19] Frequently, women in Hispanic societies experience the devastating constraints of the passive, quiet role imposed on them by a male-defined society, and sometimes that imposition looks like a choice. In the case of Spain under Franco, women—especially women writers—suffered a double imposition of silence: as women subjected to strong, conservative expectations about proper femininity and, together with male writers, as intellectuals subjected to the stern, often arbitrary Francoist censorship laws.[20]

However, as Castillo notes, there is a subversive back way out of the prison of silence, a way that confers a new function on the oppressor's tools: "The revolutionary response to silencing is resemanticization: to use silence as a weapon (to resort to silence) or to break silence with hypocrisy."[21] For women writers who do not accept the passive, quiet role, strategic silence, and the distancing that comes from it, provides a separate, safe space in which what is not said becomes more eloquent than what is said. This was the case for the famous *Carta a Sor Filotea de la Cruz* by the Renaissance Mexican poet Sor Juana Inés de la Cruz.

Silence as a feminist strategy, then, does not become a mere *callar* but a *no decir*, as Josefina Ludmer has suggested in writing about Sor Juana.[22] The distinction between these two phrasings is crucial. As Castillo suggests, *no decir* is not quite the same as *callar*, for in the case of the former, "the traversal of speech by the negative allows for a trace of its passage, maintaining [the woman's] essential self at a safe spatiotemporal distance that both permits her free play of thought and subtly establishes her own agency as the concealed subjectivity alone capable of bridging the gap of silence."[23] In other words, a carefully constructed *no decir* gives the woman writer a safe position from which she can actually say, sometimes even cry out loud, what she is not supposed to say in a male-dominated system; it also allows her to attain an ironic distance from which to analyze, understand, and expose women's oppression.[24] However, strategic silence does not mean speechlessness, because mere hermeticism alone cannot provoke any dramatic change in the marginalized situation of women. As Castillo writes, "Eventually, the woman must break silence and write, negotiating the tricky domains of the said and the unsaid, the words written down, . . . smudging the page, and the words left, for whatever reason, between the lines."[25] In other words, only a juggling of silence and speech through writing can effect change.

Such tactical deployment of the unsaid and the said—which demands a reading both of and between the lines of the text—is precisely what is at stake in Moix's narrative technique in *Julia*.[26] Her intricate weaving of *lo dicho* and *lo no dicho* must be analyzed on two fronts: first, at the level of the plot (that is, Julia's narrative and her characterization as a silent, because silenced, young woman whose incapacity to speak out leads almost to her death and ultimately to a bleak, monotonous, oppressive, and meaningless life); and second, at the level of the unwritten part of the text and the cooperation it elicits from a *lector entendido* for one of the potential meanings of the novel to be complete. As revealed through these two levels of analysis, *Julia* stands as a work that chooses "not to create a spoken/written matrix of configurative meaning and only point[s] mutely."[27]

Moix's presentation of Julia as a willfully silent young woman who fails to establish any fruitful communication with outside allies illustrates Castillo's idea that, "as a political strategy, . . . to embrace silence is clearly of limited value."[28] Even though Julia feels isolated and afraid and fails to communicate her traumas to others, she often consciously orchestrates her silences as a form of rebellion. Such is the case when she wants to antagonize her repressive bourgeois family ("Enmudecía para enfurecer a mamá"[29]) and when she refuses to communicate with men as a response to their intrusions into her life. Through Julia's display of antagonistic silence in response to the young men in her life—Andrés and Carlos, in particular—Moix raises the problem of silence as potential feminist tactic.

Against the repeated prying into Julia's world by Andrés, a teaching assistant in a Spanish language class who is clearly in love with her, for example, Julia responds with a strategic refusal to communicate: "Andrés se sentaba junto a ella: Sólo un rato, el tiempo de fumar un cigarrillo y saber en qué estás pensando. No pensaba en nada. Esa era la verdad. Pero Andrés siempre preguntaba: ¿En qué piensas? Y ella tenía que responder: En nada. No pensaba en algo que pudiera explicarle a Andrés."[30] In passages such as this one, Moix presents her protagonist as alienated from men in general, and from (hetero)sexist society in particular. Ironically, Andrés, who teaches language (a tool of communication), can elicit only silence from Julia.

Andrés, in fact, performs a particularly complex pedagogical role in the novel. As one name in a long list of heterosexual male pedagogues who turn teaching into seduction, he attempts to indoctrinate Julia into a subservient feminine position through his pedagogically inflected courtship.[31] He tries to impose his presence on Julia's life, forcing her into a role of passivity and quietness that is ultimately detrimental to communication across gender lines. To some extent, Julia falls for the allure of this passive role, accepting some of its dubious advantages—harmony and a lack of emotional agency—while she also uses that passivity as a shield against his attempts to control her subjectivity. Although at times Julia "sentía cierta ternura por Andrés," because "la adivinaba y era consciente de que prodigándole su cariño y protección, . . . sin pedirle nada, ella nunca rechazaría su presencia," she hates him "por meterse en sus cosas, preguntar qué piensas, qué haces esta tarde, qué has hecho esta mañana, ¿te ha gustado la película?"[32]

Andrés's masculine agency and privilege become obvious to Julia in the apparent ease with which he takes an active role as interrogator, a role Julia never assumes in the novel. He reads her silence and her refusal to avoid his presence as signs of feminine compliance instead of as what Julia means them to be: stubbornly chosen silence. Julia never verbalizes her recurrent irritation toward Andrés, even though he forces his way into her privacy by constantly subjecting her to his controlling gaze: "Se veía a sí misma, en clase, observada por Andrés. Se veía en el patio de la facultad, paseando o charlando con algún compañero, bajo la mirada de Andrés."[33] He assumes that he has a tacit agreement to meet her every day at the university cafeteria and designs her leisure activities. No matter how much "la irritaba el peculiar acoso de Andrés," Julia passively accepts it; she is devoid of willpower because of years of fighting her family's and society's systematic misunderstanding of her.[34] Julia chooses silence and passivity as a way to survive in an oppressive system, but this chosen silence ultimately backfires, sending her into a meaningless, suffocating existence where "[t]odos sus días eran iguales, monótonos."[35]

Toward the end of the novel, Julia concedes that "la habían derrotado."[36] This final acceptance of her defeat—after she barely survives an attempted suicide (another form of failed rebellion)—further illustrates Moix's point that "SILENCE = DEATH."[37] Although the third-person plural in her recognition of defeat ostensibly refers to her oppressive family dynamics—and, perhaps, more generally to patriarchal pressure— it also includes Julia's tyrannical alter ego: herself at age six, frozen in time as a result of a traumatic sexual assault. The claustrophobic, alienating ending of the novel leaves a hopeless Julia unable to communicate with the outside world, trapped in her own web of willful silence.

Although she ultimately fails to communicate effectively with the external world, Julia does establish an eloquent communication between her divided selves. The story is presented as a sort of interior monologue narrated in the third person, with two main focalizers: Julia as young woman and Julita from age five to age eight.[38] The dialectic, or confrontation, between the young adult and the child becomes dramatized in the form of a split character,[39] "como si Julita y ella fuesen dos personas distintas. Julia, a veces, tenía la seguridad de que Julita existía aún, de que vivía y habitaba en otro mundo inalterable, inmóvil, sin tiempo. Era como si Julita existiese con vida propia ... y desde allí ... doblegara la voluntad de Julia para que ésta hiciera, pensara y sintiera cuanto a ella se le antojara."[40] At first glance, the fact that all real dialogue occurs only in Julia's mind, between herself and the frozen memory of herself at five, suggests a short-circuited communication, a silent dialogue that never goes beyond Julia's own subjectivity. A closer reading, however, reveals the othering or splitting effect of Julia's sense of alienation from herself. Standing in for traumatic childhood, the figure of Julita is rendered an Other, alienated self. This divided character does not constitute a narcissistic doubling of self but a differentiating of self that allows the seemingly short-circuited, otherwise "silent" conversation to speak out about being sexually terrorized into silence. Hence, Julia and Julita are not images in a mirror but "dos personas distintas" (two different people) with distinct experiences, desires, and needs. Although Julia longs for happiness and love, Julita "se vengaba" (would take revenge) by forcing the young adult to relive the traumatic moments in her childhood.[41] Further, the othering metaphor allows for a queer understanding of Julia's relationship to Julita precisely as an intersubjective, intergenerational, homoerotic—albeit somewhat sadomasochistic—relationship.[42] Julita becomes a Jehova-like dominatrix who, like a "dios martirizador, ... reclamaba continuos sacrific[i]os para calmar su antiguo dolor."[43]

Julia's split subjectivity and her slips into willful silence stem from a traumatic sexual assault at age six that, among other things, brutally dramatizes the patriarchal silencing of women. The episode, possibly a rape (it is unclear from the impressionistic text), is sketched out only enough to illustrate Julia's repressed memories of the trauma. An adult male friend of the family, Víctor, sexually assaults Julita on a deserted beach, stressing his dominance over the little girl with the injunction: "No dirás nada, idiota."[44] This crucial scene offers an insight into Julia's silent personality and her will-ful reappropriation of silence as a defense against sexist intrusion. Víctor's assault and Julia's mother's subsequent violent reaction to Julia's disappearance shut her into a silent world and encapsulate her in a frozen image, recurring throughout the text, that comes to signify separation and lack of communication: "Julita, sentada en el portal de la casa, pequeña y delgada, los pies descalzos, las trenzas medio deshechas, el pan-talón corto y el jersey azul marino con un ancla dibujada en el pecho, la mirada baja, fija en dos piedras que machacaba una contra otra, la obligaba a recordar cosas así, confusas, inconexas."[45]

Andrew Bush reads this passage as "an image of obstruction," an entrapment of Julia in childhood; she is "anchored there, as the attribute or aegis on her undevel-oped breast announces."[46] But this image also emphasizes Julita's liminal position "en el portal" (at the threshold) between the interior, domestic, feminine space, and the exterior, public, masculine space, the anchor embroidered on her T-shirt signifying stagnation in a subservient gender position, subject to heterosexist terrorism. Julita's "mirada baja" (lowered gaze) further suggests how she has been shamed into sub-mission, into her "proper" feminine place. Yet Julita's insistence on remembering this childhood image of herself sitting precisely at "el portal" with "dos piedras que ma-chacaba una contra otra" (two stones that she would pound against each other) also suggests her defiance of and refusal to comply with heterosexist notions of gender dynamics.

Víctor—standing in for a more generalized patriarchal oppression—silences Julia in an especially violent and repressive way, not only rendering her incapable of say-ing anything about her rape but also making it impossible for her to express her feel-ings toward women later, as an adolescent. Bush proposes that Moix

> does not offer a vision of the male suppression of the female voice for which a reappro-priation of speech could serve as clear remedial gesture. Rather, the outpouring of speech is precisely what Moix and her autobiographical heroine, Julia, seek to control. Language may itself be the nightmare from which Julia is trying—and failing—to awake; the sweeter dream represents a contrary nostalgia for silence and a wordless world of women.[47]

Against this reading, I contend that there is absolutely no nostalgia "for silence and a wordless world of women" in *Julia*. On the contrary, the whole novel works to denounce how women are silenced and how remaining silent brings no comfort and no escape. Bush further contends that Víctor's utterance—"No dirás nada, idiota" (You'll say nothing, idiot)—is an obstruction of Julia's access to language, which is then "converted into the symptom or trope of stifled breathing."[48] Ultimately, repressed lan-guage returns in the narrative in the form of Julia's adult nightmares, "becoming itself an obsession that exceeds Julia's control."[49] However, Víctor does not obstruct Julia's access to language so much as he inflicts silence on her; his relationship to her thus functions as a metaphor for the larger silencing of women in sexist Spain.

Unlike Bush, I do not think that language is the repressed material coming out in Julia's nightmares. The repressed aspect of Julia's narrative is her desire for other women, which earlier critics of Moix's novel fail to acknowledge.[50] This general, earlier critical blindness to the lesbian theme of the novel may attest to Moix's success in encoding a forbidden topic and rendering it "silent" to a *lector no entendido*. For a lesbian writer writing about a lesbian (anti)heroine in Franco's Spain, there are perhaps no other possible devices at hand but the use of a narrative that incorporates "unsaid" themes and the "resemantization" of silence. Not saying the word "lesbian" does not imply a *callar* in Moix's narrative technique. Instead, she uses a complex method of *no decir* through her explicit writing about male homosexuality (always more visible in Francoist Spain than lesbianism[51]), and through her explorations of the role of pedagogy in the formation of Julia's queer subjectivity.

Moix diverts unsympathetic attention from Julia's desires to those of her older brother Ernesto, who is characterized as having homosexual tendencies. This diversion necessarily attracts the attention of the *lector entendido*. Ernesto's homosexuality is an open secret: Everyone from his father to the maid "understands" his tendencies and explicitly avoids naming them. For example, Ernesto's father—an avowed homophobe for whom "un hombre atento, elegante y sensible ya es un . . ."[52]—menacingly alludes to his son's effeminacy and eventually beats Ernesto while calling him "una mujerzuela."[53] Also, the younger of the maids in Julia's family, Maruja, makes explicit this open secret: "Chica, he visto de qué pie cojea tu hermanito, te lo digo a ti porque hay confianza. Tiene miedo a las mujeres, bueno, suponiendo que no sea otra cosa peor que me callo porque Dios me libre (y se santiguaba) de añadir leña al fuego y en esos casos lo mejor es ver, oír y *callar*."[54] Through this subtle metonymical gesture—saying that male homosexuality cannot be spoken about but never mentioning a word throughout the whole novel about lesbianism—Moix opens up the space for a *decir* through a *no decir* and thus sets out the first coded flag for the *lector entendido*.

Julia's silence, passivity, and gloominess are not inherent characteristics. As a child, she is talkative and lively—for instance, when she receives her mother's whimsical attention, but also when she lives with her paternal grandfather, don Julio.[55] Because of marital conflicts, an imminent separation, and Julia's younger brother's serious illness, Julia's parents take her for a year to her father's childhood home in the mountains, where the formidable don Julio lives. After a year with him and tía Elena, Julia returns to Barcelona for a summer, but as a result of her parents' separation, she goes back to live with don Julio for five years, until she is thirteen. Playing a subversive role in the socialization of Julita, the old man becomes the most influential pedagogue in the protagonist's life.

The introduction of don Julio and his unique pedagogy calls attention to all the previous, and the following, pedagogical scenes in the book; it also prompts the *lector entendido* to consider the intersection of pedagogy, seduction, and shame in the constitution of queer subjectivity. In a provocative essay on the complexities of teaching queer theory, Joseph Litvak begins with the premise that "*all* teaching, even by heterosexual men, is not just theatrical, but what it somehow seems appropriate to call 'queer,'" and concludes with, "If every teacher, even the most avant-garde queer theorist, is a disciplinarian, every teacher, even the most reactionary custodian of the eternal verities, is also a pervert."[56] Basing his claims on Eve Kosofsky Sedgwick's musings on shame and queer performativity and Judith Butler's concept of the melancholia of gender, Litvak insists that the dominant heterosexual gender dichotomy constitutes not a fixed identity "but an identification that one must be terrorized into" through "the manifold operations of homophobic shaming."[57] The *lector entendido* that Moix's novel calls forth would necessarily identify those moments in the text in which either a subtle or an overt scene of "homophobic shaming" takes place, and he or she would undoubtedly perceive those moments in which a scene of teaching and learning becomes the locus for seduction—whether queer or straight. By identifying Moix's *no decir* about Ernesto's homosexuality, the *lector entendido* recognizes the multiple scenes not only of Ernesto's but also of Julia's homophobic shaming into "proper" masculine and feminine behavior, respectively. However, the fact that the shaming mechanism fails to mold either of the siblings into heteronormativity attests to the power of shame identification for them.

Sedgwick has convincingly explained that, of all affects, shame is the one "that delineates identity—but delineates it without defining it or giving it content"—that is, without making identity an essence. She claims that, "*at least* for certain ('queer') people, shame is simply the first, and remains a permanent, structuring fact of powerfully social metamorphic possibilities."[58] Litvak provides an even clearer explanation of the power of shame identification for certain queer children. In analyzing an autobiographical childhood incident of homophobic shaming in which his father parodies a gay man in order to deter him and his brothers from homosexuality, Litvak explains:

> My father, whether he knew it or not, made a spectacle of—that is to say, homosexualized—himself. When, as often happens, the scene of instruction is also a scene of humiliation, the shame-agent can turn to, or become readable as, a shame-object, and, on some spectators, that reversal or doubling can have powerful, because equally unstable, effects.... To put it most schematically: while the effect of my father's performance on my brothers, who turned out straight, seems to have been to make them "identify with" him—that is, with his homophobic heterosexuality—the effect of that performance on me was to make me "identify with" him—that is, with his homophobic homosexuality.[59]

As in the scene described by Litvak, in *Julia*, the father repeatedly tries to make Ernesto feel ashamed of his uncharacteristic feminine behavior. According to his father, not only Ernesto's hair "es afeminado, ... todo él es afeminado."[60] The father sometimes even humiliates his son through physical violence, as has been shown. Most significantly, his humiliation of Ernesto involves the domain of pedagogy: "Papá, a fin de mes, cuando le enseñaban el boletín de notas, se enfurecía contra Ernesto y lo humillaba delante de Rafael: ... debería darte vergüenza, grandullón, gandul."[61] Although the father's anger is directed toward Ernesto's school performance, a *lector entendido* would also understand the father's efforts to shame Ernesto as a displacement of his anger toward Ernesto's failed heterosexual performance, as the text I ellided in the

quote suggests: Rafael "es más pequeño que tú, está enfermo y fíjate qué notas"—
and how masculine he is, one is tempted to add.[62]

At school, Julia's recognition of shame is the primary motivation behind her behavior and identification. On one occasion, for instance, Julia has wrapped herself within her willful silence; when one of her classmates turns to look at her intently, as if she were an odd animal, "Julia enrojecía cuando se daba cuenta y hundía la cabeza entre los hombros, fijando la mirada en el libro abierto para que los demás no advirtieran que tenía los ojos llenos de lágrimas, y se sentía sola, extraña, diferente a ellos."[63] Not only do her classmates shame Julia into difference, but "incluso los profesores, cultivaban la diferencia."[64]

Attesting to the success of the shame mechanisms that terrorize queer children into gender conformity, Moix has Ernesto participate in the shaming of his sister. He reports Julia's slovenly (masculine) garb to their mother: "Parecía un espantapájaros.... Conozco montones de chicas de su misma edad, que siendo más feas que ella dan otra impresión, se pintan, se arreglan."[65] Julia's refusal to participate in culturally dictated feminine behavior always elicits her mother's and her grandmother's ire. For instance, her mother "se quejaba ... de que Julia jamás tuviera iniciativa para comprarse un vestido, o unos zapatos, arreglarse el pelo o cualquier cosa por el estilo que Mamá calificaba como pruebas de feminidad.... Una chica debe ser coqueta y presumida, de lo contrario parece un hombre."[66] For Julia's bourgeois, vain mother, outward physical traits determine "proper" feminine behavior; for grandmother Lucía, the novel's representative of the dominant, oppressive Catholic morality of Francoist Spain, "la feminidad se demuestra en otras cosas ..., por ejemplo en la piedad hacia Dios. Una mujer que no va a misa y no reza, no es una mujer decente."[67] Further, for Julia's mother and grandmother, gender roles are also demarcated by "appropriate" reading: While Ernesto is allowed to read certain "subversive" books ("Sartre, Camus, Tennessee Williams y Françoise Sagan"), Julia is systematically denied access to them. Nevertheless, having already been indoctrinated in a certain anarchist rebellion by her paternal grandfather, Julia protests: "Si Ernesto los puede leer, yo también."[68] Yet her grandmother's logic is inexorable: "Ernesto hace mal, pero al fin y al cabo es un hombre.... Una mujer no necesita saber tanto como un hombre, así es desde que el mundo es mundo."[69] Against this systematically insidious shaming into heterosexist gender behavior, Julia's paternal grandfather's (queer) pedagogy offers an antidote that is especially apparent to a *lector entendido*.

Although don Julio keeps a stout patriarchy in his household, exerting power over his daughter Elena and his maid, he is determined to make of his granddaughter "una persona inteligente, aunque sea mujer."[70] Unlike Andrés, who through his pedagogical intervention in Julia's life seeks to seduce her into heterosexuality and gender conformity, don Julio's teacherly project contributes to the consolidation of Julia's queerness and subversive consciousness. Regardless of his openly sexist intentions to perpetuate traditional gender roles in his home, don Julio's pedagogy might be termed "perverse" in the sense that it teaches Julia how to deviate from the dominant culture.

An avowed anarchist, don Julio occupies a marginal (deviant) position with respect to the dominant world of the victors of the civil war: Julia tells the reader that he lived secluded "en las montañas desde hacía veinticinco años,"[71] where even his home "quedaba algo apartada del pueblo."[72] Julia's maternal grandmother, a conservative Catholic and the self-declared arch-enemy of don Julio, voices the winners' version of the losers' wartime activities by demonizing Julia's paternal grandfather:

> La abuela Lucía era quien peor hablaba de don Julio: Un ateo, Dios mío, un anarquista, peor aún que si hubiera sido comunista. Un sanguinario. Vosotros no podéis saberlo porque no vivisteis las terribles jornadas de la Semana Trágica. Barcelona era un río de sangre y todo por culpa de hombres desalmados como don Julio. ¿Qué culpa tienen las monjas y curas de que los políticos se tiren los trastos por la cabeza? Anarquista y además grosero.[73]

In abuela Lucía's prejudiced imagination—and by extension, in the eyes of the victors—don Julio is a pervert who shamelessly rejects political and social etiquette. Although his angry character and the respect and fear with which all his children address him ("Toda la familia, incluso Papá, lo llamaba don Julio"[74]) grant him a quasimythical status among his awestruck grandchildren, "[l]a figura potente, feroz, guerrera y cruel que [Julia] había imaginado nada en común tenía con don Julio."[75] Abuela Lucía's negative presentation of don Julio proves to be exaggerated and Manichean, as the reader soon realizes that his bad temper is only a cover-up for a wildly independent man who, positioned at the margins of the dominant society of his time, wields no effective power.

Nevertheless, don Julio's role in the giving and taking of speech is paramount to an understanding of the negotiations of communication and silence dramatized in *Julia*. Having been entrusted with his eight-year-old granddaughter, don Julio sets out to educate her. His unique pedagogical project involves turning Julita into an independent, self-sufficient, arrogant person, like himself: "Una de las cosas que voy a enseñar a mi nieta es demostrarle que puede vivir sin que nadie gobierne sus actos."[76] Don Julio is interested in the brand of pedagogy that aims at an exact reproduction of the teacher. In fact, he actively seeks to produce a miniature version of himself in Julia.[77]

Joan de Jean has intelligently criticized Jean-Jacques Rousseau's pedagogical project in *Julie ou la Nouvelle Héloïse*—a work with which *Julia* strongly resonates.[78] De Jean suggests that the most important teachers in the novel, Saint-Preux and Julie—but also Rousseau himself in his attempt to propose his new pedagogical project through that novel—partake of a model of pedagogy she calls "miniaturization." Following Claude Lévi-Strauss's notion of *bricoler*, de Jean suggests that

> miniaturization, it seems, is adopted as a result of the *bricoleur*/teacher's insecurity and his attempted rejection of risk and failure. Such excessive prudence must stem from a fear that the object being controlled could somehow step out of line (and out of control)—from a fear of the original swerve of *bricoler*. Reduction in size therefore means also reduction in fearfulness: the miniature is more easily knowable, more easily controllable.[79]

Most interestingly, for de Jean "miniaturization can be viewed as a denial of adult sexuality. The miniature it creates inspires no fear, because it is either a-sexual or not sexually threatening."[80] Thus, both Julie and Saint-Preux "control those with whom they come into contact by making them into carbon copies of themselves." If their student is a child, "those copies can only be reductions in size, or miniatures."[81] Similarly, don Julio seeks to reproduce his image by handing down his particular tradition of education through his line of the family.

Don Julio's reproduction of himself follows the male genealogy of the family: first through his son, Julia's father, whose name is also Julio, and second, through Julita, the miniature version of both. The women in the family, however, recognize don Julio's project as problematic. According to them, Julita mimics the worst aspects of don Julio's personality: "Tía Elena reprochaba a don Julio: La estás educando mal, se le han pegado tus gestos y tus palabrotas."[82] By handing down his traits—specifically, masculine traits—don Julio is in their view further "queering" Julita, turning her into an indomitable, inappropriately masculine little girl: "Decía Mamá que don Julio la había malcriado y contagiado su carácter y mala educación: Y tú eres una imitamonas. Cada vez que Julita se enfadaba y daba un golpe sobre la mesa o insultaba a Ernesto, Mamá le daba una bofetada y la llamaba doña Julia."[83] Julia proves to be the model student who exactly reproduces, albeit on a smaller scale, the traits of the teacher. And just as in *Julie,* the teacher's "inability to encourage individuality and refusal to view the student/other as anything but a projection of the teacher and his desires" eventually backfires.[84] In *Julia,* the grandfather/pedagogue's obsession with making his granddaughter into the free individual he never managed to be ultimately locks Julia into silence and ostracism.

Of course, the explicit criticisms of don Julio's pedagogy in the novel come from those people who voice the dominant culture's concerns: Julia's mother and abuela Lucía. What these characters refuse to acknowledge is the power Julia derives from her grandfather's lessons. As Julia soon realizes, many of don Julio's teachings—traditional and otherwise—prove crucial in the formation of her subjectivity. For instance, of all the disciplines that don Julio teaches Julita, Latin becomes the most prominent and most powerful one for her. Julia's passion for Latin grows as she encounters the mysteries of a new language: "Se enfrentaba con palabras misteriosas cuyo significado buscaba en un diccionario, y luego debía encontrar el orden preciso de las mismas para darles un sentido."[85] When she returns to Barcelona, Julia realizes that her knowledge of Latin has become a double-edged sword. It increases her prestige in the eyes of her abusive brothers and becomes the mediating link between Julia and her brother Rafael: "Sabe más latín que el cura del colegio," he would say in awe.[86] Because Latin has traditionally been the prerogative of the church, Julia's wielding of the oppressors' tool of power and knowledge is doubly effective, as don Julio's subversive pedagogy had probably anticipated. But at the same time, her grandfather's legacy of Latin proves to be problematic. Latin sets Julita apart from other young girls at school in Barcelona, perhaps because it is a mark of masculinity. Hence, it seems to "queer" her further.

Bush offers an interesting reading of the function of Latin:

> Latin might be regarded as a displaced figure for Catalan in this Castilian text. Within the context of Don Julio's anarchist utopia, moreover, Latin is a synecdochic figure for language in general—and the mastery of Latin for mastery in general. . . . Latin . . . is in some sense the first language that [Julita] truly acquires and represents her emergence into the world of reason. . . . [Latin] bears an implicit relationship to writing, of which it is, once again, a trope.[87]

Indeed, through Latin, don Julio hands down to Julia one of the ultimate patriarchal privileges. Her command of this language might symbolize her passage into the symbolic order of the Law of the Father. But more than a tool for writing, Latin becomes a tool for reading in Julia's hands—a game of questions and answers through which she learns to "close read." As any good "perverse" teacher (or, to continue our pun, *profesor entendido*) would do, don Julio incites Julia to be an active (*entendida*) reader, one who reads between the lines, thus signaling to the actual reader of *Julia* to do the same: "Nunca te pierdas en detalles; ése es el error de los estúpidos. Pierden el tiempo en contestar preguntas idiotas y jamás llegan al fondo de la cuestión."[88] Don Julio's advice is of the utmost importance, for it is a pointed lesson in the act of close (queer) reading. Significantly, it is a man who gives Julia a voice, a means of reading, and a tool for understanding. However, as I have discussed, he is a marginalized man. Once Julia leaves the transgressive space of her grandfather's mountain village, she returns to a world of wordlessness in which Latin in the hands of a female teenager serves not as a tool for communication but as a form of knowledge that sets her apart from her peers and codes her as *"rara"* (strange, rare, queer). Julia is back in the dominant world where Víctor's oppressive silencing overcomes her again.

Julia's insertion into school after five years of a happy, secluded life in the mountains elicits a trauma. Silence becomes a complex experience for her: She chooses it mostly as a rebellion for having been torn away from the blissful life with her grandfather, but it is also imposed on her by her classmates, who find her odd, queer. On entering the school, Julia takes a placement examination. Although the principal is astounded by her knowledge of Latin and her well-rounded education, she cannot avoid asking Julia's mother "[u]na pregunta . . . delicada: su hija . . . ¿es muda?"[89] Her mother immediately recognizes Julia's hermeticism as a rebellion and as a sign of self-marginalization. From Julia's point of view, it is a refusal to become part of a society that oppresses her: "Mamá regresó hecha una furia. Eres una salvaje, una antipática. Era cierto, pero le daba igual."[90] Julia's rebellious silence, distance, and indifference ultimately lead her to a dead end. She suffers the consequences of her isolation and her inability to open up to a community of women who could have been her allies: "No hablaba con nadie. Si le preguntaban algo contestaba con las palabras imprescindibles. Al cabo de una semana, en el colegio, le llamaban 'la que no habla.'"[91] Don Julio's masculine legacy of knowledge prevents Julia from understanding the language the other women speak. Paradoxically, then, although his teachings make her a close reader of masculine privileges, they do not teach her how to become, properly speaking, a *lectora entendida,* for a *lector entendido* would have been able to see through the dominant society's gender-dichotomizing strategies. Unfortunately, Julia cannot relate to her classmates' interest in clothes, gossip, and men. From this point on in the novel, Julia desperately tries to understand her isolation, yet fails to see that what separates her from most other women is her desire for women.

The sociopolitical context in which Moix published her novel forced her to re-semanticize silence as the only possible tool with which to write about lesbianism. In this wordless process, she needs the aid of a reader who can recognize the blanks between lines and appropriately read into them, supplying the subversive, missing information. Moix's submerged presentation of the subject proves crucial. As Linda Gould Levine perceived in one of the earlier critical treatments of this novel, the "lesbianism finally emerges as a theme treated with sensitivity and care, although definitely with a somewhat guarded allusiveness."[92] In spite of Moix's "guarded allusiveness," Julia's desire for women is there for a *lector entendido* to discern. The narrative takes the reader from Julita's childish passion for her mother, to her adoration for her aunt Elena, to her first adolescent crush on her school's principal, La Señorita Mabel, and finally, to her great passion for Eva, her college literature professor and—tellingly—her father's first love.[93]

Julia's loving relationship with her mother when she is a child is introduced in explicitly sensual language, as is her relationship with her aunt Elena.[94] Neither Julia's mother nor her aunt, however, returns Julia's passion. While Julia's mother is represented as being cold, distant, vain, and as preferring her two sons to Julia, tía Elena eventually falls in love with and marries Félix, a man who abuses her and turns her into a "persona triste y silenciosa" who "a menudo lloraba por las noches."[95] This heterosexual union enrages Julia and fills her with jealousy, developing in her "un odio asesino contra Félix, y a veces también contra tía Elena."[96] However, this event subversively allows don Julio to deliver another of his "deviant" lessons: "[Félix] hace del amor un arma de posesión, ya que la pobreza de su espíritu no le permite saciar sus ansias de dominio, y [tía Elena] justifica en él su debilidad y cobardía.... Así va el mundo. Tú ve aprendiendo."[97] And learn Julia does. Perhaps she does not learn the lesson don Julio intends, but, more important, she aptly derives from this lesson a new awareness of the dangers to women posed by heterosexuality: "La angustiaba pensar que algún día ella pudiera sentirse dominada, atada por algo o alguien."[98]

Consequently, after five years of exceptional, but ultimately detrimental, private tutoring by don Julio in the mountains, and after her traumatic entrance into school, Julia can find solace only in a kinder and more seductive pedagogue: La Señorita Mabel. The school's principal can see through Julia's desperation and knows how to console her after Rafael's death: "La señorita Mabel cogió su cabeza entre las manos y la besó."[99] Therefore, Julia's first pseudo-lesbian fantasies revolve around the "understanding" school principal, and she often wishes that "la directora fuera más cariñosa con ella, que la estrechara entre sus brazos, como el primer día de clase después de la muerte de Rafael."[100] Moix makes explicit here that "one of the classic student–teacher relationships is an association through seduction."[101]

Not surprisingly, Julia is not conscious of her feelings; she cannot name them, and she cannot even conceive of them as love: "Julia nunca se había preocupado por aquello. El amor era algo que sucedía a los demás, a los personajes de las películas, de las novelas, y a las gentes que vivían a su alrededor."[102] But if she cannot identify what is happening within herself, other people can. Eventually, even her peers single her out, as does an odd newcomer to the school: Lidia. This character comes the closest to being overtly presented as a lesbian. The adolescent fixates on Julia and becomes an abusive and possessive friend. Julia is forced to do Latin translations for Lidia in exchange for human contact, because Lidia is the only classmate who talks to her ("Tú me haces cada día la traducción de latín y yo dejo que seas mi amiga"[103]). Thus, Lidia forces Julia to pass on to her Julia's phallic power—her knowledge of Latin. Because Lidia *entiende,* she, unlike Julia, can close read the queer meaning hidden between the lines of Julia's apparently pedagogical relationship with the school principal. She announces that Julia is "la preferida de la solterona."[104] Her choice of the term "solterona" (old maid) to refer to Señorita Mabel exposes the repressed sexual content of the student–teacher relationship. Lidia uncovers the seduction at the heart of every pedagogical act and comes the closest to *decir* Julia's desires.

On recognizing the nature of Julia's fascination with Señorita Mabel and the latter's favoring of her, Lidia jealously crushes Julia's hopes to break out of her prison of silence and pain: "El miedo se apoderó de Julia, presintió una extraña y misteriosa venganza. Alguien intentaba quitarle algo que ni siquiera había llegado a poseer, algo que tan sólo había deseado."[105] As Lidia's manipulations and Julia's ostracism and silencing intensify, Julia has a nervous breakdown and subsequently leaves school. Julia's illness may represent her fear of being named, of being read as queer. Ultimately, Julia becomes a rancorous and estranged woman who relinquishes all hope of ever establishing proper communication with other human beings: "No sentía dolor, ni pena, ni ganas de llorar, sólo rencor contra sí misma por haberse dejado derrotar y por una soledad que prometía ser eterna."[106]

When Moix introduces Eva, Julia's literature professor and her father's first love, the narrative becomes more explicit in its presentation of Julia's desire; yet, it still remains a *no decir.*[107] Julia eventually starts working as a research assistant for Eva and remembers the days spent together in Eva's house "como la época más apacible de su vida."[108] Julia is attracted to Eva because, like don Julio (an admirer of Eva), she is also a "perverse" pedagogue who helps Julia to become self-assured. Eva teaches literature and forces Julia to close read when she asks her, "¿Qué te parece tal libro?, ¿o tal película?" Such questions "obligaba[n a Julia] a pensar, a razonar sobre algo exterior a ella." And Eva's teachings are not easy: "Julia debía esforzarse."[109]

Recognizing in Julia and Eva's friendship a reiteration of don Julio's "mala educación" (miseducation), Julia's mother angrily forbids Julia to visit Eva. To protect her special friendship and newly found safe space, Julia strikes a deal with her brother Ernesto (now an artist), thus establishing a subversive coalition with the other queer member of her family. Ernesto covers up the shameful scene of Eva and Julia's pedagogical seduction and desire: Ernesto and Julia tell their mother that they are at the movies together when, in fact, he socializes with men and Julia flees to Eva's house. To Julia's dismay, the trick is discovered after a year, and her mother responds in an extremely violent, homophobic, and sexist manner: Julia is to remain at home and never to go out alone.

Julia once more fails to break her silence. She does not communicate to Eva what has happened, and Eva's response to Julia's silence—though motivated by ignorance—is cruel: "Te he dicho que tengo trabajo, ¿sucede algo grave? No seas pesada. Te llamaré mañana. Buenas noches."[110] Julia's narrow world is thus shattered and, in desperation, she attempts suicide. While in the hospital, she is finally able to say something in response to her mother's unfair reproaches: "Julia empezó a gritar. Los insultos salían de su garganta sin poder retenerlos,"[111] but her reaction comes too late. After years of distance and silence provoked by oppression, Julia's cry is not effective. Her family alienates her, and Julia feels empty.

One of don Julio's apparently subversive teachings again backfires here. When his son, "para no sacar las cosas de quicio y cubrir las apariencias," had to return to the mountains after five years of separation from his bourgeois wife to take Julia back to live with the nuclear family, don Julio managed to rebel only by screaming insults against "Papá, Mamá, la abuela Lucía, la Iglesia, y la inmoralidad de la moral burguesa."[112] But his son inevitably takes Julia away amid don Julio's willful silence. Don Julio's only doubtful achievement is literally to lose his voice: "Al día siguiente estaba afónico."[113] Likewise, Julia's string of insults against her mother allow her only to feel "vacía."[114]

In these dramatic final episodes of the novel, Moix clearly denounces the oppressiveness of a heterosexist society that does not permit women to have voices of their own and that cannot conceive of women desiring other women. Julia is defeated in her silence and is thus condemned to live a meaningless life: "No había muerto, pero yacía en la cama del hospital, ciega y tullida, sin pensamientos, sin recuerdos, sin deseos. No existía, había sufrido una gran derrota y la habían desterrado a un *lugar sin nombre*, desconocido, fuera del tiempo y del espacio de los demás."[115] It is painfully ironic that Moix has Julia say, "No existía" (She didn't exist), for in the sociopolitical context in which Moix was writing, lesbians indeed did not exist as far as society was concerned. For all practical purposes, lesbians were erased from the public consciousness. In fact, Moix plays precisely with this double-edged circumstance in her careful encoding of the lesbian theme: Those readers who are invested in erasing lesbianism will fail to find it in the novel. Such readers will be complicit with Julia's family in condemning Julia to a world of silence and anonymity, to an existence in which, even if she has survived her attempted suicide, she will feel dead and disconnected from the world, to a *lugar sin nombre* (a place with no name) where her desires will remain unnamed.

In an attempt to counter the erasure of the lesbian in 1970s Spain, Moix constructs a complex narrative that, although full of gaps in information, specifically points to those gaps and cries out for a reading between the lines. Moix is relentless with her protagonist. The novel ends on a pessimistic note, with Julia feeling defeated and with the final appearance of the image of Julita stagnated, brutalized, and silenced at age six: "Y allí estaba. Como todas las mañanas, Julita había regresado"[116] turned into "un dios martirizador, un dios que reclamaba continuos sacrificios para calmar su antiguo dolor."[117] Julia survives but at the price of her freedom and without the ability to articulate her oppression.

Moix dramatizes the dangers of remaining silent, for lesbians and heterosexual women alike, through the story of Julia. This political message could not be conveyed explicitly in the Spain of 1968, so Moix resorts to the use of a complex *treta* (trick): the tactic of unsaying, a tactic that requires a lesson in reading. Through a web of blanks— "unsayings"—that point to "a vacancy in the overall system of the text,"[118] the text hails the *lector entendido* and asks her or him to supply the missing links. Just as don Julio teaches Julita not to lose herself in the details when translating Latin, Moix's text teaches us not to get lost in unimportant details but to read the coded messages in the text. It is up to the *lector entendido* to *decir*, to dare to speak the name of Julia's desires.

Notes

1. Josep María Castellet, *Nueve novísimos poetas españoles* (Barcelona: Barral Editores, 1970).

2. The books of poetry are Ana María Moix, *Baladas del dulce Jim* (Barcelona: El Bardo, 1969); *Call Me Stone* (Barcelona: Esplugues Llobregat, 1969); *No Time for Flowers y otras historias* (Barcelona: Lumen, 1971). These books were later collected in the volume *A imagen y semejanza* (Barcelona: Lumen, 1983). The short-story collection is *Ese chico pelirrojo a quien veo cada día* (Barcelona: Lumen, 1971). The novels are *Julia* (Barcelona: Editorial Lumen, 1968; rev. ed. 1991) and *Walter, ¿por qué te fuiste?* (Barcelona: Barral, 1973; rev. ed. 1992). It is worth noting that Moix's second novel merited the praise of Julio Cortázar, the renowned writer of the Latin American boom who, as a juror for the 1972 version of Barral's prestigious prize, commented that Moix's novel was one of the best manuscripts presented to the competition that year, even though it did not receive the coveted prize: Cortázar, as cited in José María Martínez Cachero, *La novela española entre 1936 y el fin de siglo: Historia de una aventura* (Madrid: Castalia, 1997), 323. And Moix's book of interviews is *24 x 24* (Barcelona: Península, 1972).

3. However, during that period, Moix remained active as a journalist, a translator, a literary critic, and an author of children's literature. For a thorough analysis of these years of Moix's supposed "silence," see Linda Gould Levine, "Behind the 'Enemy Lines': Strategies for Interpreting *Las virtudes peligrosas* of Ana María Moix," in *Nuevos y novísimos: Algunas perspectivas críticas sobre la narrativa española desde la década de los 60*, ed. Ricardo Landeira and Luis T. González-del-Valle (Boulder, Colo.: Society of Spanish and Spanish-American Studies, 1987), 97–111. Moix's 1985 collection is *Las virtudes peligrosas* (Barcelona: Plaza y Janés, 1985).

4. Moix's silence as a writer was weirdly praised by Alfredo Bryce Echenique who, on the publication of *Las virtudes peligrosas*, remarked that Moix was "una escritora que parece *haber sabido callar*, a lo largo de años, sólo para sacudirnos con unas páginas tan bellas como las que conforman la materia de este libro" (a writer who seems to *have known how to remain silent* over the years, only to jolt us with some pages as beautiful as the ones that make up this book's material): Alfredo Bryce Echenique, "Luz y Tinieblas," *Quimera* 50 (1985): 70; emphasis added. (The difference between *callar* and *no decir* is discussed later.) Also, Sandra Kingery speculates that "the halting of Moix's flood of works … may ironically have stemmed from the

democratization of Spain. . . . With Franco's death, the most obvious repressions were softened and the perceived necessity for battle, eliminated. . . . [D]eprived of the fairy-tale dragon against whom to sharpen her sword of creativity, Moix lost the challenge of her rebellious adventure": see Sandra L. Kingery, "Ana María Moix: Feminist Subversions and Feminism Subverted" (Ph.D. diss., University of Wisconsin, 1996), 230–31.

5. I use the generic Spanish singular masculine in *lector entendido* on the assumption that the term includes both male and female readers. The use of the masculine is further justified by the origin of the code term *"entender,"* as I explain later.

6. Such as Julita's fears of being abandoned by a mother who is inconsistent in her affection toward her daughter and who unfairly favors her two sons. "Mamá otorgaba su cariño a rachas" (Mom granted her love capriciously): Moix, *Julia,* 15. All translations are mine, unless noted otherwise.

7. As Levine has indicated, "In the first reading of the novel, neither the rape itself nor the lesbian theme is apparent": see Linda Gould Levine, "The Censored Sex: Woman as Author and Character in Franco's Spain," in *Women in Hispanic Literature: Icons and Fallen Idols,* ed. Beth Miller (Berkeley: University of California Press, 1983), 304.

8. This term has been aptly used by Emilie Bergmann and Paul Julian Smith in the title of their influential anthology of Hispanic queer theory, *¿Entiendes? Queer Readings, Hispanic Writings* (Durham, N.C.: Duke University Press, 1995).

9. "A hegemonic, gay model of pure Anglo-Saxon origin that generates a discourse incapable of acknowledging intercultural nuances and adaptations [of same-sex relationships]": Óscar Guasch, *La sociedad rosa* (Barcelona: Anagrama, 1995), 162.

10. "Any person capable of establishing sexual relationships with people of his or her own gender, regardless of the frequency and intensity with which those relationships take place": ibid., 160.

11. Pierre Bourdieu, "Censorship and the Imposition of Form," in *Language and Symbolic Power,* ed. John B. Thompson, trans. Gino Raymond and Matthew Adamson, (Cambridge, Mass.: Harvard University Press, 1991), 158.

12. Wolfgang Iser, *The Act of Reading: A Theory of Aesthetic Response* (Baltimore: Johns Hopkins University Press, 1978), 275.

13. Because of the persistence of censorship during the last years of the regime, most readers were alerted to the need to read between the lines. As Roberto Saldrigas notes, under Franco authors generally assumed "que había un lector que te leía entre líneas y entonces guiñabas el ojo al lector y . . . se establecía una complicidad" (that there was a reader who would read between the lines, and then you winked at the reader and . . . a complicity was established): Roberto Saldrigas, "Por los territorios de la ambigüedad," *Sociedad y nueva creación,* ed. Juan Pedro Aparicio (Madrid: Germán Sánchez Ruipérez, 1990), 221.

14. ACT UP's Spanish branch, ACTUA, was founded on 23 January 1991 in Barcelona. See Jordi Esteva and Oscar Fontrodona, "Tú sí puedes parar el SIDA," *Ajoblanco* 47 (December 1992): 25–30.

15. For a study of the actual legal and penal consequences of speaking out for Spanish queers during the last years of the Franco regime, see Gema Pérez-Sánchez, "Franco's Spain, Queer Nation?" combined issue of *Michigan Journal of Race and Law* 5, no. 3 (Summer 2000): 943–87, and *University of Michigan Journal of Law Reform* 33, no. 3 (Spring 2000): 359–403.

16. It is well known that writers in post–Civil War Spain had to confront two types of censorship: Franco's and their own. *Autocensura* (self-censorship) is a writer's anticipation of and response to a censor's potential objections.

17. In a similar cultural and historical context, Karen Van Dyck explains the effects of the Greek colonels' dictatorship on literature: "According to many accounts the dictatorship was a time in which the general population was 'feminized'; for seven years the subaltern 'experiences' of women—claustrophobia, curfews, silencing and censorship, physical restraints—became those of both genders." It follows that women writers were caught in a double bind that their male counterparts escaped. However, such "feminine" experiences of oppression allowed Greek intellectuals "to make analogies among censorship by an oppressive regime, censorship practiced in the subjection of women, and even the Freudian notion of censorship as a necessary check on the unconscious": see Karen Van Dyck "Reading between Worlds: Contemporary Greek Women's Writing and Censorship," *PMLA* 109 (1994): 46.

18. Debra A. Castillo, *Talking Back: Toward a Latin American Feminist Literary Criticism* (Ithaca, N.Y.: Cornell University Press, 1992), 2. Although Castillo bases her theories on the work of Latin American women writers, some peninsular women writers have used the same strategies as, for example, Sor Juana Inés de la Cruz and Rosario Castellanos. As I argue in this essay, Moix uses such a strategy of silence in *Julia*, although in a complex combination with moments of overt eloquence in which she represents the injustices that can accompany the silences imposed on women by an oppressive masculinist system.

19. Ibid., 37.

20. David Herzberger insightfully labels the climate in which intellectuals had to operate as one of "coerced acquiescence" with the doctrines of the regime: David Herzberger, *Narrating the Past: Fiction and Historiography in Postwar Spain* (Durham, N.C.: Duke University Press, 1995), 15. Also, Manuel Abellán provides a good account of the effects of censorship under Franco's regime in his *Censura y creación literaria en España (1939–1976)* (Barcelona: Península, 1980). For censorship and the press, see Justino Sinoya, *La censura de prensa durante el franquismo (1936–1951)* (Madrid: Espasa Calpe, 1989); and for documents on censorship, see Ramón Tamames, *España 1931–1975: Una antología histórica* (Barcelona: Planeta, 1980), 383–92. On censorship of "inappropriate" gender behavior by the Sección Femenina de la Falange, see María Teresa Gallego Méndez, *Mujer, Falange y Franquismo* (Madrid: Taurus, 1983); Giuliana di Febo, *Resistencia y movimiento de mujeres en España, 1936–1976* (Hospitalet: Icaria, 1979); and Geraldine M. Scanlon, *La polémica feminista en la España contemporánea (1968–1974)* (Madrid: Siglo XXI, 1976).

21. Castillo, *Talking Back*, 39.

22. "Decir que no se sabe, no saber decir, saber sobre el no decir: esta serie liga los sectores aparentemente diversos del texto ... y sirve de base a dos movimientos fundamentales que sostienen las tretas que examinaremos: en primer lugar, separación del saber del campo del decir; en segundo lugar, reorganización del campo del saber en función del no decir (callar)." (To say that one does not know, not to know how to say, to know about not saying: this series links the apparently disparate sections of the text ... and serves as a basis for two fundamental movements supporting the tricks that we will examine: in the first place, the separation of knowing from the field of saying; in the second place, the reorganization of the field of knowing according to that of not saying [unsaying]): Josefina Ludmer, "Las tretas del débil," in *La sartén por el mango,* ed. Patricia Elena González and Eliana Ortega (Río Piedras, P.R.: Huracán, 1985), 48.

23. Castillo, *Talking Back*, 42.

24. From a rhetorical point of view, this feminist strategy constitutes a sort of litotes. For a relevant study of how censorship generally functions as litotes and how it paradoxically creates non-naive readers, see Michael Holquist, "Corrupt Originals: The Paradox of Censorship," *PMLA* 109, no. 1 (January 1994).

25. Castillo, *Talking Back,* 42.

26. Many critics have commented on Moix's fascination with silence and its relationship to gendered positions throughout her works. Most significantly, Emilie Bergmann argues that "Julia's repression of her lesbianism is enacted by the repetitions and silences of the narrative": see Emilie Bergmann, "Reshaping the Canon: Intertextuality in Spanish Novels of Female Development," *Anales de la literatura española contemporánea* 12, nos. 1–2 (1987): 150. However, she does not establish a connection between the silences in the text and the need for a particular kind of queer reader, as the present essay does. See also Andrew Bush, "Ana María Moix's Silent Calling," in *Women Writers of Contemporary Spain: Exiles in the Homeland,* ed. Joan L. Brown (Newark: University of Delaware Press, 1991), 136–58, and Margaret E. W. Jones, "Different Wor(l)ds: Modes of Women's Communication in Spain's *Narrativa femenina,*" *Monographic Review* 8 (1992): 57–69. In addition, Sandra J. Schumm reads into what she calls the "voids within the novel" in order to psychoanalyze Julia in "Progressive Schizophrenia in Ana María Moix's *Julia,*" *Revista canadiense de estudios hispánicos* 9 (1994): 151. Unfortunately, her reading falls into a simplistic pathologizing of Julia. More convincingly, Beverly Richard Cook recently argued that Julia's silences serve as a representation of the impossibility of rape victims to verbalize their trauma: Beverly Richard Cook, "Division, Duplicity, and Duality: The Nature of the Double in Three Works by Contemporary Spanish Women Writers," in *Letras peninsulares* 11, no. 2 (Fall 1998): 657–77. In their respective studies, Melissa Stewart and Sandra L. Kingery focus on Moix's narratological deployment of silence in *Walter.* See Melissa Stewart, "[De]constructing Text and Self in Ana María Moix's *Walter, ¿por qué te fuiste?* and Montserrat Roig's *La veu melodiosa,*" in *Hispanófila* 124 (September 1998); and Kingery "Feminist Subversions," esp. 114–15, 227–28. Rosalía Cornejo-Parriego explores Moix's representation of willful silences between desiring women in "Las virtudes peligrosas": see Rosalía Cornejo-Parriego, "Desde el innominado deseo: Transgresión y marginalidad de la mirada en 'Las virtudes peligrosas,' de Ana María Moix," in *Anales de la literatura española contemporánea* 23, no. 1–2 (1998): 607–21.

Cornejo-Parriego's words about the silent desire established between two female characters in "Las virtudes peligrosas" could be extended to assess the "silent" representation of lesbian desire in *Julia:* "El amor sin palabras . . . constituye otra dimensión de la difícil supervivencia del deseo lésbico en la sociedad heterosexual: no sólo se trata de ocupar un espacio marginal, sino también de encontrar un lenguaje ex-céntrico que prevenga [su] desaparición" (Love without words . . . constitutes another dimension of the difficult survival of lesbian desire in heterosexual society: not only because it is a matter of occupying a marginal space, but because it is a matter of finding an ex-centric language that prevents (its) disappearance": Cornejo-Parriego, "Desde el innominado deseo," 613.

27. Castillo, *Talking Back,* 41. See also how, in one of the earliest reviews of *Julia,* José Batlló uses the metaphor of scent to describe the absences that I term silences: "la novela de Ana María Moix exhala un perfume extraño, desazonante, que obliga a un esfuerzo de percepción e identificación por parte de nuestro olfato" (Ana María Moix's novel exudes a strange, disquieting perfume that forces our sense of smell to engage in an effort of perception and identification). However, at the end of his review, he switches metaphors: "me atrevería a recomendar a los lectores de *Julia* que se sientan insatisfechos que se hagan examinar los tímpanos por un especialista" (I would dare to recommend that those readers of *Julia* who feel dissatisfied should have their ears examined by a specialist): José Batlló, review of *Julia,* by Ana María Moix, *Cuadernos hispanoamericanos* 83, no. 248–49 (August–September 1970): 684, 686.

28. Castillo, *Talking Back*, 42. In his creatively evocative, biographical piece about Moix, Eugenio Cobo reminds us of the Catalan writer's awareness of how silence is ineffective: "Quien ama el silencio perecerá en él. Silencio igual a mitad de suicidio" (Whoever loves silence will perish in it. Silence equals half a suicide): Eugenio Cobo, "Imagen de Ana Moix," *La estafeta literaria* 636 (15 May 1978): 21.

29. "She kept silent to infuriate mom": Moix, *Julia*, 34.

30. "Andrés would sit beside her: only a while, enough time to smoke a cigarette and find out what you're thinking. She was thinking of nothing. That was the truth. But Andrés would always ask: What are you thinking? And she would have to answer: Nothing. She wasn't thinking of something that she could explain to Andrés": ibid., 35.

31. I am thinking of the genealogy of male teachers/seducers started by the medieval *Letters of Abelard and Heloise* and continued especially with Jean-Jacques Rousseau's *Julie ou La Nouvelle Héloïse*. Quite possibly, Moix was aware of this tradition and consciously named her protagonist Julia to resonate with Rousseau's heroine. In *Julia*, however, Moix eventually subverts the pedagogical scene of seduction by making it a lesbian scene, as we shall see in Julia's student–teacher interactions with Señorita Mabel and especially with Eva. Peggy Kamuf has argued that the male heterosexual genealogy of seducer pedadogues is completed by Guilleragues's *Les Lettres Portugaises*, Madame de Lafayette's *La Princess de Clèves*, and Choderlos de Laclos's *Les Liaisons dangereuses*. For an excellent analysis of the Spanish subversive twist to the pedagogical-seduction scenes in *Julia*, see Paz Macías Fernández's comparison of Rousseau's text to Francisco de Tójar's *La filosofa por amor; o, Cartas de dos amantes apasionados y virtuosos*, "The 'Interesting Woman': Sex, Sentiment, and Ideology in the Spanish Novel of the Enlightenment" (Ph.D. diss., Cornell University, Ithaca, N.Y., 1996). For further analyses of the politics of pedagogy in Rousseau's *Julie*, see Peggy Kamuf, *Fictions of Feminine Desire* (Lincoln: University of Nebraska Press, 1982), and Joan de Jean, "*La Nouvelle Héloïse*, or the Case for Pedagogical Deviation," in *Yale French Studies* 63 (1982): 98–116.

32. Although at times Julia "felt a certain tenderness for Andrés" because "he guessed her out and was conscious that, by lavishing her with his affection and protection . . . and by asking for nothing, she would never reject his presence," she hates him "for meddling in her things, for asking what are you thinking, what are you doing this afternoon, what did you do this morning, did you like the film?": Moix, *Julia*, 27.

33. "She saw herself, in class, observed by Andrés. She saw herself in the university quad, strolling or chatting with a classmate, under Andrés' gaze": ibid., 24.

34. Ibid., 25.

35. "All her days were the same, monotonous": ibid., 189.

36. "They had defeated her": ibid., 187.

37. Significantly, Julia's tenacious silence and passivity seem to have bothered certain critics, such as Geraldine C. Nichols, who writes that "sus fobias y su pasividad la hacen tan antipática para el lector que a veces dificulta el seguir con su historia. Es precisamente por lo que tiene de real y autobiográfica esta personalidad desagradable por lo que mantiene el interés. . . . Su deformación psicológica, por extrema que sea, ejemplifica un patrón de represión por parte de los mayores" (Her phobias and her passivity make her so disagreeable to the reader that, sometimes, it is difficult to go on with her story. It is precisely because of what this disgusting character has of real and autobiography that the interest is maintained. . . . Her psychological deformation, however extreme, exemplifies the adult's pattern of repression)." Geraldine C. Nichols, "*Julia*: 'This is the Way the World Ends . . . ,'" in *Novelistas femeninas de la posguerra*

española, ed. Janet W. Pérez (Madrid: Porrúa, 1983), 113. Nichols remains deaf to Moix's strategic use of silence and proves a *lectora no entendida*, because for her Ernesto is the only homosexual character in the novel, and Julia is "ensimismada, casi cataléptica, asexual" (self-absorbed, almost cataleptic, asexual): ibid., 114. Curiously, in a later piece, Nichols retreats from her pathologizing and biographical reading of *Julia:* see Germán Gleiberg, Maureen Ihrie, and Janet Pérez, eds., *Dictionary of the Literature of the Iberian Peninsula* (Westport, Conn.: Greenwood Press, 1993), s.v. "Ana María Moix" (Geraldine Clearly Nichols), 1107–1108.

My critique of Nichols's early biographical approach to the novel does not foreclose a recognition of the similarities between the novel and Moix's life. Nichols probably based her early assessment of the biographical dimensions of *Julia* on her own interview with the writer: See Geraldine Clearly Nichols, *Escribir, espacio propio: Laforet, Matute, Moix, Tusquets, Riera y Roig por sí mismas* (Minneapolis: Institute for the Study of Ideologies and Literature, 1989). Recently, Kingery proved that Moix freely but accurately depicts her family in *Julia:* see Kingerly, "Feminist Subversions," 171 ff.

38. Several critics have devoted particular attention to the narratological complexities of *Julia* and *Walter.* See esp. Bush, "Silent Calling"; Biruté Ciplijauskaité, *La novela femenina contemporánea (1970–1985): Hacia una tipología de la narración en primera persona* (Barcelona: Anthropos, 1988); Kingerly, "Feminist Subversions," 191 ff; Jones, "Literary Structures"; C. Christopher Soufas, "Narrative Form as Feminist Ideology: Feminist Consciousness/Criticism in Laforet's *Nada,* Matute's *Primera memoria* and Moix's *Julia,*" in *Discurso: Revista de estudios iberoamericanos* 11, no. 1 (1993): 153–61; Stewart, "[De]Constructing Text and Self"; and idem, "Memory in Ana María Moix's *Julia,*" *Ojáncano* 10 (October 1995): 23–33.

39. For specific studies on doubling in Julia, see Catherine G. Bellver, "Division, Duplication, and Doubling in the Novels of Ana María Moix," in *Nuevos y novísimos: Algunas perspectivas críticas sobre la narrativa española desde la década de los 60,* ed. Ricardo Landeira and Luis T. González-del-Valle (Boulder, Colo.: Society of Spanish and Spanish-American Studies, 1987), 29–41; Cook, "Division, Duplicity, and Duality"; Schumm, "Progressive Schizophrenia," 657–77; and Michael D. Thomas, "El desdoblamiento psíquico como factor dinámico en *Julia* de Ana María Moix," in Pérez, *Novelistas femeninas,* 103–11. Margaret W. Jones also briefly dicusses doubling in "Del compromiso al egoísmo: La metamorfosis de la protagonista en la novelística femenina de postguerra," in Pérez, *Novelistas femeninas,* 132.

40. "As if she and Julita were two different people. Sometimes, Julia was sure that Julita still existed, that she lived and dwelled in another unalterable world, motionless, timeless. It was as if Julita existed with a life of her own . . . and from there . . . she would bend Julia's will so that the latter would do, think, and feel whatever she [Julita] pleased": Moix, *Julia, 55.*

41. Ibid., 186–87.

42. My reading is informed here by the eloquent interpretation in Eve Kosofsky Sedgwick, "Queer Performativity: Henry James's *The Art of the Novel," GLQ: A Journal of Gay and Lesbian Studies* 1, no. 1 (1993): 8.

43. "A tormenting god . . . would claim continuous sacrifices to calm his ancient pain": Moix, *Julia,* 56.

44. "You'll say nothing, idiot": ibid., 54.

45. "Julita, sitting at the threshold of her home, small and thin, barefoot, braids half undone, shorts and navy-blue jersey with an anchor drawn on her chest, lowered gaze, fixated on two stones that she would pound against each other, would force her to remember such confusing, disconnected things": ibid., 55.

46. Andrew Bush, "Moix's Silent Calling," 143.

47. Ibid., 137–38.

48. Ibid., 143.

49. Ibid.

50. Carmen de Urioste succinctly and accurately qualifies the main critical approaches to *Julia*: "According to traditional lines of investigation, Julia could be [and has been] read as a biographical novel, as a psychological novel with a schizophrenic protagonist, or as a social-realistic novel portraying the decadent world of the Catalan bourgeoisie during the first years of the Franco regime." In addition, Urioste proposes a queer reading of *Julia*, albeit not specifically focusing on the dynamics between "unsaying" lesbian desire, pedagogy, and formation of queer subjectivity, as the present essay does. For Urioste, "in the light of queer criticism, it is possible to analyze the novel as the representation of a sexual identity formation, that is, not only as a social construction of the character but also identity as a matter of desire": Carmen de Urioste, "Ana María Moix," in *Spanish Writers on Gay and Lesbian Themes: A Bio-Critical Sourcebook*, ed. David William Foster (Westport, Conn.: Greenwood Press, 1999), 113.

Of the other critics who directly analyze *Julia*, only Bergmann, Cook, Costa, Kingery, Levine (in "The Censored Sex"), Schyfter, Schumm, and Stewart present a significant reading of the lesbianism in the novel. Bergmann, Kingery, Levine, and Stewart provide sympathetic readings, although lesbianism is not their main subject of study. For example, in analyzing gendered variations of the Bildungsroman in Spanish novels, Bergmann acknowledges Julia's lesbianism and appropriately criticizes Moix's inscription of Julia's consciousness in Freudian terms—an inscription that leads the protagonist to repress "her lesbianism, . . . to seek a mother in limited relationships with older women, and [to deny] herself the autonomy exemplified and offered by her grandfather": Bergmann, "Reshaping the Canon," 149. Unlike Bergmann's serious engagement with psychoanalytic theory, Schyfter and Schumm develop a problematic pseudo-psychoanalysis of the character of Julia, whom they both condemn as irrecoverably pathological. Similarly, although she criticizes blaming-the-victim approaches to the analysis of Julia, Cook still pathologizes the character's lesbianism.

Other critics either do not mention lesbianism at all or do so in passing, in a footnote, or as a pathological state. It is worth mentioning the creative circumlocution in Jones's excellent essay "Del compromiso al egoísmo" to avoid using the word "lesbianism": "La Julia mayor es una persona . . . con una decidida preferencia por las mujeres (una preferencia con implicaciones sexuales)" (The older Julia is a person . . . with a resolute preference for women [a preference with sexual implications]): Jones, "Del compromiso al egoísmo," 128–29. This circumlocution is particularly telling because Jones does use the word "lesbianism" in her essay to refer to another writer's work. In my opinion, Jones's clever word choice confirms my contention that Moix's first novel purposefully avoids naming Julia's desire to elicit the cooperation of a particular kind of queer reader. By contrast, María Dolores Costa's supposedly queer-positive entry for *The Gay and Lesbian Literary Heritage* unfairly claims that "Moix unwittingly regenerates the notion that lesbians are not women who love women, but women who hate men": María Dolores Costa, "Spanish Literatures," in *The Gay and Lesbian Literary Heritage: A Reader's Companion to the Writers and Their Works, from Antiquity to the Present*, ed. Claude J. Summers (New York: Henry Holt, 1995), 670.

The most egregious pathologizing analysis of *Julia* can be found in Pablo Gil Casado's relatively recent book, *La novela deshumanizada española (1958-1988)* (Barcelona: Anthropos, 1990). In this work, Gil Casado problematically classifies *Julia* under the category "La psicopatía" (psychopathology)—a group of works that includes novels that focus on "la anormalidad psíquica, representando su patología, manifestaciones o tratamiento" (psychic abnormality, representing its pathology, manifestations or treatment): Gil Casado, *La novela*, 200. He further accuses the protagonist of displaying "conducta histérica" (hysterical behavior), laments that "la predisposición de Julia al llanto peca de más" (Julia's predisposition to crying is excessive), and criticizes Moix for lacking "lo que se llama voluntad de selección narrativa," (what is called a capacity for narrative selectivity): Gil Casado, *La novela*, 209–10. Gil Casado's sexism and homophobia is comically highlighted elsewhere in his work when he refers to the lesbian relationship narrated in Esther Tusquets's *El mismo mar de todos los veranos* as "un intenso amor violeta" (an intense lavender love): Gil Casado, *La novela*, 203.

   See Bellver, "Division, Duplication, and Doubling"; Bergmann, "Reshaping the Canon"; Bush, "Moix's Silent Calling"; Cook, "Division, Duplicity, and Duality"; Costa, "Spanish Literatures"; Gil Casado, *La novela*; Jones, "Different Wor(l)ds," "Ana María Moix: Literary Structures and the Enigmatic Nature of Reality," *Journal of Spanish Studies: Twentieth Century* 4 (1976): 105–16, and "Del compromiso al egoísmo"; Kingery, "Feminist Subversions"; Levine, "The Censored Sex"; Juan Antonio Masoliver Rodenas, "La base sexta contra Ana María Moix," *Camp de l'Arpa* 9 (January 1974): 9–12; Nichols, "The Way the World Ends"; Schumm, "Progressive Schizophrenia"; Sarah E. Schyfter, "Rites without Passage: The Adolescent World of Ana María Moix's *Julia*," in *The Analysis of Literary Texts: Current Trends in Methodology. Third and Fourth York College Colloquia*, ed. Randolph D. Pope (Ypsilanti, Mich.: Bilingual Press/ Editorial Bilingüe, 1980), 41–50; Christopher C. Soufas, Jr., "Ana María Moix and the 'Generation of 1968': *Julia* as (Anti-)Generational (Anti-)Manifesto," in Landeira and González-del-Valle, *Nuevos y novísimos*, 217–28; Stewart, "Memory in *Julia*"; and Thomas, "El desdoblamiento psíquico." For the earliest pathologizing analysis of the protagonist, see José Domingo, "Narrativa española: Aires de Barcelona," *Ínsula* 287 (October 1970): 6–7.

   51. As the Spanish feminist Carmen Alcalde explains: "El lesbianismo no lo consideran [en España], creen que no es nada, que son juegos, no se lo toman en serio.... No entienden que una mujer guste a otra mujer" (They don't consider lesbianism [in Spain], they think it's nothing, that it's a game, they don't take it seriously.... They don't understand that a woman would like another woman): Linda Gould Levine and Gloria Feiman Waldman, *Feminismo ante el Franquismo: Entrevistas con feministas de España* (Miami: Universal, 1980), 36.

   52. "An attentive, elegant, and sensitive man must be a ...": Moix, *Julia*, 53.

   53. "A worthless female/a prostitute": ibid., 129.

   54. "Girl, I've figured your brother out, and I'm telling you because we trust each other. He's scared of women—well, supposing he's not something worse, which I will not say, because, God prevent me (and she crossed herself) from fanning the fire. In these kind of cases it's better to watch, listen, and *remain silent*": ibid., 42; emphasis added.

   55. Ibid., 33.

   56. Joseph Litvak, "Discipline, Spectacle, and Melancholia in and around the Gay Studies Classroom," in *Pedagogy: The Question of Impersonation*, ed. Jane Gallop (Bloomington: Indiana University Press, 1995), 19–27; Judith Butler, *Gender Trouble: Feminism and the Subversion of Identity* (New York: Routledge, 1990).

   57. Litvak, "Discipline," 21.

   58. Sedgwick, "Queer Performativity," 12, 14.

   59. Litvak, "Discipline," 21–22.

   60. "Is effeminate ... the whole of him is effeminate": Moix, *Julia*, 37.

   61. "Dad, at the end of the month, when they would show him their report cards, would get infuriated with Ernesto and would humiliate him in front of Rafael:... You should be ashamed of yourself, overgrown loafer": ibid., 72.

62. "He's younger than you; he's ill, and look at his grades": ibid.

63. "Julia would blush when she realized and would bury her head between her shoulders, fixing her gaze on the open book so that the others wouldn't notice that her eyes were full of tears, and she would feel alone, strange, different from them": ibid., 131.

64. "Even the teachers would cultivate the difference": ibid., 132.

65. "She looked like a scarecrow. . . . I know a bunch of girls her age who, being uglier than her, give another impression, they wear make up, they dress up": ibid., 138.

66. "Would complain . . . that Julia never had the initiative to buy herself a dress, or some shoes, to fix her hair or any other such thing that mom would classify as proofs of femininity. . . . A girl ought to be coquettish and vain; otherwise she seems like a man": ibid., 125.

67. "Femininity is demonstrated in other things . . . , for example, in her piety toward God. A woman who doesn't go to church and doesn't pray is not a decent woman": ibid., 139.

68. "If Ernesto can read them, so can I": ibid., 141.

69. "Ernesto is wrong to do that, but, after all, he is a man. . . . A woman does not need to know as much as a man; it has been that way since the world began": ibid.

70. "An intelligent person, even though she is a woman": ibid., 88.

71. "In the mountains for twenty-five years": ibid., 74.

72. "Was a bit remote from the town": ibid., 76.

73. "Grandmother Lucía was the one who said the worst things about don Julio: an atheist, my God, an anarchist, even worse than if he had been a communist. A bloodthirsty person. You could not know it because you did not live through the horrible events of the Tragic Week. Barcelona was a river of blood and all because of heartless men like don Julio. How could nuns and priests have been at fault for politicians' fights? An anarchist and, furthermore, a rude person": ibid., 74.

74. "The whole family, even Dad, would call him don Julio"; Ibid.

75. "The powerful, ferocious, warlike, and cruel figure that [Julia] had imagined had nothing in common with don Julio": ibid., 75.

76. "One of the things I am going to teach my granddaughter is to demonstrate to her that she can live without anybody ruling her actions": ibid., 81.

77. As Jane Gallop has indicated, following Bourdieu and Passeron's theory, "education involves, not only the specific case of the student as reproduction of the teacher, but the more general case of the student as impersonation of an educated person, taking on and reproducing the style and tastes of a class": Jane Gallop, "Im-Personation: A Reading in the Guise of an Introduction," in *Pedagogy: The Question of Impersonation* (Bloomington: Indiana University Press, 1995), 4. Don Julio, however, is a pedagogue who is particularly concerned with subversively educating Julia in his anarchist ideology. He deliberately pits her against the conservative, fascist world represented by Julia's mother's side of the family. Thus, his reproduction is a perverse one. Nevertheless, Moix might have intended a veiled criticism of the ideologically opposed grandparents. By involving the grandchildren in their "war," don Julio and abuela Lucía perpetuate the divide between *las dos Españas* (the two Spains).

78. Joan de Jean, "*La Nouvelle Héloïse,* or the Case for Pedagogical Deviation," *Yale French Studies* 63 (1982): 98–116.

79. De Jean refers to the original meaning of the verb *bricoler* and its derivatives, which suggest deviation from a set course or a surprise. Thus, in billiards, a *coup de bricole* means a "shot off the cushion," and the idiom *par bricole* means "indirectly, unfairly, by a fluke": *Cassell's French–English, English–French Dictionary* (New York: Macmillan, 1981), 110. De Jean, "The Case for Pedagogical Deviation," 106.

80. De Jean, "The Case for Pedagogical Deviation," 114.

81. Ibid., 110.

82. "Aunt Elena would reproach don Julio: You are educating her badly, she's picking up your gestures and swear words": Moix, *Julia*, 88.

83. "Mom said that don Julio had educated her badly and had given her his disposition and rudeness: and you are a copycat. Every time Julita got angry and hit the table or insulted Ernesto, Mom slapped her and called her doña Julia": ibid., 96.

84. De Jean, "The Case for Pedagogical Deviation," 109.

85. "She confronted mysterious words whose meaning she looked up in a dictionary, and she later had to find the precise order of the words to make sense out of them": Moix, *Julia*, 90.

86. "She knows more Latin than the priest at school": ibid., 91.

87. Bush, "Moix's Silent Calling," 146–47.

88. "Never get lost in details; that's the mistake of stupid people. They waste their time answering idiotic questions, and they never get to the bottom of the problem": Moix, *Julia*, 106.

89. "A delicate . . . question: your daughter. . . . Is she a *mute*?": ibid., 110; emphasis added.

90. "Mom returned infuriated. You are savage, disagreeable. It was true, but she didn't care": ibid.

91. "She didn't speak to anyone. If they asked her something, she gave the shortest possible answer. After a week at school, they called her 'the one who doesn't speak'": ibid., 111.

92. Levine, "The Censored Sex," 305.

93. Kingery's thorough research and candid personal interview with Moix allows one to establish a curious—although decidedly unimportant for the analysis of the novel—biographical identification of Julia's passion for Eva with the real relationship between Moix and Esther Tusquets: See Kingery, "Feminist Subversions," 67–68, 238 n. 21.

94. Moix, *Julia*, 16–17, 85.

95. "A silent and sad person [who] often cried at night": ibid., 105.

96. "A murderous hate against Félix, and sometimes also against aunt Elena": ibid.

97. "[Félix] makes a possessive weapon out of love, because his meanness of spirit does not allow him to satisfy his desire for domination, and [aunt Elena] justifies her weakness and cowardice through him. . . . That's how the world goes. Learn from this": ibid., 106.

98. "It distressed her to think that someday she could feel dominated, tied down by something or someone": ibid.

99. "Miss Mabel held her head in her hands and kissed her": ibid., 134.

100. "The principal was more affectionate with her, that she would hold her in her arms, like the first day of class after Rafael's death": ibid., 135.

101. De Jean, "The Case for Pedagogical Deviation," 98.

102. "Julia had never worried about that. Love was something that happened to others, to the characters in films and novels and to people who lived around her": Moix, *Julia*, 142.

103. "You do the Latin translation for me every day, and I will allow you to be my friend": ibid., 146.

104. "The old maid's pet": ibid., 149.

105. "Fear overtook Julia; she had a premonition of a strange and mysterious vengeance. Somebody was trying to take away something that she hadn't even gotten to possess, something that she had only desired": ibid.

106. "She felt no pain, sorrow, or need to cry, only rancor against herself for having allowed herself to be defeated and for a solitude that promised to be eternal": ibid., 153.

107. Ibid., 160.

Julia's father proves to be a failed student of don Julio and of Eva, because, against his father's better judgment, he did not marry Eva. Instead, he chose a marriage of convenience that, as the novel exposes, ends as a resounding failure.

108. "As the most peaceful time of her life": ibid., 176.

109. "What do you think of that book? Or that film? [Such questions] would force Julia to think, to reason about something outside of her": ibid.

110. "I've told you I have work to do. Has something serious happened? Don't be annoying. I'll call you tomorrow. Good night": ibid., 182.

111. "Julia started to scream. Insults came out of her throat without her being able to stop them": ibid., 184.

112. "in order not to get things out of proportion and to keep appearances" and "Dad, Mom, grandmother Lucía, the church, and the immorality of bourgeois morality": ibid., 108.

113. "The following day he had lost his voice": ibid.

114. "Empty": ibid.,185.

115. "She hadn't died, but she lay on the hospital bed, blinded and crippled, with no thoughts, no memories, no desires. She didn't exist; she had suffered a great defeat, and they had banished her to *a place with no name,* unknown, away from the time and space of others": ibid., 186; emphasis added.

116. "And there she was. Just as she did every morning, Julita had returned": ibid., 189.

117. "A tormenting god, a god who claimed continuous sacrifices to calm his ancient pain": ibid., 190.

118. Wolfgang Iser, *The Act of Reading: A Theory of Aesthetic Response* (Baltimore: Johns Hopkins University Press, 1978), 182.

Janis Breckenridge

---

7   Outside the Castle Walls:
     Beyond Lesbian Counterplotting in
     Cristina Peri Rossi's *Desastres íntimos*

Despite contemporary attention afforded Latin American women's writing, not only the literary canon but also feminist theory and criticism have until recently ignored lesbian writing, refusing to acknowledge its existence. Although this situation gradually continues to improve, much work remains to be done in Latin American lesbian studies. The bibliographical and sociological work published by David William Foster has opened the way for such recently published anthologies as *¿Entiendes? Queer Readings, Hispanic Writings,* which contains five essays on lesbianism in Latin American and Latina writing, and *Sex and Sexuality in Latin America,* with three essays on lesbian presence in Latin American culture.[1] These pioneering works not only testify to the existence of homosexual literature in Latin America; they also call for its critical recognition. Nevertheless, with the current emphasis on queer theory, lesbian writing as a separate and distinct category remains both undertheorized and underanalyzed.

This general neglect of Latin American female homosexuality also surrounds the Uruguayan writer Cristina Peri Rossi, who has hinted at her lesbian sexual orientation in interviews and who consistently publishes homoerotic fiction. With the exception of Inmaculada Pertusa, Mary Gossy, and Amy Kaminsky, who have specifically analyzed the homosexual aspect of Peri Rossi's works, these texts have been studied primarily in terms of politics, gender, and eroticism while the lesbian content has invariably been overlooked. Noting that not all of Peri Rossi's poems and stories offer lesbian thematic content, Kaminsky states, "One might be a respectful and serious reader of her work without much taking into account that content.... In fact, most of the criticism of Peri Rossi's writing ... does just that."[2] Although she emphasizes nonphallic sexuality, Peri Rossi often encodes her lesbian works by employing the traditional male narrative voice while maintaining the female body as the desired object. Working within the existing narrative paradigm, Peri Rossi simultaneously deconstructs this system by virtue of being a female author. She effectively questions rigid gender positioning at the same time that she challenges the traditional narrative structure itself. As Kaminsky explains, the refusal to accept gender as absolute enables multiple readings of her work. However, I will demonstrate that a lesbian reading of Peri Rossi's corpus remains both plausible and rewarding.

Although the debate over the characteristic features of lesbian narrative continues, I find an adequately broad and applicable definition in Terry Castle's *The Apparitional Lesbian: Female Homosexuality and Modern Culture* (1993).[3] As Castle studies what she considers to be the paradigmatic lesbian novel, Sylvia Townsend's *Summer Will Show,* she reformulates the intrinsic gender bias present in the "erotic triangle."[4] This narrative pattern, analyzed by Eve Kosofsky Sedgwick in *Between Men: English Literature and Male Homosocial Desire* (1985), reflects the triangular structure inherent in patriarchal society.[5] Sedgwick maintains that, in canonical European literature, bonding between men occurs through women. Paradigmatic male–female–male relationships ensure normative (nonsexual) male bonding through insistence on woman's mediation. Departing from René Girard's triangular schematization of the European canon, Sedgwick focuses on "male homosocial desire within the structural context of triangular, heterosexual desire."[6] This triangular desire necessarily positions the female between men and posits hierarchical relations. In this way traditional narrative structure subordinates women and prevents female bonding.

By emphasizing that canonical literature facilitates male homosocial bonding while impeding possible homosexual relations, Sedgwick exposes societal and literary homophobia. Although she mentions women's marginalization in these canonical texts, she intentionally does not treat female homosexuality. Openly acknowledging that "the exclusively heterosexual perspective of the book's attention to women is seriously impoverishing," she justifies this omission by stating that lesbianism does not fit into the structure of her argument.[7] Responding only in part to Girard's challenge that "an attempt should be made to understand at least some forms of homosexuality from the standpoint of triangular desire," Sedgwick limits this study to male homosocial relationships.[8] She concludes that canonical fiction serves to uphold patriarchal social structures by testifying against male homosexuality.

It remains for Castle to postulate further that, "in the absence of male homosocial desire, lesbian desire emerges."[9] Accordingly, she affirms that the basic principle underlying lesbian narrative involves the suppression of male homosocial (though not homosexual) bonding. Defining lesbian fiction as underread and underappreciated works standing in an inverted relationship to canonical texts, she states that, "by plotting against what Eve Sedgwick has called the 'plot of male homosociality,' the archetypal lesbian fiction decanonizes, so to speak, the canonical structure of desire itself. . . . It documents a world in which men are 'between women' rather than vice versa."[10] Castle's provocative thesis proposes a "subverted" triangulation that makes female bonding possible by plotting men between women.[11] In this unconventional paradigm the repositioning of characters suppresses male bonding. The subversive lesbian presence disrupts traditional relationships and realigns narrative codes.

Castle's argument is convincing and effective until she attempts to broaden this underlying principle into a prescriptive classification for existing lesbian fiction. Castle recognizes only a mimetic context for lesbian desire. Identifying two basic plots, as premarital or postmarital homosexual relations, she delineates contrasting elements to characterize each. Creating rigid dichotomies, she defines the adolescent lesbian novel as "dysphoric" counterplotting where male homosocial desire ultimately reasserts itself. Castle contends that these texts depict "female homosexual desire as a finite phenomenon—a temporary phase in a larger pattern of heterosexual *Bildung*."[12] In other words, experimental lesbian relationships facilitate sexual development but are ultimately abandoned for the heterosexual union sanctioned by society. In contrast, Castle identifies the "euphoric" conversion novel containing a comic or utopian lesbian counterplot. Such texts imagine a new world where male bonding has no place. Eliminating male homosocial bonding entirely, this textual paradigm favors permanent homosexual relationships between female characters.

However, Castle proceeds to deconstruct her own argument. Having identified the existence of "two basic mimetic contexts in which, in realistic writing, plots of lesbian desire are most likely to flourish," she later claims that in fact lesbian fiction "masquerades" as realistic while truly exhibiting fantastic, allegorical, or utopian tendencies.[13] Further, she footnotes recognition that her categories fail to describe adequately as important a work as Radclyffe Hall's classic *A Well of Loneliness*, and she admits that the category of lesbian epic perhaps could also be considered.[14] Even with this addition Castle's view remains too narrow. Classifying only writings that directly narrate lesbian romance, she does not allow for the creativity and complexity characteristic of much lesbian fiction. As exemplified by Peri Rossi's works, many lesbian texts resist direct portrayal of their subversive content and offer innovative plots that Castle's paradigms do not foresee.

Castle's strictly defined paradigms of lesbian counterplotting fail to account for texts that encode desire for the female body in the more widely accepted terms of heterosexual desire. Male-voiced lesbian erotic novels such as Peri Rossi's *Solitario de amor* break gender and sexual categories bound in literature.[15] This technique, not unique to Peri Rossi, has received the critical attention of Lillian Faderman, whose chapter "In the Closet: The Literature of Lesbian Encoding" examines the language of reticence. Faderman asserts that the lesbian writer has often "purposely encoded her lesbian subject matter so that it is veiled to the majority of the population yet often decipherable by the reader who has knowledge of the writer's homosexuality and understands her need to hide her lesbian material."[16] Whether accomplished through deliberate gender suppression (Faderman's "bearded pronoun"), double entendres, or other narrative tricks, the widespread use of encoding points to universal homophobia that forces writers to obscure lesbian themes.

Furthermore, Castle's paradigms imagine female characters defined only through men: They are either curious adolescents who afterward choose heterosexual union or previously married women who espouse lesbian love. Limited by these heterosexual and homophobic parameters, the lesbian subject as a fluid narrative possibility remains restricted. No place exists for the postmodern lesbian subject, the "figure beyond the phallocentric categories of gender" described by Marilyn Farwell.[17]

I will now offer my reading of two lesbian short stories published in Peri Rossi's most recent collection, *Desastres íntimos*. Both "El testigo" (The witness) and "La semana más maravillosa de nuestras vidas" (The most wonderful week of our lives) showcase lesbian counterplotting.[18] Departing from Castle's notion that this subversive narrative reformulation constitutes the principle underlying women's homosexual literature, I will first demonstrate how Peri Rossi eliminates male homosocial bonding in these tales. Subverting the canonical narrative structure as defined by Girard and Sedgwick, Peri Rossi plots each story's solitary male character between women. In this way, these texts can be studied as lesbian fiction. However, I will then show how Peri Rossi goes beyond Castle's paradigms for lesbian narrative. With "El testigo," Peri Rossi constructs a disturbing allegorical tale representing the homophobic violence perpetrated against female homosexuality in both literature and society. Although clearly "postmarital," this non-utopian text cannot be classified as a euphoric tale because of the ruthless attempt to reassert heterosexual norms. Instead, the story exposes the violence and antifeminism present in both society and the traditional narrative structure. In contrast, "La semana más maravillosa de nuestras vidas" humorously relates an affair between two professional women, one lesbian and the other married. Neither a pre- nor a postmarital situation, this euphoric text refuses to subscribe to the utopian "happy ever after" ending, instead humorously depicting a short-lived homosexual liaison. Narrating women's autonomous active sexual desire rather than their traditional passive positionality as desired object, this text challenges established thematic and structural elements as it explores new possibilities in lesbian fiction.

In contrast to many of Peri Rossi's male-voiced narratives, "El testigo" does not encode lesbian desire through a heterosexual narrative framework. Rather, as the title indicates, the story uses first-person narration to depict lesbian relationships witnessed from an outside position. The anonymous adolescent male describes his experience growing up in a lesbian household. From the opening sentence, the narrator alludes to this subversive family structure, stating that "Me crié entre las amigas de mi madre."[19] Following this destruction of the traditional familial triangle (father–mother–son), a continual parade of women replaces the privileged male position. In this way, the canonical male–female–male narrative structure disappears. With the father's absence, the son remains isolated, with no possibilities for male homosocial bonding, while the mother gains the freedom necessary to initiate relationships with other women. No longer serving as mediator, she explores her (homosexual) desire.

Peri Rossi depicts the mother's eroticism from the male child's perspective. His inability to break free of societal stereotypes forces the narrative to remain trapped in conventional female casting. Despite the story's subversive lesbian content, each woman in turn represents a stereotypical image. At first the son describes the household as idyllic; women are preferred to men because they provide a tender, nurturing environment. With childlike innocence and acceptance the son gratefully states, "Me gusta que no haya otros hombres en la casa. . . . Las mujeres son mucho más dulces."[20] Thankful to have escaped the stereotypical violent father or demanding male lover, he voices appreciation for the maternal "amigas," or "friends." Although he avoids culturally loaded terms (such as "marimacha," a derogatory term that corresponds roughly to "butch") that allude to sexual orientation, the narrator nevertheless proceeds to describe both butch and femme figures. Invoking the notorious image of the mannish lesbian, the narrator recalls a woman who was both "viril" (virile) and "muy fuerte" (very strong). However, he prefers a woman to be "más bella y más inteligente."[21] These other women, especially Helena, uphold the stereotype of the helpless female who needs protection.

So as not to provoke the son's (or patriarchal society's) curiosity, lesbian desire remains intentionally silenced, hidden behind the closed bedroom door. This secrecy and dissimulation recalls the proverbial closet metaphor for homosexuality. A linguistic silence also pervades the text, for words such as "homosexual" and "lesbian" never appear. The male narrator, unwilling to legitimize these relationships, refuses to name them. By calling his mother's lovers "amigas," he attempts to deny their sexuality while emphasizing the emotional bonding between women.[22] Nevertheless, the son gradually demonstrates awareness, jealousy, and increasing hostility as he goes through puberty and sexual awakening. His interest in Helena (who significantly is the only named character in the story) provokes rivalry with the mother. No longer naive, the jealous son becomes an imaginative voyeur. Although he never directly witnesses the amorous scene, he spies on the female lovers mentally and envisions what must be occurring. Recognizing that the closed door remains permanently blocked to him (and, by extension, to all other males), he angrily exclaims, "Yo era el excluido, el rechazado, el ausente."[23] Ironically, although the adolescent male narrator of "El testigo" holds a position of power within the story's structural framework, he acknowledges his impotence. Traditionally, the (male) narrative voice claims language in order to constitute himself as an authoritative subject. However, the undeniable presence of lesbian desire forces the son to perceive and portray himself as the excluded third member of the familial triangle.

Finally, the reader witnesses the displaced male's refusal and attempted destruction of lesbianism. Violently invading the bedroom, he first attempts to control lesbian sexuality and then forcefully to impose heterosexual norms. Not content with exposing the women's naked corporeality, he insists that they perform sexually for his visual pleasure. This demand mirrors exploitative techniques used in lesbian pornography, where women come together not to service each other but to please the voyeuristic male. Positioning himself as "la tercera figura del tríptico" (the third figure in the tryptic), he tries to eradicate lesbian sexuality through brutal rape. Reducing the women to objects, the son's pleasure results from the attempted annihilation of their sexual autonomy and desire. Ironically considering himself an empowered representative of society, he then abandons the women. Significantly, it is now the son who closes the door on the lesbian couple as he asserts, "Ya soy todo un hombre.

El que faltaba en esta casa."[24] With this declaration he hopes to reestablish his status as the privileged male, and he deliberately conceals the women's disruptive presence.

This final scene's exaggerated nature, which on a textual level remains forced or unconvincing, points to the text's allegorical nature. The title "El testigo" highlights not only the narrator as witness to his mother's illicit and forbidden lesbian relationships, but also the reader's involvement as a silent and passive witness to societal and literary suppression of lesbian desire. This implication, as much as the sexual violence within the text, disturbs and shocks the reader.

Castle's paradigms fail to account for this complex text, which goes beyond narrating female homosexual romance. Lesbian in structure, having subverted canonical narrative triangulation, the story fails to present lesbian themes and is unable to depict homoeroticism. Although it presents a postmarital situation, the text cannot be classified as euphoric. Male homosocial bonding remains permanently blocked, yet the story does not relate a lesbian plot. Instead, it narrates the displaced male's attempt to eliminate female homosexuality. The tale functions antimimetically by instructing its readers through allegory. Read as a fictional continuation of Sedgwick's analytical framework, "El testigo" explores in a specifically lesbian context the upholding of homosocial bonding and the condemnation of the homosexual. The son accepts the mother's companions as "amigas," but he reacts violently when faced with their undeniable homosexuality.

In contrast to the male-voiced "El testigo," "La semana más maravillosa de nuestras vidas," which explores agency in female homosexual desire, is narrated by a lesbian subject. This lighthearted tale celebrates lesbian sexuality as it depicts a passionate but brief affair between two professional women. Frank, the single male character, is portrayed from the perspective of his wife's lesbian lover and exists as the excluded member of the narrative triangle. Thus, he is denied the structural power position given the narrator of "El testigo" and receives marginal treatment. Uncertain about Frank's perceptions and motives, the narrator portrays him ambivalently. She humorously justifies this ambiguity by confessing her limited knowledge of the opposite sex.

In giving voice to this lesbian subject, Peri Rossi realigns narrative codes. Traditionally a male and not a female prerogative, agency has been reassigned. Peri Rossi successfully realizes John Deredita's challenge that "la innovación debería tocar en especial al *sujeto* hablante y deseante."[25] In contrast to many earlier works, in this story she no longer conceals lesbian desire through ambiguity and encoding.

In addition to structural transformation, "La semana" offers thematic innovation. As the lesbian subject gives voice to her autonomous desire, the text examines lesbian identity. The narrator protests against the linguistic deficiency surrounding homosexual relationships. Explaining that she and Lucía cannot be considered married because laws and customs do not exist for such a pairing, she says: "El hecho de que no exista una palabra para nombrar esta clase de relación es la prueba de su autenticidad. Lucía y yo somos *amigas*."[26] The subversive and sarcastic reappropriation of the term "amiga" demonstrates the narrator's defiance of societal repudiation of lesbian sexuality. This cliché, as illustrated in "El testigo," insinuates that only platonic emotional bonding occurs between women. However, its ironic pronunciation by a lesbian subject converts this euphemism into a condemnation of homophobic intolerance. Further, unable to comprehend Eva's ambiguous sexuality, the narrator denies affinity between married women and lesbians. Declaring to Eva that "somos especies diferentes. Como los hombres y las mujeres," she asserts her difference and proudly affirms her lesbian identity.[27]

Unlike "El testigo," which chronicles an attempt to prohibit lesbian eroticism, "La semana" foregrounds physical attraction between women. After meeting at a gay bar, the protagonists engage in constant sexual activity. The narrator shamelessly enumerates their many variations: "de pie, en la cama, de espaldas, sobre la alfombra, contra la nevera, ella arriba, yo abajo, yo arriba, ella abajo, desnudas o con las prendas de lencería erótica."[28] Emphasizing carnality, the narrator and Eva do not value conversation or the discussion of relevant matters. Purely physical coupling substitutes for emotional bonding between these women.

Empowered by her marriage of convenience, Eva actively engages in such amorous pursuits. She explores her lesbian eroticism, freed from dominating men who seek to demarcate their power. While complaining that Eva refuses to disclose these extramarital affairs, Frank says, "No me lo diría por nada de este mundo. . . . En eso consiste su placer."[29] Silencing the details of these relationships becomes Eva's prerogative. Not forced to hide her sexual activity for security, as are the lovers in "El testigo," she consciously chooses to remain silent. Eva's power lies in her ability to manipulate the narrative triangle. She maintains a permanent heterosexual, societally sanctioned bond while playing games in the homoerotic sphere. In this way, Eva participates in canonical triangular desire even as she takes advantage of it. The narrator, unable to identify with this power play, flees from her.

Similar to their shortcomings vis-à-vis "El testigo," Castle's paradigms fail to locate "La semana." With one protagonist refusing to define herself through men and the other remaining married, neither a pre- nor a postmarital situation exists. Complicating lesbian narrative triangulation, Peri Rossi plots temporary homosexual bonding. Conversely, a permanent union exists between husband and wife, the primary and stable alliance. Although comic, this non-euphoric story resists utopian closure, depicting a failed homosexual liaison rather than a happy-ever-after situation. In this way the text seemingly favors homosociality while supporting a patriarchal society. However, the narrator's carefree attitude as she abandons her lover for her complicity in patriarchal institutions enables a lesbian reading. Unscathed, she remains faithful to her lesbian identity. Rather than feel sorry for herself, she expresses pity for the flowers, the innocent victims of this erotic game.

Thus, Peri Rossi goes beyond Castle's counterplotting and offers new possibilities in lesbian literature. While "El testigo" portrays the hostility and violence inherent in heterosexist canonical literature and the society it reflects, "La semana" joins a tradition of lesbian exile writing, from Gertrude Stein through Sylvia Molloy. These short stories reflect the historical development of lesbian fiction in general and the evolution of Peri Rossi's corpus in particular. Whereas early works veiled their lesbian content by offering indirect and often encoded accounts, recent works have become progressively more overt. Further, rather than concentrate on the hostility present in homophobic society, these narratives reflect lesbian experience and reality. Unlike "El testigo," which presents disturbing violence, "La semana" offers a gay (in every sense of the word) outlook. Peri Rossi shows that lesbian fiction must do more than merely eliminate male homosocial bonding. To be truly revolutionary, this subversive literature must go beyond simple realignment of the triangular structure by transforming both narrative voice and theme.

Notes

1. Emilie L. Bergmann and Paul Julian Smith, eds., *¿Entiendes? Queer Readings, Hispanic Writings* (Durham, N.C.: Duke University Press, 1995); Daniel Balderston and Donna Guy, eds., *Sex and Sexuality in Latin America* (New York: New York University Press, 1997).

2. Inmaculada Pertusa's article, "Revolución e identidad en los poemas lesbianos de Cristina Peri-Rossi," *Monographic Review/Revista Monográfica* 7 (1991): 115–33, foreshadows the in-depth treatment of lesbianism in her dissertation "Escribiendo entre correintes: Carme Riera, Esther Tusquets, Cristina Peri Rossi y Sylvia Molloy" (Ph.D. diss., University of Colorado, 1996). Mary Gossy's article "Not So Lonely: A Butch–Femme Reading of Cristina Peri-Rossi's Solitario de Amor," in *Bodies and Biases: Sexualities in Hispanic Cultures and Literature,* ed. David William Foster and Roberto Reis (Minneapolis: University of Minnesota Press, 1996), identifies the male-voiced narrator as lacking an anatomical penis while possessing the lesbian phallus. Amy Kaminsky's chapter "Cristina Peri-Rossi and the Question of Lesbian Presence," in *Reading the Body Politic: Feminist Criticism and Latin American Women Writers* (Minneapolis: University of Minneapolis Press, 1993), looks at the intersection of politics, gender, and sexuality in Peri Rossi's works.

3. Terry Castle, *The Apparitional Lesbian: Female Homosexuality and Modern Culture* (New York: Columbia Press, 1993).

4. Sylvia Townsend, *Summer Will Show* (1936; repr., New York: Viking, 1987).

5. Eve Kosofsky Sedgwick, *Between Men: English Literature and Male Homosocial Desire* (New York: Columbia University Press, 1985).

6. Ibid., 16.

7. Ibid., 18.

8. René Girard, *Deceit, Desire, and the Novel: Self and Other in Literary Structure* (Baltimore: Johns Hopkins University Press, 1965), 47. In later works, such as *Epistemology of the Closet* (Berkeley: University of California Press, 1990), Sedgwick extends her analysis to include male homosexual relationships.

9. Castle, *Apparitional Lesbian,* 85.

10. Ibid., 90.

11. Interestingly, this series of theoretical propositions parallels Castle's notion of the elimination of male bonding within literature itself. Castle's reworking of Sedgwick, itself a reformulation of Girard's classic study of triangular desire, forms a subverted triangulation of theoretical frameworks, which in turn allows a general theory of lesbian narrative to emerge.

12. Castle, *Apparitional Lesbian,* 85.

13. Ibid.

14. Radclyffe Hall, *A Well of Loneliness* (London: Virago, 1928; repr. New York: Anchor, 1990).

15. Peri Rossi, *Solitario de amor* (Barcelona: Seix Barral, 1998). This technique also appears in Peri Rossi's homoerotic poetry, such as *Evohé: Poemas Eróticos* (Montevideo: Girón Editorial, 1968).

16. Lillian Faderman, ed., *Chloe plus Olivia: An Anthology of Lesbian Literature from the Seventeenth Century to the Present* (New York: Penguin Books, 1994), 444–45.

17. Marilyn Farwell, *Heterosexual Plots and Lesbian Narratives* (New York: New York University Press, 1996), 64.

18. "El testigo" first appeared in *Cuentos eróticos* (Barcelona: Ediciones Grijalbo, 1988). In this chapter, I quote from the versions of "El testigo" and "La semana más maravillosa de nuestras vidas" in Cristina Peri Rossi, *Desastres íntimos* (Barcelona: Editorial Lumen, 1997). The translations are mine, as *Desastres íntimos* has yet to be translated into English.

19. "I grew up among my mother's female friends": Peri Rossi, "El testigo," 59.

20. "I'm glad that there are no men in the house. . . . Women are much sweeter": ibid., 59–60.

21. "Prettier and more intelligent": ibid., 61.

22. In this way the male narrator follows in the footsteps of the theorists Audre Lorde and Lillian Faderman, for whom the concept of lesbian does not necessarily imply erotic involvement.

23. "I was the one excluded, rejected, absent": Peri Rossi, "El testigo," 65.

24. "Now I am a real man. The one that was missing from this house": ibid., 70.

25. "Innovation should especially touch upon the speaking and desiring *subject*": John F. Deredita, "Desde la diáspora: entrevista con Cristina Peri-Rossi," *Texto crítico año* 4, no. 9 (1978): 138. The translation is mine.

26. "The fact that no word exists to name this type of relationship is proof of its genuineness. Lucía and I are *friends*": Peri Rossi, "La semana," 78.

27. "We are different species. Like men and women": ibid., 79.

28. "Standing up, in bed, back to back, on the rug, against the refrigerator, she on top, me underneath, me on top, her underneath, naked or in erotic lingerie": ibid., 73.

29. "She wouldn't tell me about it for anything. . . . Her pleasure consists in exactly this": ibid., 98.

Regina M. Buccola

---

8   "He Made Me a Hole!"
Gender Bending, Sexual Desire,
and the Representation
of Sexual Violence

Feminist theories of dramatic criticism have been mushrooming since the early 1980s. One of the issues that tends to recur in such critical analyses is a concern with the representation of female sexuality. Drawing on the film theory of critics such as Teresa de Lauretis and Laura Mulvey, who posit a normative spectator/subject position gendered male, a number of critics question the possibility of successfully depicting female sexuality on the stage in a manner that does not simply reify oppressive notions of women as sexual objects (of the male gaze).[1] Positing the theater as a sort of feminist workshop where possible approaches to addressing or actively combating gender oppression can be experimented with, Jill Dolan contends, "The theatre, in its peculiar position as the mirrored stage, reflective of 'real life' while not *being* real life, is an appropriate place for feminists to continue this ideological investigation."[2] On a related note, many feminist theorists—including Cheryl Clarke, Jeanie Forte and Dolan herself—have posited the homosexual subject position as a viable place from which to explore sexual desire unfettered from the binaries of dominance and submission, voyeur and object of the gaze, male and female.

Echoing feminist film theorists, Dolan continues her discussion of the theater as the mirrored stage by positing that "the theatrical mirror is really an empty frame. The images reflected in it have been consciously constructed according to political necessity, with a particular, perceiving subject in mind who looks into the mirror for *his* identity."[3] Posing questions that will be critical for this analysis, Dolan concludes her article by returning to the fact that men are invited to identify with the image in the mirror. To complete the identification process, they must perceive women as the objects of their desire. Can men extricate themselves from this process to look clearly at sexual difference? Might they be willing to give up their privileged subjectivity, to consider women's desire, or lesbians, as the subject of representation?[4]

I would push these questions further still. Given the highly persuasive arguments that de Lauretis and Mulvey, among others, have made about the way in which both men and women are socialized to perceive women as the objects of male desire, can women extricate themselves from this process to look clearly at their own sexuality? What sort of representational strategies does it take to empower women to break out of their socially constructed roles as sex objects to consider their own sexuality as the subject of representation?

Sue-Ellen Case quite rightly points out that most of the feminist work on the issue of representational subject positionality "has only revealed the way in which the subject is trapped within ideology and thus provides no programs for change."[5] Case goes on to provide just such a program, which hinges—as most attempts to address women as desiring subjects do—on the representation of lesbian sexuality.[6] Case labels the lesbian roles of butch and femme a "dynamic duo" that, in her view, offers "precisely the strong subject position the movement requires."[7] A number of feminist theorists followed Case's lead in the 1990s, answering her call to clarify the nature of this dynamic duo, "particularly in relation to the historical and racial relations embedded in such a project."[8]

Lesbian feminist theory has undergone a series of sea changes in the past three decades. Initially construed in the '60s as an alternative to heterosexuality and its corollary, patriarchal oppression, by the 1970s even the logic of the lesbian couple had roused the ire of egalitarian-minded feminists who contended that the butch–femme dyad simply aped the dichotomous—and hierarchical—male–female heterosexual couple. Suppressing the complex realities of lesbian sexual desire, feminist theorists focused on a streamlined form of female identification sanitized of its politically incorrect sexual habits and urges. At the same time, white feminist theorists made common cause with oppressed women of color, which had the unintended result of collapsing the oppression women face under patriarchy with the oppression racial and ethnic minorities experience in a white-dominant world. By the late 1980s this tide, too, had turned, and the '90s ushered in a meticulous process of dismantling feminist theory qua monolith that had produced a proliferation of feminisms grounded in the particularities of identity, including gender, race, class, sexual preference, and age.

In this chapter, I test the practical application of feminist theories about the potential for female empowerment in the theatrical representation of sexual violence and lesbian sexual desire. I do this via an analysis of Cherríe Moraga's play *Giving Up the Ghost*, a particularly rich text for such a purpose because of its complex exploration of the trauma of sexual abuse and its attempt to model a woman's psychological transition from perhaps the single most objectified position she could occupy (rape victim) to empowered sexual subject.[9] Originally performed in 1989, Moraga's play forecast many of the ideological battles fought within feminism's various camps during the 1990s, grappling in painfully honest, and therefore not necessarily comforting, ways with nonnormative sexual desire, sexual violence, and the sometimes volatile compound of sexual and ethnic identity.[10]

Case is sensitive to the fact that many feminists resist the inscription of their ideas in the academic tablet labeled "theory" because it seems too detached from feminist activism. There is a substantial positive, practical element to Case's theorizing: Rather than simply criticizing the dominant sociopolitical and cultural modes, she suggests alternatives to them. She consistently comes down on the side of change, articulating specifically what she is *for* rather than merely what she is *against*. Drawing on Aristotle's *Poetics* as the cornerstone of traditional theater (which Case describes as male-centered and oppressive to women in many of the same ways that Mulvey, de Lauretis, and others have demonstrated traditional film narratives to be), Case calls for a " 'new poetics' that would accommodate the presence of women in the art, support their liberation from the cultural fictions of the female gender and deconstruct the valorisation [*sic*] of the male gender."[11] If the goal is to make women subjects rather than objects of cultural production in the context of theatrical representation, Case asks, "doesn't this cultural revolution necessitate a new form and perhaps even a new discourse for women?"[12]

I would respond with a resounding yes. Like Case, I am interested not merely in crying foul—pointing out potential problems in the representation of female sexuality—but in positing ways of both representing women as desiring subjects and, more specifically, creating a safe space within which to articulate the experience of sexual abuse. Because this is a key issue for women attempting to reclaim their potency as sexual, desiring subjects, how is it to be addressed in the context of feminist theater? Given the fact that many pornographic materials rely on depictions of violent sexual acts (rape, bondage, mutilation, torture), how is one to depict incidents of sexual violence without reinscribing the very objectification of women set in motion by the abusive act itself?

In 1988, Catharine MacKinnon and Andrea Dworkin drafted a model ordinance, "making pornography actionable as a civil rights violation, [which] defines 'pornography' as 'the graphic sexually explicit subordination of women through pictures and/or words.'"[13] The ordinance provides a list of problematic representations of women and sexual acts, including visual depictions and verbal descriptions (oral and written) of women " 'presented as sexual objects tied up or cut up or mutilated or bruised or physically hurt.'"[14] One of the problems with this definition is that any attempt on the part of women to describe sexual abuse that they have suffered (for the purposes of expunging the experience or seeking self-healing, for instance) could—perversely—be rejected or censured as pornographic exploitation. As Dolan puts it, "If power adheres in sexuality, and cultural feminists assume power leads to violence against women, it becomes politically and artistically necessary to attempt to disengage representation from desire."[15] However, given that sexual desire inheres in human identity—indeed, it serves to define the politico-sexual identity of the lesbian—such a schism in the representation of women as active occupants of the subject position hardly seems politically or artistically viable.

Sizing up lesbian feminists' attempts to reclaim desire outside of the power dynamics of heteronormativity, Cherry Smyth observes:

> Queer politics have also redefined the construction of the gaze. One of the most significant aspects of queer is address. It is not telling the straights how we live and love to gain their acceptance, as the campaign for positive images attempted in the 1980s, but speaking to ourselves with our own self-referential humour and irony, regardless of whether they "get it" or not. It is not coming out to them, but on to ourselves.[16]

Lesbian desire gazes with a difference. Only by repeatedly staging images that reveal its lusts and its fears, its pleasures and its pains, and showing the kaleidoscopic ways in which those images can be received and interpreted, will ground be gained in breaking free of a default gaze that is male, straight, and white.

Moraga's *Giving Up the Ghost* is a good case study for these theoretical concerns because it is a play that involves most of the issues taken up by the feminist dramatic critics and theoreticians discussed thus far: lesbian sexuality, sexual abuse, and oppression or vicitimization of women by other women. I intend to focus in particular on how Moraga's depiction of sexual violence against women intersects both with the play's representation of lesbian sexual desire and with its visceral recreation of heterosexual violence. This intersection problematizes the representation of female sexuality and, ultimately, lesbianism itself. Moraga's powerful and relentlessly realistic play reveals some of the flaws in the logic that equates lesbian sexuality with liberatory sexuality. The surrender implied in the play's titular phrase "giving up" is not borne out by the central character's struggle toward psychological and sexual wholeness or by the unflagging efforts of Moraga herself to negotiate the white heterosexual patriarchy as a butch Chicana lesbian.[17] Oppression—of her cultural and sexual identity—is the ghost that is left behind.

Giving Up the Ghost is a nonlinear series of monologues (the characters rarely interact, although they are supposed to make it clear to the audience that they hear one another) by three characters: Marisa, a twenty-something-year-old Chicana lesbian; Corky, Marisa's younger self; and Amalia, a heterosexual Chicana in her late forties. Corky takes on a wide variety of roles as both the subject and object of sexual desire over the course of the play (*cholo*, lesbian, rapist, rape victim, *chingón*, etc.). The depictions of these various roles are the representational moments in the play's narrative that most directly complicate its representation of female sexuality. As it stands in its most recently published form, Moraga's text poses problems with its representation of female sexuality, leaving the door open for an array of potentially problematic interpretations or responses, including the assumption of heterosexual desire and physical interaction as implicitly or even necessarily oppressive, and the depiction of destructive heterosexist-based role-playing within lesbian relationships.[18] However, these potentially negative representations co-exist with feminist theatrical strategies aimed at circumventing the possibility that the characters will be viewed from the perspective of the male gaze.

One of the strategies Moraga employs in *Giving Up the Ghost* that disrupts the adoption of a standard spectator position with respect to the play's action is the complete destruction of linear temporality with respect to the events described. Although the key events are all clearly in the past, they are described largely out of chronological sequence (a strategy aided and abetted by the fact that two of the three characters on stage are the same person at different ages). Yet one can piece together their chronological "reality," and this sometimes has important implications for the representation of the characters' sexuality, particularly Corky/Marisa's. For instance, Moraga makes it abundantly clear that Corky was an active lesbian prior to her sexual assault by a school custodian. This removes the possibility of a hegemonically comfortable interpretation of her lesbianism as a response to sexual abuse—a "she was driven to it" dismissal of the possibility that lesbian sexuality is a free choice or natural desire.

The monologue in which Corky discusses her awakening to lesbianism via sexual play with her older cousin Norma serves as the prelude to her description of her rape. She begins by explaining that she was at school after hours in the first place "trying to be helpful 'n' all to the nuns / I guess cuz my cousin Norma got straight A's / 'n' was taking me into her bed by then / so I figured ... that was the way to go."[19] So, Corky is in a position to be raped in the first place because she is trying to impress her cousin, the academic overachiever, with academic involvements of her own in the interest of preserving their sexual relationship. Corky goes on to add—*before* describing the rape—"anyway Norma was the only one I ever tole / about the janitor doing it to me / 'n' then she took it away for good."[20] So, Corky's attempt to turn to another woman for comfort after her sexual assault is met with a rebuff that is directly connected to her sexual identity; she is "punished" by the removal of the positive sexual relationship in her life. Thus, Corky's rape narrative is preceded by an account of her subsequent rejection as "damaged goods."

The stage directions in the most recent edition of *Giving Up the Ghost* make it clear that the actor portraying Corky should not only describe the rape scene in very explicit terms but also demonstrate—act out—what happened. One stage direction, for instance, reads, "She stands with her legs apart, her pelvis pressed up against the edge of the 'desk.'"[21] The janitor tells Corky in Spanish (though she notes "somet'ing was funny / his Spanish I couldn't quite make it out"[22]) that he wants her to hold together a broken drawer so he can fix it. Ironically, he breaks *her* on the strength of this ruse.

Corky describes the way he "sits behind me on the floor / 'n' reaches his arm up between my legs."[23] In a disarming conflation of this instance of sexual violation and her prior, positive sexual interaction with Norma, Corky describes "this guy's arm up between my legs / 'n' then it begins to kina brush past the inside of my thigh ... the skin is so soft I hafta admit / young kina like a girl's like Norma's shoulder."[24] In addition to this disturbing linguistic conflation of her lesbian lover and her rapist, the stage direction further indicates that these lines are to be delivered "almost tenderly."[25] In a culture that dismisses the reality of the sexual exploitation of women by claiming that they "want" it, such a representation of sexual violence by the victim dances dangerously close to reifying such oppressive, misogynistic views. However, this is part and parcel of the painful honesty in Moraga's writing, both here and in her autobiographical and theoretical works. Corky is young and does not know that she cannot trust this man, this adult member of her school, the place where she is accustomed to following the orders given to her in an effort to impress Norma. Because her only sexual experiences have been with Norma, her analogy of the flesh on the janitor's groping arm to that of Norma's shoulder serves as one of her only clues that his intentions with her are explicitly sexual.

The rapist first probes Corky's genitals with a screwdriver, and she recalls her mounting confusion and fear: "The arm was so soft but this other thing . . . "[26] Speaking in English now, "His accent gone,"[27] the janitor orders Corky to lie down, and she is "relieved when I hear the metal drop to the floor . . . 'n' I open my legs wide open / for the angry animal that springs outta the opening in his pants."[28] Corky had earlier conceptualized girls as animals; she now transfers this image to the male genital. Her own genitals become "a face with no features / no eyes no nose no mouth," but that are "supposed to be a mouth."[29] The spectator watches here as Corky describes her descent from her earlier identification with the dominant male position and its attendant capacity to perceive woman as other—as animal—to a recognition of the disempowered gender-role realities to which her own body betrays her. Corky ends her rape narrative by crying, "He made me a hole!"[30]

Corky, who up to this point in the play has characterized herself as the knife-toting *cholo*—a "stone butch" in lesbian parlance—has been forced into the biology, emotionality, and violability of the femininity she has shunned and to which she has considered herself superior. Addressing the femme lesbian Amber Hollibaugh in a published conversation, Moraga reveals that, from her perspective, "To be butch, to me, is not to be a woman. . . . She doesn't want to feel her femaleness because she thinks of you as the 'real' woman and if she makes love to *you,* she doesn't have to feel her own body as the object of desire."[31] The ellipsis covers only a sentence in which Moraga sets up the butch–femme dynamic; it is intriguing that even here she elides herself from the sexual equation. She begins speaking of her own experience as a butch, but then switches to the butch universal while continuing to address the specific femme with whom she is talking, "you," Amber.

Ruminating on the butch experience, Ann Cvetkovich speculates:

> To what extent does the stone or untouchable butch who resists being touched, also resist being made to feel, in part because feeling is associated with vulnerability and femininity? Emotional untouchability can be the public side of sexual untouchability when the butch lesbian's (female) masculinity depends on and is defined by her refusal to be made emotionally vulnerable or to display feeling publicly or openly.[32]

In essence, then, Corky's rapist messes with her sense of both her gendered (*cholo* versus girl) and her desiring self. She resists and rejects vaginal penetration, describing how Norma would show her "how wide and deep like a cueva hers got . . . only with me she said"[33] as opposed to her own genitalia marked only by "little lines"[34] where the caverns and fissures of Norma's sexually responsive body were. Corky's rapist violates the taut smoothness of her virgin genitals and her *cholo* denial of those biological gender markers.[35]

Discussing the myth of La Malinche, which figures so prominently in *Loving in the War Years* and which provides a cultural context for Corky's visceral, negative characterization of her female sexuality, Nancy Saporta Sternbach says that La Malinche is "the mythical, even metaphorical mother, her flesh serving as a symbol of the Conquest, the rape of Mexico"[36] As in the Malinche myth, Corky's rapist takes her self-confidence, which she perceives to be linked to her masculinized identity as the impenetrable *cholo*, making her into a subjugatable woman by making her "a hole." This term creates a negative image of heterosexuality and re-inscribes the notion of woman as *chingada*, the locus of passivity, violability. One can read Corky's cry, "He made me a hole!" in the sense that he *gave me* a hole or in the sense that he *turned me into* a hole. Both readings suggest a disempowering notion of female sexuality and woman in general as void, as endlessly violable space.

Yvonne Yarbro-Bejarano suggests that the play "explores the ways in which Chicanas' sexuality—both lesbian and heterosexual—has been distorted and repressed. . . . The quote and dedication at the beginning of the play introduce central images of imprisonment and longing for freedom: sex as a prison and women who hold out the possibility of release."[37] Such a woman-centered understanding of liberatory sexuality still leaves heterosexual women high and dry, though, because it is *women* who hold out the possibility of release. This is a common position in feminist theory. A succinct articulation of the basic stance is provided by Cheryl Clarke, who speaks of the "life of servitude implicit in Western, heterosexual relationships."[38] Doesn't this, however, constitute the abandonment of heterosexual women?

Many critics point to the representation of lesbian desire as a means of disrupting the spectatorial assumption of the male gaze by depicting women as "the bearer of the look" and as seeking the desiring gaze of one another.[39] Although this is a viable way to subvert the spectatorial status quo, are the only empowering options for feminist theatrical representations lesbianism and celibacy? As a heterosexual feminist, I feel compelled to say no, lest I be left to accept the impossibility of empowering representations of my sexual identity. Representations of even lesbian sexuality that are ultimately destructive or disempowering for at least one of the parties involved because of the way in which the depicted relationships mimic hierarchical heterosexual relations make it even less acceptable to use lesbian sexuality as the default representational strategy for women's sexual empowerment. *Giving Up the Ghost* makes it all too clear that women are capable of hurting each other in sexual situations, too.

Early in the play, the Corky character describes a truly disturbing instance of "pretend" play with her male pal, Arturo (Tury). Revealing the origins of her *cholo* stance, Corky proudly reports that, though "in reality" she was "little . . . and a girl," in her mind she was "big 'n' tough 'n' a dude."[40] One of her and Tury's favorite Saturday pastimes was to "make up our own movies . . . we'd capture these chicks 'n' hold 'em up for ransom / we'd string 'em up 'n' make 'em take their clothes off / 'strip' we'd say."[41] As Yarbro-Bejarano points out:

Corky identifies with the males in her culture . . . her appropriation of the subject role as well as her attraction to women are inscribed within the gender roles assigned in Chicano culture and the culture at large. Her attraction to women is played out in contexts of violence and dominance.... She relates the excitement to the movies she loves.... She sees the freedom of the "dude" she identifies with as the freedom to see women as Other.[42]

Or, as Corky puts it, she acquires the male freedom "to see a girl kina / the way you see / an animal."[43] Such an understanding of "girls" suggests not only difference but also a hierarchical relationship: Men are superior to women as humans are superior to animals.

Corky goes on to describe a time that she and Tury "stripped for real."[44] This introduction sets the spectator up to expect a sexual scene between the two of them; however, that is not what happens. Instead, Corky describes her complicity in the abuse of a three-year-old neighbor girl, Chrissy. Tury suggests this new twist in their role-playing and, although Corky "wasn't that hot on the idea,"[45] she still goes along with him. In a descriptive image that resonates with her earlier characterization of girls as animals, Corky says that they roamed the neighborhood, "looking for prey." Corky calls Chrissy into a shed in a "real syrupy-like" voice; holding her hand, Corky tells the child "we think she's got somet'ing wrong with her / 'down there.'" Corky is the one who pulls down "her little shorts . . . 'n' then her chones." Then Tury "sticks" his fingers on the child's genitals. The child looks to Corky for confirmation that this is okay, "like I was her mom or some'ting." Suddenly struck by the overwhelming ramifications of what they are doing, Corky stops Tury and tells Chrissy, "You're fine really there's nut'ing wrong with you."[46]

This scene is extremely unpleasant, but it is also an example of Moraga's unflinching realism. Children—regardless of ethnic background, class status, and sexual preference—do, in fact, engage in sexualized play, trying on the various sexual roles that appeal to them. Thus, this portrayal of Corky as a quasi-rapist herself is not "antifeminist" on Moraga's part, but realistic.[47] The truth in this dramatic moment gives the lie to any glib notion of women's identification and consequent interactions as guarantors of sexual security. Sexual ethics reside not in preferences or desires, but in the control exerted over those impulses. Sexuality and its politics are messy businesses, and Moraga is not content to depict them in anything less than the full splendor of their complexity.

Yarbro-Bejarano asserts that "the absence of male characters in the play avoids the representation of women as objects of male desire and focuses on the desire of female subjects."[48] This is a really easy out—much too easy, as a matter of fact, given incidents such as the one with Chrissy and Corky's complete identification with the dominant, male sexual subject position. Clearly, if one accepts the argument that even women are socialized to gaze from the male perspective—to find the same things desirable that men find desirable, as Corky clearly does—the mere absence of a literal man on the stage would not by any means completely eradicate the possible objectification of the female characters in the play.

Even assuming an all-female audience,[49] what about the fact that males (Corky's friend Tury, Amalia's old lover in Mexico) are invoked in the play? What about the fact that Corky herself both takes on the male *cholo* persona and subjects a young girl to sexual abuse in "pretend" play modeled on scenes from her favorite Western films, which certainly objectify women?[50] Corky is a lesbian who chooses to identify with the dominant male as a desiring subject. She further takes on the belligerent stance of a *cholo*, which, Yarbro-Bejarano notes, "stands as a sub-culture in oppositional relationship to both the Chicano and the dominant culture. It represents a stance of resistance to cultural assimilation and the social, racial, and economic discrimination of the dominant culture as well as rebellion against the traditional values of the Mexican culture of the youths' parents."[51] In other words, Corky engages in multilevel rebellion against both her familial culture and the larger oppressive culture within which that culture has been circumscribed.

This sounds impressively empowering, yet even as Corky resists two of the forces that act to define her, to prescribe her sociocultural role, she also adopts (in taking the *cholo* stance) identification with the *chingón*, the masculine. This seems a somewhat understandable or even natural response in an impressionable young woman attracted to women with no cultural representations of such a dynamic other than the heterosexual ones—especially given the argument developed by de Lauretis, Mulvey, and others that, regardless of sexual orientation, both men and women are socialized to see women as sexual objects. However, it leads Corky to adopt many of the misogynistic characteristics of that macho subject position.[52]

Moraga explores and challenges the assumptions that inhere in theorizations of lesbianism, maternity, and sorority as models for equitable interaction. Taking issue with the elision of female sexual desire that frequently occurs in such theoretical idealizations of woman-identified woman, de Lauretis helpfully catalogs the traits such female sociality—stripped of its sexuality—is supposed to possess: "sisterly or woman-identified mutual support, antihierarchical and egalitarian relationships, an ethic of compassion and connection, an ease with intragender affectionate behavior and emotional sharing, a propensity for mutual identification, and so forth."[53] Moraga writes freely about the ways in which she, personally, fails to fit this mold and with equal frankness paints Corky in broad strokes as a woman-identified woman who must fight to suppress urges to dominate and abuse.

As Moraga and Hollibaugh reflect in the introduction to a published conversation about "sexual silences in feminism": "Heterosexuality is both an actual sexual interaction *and* a system. No matter how we play ourselves out sexually, we are all affected by the system inasmuch as our sexual values are filtered through a society where heterosexuality is considered the norm."[54] Later in the introduction, Moraga and Hollibaugh point out that even heterosexuality can exist independent of heterosexism.[55] Corky is a very real, and therefore ethically imperfect, lesbian who has been infected by heterosexism even though she has resisted heterosexuality. With the support of her compassionate, supportive lover, Amalia, she is beginning to sort out the distinctions among these sexual subjectivities by the play's final scenes.

Yarbro-Bejarano notes, "Up to the time of the rape, Corky had thought it could never happen to her because she had denied her femaleness, rejecting the role of chingada and identifying with the chingón, the active, aggressive, closed person who inflicts the wound. The rape brings home Corky's sex to her as an inescapable fact, confirming her culture's definition of female being as taken."[56] Because it is the nature of spectatorial socialization to identify with the *chingón*—the aggressor—rather than the victim, this representation of Corky's sexuality reinscribes the very oppressive social constructions of female sexuality to which she originally stands in opposition.[57]

Barbara Freedman suggests that theater is a deconstructive space that, by its very nature, is capable of disrupting the placidity of the male-defined gaze. In a passage that resonates with Moraga's text on many levels, Freedman writes:

> Theatre tells the story of a rape which has always already occurred, thereby involving us in a series of gazes which splits and displaces our own. . . . Theatre calls the spectatorial gaze into play by exhibiting a purloined gaze, a gaze that announces it has always been presented to our eyes; is designed only to be taken up by them. The spectatorial gaze takes the bait and stakes its claim to a resting place in the field of vision which beckons it—only to have its gaze fractured, its look stared down by a series of gazes which challenge the place of its look and expose it as in turn defined by the other. . . . Theatre has no allegiance but to ambivalence, to a compulsion to subvert its own gaze, to split itself through a reflected image.[58]

The virtual play-within-a-play in which Corky narrates the story of her rape while her older self watches from the same stage is a species of the subversion of the gaze that Freedman describes. This already fractured, reflected self—Corky and Marisa— further splits and reflects the rape narrative by recounting it in an almost tag-team fashion.

Marisa begins by announcing, "Got raped once. When I was a kid. Took me a long time to say that was exactly what happened. . . . I guess I never wanted to believe I was raped."[59] Yet the younger, on-stage reflection of Marisa in the person of Corky immediately undercuts this statement of fact by proceeding to both describe and physically represent the rape act. Corky is Marisa's younger self, and she does acknowledge what happened to her. The audience, however, is offered a sort of comfort even in the midst of Corky's relentless description of her rape by virtue of the fact that her older self, Marisa, is present and safe. Moraga actively suggests the possibility of comfort even at this heightened moment by directing that Marisa approach Corky, wrap a rebozo around her shoulders, and hold her younger self.[60]

Moraga's example of the way in which Freedman's suggestions for calling the male gaze into play might be staged make the utility and feasibility of Freedman's ideas clear to me in provocative ways.[61] I can also see in them a way to achieve Dolan's objective of smashing the mirror that is held up for the spectatorial gaze. The fracturing of the subject position described earlier occurs on a number of levels in Moraga's play. Corky/Marisa is literally a split subject: Two different actors on the stage portray the same person at different stages of development. Further, Corky herself is a twice-split subject. The stage directions indicate that Corky is Marisa's teenage self, but she portrays two different versions of that self—prepubescent and adolescent.

Yarbro-Bejarano notes that she is supposed to be twelve in the first act and seventeen in the second.[62] Corky provides Marisa's background: She describes both her awakening to lesbian sexuality and both instances of her past sexual abuse. These descriptions of sexual violence constitute another splitting of subjectivity, as Corky is the aggressor in one instance and the victim in the other.

With respect to the play, Yarbro-Bejarano concludes that "the relationship with the audience, designated 'the people' and included in the cast of characters, extends the promise of community. . . . If the play is performed to an all-women audience . . . the spectators participate in the ritual of painful self-revelation and healing self-discovery in and for a community of women."[63] And what if the play is not performed before an all-women audience? Is it possible that Corky's painful revelations will be reconfigured as pornographic? If one does suppose an all-women audience, might her visceral descriptions of sexual abuse be perceived as pornographic even by women in the audience who have been socialized on sadomasochistic sexual stimulation even in mainstream media (for instance, in Calvin Klein cologne and Victoria's Secret lingerie ads)? And what of lesbian audience members who are drawn erotically to sadomasochistic rituals? Is it not possible that Corky's representation of her rape as the annihilation of her self-assured subjectivity into "a hole" will further oppress female spectators who perhaps have been similarly abused? Jeanie Forte poses the further general questions: "Learning that female spectators are in fact in the audience, can we assume that feminism, or even a readiness for feminism, is a condition of their consciousness? . . . What performative measures are necessary to awaken that consciousness in political terms?"[64]

Writing specifically about television and film, Annette Kuhn distinguishes between a spectator and an audience member. In her formulation, it is the social act of going to the cinema or tuning the television to a program that people are watching simultaneously across the nation (or, I might add, entering a theater) that makes those individuals audience members. She claims that these audience members become spectators "in the moment they engage in the processes and pleasures of meaning-making attendant on watching a film or TV programme."[65] Kuhn points here to a key shift that needs to take place in the mentality of the audience members to awaken political consciousness. Clearly, there is no reasonable way to determine whether the people attending a production are there to absorb it passively or intellectually engage with it. Therefore, actively encouraging the audience members to engage with a production in such a way that they become spectators is the responsibility of those who mount the production.

Yarbro-Bejarno's comments about "community" and the potential for group healing along with self-discovery through a theatrical experience suggest the possibility for an interactive, empowering approach to theater that could bring about such a shift in the level of the audience's engagement.[66] In figuring the audience and actors as a community, eliding the traditional conception of those normative roles within the space of theatrical performance, Yarbro-Bejarano opens the door to a different kind of theatrical experience that may well crack the mirror, shatter the hegemonic white, heterosexual, male spectator frame. The key to a feminist, woman-empowering representation may lie not in the representation itself, but in the relationship between those staging that representation and those viewing it.[67] Spectators who are not allowed to remain passive—not allowed simply to "gaze" but are asked to take part in the performance in some way that requires that they think critically about what they are seeing and what its implications are for them, their lives, their relationships—are likely to leave the performance with an altered consciousness of the issues taken up. They are certainly more likely to think about what they are experiencing at the time of the theater event if they are being called on to play some role in it, and are likely to have a new set of associations with and responses to the issues the performance addresses when they encounter them later, in "real life."

For example, Natalie Schmitt describes a performance that seems to me to suggest a way to secure a more proactive response to the representation of women vicitimized by sexual abuse than the standard spectator–performer dichotomy that is constantly haunted by the potential for the male gaze. The At the Foot of the Mountain women's collective once put on a production in which "the group requested audience members to stop the performance whenever it elicited a recollection of having been raped and to narrate that experience."[68] *Giving Up the Ghost* was developed through the Broadcloth Series hosted by At the Foot of the Mountain Theatre in Minneapolis. So there is already a connection between that theater's experimental approach and Moraga's play. However, even this approach could prove traumatic for people who are not prepared psychologically to acknowledge openly and discuss a rape experience. Further, not all audience members would have had such an experience.

Another strategy was effectively employed in Kathleen Ross's play *Rational Malaise*, staged in Chicago in 1994. The play consisted of a series of disconnected short pieces, including a lengthy monologue titled "Lip Bomb" that featured a lone female character trying to trace the origin of "the momentum of a nameless fear having its way with me."[69] She addresses the audience directly throughout while simultaneously frankly confessing a borderline misanthropic fear of people and of being seen by them. By default, then, the audience is identified with her and her experience because she would not be addressing them if they were "people" external to herself. Although she reveals a number of disturbing things about herself and her life (including suicidal depression), she never goes to the heart of the matter, never identifies the source of the depression and the terror and the death drive. However, the play concludes with a car alarm relentlessly going off outside her open window, delivering various mechanized warnings about violating the "perimeter" and then the "security" of the vehicle and culminating in the hysterically repeated announcement "I'VE BEEN TAMPERED WITH"[70]—a locution no car alarm would ever deliver but that a raped woman well might. No rape scene is ever seen or described, yet the audience is still drawn into sympathetic identification with this deeply troubled woman and then brought to the discovery of its basis in sexual assault without ever having to witness its literal reenactment.

I think the development of a communal theatrical experience that directly engages the spectator is the direction to take to recuperate a secure female subjectivity in which to speak many aspects of women's experience, including sexual violence. Like Dolan, I am not satisfied with an approach like MacKinnon and Dworkin's, which posits that issues of sexual violence cannot be represented effectively without rein-scribing the original oppression or subjugation of women. But neither am I convinced that any of the standard theories of representation governing theatrical performance are completely compatible with the kinds of issues a play such as *Ghost* takes up. I think interactive performative strategies such as those discussed earlier, in tandem with the strategies of fracturing the subject positions and disrupting the linear pro-gression of the narrative that Moraga employs, however, might be a way to secure a more powerful subject positionality for female characters and audience members alike. The proof lies in future productions and critical responses to them: It is only by repeatedly testing theory against experience—be it lived or theatrical—that we can arrive at a truly empowered position regarding women's sexual selves in all of their various manifestations.

Notes

1. See particularly Teresa de Lauretis, "Desire and Narrative," in *Alice Doesn't: Feminism, Semiotics, Cinema* (Bloomington: Indiana University Press, 1981); Laura Mulvey, "Visual Plea-sure and Narrative Cinema," *Screen* 16, no. 3 (Fall 1975). Interestingly, Mulvey seems to deny the applicability of her theories of "the look" to drama in "Afterthoughts on 'Visual Pleasure," *Framework* 15–17 (1981): 12–15. Mulvey says that the earlier article was focused on "a desire to identify a pleasure that was *specific to cinema,* that is the eroticism and cultural conventions sur-rounding the look": Mulvey, "Afterthoughts," 15; emphasis added. Feminist drama critics including Jill Dolan, Sue-Ellen Case, and Gayle Austin all precede me, however, in locating this same pleasure in theatrical representations, as well.

For related theories, see, for instance, Gayle Austin, *Feminist Theories for Dramatic Criticism* (Ann Arbor: University of Michigan Press, 1990); Sue-Ellen Case and Jeanie Forte, "From For-malism to Feminism," *Theater* 16, no. 2 (1985); Jill Dolan, *The Feminist Spectator as Critic* (Ann Arbor: UMI Research Press, 1988); and Jeanie Forte, "Realism, Narrative, and the Feminist Playwright—A Problem of Reception," *Modern Drama* 32, no. 1 (1989).

The notion of the male gaze has become a staple of feminist film, dramatic, and cultural (that is, advertising) criticism. The theory derives originally from Mulvey's analyses of "the look," which de Lauretis further elaborates in *Alice Doesn't.* In an often quoted passage, de Lauretis writes, "The woman is framed by the look of the camera as icon, or object of the gaze: an image made to be looked at by the spectator, whose look is relayed by the look of the male charac-ter(s). The latter not only controls the events and narrative action but is 'the bearer' of the look of the spectator": De Lauretis, *Alice Doesn't,* 139.

2. Jill Dolan, "Gender Impersonation Onstage: Destroying or Maintaining the Mirror of Gen-der Roles?" *Women and Performance* 2, no. 2 (1985): 7.

3. Ibid.

4. Ibid., 9.

5. Sue-Ellen Case, "Toward a Butch–Femme Aesthetic," in *Making a Spectacle: Feminist Essays on Contemporary Women's Theatre*, ed. Lynda Hart (Ann Arbor: University of Michigan Press, 1989), 282.

6. See, for example, Teresa de Lauretis, "Sexual Indifference and Lesbian Representation," in *Performing Feminisms: Feminist Critical Theory and Theatre*, ed. Sue-Ellen Case (Baltimore: Johns Hopkins University Press, 1990); Jill Dolan, "Lesbian Subjectivity in Realism: Dragging at the Margins of Structure and Ideology," in Case, *Performing Feminisms*; and Forte "Realism."

7. Case, "Toward a Butch–Femme Aesthetic," 283.

8. Ibid.

9. Cherríe Moraga, "Giving Up the Ghost," in *Heroes and Saints and Other Plays* (Albuquerque: West End Press, 1994).

10. For an insightful reprisal of the various ideological shifts that have occurred within feminist theory over the past thirty years, see Judith Roof, "1970s Lesbian Feminism Meets 1990s Butch–Femme," in *butch/femme: Inside Lesbian Gender*, ed. Sally R. Munt (London: Cassell, 1998); and Sue-Ellen Case, "Making Butch: An Historical Memoir of the 1970s," in Munt, *butch/femme*.

11. Sue-Ellen Case, *Feminism and Theatre* (New York: Routledge, 1988), 114–15.

12. Ibid., 128.

13. Catharine A. MacKinnon, *Only Words* (Cambridge, Mass.: Harvard University Press, 1994), 121, fn. 32.

14. Ibid.

15. As Dolan explains in an endnote, she prefers to refer to theoreticians such as MacKinnon and Dworkin as "cultural feminists" rather than as "radical feminists" because the former term "articulates the desire to separate women's culture—both its art and its everyday experience—from the dominant culture." This is not how MacKinnon or Dworkin typically formulate their theoretical stance. See Dolan, *Feminist Spectator*, 61, 134, fn. 8.

16. Cherry Smyth, "How Do We Look? Imaging Butch/Femme," in Munt, *butch/femme*, 84.

17. As Catherine Wiley observes, the title "refers to personal as well as cultural phantoms. . . . 'Giving up the ghost,' then, involves abandoning the nostalgia that keeps us from living in the present": see Catherine Wiley, "*Teatro* Chicano and the Seduction of Nostalgia," *MELUS* 23, no. 1 (Spring 1998): 106, 113.

18. The play has gone through a variety of permutations in performance and publication. It was most recently published in 1994 in a collection of three of Moraga's plays. The introductory matter to the text in the 1994 edition explains that the play was originally conceived in a workshop hosted by At the Foot of the Mountain Theatre in 1984. The play's text was first published in 1986, but the introduction's final sentence notes that the 1994 version is based to a large extent on the Theatre Rhinoceros production staged in San Francisco in early 1989.

19. Moraga, "Giving Up the Ghost," 26.

20. Ibid.

21. Ibid., 27.

22. Ibid., 26.

23. Ibid., 27.

24. Ibid.

25. Ibid.

26. Ibid., 28. The ellipsis that concludes the quote is original to the text.

27. Ibid., 27.

28. Ibid., 28.

29. Ibid., 29.

30. Ibid.

31. Amber Hollibaugh and Cherríe Moraga, "What We're Rollin' around in Bed with: Sexual Silences in Feminism," in *The Persistent Desire: A Femme–Butch Reader*, ed. Joan Nestle (Boston: Alyson Publications, 1992), 248.

32. Ann Cvetkovich, "Untouchability and Vulnerability: Stone Butchness as Emotional Style," in Munt, *butch/femme*, 160.

33. Moraga, "Giving Up the Ghost," 28.

34. Ibid., 29.

35. Describing Moraga's discussion of her own refusal to be penetrated in her autobiographical work *Loving in the War Years* (Boston: South End Press, 1983), Ann Cvetkovich notes, "For Moraga, the physical dimensions of sexual acts have emotional, as well as sexual, meanings; she extends the imagery of the body/vagina's permeability to the heart and imagines not feeling anything as the physical effect of growing a callous around her heart"; see Cvetkovich "Untouchability and Vulnerability," 162.

36. Nancy Saporta Sternbach, "'A Deep Racial Memory of Love': The Chicana Feminism of Cherríe Moraga," in *Breaking Boundaries: Latina Writing and Critical Readings*, ed. Ascunción Horno-Delgado and Eliana Ortega (Amherst: University of Massachusetts Press, 1989), 48–61. Sternbach's discussion of La Malinche is on p. 52. For further analysis of the La Malinche myth and its significance for the Chicana feminist movement, see Cherríe Moraga, "A Long Line of Vendidas," in idem, *Loving*, and Norma Alarcón, "Chicana's Feminist Literature: A Re-Vision through La Malintzin/or Malintzin: Putting Flesh Back on the Object," in *This Bridge Called My Back: Writings by Radical Women of Color*, ed. Cherríe Moraga and Gloria Anzaldúa (New York: Kitchen Table–Women of Color Press, 1983).

37. Yvonne Yarbro-Bejarano, "Cherríe Moraga's *Giving Up the Ghost*: The Representation of Female Desire," in *Third Woman* 3, nos. 1–2 (1986): 114.

38. Cheryl Clarke, "Lesbianism: An Act of Resistance," in Moraga and Anzaldúa, *This Bridge Called My Back*, 128.

39. Celebrating as do many feminist critics (including Hélène Cixous) Marcel Proust's interference with the presumed heterosexual male subject position in narrative discourse, Monique Wittig notes the manner in which he "made 'homosexual' the axis of categorization from which to universalize. The minority subject is not self-centered as is the straight subject. Its extension into space could be described as being like Pascal's circle, whose center is everywhere and nowhere . . . an effect comparable to what I call an out-of-the-corner-of-the-eye perception": see Monique Wittig, "The Point of View: Universal or Particular?" *Feminist Issues* 3, no. 2 (1983): 65.

40. Moraga, "Giving Up the Ghost," 8.

41. Ibid., 7. In a published conversation with Amber Hollibaugh, Moraga reveals that "growing up what turned me on sexually, at a very early age, had to do with the fantasy of capture, taking a woman, and my identification was with the man, taking": see Hollibaugh and Moraga, "What We're Rollin' around in Bed with," 245. Moraga, then, paints from experience Corky's highly realistic, complicated journey into sexual selfhood. For an equally gritty account of butch fantasies, see Jan Brown, "Sex, Lies, and Penetration: A Butch Finally 'fesses Up," in Nestle, *Persistent Desire*.

42. Yarbro-Bejarano, "Representation of Female Desire," 115.

43. Moraga, "Giving Up the Ghost," 8.

44. Ibid., 9.

45. Ibid., 10.

46. Ibid.

47. "Institutionalized feminism is all too frequently getting to 'draw the line' of sexual possibility. Beyond the line lurks the 'excessive,' which seems to reside in those instants when gender is subject to sexual play (butch–femme), in visual displays of the cohesion of desire and violence, of the points at which pleasure and danger intersect, of the moments when sex and rage are undifferentiated. This territory has been so thoroughly masculinized by some feminisms that explorations into it are frequently dismissed as antiwoman and antifeminist": see Joan Parkin and Amanda Prosser, "An Academic Affair: The Politics of Butch–Femme Pleasures," in Nestle, *Persistent Desire*. I am not engaged in a condemnation of frank depictions of sexual interactions; rather, I am calling for a theatrical theory and practice that can accommodate the sometimes problematic aspects of all of our sexual conduct, straight and queer. Just as Parkin and Prosser assert that butch/femme need not be an oppressive dynamic, I maintain that depiction need not constitute reinscription in the case of sexual violence.

48. Yarbro-Bejarano, "Cherríe Moraga's *Giving Up the Ghost*," 115.

49. Yarbro-Bejarano notes that the first performance was, in fact, for an all-women audience: see ibid., 119.

50. As Dolan points out, neither a simple inversion of the normative gender hierarchy nor the adoption of masculine power by a female subject is sufficient for addressing the issue of representing female sexuality, because "simply switching gender roles, and gender values, continues to bind representation to the system of sexual difference that gives it shape.... Reorganizing this binary opposition so that the weaker term is placed in the theoretically powerful position does nothing to deconstruct the dichotomy. It simply exchanges the placement of the terms": see Dolan, *Feminist Spectator as Critic*, 64.

51. Yvonne Yarbro-Bejarano, "The Female Subject in Chicano Theatre: Sexuality, 'Race,' and Class," in Case, *Performing Feminisms*, 147, fn. 42.

52. In an interview devoted to discussion of *Giving Up the Ghost* and *Loving in the War Years*, Moraga asserted that "on some level you should be able to empathize with your enemies in order to write that conflict as the conflicts experienced in life. You don't have to like them or even agree with them, but if you are going to show what happened, then you need to do that": see Luz Maria Umpierre, "Interview with Cherríe Moraga," *Americas Review* 14, no. 2 (Summer 1986): 59.

53. Teresa de Lauretis, "Fem/Les Scramble," in *Cross-Purposes: Lesbians, Feminists, and the Limits of Alliance*, ed. Dana Heller (Bloomington: Indiana University Press, 1997), 44.

54. Hollibaugh and Moraga, "What We're Rollin' around in Bed with," 243.

55. Ibid., 244.

56. Yarbro-Bejarano, "Female Subject," 147.

57. Gayle Austin, for example, discusses the fact that plays by heterosexual men tend to depict women as the goal—or, at least, as part of the goal—motivating the action of the plot or to vilify them as bitches or whores. Modifying Judith Fetterley's literary theory of the resisting reader and applying it to the female theatergoer, Austin says that it is only by going against the grain and resisting such representations that women can intellectually engage with the production as women. The only other option is to twice remove themselves from the subject position by first identifying with the male protagonist, and second accepting the subsequent objectification (or worse) of the women in the play: see Gayle Austin, "Feminist Literary Criticism: The 'Resisting Reader,'" in *Feminist Theories*, 21–37.

58. Barbara Freedman, "Frame-Up: Feminism, Psychoanalysis, Theatre," in Case, *Performing Feminisms,* 74.

59. Moraga, "Giving Up the Ghost," 25.

60. Ibid., 29.

61. This application of Freedman's theories to Moraga's text is entirely my own. I have seen no indication that Moraga was deliberately employing these theoretical formulations in her script.

62. Yarbro-Bejarano, "Cherríe Moraga's *Giving Up the Ghost,*" 115. Indicating Moraga's agreement with her interpretation, Yarbro-Bejarano writes, "After discussing the paper with Moraga, *we* decided . . . ": see ibid., 120, fn. 3; emphasis added.

63. Ibid., 119.

64. Forte, "Realism," 122.

65. Annette Kuhn, "Women's Genres: Annette Kuhn Considers Melodrama, Soap Opera and Theory," in *Screen* 24 (January–February 1984): 23.

66. Twentieth-century theater history includes a number of attempts to craft the theater into a didactic, socially critical space. Bertolt Brecht's theatrical experimentation is relevant here, as is Augusto Boal's more recent work in what he calls "the theatre of the oppressed": see Augusto Boal, *Theatre of the Oppressed,* trans. Charles A. and Maria-Odila Leal McBride (New York: Theatre Communications Group, 1985).

67. Peggy Phelan, for example, dismisses the male gaze as the starting point for an interrogation of issues of representation and suggests instead "a reexamination of the economy of exchange between the performer and the spectator in performance": see Peggy Phelan, "Feminist Theory, Poststructuralism, and Performance," *Drama Review* 32, no. 1 (Spring 1988): 111.

68. Natalie Crohn Schmitt, *Actors and Onlookers: Theater and Twentieth-Century Scientific Views of Nature* (Evanston, Ill.: Northwestern University Press, 1990), 27.

69. Kathleen Ross, *Rational Malaise* (Chicago: Splinter Group Studio, 1994), 31.

70. Ibid., 35.

Part III

Sites of Resistance

Karina Lissette Cespedes

---

9   *Bomberas* on Stage:
Carmelita Tropicana Speaking
in Tongues against History,
Madness, Fate, and the State

Who is Carmelita Tropicana?

> I couldn't stand in front of an audience, wear sequined gowns, tell jokes . . . But she could.
>
> She who penciled in her beauty mark, she who was baptized in the fountain of America's most popular orange juice, in the name of Havana's legendary nightclub, the Tropicana, she could. She was a fruit and wasn't afraid to admit it.
>
> She was the past I'd left behind. She was Cuba. Mi Cuba querida.

These are the words of a 150 percent Cubanita named Alina Troyano and her fruity alter ego, Carmelita Tropicana, mastering a performance space and language that speaks so directly to many Cubans residing in the United States who experience being outsiders within normative notions of *cubanidad* (Cubanness). The sensational Carmelita Tropicana, self-proclaimed songbird of Cuba, emerged in feminist and queer performance spaces in New York City in the 1980s, where she initially went looking for girls but instead found theater.[1] Troyano adopts Carmelita Tropicana as an alter ego in a number of performance pieces, such as the radio show "Cheet Chat with Carmelita," the film *Carmelita Tropicana: Your Kunst Is Your Waffen,* and the solo performance *Milk of Amnesia.* Troyano's performances impel her audiences to confront issues of multiple identities while illuminating, through a critical dissection of race, gender, and cultural stereotypes, the experiences of lesbian and progressive Cubanas transplanted to the United States. Troyano addresses the systematic and multiple amnesia of Cubans and Cuban Americans in the United States, who, delineated by epoch of migration and hence racial, class, and (anti)revolutionary positioning, have made a politics and cultural movement out of erasing from their exilic imaginations the lives of the many Carmelita Tropicanas who queer the Cuban American scene.

Using the genres of camp and *choteo,* the solo performance *Milk of Amnesia* is at times theatrical and at other times autobiographical.[2] It depicts the journey of both Carmelita Tropicana and Alina Troyano to Cuba many years after leaving the island. Regarding *Milk of Amnesia,* Troyano has stated that her "schizophrenia blossomed, and [she] was able to combine the voices of Carmelita with . . . that of the writer, and sprinkle it with assorted animals whose voices gave us a glimpse of Cuban History."[3] Troyano's/ Carmelita's return to Cuba is schizophrenic, filled with amnesia, flashbacks, and speaking in tongues—the tools needed to explore psychic trauma and the haunting of memory produced by twentieth-century migration to the United States and by the phantasmic residue of Cuba's colonial history.[4]

Troyano's return to the island alongside her alter ego captures a sense of the nation's historical, patriarchal, and colonial amnesia for queer and diasporic left-leaning Cubanas. Her exploration of multiple amnesia is exercised in the character of Carmelita Tropicana and manifested through possessions of her body, or *montados,* by non-human characters.[5] The cajoling of the animals points to the paradox of tracking through time and across all historical forces that which makes its mark by being there and not there at the same time.[6] At the center of Troyano's schizophrenia is a cajoling spirit persuading us to reconsider (if only to get some peace) the legacy on which Cuban subjectivity is formulated. Such is the haunting of history and "exilic" memory.

No Es Fácil: The Politics of "Exilic" Memory

I see a field in the distance. Palm trees, two peasants, and an ox. It reminds me of Southeast Asia, Vietnam. I never been there. But who knows where memories come from.[7]

When confronting the complexities of life, Cubans, both on and off the island, often use the phrase *"No es fácil"* (It's not easy).[8] In *Milk of Amnesia,* Troyano uses *"No es fácil!"* to capture the dilemmas presented by Cuba's multitude of contradictions during the *período especial* (special economic period) of the 1990s. Confirming that life is complicated, or *"no fácil,"* according to Avery Gordon, is perhaps the most important theoretical statement of our time: "It is a theoretical statement that guides efforts to treat race, class, gender and sexual dynamics and consciousness as more dense and delicate than those categorical terms often imply."[9] It requires addressing the limitation of these standard categories of analysis when addressing Cuba. Moreover, it suggests that Cuban "exilic" memories tend to be more psychically complex than merely politically misguided.

Cubans in the U.S. live in memory, and those memories definitely have a politics.[10] The cultural critic José Muñoz has keenly noted that Cubans in the United States have lived in Cuba through the medium and power of memory. This is especially true of those who make up what Gustavo Pérez-Firmat has called the 1.5 generation, those born on the island but raised in the United States after 1959.[11] That generation's Cuban identity and "exile" has been learned and lived through the memories of an older generation and modified through American mass culture.[12] According to Muñoz, many Cubans have

> lived in Cuba through the auspices of memory . . . "exilic" memory has reproduced Cuba as a collection of snapshots, disembodied voices over the phone line, and, most vividly, exilic memories. The ephemera and personal narratives that signify "Cuba" resonate as not only possessing a certain materiality, but also providing a sense of "place."
>
> Anyone who is familiar with Cuban exile communities knows that Cubans live in memory. Furthermore, that memory has a strange spatiality for the Cuban exile who inhabits North American territory but, nonetheless, has powerful associations, identifications, and affiliations with the island. Or, more nearly, a memory of the island.[13]

Cuban American memory is a politics of nostalgic reconstruction and fabrication in which, for some, prerevolutionary Cuba is imagined as an ideal and lost homeland, and for others revolutionary Cuba of the 1960s and '70s signifies home.[14] In addition to the materiality of "exilic" memories that Muñoz illustrates, J. A. Solis-Silva has written specifically about the discourse of a financially and politically powerful segment of Cuban American enclaves in the United States:

> The Cuban community [in the United States] for years has tended to substitute the critical study, reflection, and discussion of Cuba for the easy demonization of the present Cuban government, the loud and empty diatribe, the insulting epithets, the comfort of repeated cliches. The broadcast media has contributed to this situation in no small measure. . . . What would, otherwise, be the difference between a Cuban government that physically jails its dissidents and a Cuban community [in the United States] that psychologically jails those whose ideas and methods it finds unsettling?[15]

To these strange spatialities and discourses of Cuban American "exilic" memory and ideological policing Troyano affixes a consideration of the politics of memory that reconstructs Cuba and *cubanidad* while defying right-wing propaganda. Hence, *Milk of Amnesia* is as much about collective memory as it is about individual memory.[16]

Camp(y) *Choteo*

Troyano's exploration of memory in *Milk of Amnesia* uses both camp and *choteo* to refashion her sense of *cubanidad*. Although camp is primarily portrayed as a North American gay male performance practice, Muñoz argues that camp—and especially lesbian camp[17]—is an ideological and survivalist practice for all queers. Camp, like *choteo*, is a strategy of disidentification that enacts identity through the powerful rhetorics of parody and pastiche. The roots of *choteo*, according to Fernando Ortiz, originated from Locumi terminology to signify a range of activities that include tearing, talking, throwing, spying, and playing.[18] *Choteo* can be a fierce style of colonial mimicry that is simultaneously a form of resemblance and menace. The campy *choteo* within the performance relies on humor to examine queer social and cultural forms.

Both forms possess a disruptive potential as they mediate between the spaces of identification and total disavowal of the dominant culture's normative identificatory modes.[19] Troyano's use of *choteo* is consistent with the way in which U.S. queer people of color stand in opposition to hegemonic white queerness. Exploring and understanding the Cuban cultural practice of *choteo*—what many U.S. communities of color refer to as "the dozens," or signifying—provides the racial and class contexts for the nuances of Troyano's performance. Comparison of Troyano's performance to North American camp allows for only a partial translation, or framework, for understanding the cultural performance of campy *choteo* practiced among queer Cubans. As a campy *choteo*, *Milk of Amnesia* defies the binary of resistance and assimilation in ways that allow Troyano to negotiate among Cuban identity practices, the dominant culture, and the silences and contradictions of nation-states.

Just one of the many instances of Troyano's campy *choteo* occurs midway through the performance of *Milk of Amnesia*, when Carmelita, in excessive layers of clothing at a Miami International Airport gate, says, "The multitude of the Cuban diaspora is going back, holding on to plastic bags ... [shouting] ... follow the Maalox! Follow the Maalox!" Carmelita continues:

> The Cuban diaspora that's going back holding on to plastic bags with medicines and the most magnificent hats. I am so underdressed. These people are so dressed: shirts on top of pants on top of skirts. . . . I discover my people are a smart people. They can weigh your luggage and limit you to 44 pounds but they cannot weigh your body. The layered look is in ... soy una tienda ambulante [I am a traveling store]. I've my Easter bonnet with toilet paper on it. I'm a walking Cuban department store. Tampons and pearls, toilet paper, stationery supplies ... and next to me was a woman with a pressure cooker on her head.[20]

This "layered look" is a hilarious play on the elaborate hats that Cuban women devise to allow them to take surplus items to the island. On stage, Carmelita wears a version of one of these hats, gracefully trimmed with what in Cuba can be considered luxury items: toilet paper, tampons, plastic pearls. Carmelita's hat, and its parody of such a sensitive issue as scarcity on the island as a result of the embargo, is one of those "*no es fácil*" moments that play on the politics of spatiality and discourse and that points to the survivalist practice and self-fabrication of a Cuban lesbian in diaspora.

The "Pingalito Drag"

The "Pingalito drag" is another example of Troyano's critical campy *choteo*. This *choteo* of the loud, hyper-heterosexual Pingalito renders a reading of Miami Cuban maleness as a part of nostalgic national appropriateness. The name Pingalito is the diminutive form of the Cuban slang word for penis, yet the performance is concerned with more than simple gender difference. The Pingalito drag also parodies identities across race and class. The depiction of the lost exilic homeland and its politics via a drag performance creates an opulent scene of cross-identification that is, in one manner of speaking, queer.[21] Pingalito appears on stage wearing the assigned nostalgic and appropriate national dress of the Cuban man: the emblematic *guayabera* shirt, cigar, and hat. Pingalito informs the audience that Carmelita has been hospitalized because of her amnesia and describes his relationship to her as her former bus driver in Havana. To aid in Carmelita's recovery, he has brought with him a paper "Facts About Cuba" placemat with a map of the island from Las Lilas, a Miami restaurant that is an icon for the entrepreneurial success of the white Cuban middle class who settled in Miami during the 1960s. Pingalito reads the facts about Cuba printed on the place-mat with a sensational and exaggerated Cuban Spanish cadence in his English accent:

> Fact number one. . . . Cuba is known as the Pearl of the Antilles because of its natural wealth and beauty. And, the first thing we learn as little children is that Christopher Columbus landed on our island, and said . . . this is the most beautiful land human eyes have seen.[22]

Adding his own commentary about Cuba's beauty, Pingalito refers to the human landscape of Cuban women's bodies: "Women in Cuba are like cars, big like Cadillacs, no Toyota or Honda, with behinds you could carry daiquiris on." He continues:

> Tongolele. I swear to you people, or my name is not Pingalito Betancourt, you could put a tray of daiquiris on Tongolele's behind and she could walk across the floor without spilling a single drop. That, ladies and gentlemen, is landscape. For that you give me a gun and I fight for that landscape.[23]

It is on the body—specifically, on the buttocks—of the famous Cuban mulatta exotic dancer Tongolele that heteronormative and racialized fantasies are deployed. The focus on Tongolele's buttocks is important, because it exemplifies Cuba's slippery racial signifiers, where the black/mulatta's body comes to serve as an icon for hyper-sexuality.[24] It is the protruding buttocks that audiences paid to see—and later used to fantasize about the uniqueness of Tongolele's genitalia. Exaggerated buttocks point to what are believed to be the hidden sexual signs, both physical and temperamental, of the black woman. This association is a powerful one in a nation in which women's sexuality is linked to the image of the buttocks, and the quintessential buttocks are Tongolele's.

Fact number two on Pingalito's placemat includes a further reference to race by implying that most Cubans have African ancestry. "Spanish is the official language of Cuba," Pingalito reads, adding that his favorite expression in Spanish is *"Oyeme mano! ¿Y tu abuela dónde está?"* (Hey, bro! And where's your grandmother?). This brings Pingalito to fact number three: Three-fourths of all Cubans are white of Spanish descent. "And a lot of these three-fourths have a very dark suntan all year round," Pingalito comments. "When they ask me: Pingalito, and where's your grandmother? I say *Mulata y a mucha honra.* Dark and proud."[25]

By pointing out the racial and social location of his grandmother, Pingalito plays on the hypocrisy of official renderings of history and the policing of historical and racial representations. Although most Cubans willingly trace their European heritage to Spain, there is a tendency to erase from official national history the African and indigenous parts of that heritage.[26] Troyano's performance of Pingalito helps give her access to aspects of *cubanidad* that provide a critical reading of the complexities of racial identities and the systems of power that fuel notions of masculinity. In Pingalito's monologue about race on the island, the *choteador*, through mockery and exaggeration, satirizes the politics of polite racism in everyday Cuban life. Yet Pingalito is also the character through which Troyano attempts to parody, mimic, and menace heteronormative, sexist, and racist national identifications.[27] His monologue represents a national character that is recognizable as a Cuban form of masculine jingoism in all of its bigotry, narrow-mindedness, and dogmatic racism.[28] As a national historian, Pingalito provides an "official" history of the island and goes as far as to question subtly the Eurocentric perspective of that history. But, Pingalito is able to lay claim to *cubanidad* through an articulation of *mulataje* and a performance of heterosexual maleness anchored within the national character. In contrast, Carmelita's amnesiac claim to *cubanidad,* as her name implies, occurs through the specter of the infamous Tropicana nightclub in Havana, where Cuban women's bodies, like Tongolele's, have historically performed superfemininity and heteronormativity. The famous Tropicana dancers—black, mulatta, and "white"[29]—are still commodified as Cuban cultural icons by international tourists with both Marxist and capitalist leanings.

Drag performances such as that of Pingalito, which are already layered onto the construction of Carmelita, contribute to Troyano's queerly assembled self. Troyano's portrayal of Pingalito and Carmelita is a performance of queer identity and sexuality against the backdrop of amnesia and the misogynist, racist, and homophobic violence of national memory and heteronormative community. Her performances complicate the gendered drag by highlighting the location of these two characters within *cubanidad.* As an older, light-skinned, Miami-based Cubano, Pingalito might very well be sheltered within the city's right-wing Cuban politics and imaginary. But where might Troyano/Carmelita, a Cuban lesbian with progressive politics who publicly outs herself as anti-embargo, fit within the imagination of the Cuban exilic community in the United States?

Space and Discourse: *Que Soy de Aquí, Que Soy de Allá*

Through personalities such as Pingalito and Carmelita Tropicana, Troyano attempts to negotiate the complex terrain of history and nation for Cubans in the United States. As Emma Pérez has pointed out, the work of queer women of color in the United States emerges from *"un sitio y una lengua"* (a political space and discourse) that rejects colonial ideology and patriarchy—sexism, racism, homophobia.[30] Troyano emerges from a disidentified *sitio y lengua* that rejects normative *cubanidad* while simultaneously rooting herself in what Pérez describes as the words and silences of Third World–identified women in the United States who create a place apart from white men and women and from men of color. Through the medium of Carmelita, Troyano provides a *sitio y lengua* for queer and diasporic Cubanas that challenges conventional notions of "exile," *cubanidad,* and U.S. assimilation.

In the following passage, Troyano recalls the childhood incident in a U.S. parochial school that led to the onset of her memory loss:

In the morning I went to school. Our Lady Queen of Martyrs. That's when it happened. In the lunchroom. I never drank my milk. I always threw it out. Except this time when I went to throw it out, the container fell and milk spilled on the floor. The nun came over. Looked at me and the milk. Her beady eyes screamed: You didn't drink your milk, Grade A pasteurized, homogenized, you Cuban refugee.

   After that day I changed. . . . If I closed my eyes and held my breath I could suppress a lot of the flavor I didn't like. This is how I learned to drink milk. It was my resolve to embrace America as I chewed on my peanut butter and jelly sandwich and gulped down my milk. This new milk that had replaced the sweet condensed milk of Cuba. My amnesia had begun.[31]

Carmelita's/Troyano's amnesia begins with the materials systematically used to ensure homogeneity and assimilation. The milk, a whitewashing elixir that forces down the peanut-butter-and-jelly sandwich, symbolizes the coercion she feels to abide by U.S. assimilationist dictates. Clearly, the Grade A pasteurized, homogenized milk denotes the cultural and linguistic amnesia Carmelita experiences in the United States.[32] This homogenized milk is antithetical to Carmelita's memory of the sweet condensed milk she drank as a child. Yet in addition to this cultural-linguistic amnesia, the sweet condensed milk is a marker of a historical amnesia concerning Cuba. The challenge to forced acculturation is only part of Troyano's critique. Farther into the performance, Carmelita once again describes her memories of Cuba through the metaphor of condensed milk as she simultaneously remembers a prerevolutionary song about the pleasures awaiting tourists on the island. She muses:

My homeland, the place that suckled me as a newborn babe. In the distance, I hear the clink, clink, clink of a metal spoon against glass. It is my Mami stirring condensed milk with water . . . the milk beckons me. I feel a song coming on.

Carmelita sings:

How would you like to spend the weekend in Havana?
How would you like to see the Caribbean shore?
Come on and run away over Sunday.
Where the view and the music is tropical.
You'll have a heart attack at your office on Monday.
But you won't. No you won't be the same anymore.[33]

Symbolically, the condensed milk is a counterstancial proposition to the social and psychic conditions of Cubans in the United States as an "Other."[34] The association between Carmelita's memory of the sugary elements of condensed milk as representative of home, followed by the song affiliated with tourism on the island, suggests yet another layer of haunting irony. Sugar and tourism point to the two most vital economic factors sustaining the Cuban nation-state. The condensed milk of Cuba points to the legacy of sugar as the primary crop on which the national economy was and is dependent. Cuba's condensed milk is soured with the history of enslavement, the mechanism used to produce the sugar needed to fill each can, with its thick and heavy contents.[35]

The theme of tourism, initiated by the song "How Would you Like to Spend a Weekend in Havana?", is continued later in the performance through an examination of contemporary tourism. As Carmelita/Troyano describes walking through the colonial sector of Havana, she comments on feeling like a tourist in her own country and the contradictions of the special economic period that the island confronted in the 1990s. A young woman approaches her, and she remarks:

> A girl about fourteen asks me for my pintalabios. I part with my Revlon number forty-four "Love that Red" lipstick. I eat at La Bodegita with two Cuban artists . . . the new currency is the dollar. . . . [Later,] who do I see coming into [the hotel]? . . . Pintalabios, Revlon number forty-four. . . . I'm pissed but then I reconsider . . . maybe the lipstick got her a steak dinner.[36]

Troyano returns to her hotel. The contrast of the day's events—the hotel's luxury, seeing the young woman who had asked for her "pintalabios" walk into the hotel with a tourist for the suggested purpose of sex work, and the thought of the disparity of the exchange (sex for food)—sends her into another attack. The blue tiles in the hotel make her feel sick. She remembers a hospital operating room and its blue tiles—the fear of it all as a child. In the hotel dinning room, the song "Lágrimas Negras" is playing. She last heard it at Gloria Estefan's restaurant in Miami. She goes over what she has learned; one thing is the slang word for dyke: "*bombera.*" As she contemplates this, the pork sandwich she is eating becomes animated, and she is transported to the subjectivity of a special period pig. The pig is boxed and can see only blue tiles. Such moments in the performance demand that questions of psychic interconnectedness through historical complexities not be overlooked.

A *Bombera*, a Pig, and a Horse

With their amnesic connection to the United States and Cuba through sugar and tourism, both milks illustrate a profound sense of displacement that marks Cubanas in diaspora. And linked to the displacement within these nations emerges the need also to make central the place and discourse of sexuality. Through her performance, Troyano weaves a complex analysis of sexuality that not only includes the commodification of Cuban women's bodies through Cuban men's sexism (that is, Pingalito) and the national dependence on tourism, but also situates queerness within these scenes. She demonstrates that, for queer women of color, issues of nation, race, sexuality, and class are always already interconnected. While in Havana, Troyano/Carmelita begins to recover the memory of her queerness, the memory of having a crush on a woman before her family left the island. When Carmelita's libido in diaspora responded to a woman's touch, the memories that might have explained that desire were not available. Back in Cuba, however, Troyano/Carmelita remembers that

[she] heard her footsteps. She had long hair tied into a ponytail, red lips, and dreamy eyes like a cow. I ran to her and jumped on her and kissed her creamy cheeks. . . . My heart was beating fast, I was sweating. I knew then that that was no ordinary kiss.[37]

Toward the end of the performance, Carmelita says:

Ochún is the [African/Yoruban] goddess of the sea. No, that's Yemayá. Ochún is like the Caridad del Cobre [the patron saint of Cuba] and if you want to get the love of your life you have to leave honey under your bed for five days. You get the love you want and the cucarachas you don't.

And, the slang word for dyke is bombera, firefighter. So, maybe if I yell, Fire, would all the dykes come out now?[38]

This passage points not only to the history of religious and spiritual syncretism in Cuban culture, but also to the invisibility within the nation's history and spiritual practices of lesbian desire. The ritual of leaving honey under the bed is a popular one used to attract a lover. But Troyano describes the ritual, which is usually practiced within a heterosexual context, as one that unexpectedly draws cockroaches (*cucarachas*)—the pestilence of patriarchy and heteronormativity.

Troyano addresses the historical erasure of queers from *cubanidad* in the performance not only through human characters, but also through various animal characters. To dramatize Carmelita's amnesia, Troyano creates a psychosocial condition called Collective Unconscious Memory Appropriation Attacks (CUMAAs), which Carmelita first experiences after her accident and subsequent amnesia. These CUMAAs are responses to the phantomness of lesbian Cubanas within official Cuban and Cuban American history and identity. For Carmelita, the CUMAAs are activated during unlivable moments in which she cannot maintain her wholeness. The ghostly and haunting legacy of Cuba's colonial history triggers these attacks without notice.[39] It is important to read the language, movement, shapes,[40] and flesh of Troyano/Carmelita's CUMAAs as significant, yet historically excluded, portions of Cuba's history.

These difficult situations transport Carmelita into the bodies of animals that endure, much as she does, *períodos especiales* in Cuba's history. One CUMAA transports Carmelita into the memory and subjectivity of a conquistador's horse during European colonization in the midst of a Native American massacre. It is followed by the CUMAA mentioned earlier that transports Carmelita into the mind of a pig being raised as livestock in a small Havana apartment during the *períodos especiales*, which the island endures during the 1990s.

The CUMAAs allegorize Troyano's/Carmelita's feelings of invisibility, numbness, amnesia, and phantomness within *cubanidad* as a dyke in diaspora. They represent what Gloria Anzaldúa describes as the psychic spaces, for lesbians of color, of speaking in tongues and being thrown at the feet of madness, fate, and the state.[41] By speaking in different tongues, all of Troyano's characters become the space for emerging personalities that invoke unofficial histories of different social periods and racial, social, sexual, and political locations within *cubanidad*. Troyano constructs the CUMAAs to signal the collective memory that resists official, hegemonic channels of Cuban history.[42] She says, "My vocal chord, my tonsils, The pig and I. . . . We are all connected not through AT&T, E-mail, Internet, or the information superhighway, but through memory, history, herstory, horsetory."

Carmelita shadowboxes as she recites a poem:

> I REMEMBER
> QUE SOY DE ALLÁ
> QUE SOY DE AQUÍ
> UN PIE EN NUEVA YORK (A FOOT IN NEW YORK)
> UN PIE EN LA HABANA (A FOOT IN HAVANA)
> AND WHEN I PUT A FOOT IN BERLIN
> I AM CALLED
> A LESBISCHE CUBANERIN
> A WOMAN OF COLOR AQUÍ
> CULTURALLY FRAGMENTED
> SEXUALLY INTERSECTED.[43]

Much like the conquistador's horse and the *período especial* pig, Troyano as a lesbian is outside official history. Her subjectivity is phantasmic and denied.

With the CUMAA, Carmelita regains all of her memory. Her amnesia is gone. But to regain who she is, Troyano/Carmelita must remember the colonial and modern chaos. Carmelita's return to Cuba triggers the nostalgia: the "need for even the crack in the sidewalk to recognize [her]"[44] and the structure of feelings for a Cuba that never was—a Cuba that can be articulated only outside the island, in diaspora. Queer diasporic Cubanas, like Troyano, negotiate *cubanidad* in ways that reconfigure history, memory, and nostalgia. Troyano dismantles hegemonic definitions of Cubanidad by creating a *sitio y lengua* for U.S. diasporic Cubanas that moves beyond the traditional heteronormative notions of the nation. Carmelita, known as a cultural terrorist and a Carmen Miranda cloaked in dangerous fruit,[45] does not hesitate to remind the audience of her various identities: nightclub performer, *choteadora*, female/male impersonator, lesbian, U.S. Latina y Cubana. Troyano and Carmelita Tropicana record and perform the lesbian body, moving within multifaceted appropriations and restructurings of conventionally heterosexual cultural signifiers, modes, and discourses.

Notes

Acknowledgments: I thank Caridad Souza for reading earlier versions of this paper. Her friendship and vision are always an inspiration. Also, sincerest thanks to Sara Jane Cervenak for her friendship, overwhelming attention to ghostly matter(s), and willingness to share her personal library.

Epigraph: Carmelita Tropicana (Alina Troyano), "Milk of Amnesia: Leche de amnesia," *TDR* (*The Drama Review*) 39 (Fall 1995): 94–112.

1. David Roman, "Carmelita Tropicana Unplugged (Performance Artist Alina Troyano Interview)," *TDR* 39 (1995): 83–94.

2. See José Esteban Muñoz, "Sister Acts: Ela Troyano and Carmelita Tropicana," in *Disidentifications: Queers of Color and the Performance of Politics* (Minneapolis: University of Minnesota Press, 1999). See also idem, "No es fácil: Notes on the Negotiation of Cubanidad and 'Exilic' Memory in Carmelita Tropicana's 'Milk of Amnesia,'" *TDR* 39 (Fall 1995): 76–83.

3. Alina Troyano, "Introduction," in Alina Troyano with Ela Troyano and Uzi Parnes, *I, Carmelita Tropicana: Performing between Cultures,* ed. Chon Noriega (Boston: Beacon Press, 2000), xxii.

4. Avery F. Gordon, *Ghostly Matters: Haunting and the Sociological Imagination* (Minneapolis: University of Minnesota Press, 1997).

5. *Montado* refers to the possession of the body by spirits or the Orishas within Yoruban spiritual practices exercised in Cuba and in diaspora.

6. Gordon, *Ghostly Matters.*

7. Tropicana, "Milk of Amnesia," 100–101.

8. See Muñoz, "No es fácil," 76–83.

9. Gordon, *Ghostly Matters.*

10. See Jonathan Boyarin, *Remapping Memory: The Politics of Time and Space* (Minneapolis: University of Minnesota Press, 1994), and Muñoz, "No es fácil."

11. Gustavo Pérez-Firmat, *Life on the Margin: The Cuban-American Way* (Austin: University of Texas Press, 1994).

12. See Chon Noriega, "Very Good with the Tongue: *I, Carmelita Tropicana: Performing between Cultures,*" in Troyano et al., *I, Carmelita Tropicana,* and Pérez-Firmat, *Life on the Margin.*

13. Muñoz, "No es fácil," 76.

14. Yet more often than not, these memories of Cuba within the United States are designed to diminish the benefits of the Cuban revolution. A third imaginary—that of the U.S. left—has created an imaginary, utopic socialist Cuba without political, social, and ideological contradictions.

15. J. A. Solis-Silva, "Democracy, Dialogue and the Cuban Community," in *Apuntes Postmodernos/ Postmodern Notes* 1, no. 1 (1990): 14–18.

16. Muñoz, "No es fácil."

17. Muñoz draws on the work of Pamela Robertson to claim that camp is not only a gay male practice but also a lesbian–feminist critique of gender construction, performance, and enactment. Thus, Troyano's use of camp can be read as lesbian camp, because it stands as different from gay male camp: ibid.

18. Ibid.; Fernando Ortiz, *Glosario de Afronegrismo* (Havana: Imprenta El Siglo XX, 1924).

19. Muñoz, "No es fácil."

20. Tropicana, "Milk of Amnesia," 100.

21. José Esteban Muñoz, "Flaming Latinas: Ela Troyano's *Carmelita Tropicana: Your Kunst Is Your Waffen* (1993)," in *The Ethnic Eye: Latino Media Arts,* ed. C. A. Noriega and A. M. López (Minneapolis: University of Minnesota Press, 1996), 129–42.

22. Tropicana, "Milk of Amnesia," 96.

23. Ibid.

24. Medical discourse has marked the genital organs as a site of "difference" and demarcation of blackness. The genitalia of the black body, which provoked fear of degeneration in the nineteenth century, reemerged at the end of the twentieth century not as frightening but still as "other," exotic, and as folkloric. The focus on Tongolele's buttocks, for example, is telling in that it triggered a causal history connected to the polemic of race and "womanhood."

25. Tropicana, "Milk of Amnesia," 96.

26. Near-complete silence surrounds the serious consideration of indigenousness and Cuban/Cuban American national identity.

27. In Cuba, claiming *mulataje,* as Pingalito does, can also be problematic. It is similar to (but not exactly like) claiming *mestizaje* in Latin American countries in which national identity revolves around an articulation of being Mestizo while the native Indian population remains socially and economically subordinated.

28. José Esteban Muñoz, "Choteo/Camp Style Politics: Carmelita Tropicana's Performance of Self Enactment," in *Women and Performance* 7, no. 2 (1995): 39–52.

29. The terms "black," "mulatta," and "white" do not truly explain or represent the phenotype and pigment hierarchies that organize Cuban society.

30. Emma Pérez, "Sexuality and Discourse: Notes from a Chicana Survivor," in *Chicana Lesbians: The Girls Our Mothers Warned Us About,* ed. Carla Trujillo (Berkeley, Calif.: Third Woman Press, 1991).

31. Tropicana, "Milk of Amnesia," 95.

32. Muñoz, "No es fácil."

33. Tropicana, "Milk of Amnesia," 100.

34. Muñoz, "No es fácil."

35. The process of canning predates the abolition of slavery in Cuba. The process was developed and mechanized by Nicolas Appert of France in 1809.

36. Tropicana, "Milk of Amnesia," 102.

37. Ibid, 105.

38. Ibid, 107.

39. Avery Gordon has not established transhistorical or universal principles for theorizing haunting. Rather, her work has endeavored to represent the structure of feeling, which somewhat resembles what it feels like to be the object of a social totality vexed by the phantoms of modernity's violence. Gordon stresses that, although it is true that social life's complications are "overdetermined," what is of importance is the exploring of the particular institution and individual mediation, a social structure and a subject, and history and a biography. In haunting, organized forces and systemic structures that appear removed from us make their impact felt in everyday life in a way that confounds our analytic separations and confounds the social separations themselves.

40. In *Symmetry, Causality, Mind* (Cambridge, Mass.: MIT Press, 1992), Michael Leyton suggests that the mind needs to assign a causal history to shapes that explains how the shape was formed. Hence, shapes, along with place and discourse, are used by the mind to recover the past; thus, shapes form a basis for memory. Leyton provides a consideration of the power of memory that is close to Gordon's assessment, which dares to include the aura and energy of objects and images as possessors of social memory and imbued with the spirit of life's complexity. Hence, one can read Troyano/Carmelita's Collective Unconscious Memory Appropriation Attacks as significant portions of Cuba's History.

41. Gloria Anzaldúa, "Speaking in Tongues: A Letter to Third World Women Writers," in *This Bridge Called My Back: Writings by Radical Women of Color,* ed. Cherríe Moraga and Gloria Anzaldúa, 2nd ed. (New York: Kitchen Table Press, 1984).

42. Muñoz, "No es fácil."

43. Tropicana, "Milk of Amnesia," 108–9.

44. Ibid., 105.

45. Roman, "Carmelita Tropicana Unplugged," 83.

María Claudia André

10 Empowering the
Feminine/Feminist/Lesbian
Subject through the Lens:
The Representation of Women
in María Luisa Bemberg's
Yo, la peor de todas

When I speak of the erotic, then I speak of it as an assertion of the lifeforce of women; of that creative energy empowered, the knowledge and use of which we are now reclaiming in our language, our history, our dancing, our loving, our work, our lives.

—*Audre Lorde*

Few people have accomplished so much in the paths of feminism and filmmaking in such short-lived careers as the extraordinary Argentine film director, scriptwriter, and producer, María Luisa Marta Carlota Bemberg. Born on 14 April 1922 to an upper-class family, Bemberg followed in the footsteps of her well-known aunt, the writer and editor Victoria Ocampo. Her rebellious spirit and artistic talent began to develop at a very early age, growing steadily through the years, especially after she read Simone de Beauvoir's *The Second Sex*, a pivotal text that launched her into the path of feminism.[1] As Bemberg herself admits, "I will never be able to adequately express my appreciation for that book. It was like a dam that burst."[2] In fact, during the 1970s, several years after Ocampo had begun voicing the first feminist concepts and ideology among the highly educated elites of Buenos Aires, her niece and some of her intellectual friends founded Argentina's first Feminist Youth Organization (Asociación Juventud Feminista Argentina).[3] Through the years, Bemberg worked sporadically in several theater productions as a costume and set designer; however, because of the domestic responsibilities of raising four children on her own, she was unable to begin her screenwriting and filmmaking vocation professionally until she was almost sixty. Throughout her life and artistic career, Bemberg remained active in the feminist cause, tirelessly pursuing the worthy task of changing women's subjectivity within the social and political sphere. In several interviews, the director expressed that her primary intention was to show women different ways to channel their emotions and passion into political struggles, and to set an example through her films and through her own personal lifestyle for younger generations of women to follow.

Tapping into the literary and cinematic production of her times, Bemberg's filmography challenges some of Argentina's long-held social and political values exploring the need to redefine individual and national identities. According to Gustavo Fares, "Literary fiction produced in Argentina during the last two decades searches for two kinds of identities: that of the individual and that of the country as a whole. In the first kind of examination of identity, that of the individual, the issues of sex and gender are very important; in the second identity, that of the country as a whole, history plays a fundamental role."[4] As this chapter will examine, Bemberg takes the notion of identity a step further. Her corpus not only questions the nature of power, exposing the hypocrisy of traditional gender constructions, but through the effacement of prescribed subjectivities it generates alternative ways to approach controversial issues such as homosexuality and lesbianism.

This chapter will also explore how Bemberg's films, apart from reflecting on the constant and essential paradox of being a woman in a male-dominated society, aim both to subvert and to deconstruct patriarchal binary systems in favor of an alternative representation of feminine eroticism and desire. Such disruptive discourse manifests most prominently, perhaps, in *Yo, la peor de todas*, the last of her three historical films. In analyzing this outstanding production, I will focus on some of the cinematic techniques Bemberg devised to dismantle codified constructs of women in pursuit of a polysemic figure with which identity and gender limitations may be expanded or transformed into a whole realm of possibilities. A brief outline of the director's artistic production should also be considered to appreciate her distinctive commitment to the feminist cause as well as the consistent urgency and energy in search for a personal voice to express her vision.

Bemberg's first scripts, *Crónica de una Señora* (Chronicles of a lady; 1972) and *Triángulo de cuatro* (Triangle of four; 1974), present a sharp ideological standpoint as well as an identifiable autobiographical element; both reflect on the hardships of women dealing with marital infidelity and divorce in the extremely judgmental society of the Argentine upper class. A product of that society, Bemberg felt that the topic of marriage needed to be questioned, because "marriage has always been a form of prostitution, disguised under love and care. Divorce will change this. Women will not be able to feel safe in marriage. They will not consider their certificate as a kind of B.A., a meal ticket."[5] Dissatisfied with how her female characters were portrayed by male directors, she also took the initiative to place herself behind the lens and start directing her own scripts.

After producing two experimental short films, *Mundo de mujeres* (Women's world) in 1972 and *Juguetes* (Toys) in 1974, Bemberg was ready to film *Señora de nadie* (Nobody's wife), a full production with a more radical story about the hardships of a liberated woman searching for personal freedom. The film had to be postponed, however, because the script was censored under the military regime for suggesting alternative lifestyles for women and for portraying a homosexual. "They told me that it was a very bad example for Argentine mothers, and that we couldn't put a *maricón* in the film," Bemberg recalls. "The colonel said that he would rather have a son who had cancer than one who was a homosexual, so I couldn't do it."[6] In 1980, Bemberg traveled to the United States, where she studied acting with Lee Strasberg, and soon after her return to Argentina, she directed and produced *Momentos* (Moments, 1981) another intense psychological exploration of marital and extramarital relationships in modern society.

Under the new democracy of President Raúl Alfonsín, Bemberg was finally able to release the previously censored film and, two years later, the internationally acclaimed *Camila* (1982), a groundbreaking production that gained her worldwide recognition through an Academy Award nomination as Best Foreign Film. The script is based on the dramatic true story of the forbidden love of Camila O'Gorman, an aristocratic young woman who, after eloping with her confessor, is caught and executed without a trial for her disregard for society's pivotal institutions. The highly political production contextualized during Argentina's first dictatorial regime demonstrates how true love can become a revolutionary and powerful means of liberation within a society in which patriarchal canons are institutionally reinforced. Bemberg selected the character because, "Camila was a transgressor, she broke the received pattern of Argentine, not to mention feminine decorum. Not only did she enjoy a love affair with her priest, but her actions fought the paternalistic order—another triangle—of family, church and state."[7]

Miss Mary (1987), another distinctive example of patriarchal rule, explores the subjection and repression of bourgeois women in Argentina during the 1940s. In this semiautobiographical co-production, Bemberg re-creates the life of a British governess who, while packing her bags to return to England in 1945, reminisces about the summer of 1938, when she was hired as a private tutor for two young upper-class girls. In addition to re-creating the historical events that led to the presidency of Juan Domingo Perón, the film explores a variety of sociopolitical issues, dealing with Argentine oligarchy's delusional and eccentric behavior. As Mark Szuchman notes:

> The film explores the antinomies of asserted values and behavioral practices. This central opposition is manifested in various ways but always within the frame of ethical opposites, of morality and lasciviousness, of conservatism in public and licentiousness in private, of affinity for Fascist hierarchies in the thirties and support for liberal democracies in the forties. Bemberg explored these dyads through longitudinal portrayals of Argentine mores.[8]

Seeing how upper-class values affected the middle class, Bemberg felt compelled to examine the mechanisms that led to the institutionalization of women's subjection and to sexual repression. She considered the latter, in fact, to be the foremost repression: "It is very hard to imagine how a person can be free if s/he is sexually repressed."[9]

Constantly seeking to explore the many ways in which hegemonic institutions manipulate women's subjectivity, the hard-core feminist found the perfect example of patriarchal injustice and abuse in the historical figure of the Mexican nun Sor Juana Inés de la Cruz. In 1990, Bemberg, by now a well-known filmwriter and established director, began her third and last historical film, *Yo, la peor de todas* (I, worst of all) based on *Sor Juana Inés de la Cruz; O, Las trampas de la fe* (Sor Juana; or, the traps of faith, 1988), the biography by the Mexican Nobel Prize winner Octavio Paz.[10] The film was originally acclaimed for its magnificent depiction of colonial Mexico, as well as for its outstanding portrayal of Latin America's first feminist and exceptional poet of the Spanish Golden Age. True to historical accounts, Bemberg's production re-creates the life of Juana Inés Ramírez de Asbaje, a woman of remarkable genius who rejected the glamorous life of the seventeenth-century Spanish court to enter the convent of the Jeronymite Order to pursue her academic interests. Convent life was then the only alternative to marriage and the only place where women were allowed to read and write—and, in extreme exceptions such as Sor Juana's, to produce intellectual work.

The film's first scenes show a lively young woman in her prime: passionate, beautiful, self-reliant, and even vain in her attitude toward her right to have free access to the wonders of the world. Sor Juana's quick mind baffles those who try to outsmart her, yet her charming ways, powerful personality, and marvelous intellect attract everyone who makes her acquaintance. Her scientific curiosity gains her the admiration of the most outstanding scholars and writers of the New World; at a time when very few men could read and write, Sor Juana's personal library exceeded three thousand volumes. Despite her fame as a poet and playwright, however, the nun had to defend her vocation constantly within a society in which the Hispanic Inquisition was still in order and the realm of academia was strictly reserved for men. Sor Juana's literary productions defied the norm during a period in which even mystic poetry was strictly controlled. Indeed, as Emilie Bergmann evaluates, "What was remarkable about Sor Juana's writing was her clear awareness of her decisions to depart from the norm, and her unflinching confrontation with the consequences of those decisions."[11]

The highly sensuous tone of her poetry, her profane plays, and her nontraditional writing created havoc within the clergy and deep envy among her peers.[12] In addition, her interest in esoteric sciences such as astronomy, mathematics, and philosophy was not only unusual but potentially heretical, because it challenged the doctrines of the Hispanic Counter-Reformation. As expected, her defiant attitude and insolent behavior toward ecclesiastical authorities finally brought extremely serious consequences.[13] Subject to convent intrigues of which she seems to have been completely unaware, and once bereft of the protection of the viceregal couple, Sor Juana was forced by higher representatives of the church to give up her writing and her books to avoid the Inquisition's scrutiny. Soon after the vicereine's departure, the helpless nun inevitably fell to the archbishop's demands to renounce her scholarly aspirations publicly. In a dramatic scene, Sor Juana, with a desolate expression on her face, stands in her cell while being dispossessed of her books, her compass, and her telescope, among other beloved tools for learning, which she had previously manifested to love as her children. Once her cell is as barren as her spirit, the poet is prepared to admit in front of the Holy Tribunal her sacrilege of having joined the convent only to pursue her intellectual vocation. The Jesuit Diego Calleja, Sor Juana's first biographer reports, "She sold her books to provide for the poor. She became humble and pious, and she began to scourge her own flesh. In short, the renunciation was so complete that she lost her spirit and came to believe that she was 'the worst of all.'"[14] We see a defeated Sor Juana a few years later on her knees, scrubbing floors (to the pleasure of her confessor, Father Antonio Núñez de Miranda), and helping those dying of cholera, the illness that had finally claimed her life by 1695.

Using history as a pre-text for the cinematographic representation of an outstanding woman, Bemberg mediates between real and fictional character, intentionally focusing the film on the nun's controversial relationship with the Spanish Vicereine María Luisa Manrique de Lara y Gonzaga, the Marquise of la Laguna, Sor Juana's protector and erotic muse. Through the years, the Mexican nun's sensual poetry and enigmatic personality have been the topic of multiple critical studies in a wide variety of fields. As Bergmann notes, "Scholars and biographers from Calleja in the eighteenth century to Paz in the twentieth have struggled with the problem of identifying Sor Juana's powerful intellect as 'masculine' together with the troubling perception of homoerotic desire as masculine-identified sexuality toward the women to whom she dedicated love poetry and verbal portraits."[15] The poet's identity is still a controversial topic among scholars; even more recently, literary critics have begun to disagree about Paz's interpretation and Bemberg's cinematic representation of Sor Juana's writings. Bergmann, for example, views Paz's biography as strongly homophobic, and Elena Martínez argues that the Nobel Prize-winner went to great lengths to avoid raising the possibility of Sor Juana's lesbianism.[16] Other critics, such as Susana Ramírez, have concluded that, while Paz energetically rejects the possibility of Sor Juana's homosexual tendencies toward the viceroy's wife, Bemberg's film leaves the issue somewhat underdeveloped and unresolved (focusing mainly in the conflict between the church and the state).[17] Adding to the controversy, Nina Scott argues that, "whereas Paz maintained that the passion of Sor Juana's verses to María Luisa was strictly poetic convention, Bemberg's film portrays a definite physical attraction."[18]

In several interviews published after the film's release, the feminist director maintained that she had followed Paz's premises, thus denying all homoerotic interpretations of Sor Juana's biographical accounts. Fortunately, to the nun's benefit, the question about her sexual tendencies will probably forever remain unanswered—even if "Sor Juana's lesbianism is taken for granted by Latino/a and Spanish American lesbian and gay poets who have adapted her as their patron saint," and despite the fact that Paz has dared to claim that "it is futile to try to learn what her true sexual feelings were. She herself did not know."[19] At this juncture, we probably should come to terms with all these opinions and, as thoughtful and concerned critics and feminists, acknowledge the fact that we do not know—or perhaps cannot agree—

about just who is a lesbian. As Karla Jay and Joanne Glasgow have asked: "Is she a woman whose erotic desires are for other women, or is she a 'woman-identified woman'? Is she a woman at all, if woman is a heterosexist language construct? And if this term is so problematic, how can one hope to define or label a lesbian text?"[20]

Departing from this notion of the diversity of the lesbian experience, we owe it to both women, the poet and the director, to search beyond the basic premise of specific gender constructions and begin to focus on the real possibilities that Bemberg's poly-valent characterization of Sor Juana offers to feminist criticism. Obviously, the film-maker's portrayal of the Mexican nun does not intend to clarify or take a stand about the character's sexuality. To the contrary, it intends to disrupt bipolar dualisms and erase every conceivable oversimplification or reductionism that might restrain the poet's identity. In this respect, one can appreciate the skill with which Bemberg manip-ulated Sor Juana's literary tools to reconstruct a visual, cinematic version of the poet's life.[21] By presenting an alternative subject who resists categorization, the feminist director challenges the idea of sexual indifference that, according to Luce Irigaray, pro-poses that in a patriarchal society there is only one representation of the sexual, for even the category "woman" exists within heterosexual economies of male subject and female subject.[22]

Historians of sexuality agree that the need for gender and sexual categorization had become more important by the end of the nineteenth century, after the emergence of "Sapphism." By then, both the medical and legal professions had begun to define, con-trol, and regulate all forms of sexuality, placing the church as the arbiter of morality. In fact, in the sixteenth and seventeenth centuries, women were free to love each other without fear of social stigma. Platonism emphasized that what romantic friends loved so passionately in each other was the soul, while gender in itself was quite irrel-evant. Yet, as Lis Whitelaw observers, "it was believed by women as well as men that such a bond was more easily formed in same sex relationships."[23] Unable to resolve the problematic issue of whether such writings conveyed expressions of love or same-sex desire, feminist and lesbian critics on the seventeenth and eighteenth centuries have consistently turned to the tradition of "romantic" or "Platonic" friendship, par-ticularly in the writings of well-known or aristocratic women.[24]

Most likely, works such as Denis Diderot's *La Religiouse* (1760),[25] a masterpiece of the erotic, had some influence on the original perception that convent life promoted sexual deviance and sexual encounter between women, because convents provide "an ideal means of maintaining the pornographic myth that acts between women only take place when men are hard to come by."[26] Bemberg's representation of convent life completely eradicates and contradicts such notion. The film re-creates an animated setting of a convent in colonial Mexico by constructing visually arresting scenes of secular and ecclesiastical interrelationships within the confinement of a physical space where women are able to receive visitors and even learn music, drama, and dance. In fact, spatial symbolism is particularly relevant in the metaphoric representation of Sor Juana's convent cell as an individual and mutual place of study, a room of her/their own."[27]

As the nun and vicereine's relationship progresses, this intimate and secluded room, far removed from male dominion, gradually becomes a site of feminine liberation where both women spend hours in endless conversation, exploring the freedom of boundless love and mutual understanding. Sexual identification and friendship between these unique characters from different worlds seems peculiar; yet, the vicereine compares how both had their paths dictated for them by age twenty and how they must equally acquiesce to the demands of their respective social status. As a member of the clergy, the nun must live secluded in the convent, obeying ecclesiastic regulations, while the vicereine, representing the Spanish Crown, is forced to live in the palace and follow the court's protocol. One wears a veil and the other a crown; however, these symbols of "power" hold the mind within, not allowing thoughts to rise and soar above the imposed conventions. A secret pact of long-lasting friendship is then sealed within the convent walls, a mutual union of the souls, the embrace between the sacred and the profane, the Spanish and the Mexican, seen once again as a projection of Latin America's constant duality between European and Indian. It is interesting to consider how María Luisa (the vicereine's namesake) Bemberg's own life mirrors the experiences of these women. Bemberg was also an upper-class intellectual growing up in a patriarchal society ruled by the morals and values of Catholicism; she married at twenty; and she was subjected to the censorship of Argentina's authoritarian regime.[28]

Social dualism, or the notion of the double self, is a fairly common trope in Latin American literature, because from the divided being alternative networks or possibilities of exchange can be produced. Throughout the film, duality and doubleness between these women is emphasized through dialogue and eloquent imagery, but it becomes perhaps most evident in a scene in which Sor Juana, before her ultimate trial, asks Father Miranda, "What do they want from me?" He answers, "God wants a different Juana." The nun then inquires, "Different from the one who loved herself too much?" In an admonishing tone, the confessor responds, "Yes! You loved that woman too much! . . . For a nun to love a worldly object is an infidelity to the Divine spouse." Defeated, she admits, "Yet, the more I loved her, the nearer I felt to God." Duality, as reflected in this dialogue, is aimed at stressing and reinforcing the character of the erotic discourse projected in some of the earlier scenes. By openly admitting the depth of her love to her confessor, Sor Juana corroborates the true nature of her feelings. Such an affirmation acknowledges the integration of other aspects of her personality that neither deny nor conflict with God (as the clergyman proposes). In fact, according to the nun's interpretation, her feelings serve as a corroboration of his or her existence. On confessing her female self as reconstructed through and by the identity of another woman instead of God's, Sor Juana is not only transgressing the canonical values and doctrines of the Catholic church, but she is also projecting herself deeper into the margins of the unaccepted—that is, the recognition of a divided self.

It is precisely in this scene that perceptive viewers are supposed to fill in the gaps marked by the narrative ellipsis and search for both, the implicit and explicit meaning that manifests between revelation and concealment. The lack of a concrete gender identification or definition becomes as problematic for Bemberg's audience as it has been, through the years, for Sor Juana's critics and admirers. To clarify this notion, we should perhaps consider Jean Franco's comment about the nun's self-referential position within her literary production, as it easily applies to the director's biographical interpretation. In the works of both women, "the fictionalization of the 'I' and the system of representation that worked through allegorical 'characters' were necessary masks which served as a form of concealment and a unique way to produce a new kind of writing subject."[29] Indeed, as Leigh Gilmore has noted, the autobiographical "I" is a linguistic shifter that does not produce a proper referent because "the autobiographical code of referentiality deploys the illusion that there is a single *I*, sufficiently distinct from the *I* it narrates to know it and to see it from the vantage of experience. . . . All of this depends on not looking too closely at the profound shakiness caused by the motion of these *I*'s."[30] However, critics such as Elena Martínez maintain that the motif of the divided self reiterates the interdependency of the lesbian identity, because the lesbian theme "is textualized through the possibility of exchanging the 'I' and the 'you' as well as in the insistence on the first person plural 'we' as the result of the unification of the 'I' with the 'you.'"[31]

In *Autobiographics: A Feminist Theory of Women's Self Representation*, Gilmore analyzes the experiences described in mystic texts of the time, in which fusion and exchange of both male and female is insisted on because both God and the soul escape all confines of male discourse and gender representation: "The body of Christ, as the ground of mystical experience, provides the occasion for what can be called a counterdiscourse of gender. That is, according to the Bible, in Christ there is no male or female, and in the mystic's self-representation of the relationship between Christ's body and her own, there is both male and female."[32] By interchanging the feminine and the masculine within a single, preconceived body, the mystic representation resists the duality and finality of gender constructions to place itself outside the phallic frame of reference. Paul Smith and Gilmore agree that mysticism provides the only possibility of transcendence allowed to women in Western culture, as they are constantly mediated and inscribed through a body that can redeem its physicality only when transformed into a vessel for the manifestation of sublime experience, (or what contemporary feminist theory calls "feminine rapture").[33] Smith endorses Irigaray's perception that the Christian mystical tradition inadequately disrupts the homosexual economy of Western patriarchy because it fails to create or make room for a new female imagery. Mysticism at least provides a privileged space for the articulation of women's desire and may be "the only place where 'woman' relates to an Other speaking and acting as both object and subject." However, even when this temporary merging dissolves differences, we must remember that this space is always "unstable and shifting, by no means 'beyond' the ravages of patriarchy."[34]

If feminism and feminist theory are set to make room for women's discourse, and to create such imagery, we may want to explore how Bemberg, by treating sexuality and gender as fluid and interchangeable entities, dismantles the ideological parameters that hinder the production of new modes of feminine representation. When Sor

Juana admits to her confessor that she finds her spiritual freedom and intellectual motivation in the process of self-recognition through another woman's identity instead of as a subject of God, Bemberg's character is clearly disrupting artificial hierarchies that strictly bind and restrict female desire to the rigorous morality codes of the Catholic church. Once Sor Juana has been displaced outside the web of ideology marked by hegemonic discourses, the director grants her heroine the agency for change, or "subject repositioning," and releases her from the limiting definitions of the heterosexual. The feminist film critic Teresa de Lauretis believes that subject repositioning should be the priority for feminist criticism, because until such an exercise takes place, women will continue to be perceived in terms of masculine definitions that are incapable of ideological or political change.[35]

Considered one of the most heavily burdened bearers of meaning in culture, the human body—in particular, the female body—is restricted to a regulatory set of meanings imposed by heterosexuality in direct relation to men's needs. To this fact we owe the lack of overt interest in the critical analysis of lesbianism and homosexual desire. In contemporary culture, the lesbian retains a kind of "ghost effect"; she is an elusive figure who is difficult to spot or name. Constantly displaced, the lesbian is "never with us, it seems, but always somewhere else: in the shadows, in the margins, hidden from history, out of sight, out of mind, a wanderer in the dusk, a lost soul, a tragic mistake, a plain denizen of the night. She is far away and she is dire."[36] Feminist theories of the subject and of subjectivity have perceived lesbianism in films and literature as a ghostly presence that is consistently out of focus and evanescent. According to Diana Fuss, the tentative act of disclosure of the lesbian subject is invariably affected by a radical concealment, as the word "homosexuality" stands in for that which stands without. Or, as Judith Butler explains, the term itself "constructs such exclusion by prominently including the contaminated other in its oppositional logic. . . . Paradoxically, the 'ghosting' of homosexuality coincides with its 'birth,' for the historical moment of the first appearance of the homosexual as a 'species' rather than a 'temporary aberration' also marks the moment of the homosexual's disappearance—into the closet."[37]

Even conventional heterosexual–homosexual binaries are constructed on oppositional foundations that are basic to the survival of a symbolic order based on a logic of limits, margins, borders, and boundaries. Endorsing Laura Mulvey's theories, Patricia White notes that, within the binary stranglehold of sexual difference, lesbianism constitutes an *im*possible deviance because it has been neatly assimilated to accommodate "the masculinization of the spectator position."[38] While evaluating the problematic aspects of devising strategies of representation of feminine sexuality and desire, we must also consider Bemberg's position as an upper-class woman and controversial artist working within the restrictions of a highly regimented society in which the term "homosexuality" (even less, the idea of lesbianism) and the questioning of gender are not issues to contend with.[39] Bemberg manages to solve this dilemma by deconstructing gender limitations and openly inviting the viewer to conceive the possibility of an "ex-centric" Sor Juana. In fact, without rewriting Sor Juana's essence or simply jumping at the chance to film a scene of passion between the two women, the filmmaker draws on the nun's sensuous poetry and enigmatic personality to accentuate the erotic. Bergmann introduces a clear definition of the way in which the film portrays the dynamics between the nun and the vicereine:

> The cinematic interpretation of the relationship between the patroness and poet ensures that this threat (of a love relationship) is only a delusion of leering, misogynistic clerics and does not implicate Sor Juana as desiring subject.... The chastity of the Hispanic "Décima Musa" is protected, and she is depicted as acting only on exclusively heterosexual desire: when the Condesa de Paredes kisses Juana, she does not return the physical gesture.[40]

Fully aware of the implications of inscribing an overtly lesbian character in her productions, Bemberg opted to exceed the narrativization or representation of female sexuality by disembodying her Sor Juana in a fashion that has been quite popular among contemporary Latin American women writers.[41] In her analysis of Teresa de la Parra's corpus, Sylvia Molloy says that, "by highlighting what is secret, clandestine, conspiratorial, on the threshold, as it were, of a relatively nonthreatening text, [de la Parra] is offering not only clues to her literary strategy but a lesson in discriminating reading, an invitation to decode an oeuvre, a life, that permanently borders on the unsayable."[42] Uncomfortable with the limits of interpretation regarding feminine eroticism, Bemberg's film aims to defer and displace desire, allowing it to manifest in a variety of ways that are neither physical nor sexual. Audre Lorde's essay on the uses of the erotic as power concludes that the erotic not only functions as a main source of creative energy; it also provides "the power which comes from sharing deeply any pursuit with another person. The sharing of joy, whether physical, emotional, psychic, or intellectual, forms a bridge between the sharers which can be the basis for understanding much of what is not shared between them, and lessens the threat of their difference."[43] The (meta)physical representation of Sor Juana evades the context of sexual desire, thus serving as a referential network of border crossings and ramifications, a multisemic personality that contemporary gay and feminist critics may refer to as "queer."[44] However, Bemberg's queer or androgynous character, who sees her own body as an "abstract," is far from sexless.[45] In her self-conscious representation, the nun perceives androgyny as the only way to evade the confrontation between her repressed femaleness and the many opportunities for self-realization offered by the masculine.[46] As the child of Hermes, god of science, eloquence, and cunning, and Aphrodite, goddess of love and beauty, the poet's multiple identity is manifested through a self-explanatory dream in which she admits, "as I could not dress as a man, I dressed as a nun"—or, as the vicereine will conclude, "I never met anyone like you. More poet than nun, more nun than woman."

Franco believes that Sor Juana followed no consistent paths and that only when it was convenient did she "[draw] attention to the fact that she was a woman; at other times she deployed an impersonal subject or adopted a male persona."[47] To her own benefit, Sor Juana (like Bemberg) disrupted the dualisms of mind and body, male and female, even writing and desiring in a variety of ways to match her own purposes and needs. Several critics believe that Sor Juana's desire to dress in men's clothing was a sign of her homosexual tendencies. This notion is not completely valid, however, because we are unable to determine whether this was in fact the case or whether the poet viewed cross-dressing as a means of self-empowerment that would allow her to act as she pleased (like the French writer George Sand, who began to dress in men's clothes to get cheaper seats at the theater).

As Sor Juana uses riddles, metaphors, and myriad semantic tropes to construct each verse of her poetry, Bemberg manipulates lights, music, and props to create a filmic discourse that draws an almost imperceptible line between eroticism and spirituality. Both women camouflage their intellectual production in highly resourceful ways, by consciously creating polysemic texts that simultaneously resist and subject, wisely balancing aggression and subordination, sliding from the private into the public, from the feminine into the masculine. Within the nun's poetry as well as within Bemberg's film, symbols, allegories, and imagery play a significant role in the portrayal of multiple subject positions. One the many powerful allegories is presented through the symbolic crown of Quetzal feathers (sacred bird of Mexico) that Sor Juana receives as a gift from the Spanish vicereine. "The Phoenix of Mexico"[48] accepts the crown "through the bars of her visiting parlor," and after she puts it on her head, she dances and bows at her guests, ironically stating, "Montezuma lies prostrate at the conqueror's feet." Sor Juana, the Mexican "rare bird" in captivity,[49] is the majestic and exotic creature whose culture has been subdued (as she has herself) and conquered by the Spanish power.[50] This powerful allegory is later recalled when the viceroy visits Sor Juana before his return to Spain. Apologizing for his wife's absence, he explains, "María Luisa is very upset. since she has fallen in love with Mexico." Sor Juana responds, "Mexico will not be the same without her, it will sink into the lake." And so she does. Once devoid of the viceregal protection, the nun falls victim to conventual intrigues and finally yields to the archbishop's wrath. She distributes all of her possessions, forsaking her lifelong pursuit of universal knowledge to enter the spiritual path.

Representations of female desire and sexuality in Bemberg's cinema (and Sor Juana's writings) make it apparent that repression rather than expression marks a woman's life, and that it is only through transgressions that her identity may change and evolve. Chris Straayer suggests that feminist film theory has much to gain from considering lesbian desire and sexuality, because "women's desire for women deconstructs male/female sexual dichotomies, sex/gender conflation, and the universality of the Oedipal narrative. Acknowledgement of the female initiated active sexuality and sexualized activity of lesbians has the potential to reopen a space in which straight women as well as lesbians can exercise self-determined pleasure."[51] Still, female artists—particularly, lesbians—feel forced to hide their identities to survive within a heterosexual culture that perceives lesbianism as a threat because it defies traditional constructions of femininity and motherhood. Terry Castle explains that lesbians, even more so than gay men, are difficult to see because their image has been made invisible by culture. "It would be putting it mildly to say that the lesbian represents a threat to patriarchal protocol," Castle writes. "Western civilization has for centuries been haunted by a fear of 'women without men'—of women indifferent or resistant to male desire." Thus, "politically speaking, the lesbian is usually treated as a non-person—without right or citizenship—or else a sinister bugaboo to be driven from the scene at once."[52] Guilt is one method used to keep woman in her place; another tactic is to depict women who do not wish to conform as masculine, abnormal—that is, "lesbian." Lillian Faderman notes that twentieth-century fiction has played "a significant role in keeping women down through associating feminism with lesbianism and lesbianism with everything horrible."[53] To conceive any feminine identity beyond the limitations proscribed by patriarchal structures, feminine–feminist discourse has found ambiguity and multiplicity as two essential tools to explore and exploit transgression. However, within the areas of film and literature, women are still searching for languages of representation to challenge, deconstruct, and do away with fixed icons imposed by male productions.

Yo, la peor de todas continues the feminist tradition of Bemberg's work, yet it clearly suggests the possibility of a culture of sisterhood, reaffirming the feminine and taking it to a deeper level. The film whispers transgression, suggesting the crossing of boundaries as a denial of male-constructed subjectivity of women. If we are determined to find the truth behind the conventions of patriarchal discourse, we should, as feminists and critics, begin to explore the possibilities offered and exploited in feminist films such as *Yo, la peor de todas*. It is only through the deconstruction of these conventions that may we begin to articulate a distinctive sexual economy as an alternative to the heterosexual. Once we have accomplished this task, we will be able to evaluate to what extent (if any) the thematic departure from heterosexual to same-sex relations produces disturbances of gender conventions through the imaginary construction of a "different" economy of desire.[54]

In proposing female characters who finally dare to confront their inner selves in the quest for autonomy, Bemberg reflects on the self-evolutionary process followed by women in the deconstruction of a patriarchal system that seeks to suppress their intellectual development. As a true artist and feminist, Bemberg has portrayed women ahead of their times, who, in seeking to defend their basic need for self-development, have been forced to confront oppressive social and political forces: the Inquisition, Peronism, militarism, etc. Joining in the common preoccupation of her contemporaries, Bemberg explores identity issues that clearly relate to gender, politics, and history. As Fares notes, "The last thirty years of Argentine literature is frequently played along the thematic axis of sexuality, and often the sexuality is one marked by deviation, aberration, and by its relationship with violence."[55] By opening the film's interpretation to a whole realm of possibilities, the feminist director is making room for new female imagery while creating an eccentric space in which feminine desire might be allowed to manifest in a plurality of forms and remain free of ideological restrictions. As Bemberg herself concludes, "In these six feature films, I propose images of women that are vertical, autonomous, independent, thoughtful, courageous, spunky."[56] Like Bemberg, the Argentine director's heroines are audacious and energetic women who are able to overcome their own insecurities and fears, each serving as a role model for those who dare to be different.

Notes

Epigraph: Audre Lorde, "Uses of the Erotic: The Erotic as Power," in *The Lesbian and Gay Studies Reader*, eds. Henry Abelove, Michéle Aina Barale, and David M. Halperin (New York: Routledge, 1993), 339–43.

1. Simone de Beauvoir, *The Second Sex*, trans. H. M. Parsley (New York: Knopf, 1953; repr. New York: Vintage Books, 1980).

2. Caleb Bach, "María Luisa Bemberg Tells the Untold" (interview), *The Americas* 46, no. 2 (March 1994): 22. See also Marcela Kogan, "Contra viento y marea," *Americas* 35 (1985): 37.

3. Cecilia Grierson, Argentina's first female doctor, founded the First Feminist Party in 1919, and in March 1936 Victoria Ocampo, María Rosa Oliver, and Susana Larguía founded the Argentine Women's Union. Months later, Ocampo, whom many considered the most influential woman of letters and a cultural icon, delivered "Woman and Her Expression," a poignant address in which she called for gender equality. See Doris Meyer, *Victoria Ocampo: Against the Wind and the Tide* (Austin,: University of Texas Press, 1990). According to Leila Guerriero, Bemberg's biographer, it was in these meetings that she began the path of self-discovery and empowerment that finally transformed her into a true feminist: Leila Guerriero, "María Luisa Bemberg," in *Mujeres argentinas: el lado femenino de nuestra historia* (Buenos Aires: Alfaguara, 1998).

4. Gustavo Fares, *Contemporary Argentinean Women Writers* (Gainesville: University Press of Florida, 1998), 1.

5. Nisa Torrents, "One Woman's Cinema: Interview with María Luisa Bemberg," in *Knives and Angels: Women Writers in Latin America*, ed. Susan Basnett (New York: Zed Books, 1990), 174.

6. Ibid., 161.

7. See Donald F. Stevens, "Passion and Patriarchy in Nineteenth-Century Argentina: María Luisa Bemberg's Camila," in *Based on a True Story: Latin American History at the Movies*, ed. Donald Stevens (Wilmington, Del.: SR Books, 1997), 85–102. See also Karen Jaehne, "Love as a Revolutionary Act," *Cineaste* 14 (1986).

8. Mark D. Szuchman, "Depicting the Past in Argentine Films: Family Drama and Historical Debate in *Miss Mary* and *The Official Story*," in Stevens, *Based on a True Story*, 173–200.

9. Torrents, "One Woman's Cinema," 173.

10. *Yo, la peor de todas* was produced by Gilbert Marouani and Litat Stantic. The script was written by Bemberg and Antonio Larreta. For the biography, see Octavio Paz, *Sor Juana, or The Traps of Faith* (Cambridge, Mass.: Belknap Press, 1988), or the original, *Sor Juana Inés de la Cruz; o, las trampas de la fe* (Barcelona: Seix Barral, 1982).

11. Emilie Bergmann, "Sor Juana Inés de la Cruz: Dreaming in a Double Voice," in *Women, Culture and Politics in Latin America*, ed. Emilie Bergmann et al. (Berkeley: University of California Press, 1990), 151–73.

12. In her excellent essay on Sor Juana's life and works, Jean Franco writes, "Other nuns criticized Sor Juana's handwriting because it resembled that of a man and was therefore an indication of her transgression of boundaries": Jean Franco, "Sor Juana Explores Space," in *Plotting Women*, ed. Jean Franco (New York: Columbia University Press, 1989), 33–38.

13. In 1690, she was commissioned by an anonymous person to write a critique of a sermon delivered in 1650 by the Portuguese Jesuit Antonio de Vieyra. In this essay, later published under the title *Carta Atenagórica* (Athenagoric letter, named for its excellence worthy of Athena, the Roman goddess of wisdom), Sor Juana not only questioned but also challenged Father

Vieyra's theological views. The bishop of Puebla, Manuel Fernández de Santa Cruz, replied to Sor Juana's letter with one of his own, signed using the pseudonym Sor Filotea de la Cruz. The letter reveals his admiration for the nun's erudition and rhetorical dexterity, but it aims to discourage her interest in profane literature. This attack brought about Sor Juana's famous autobiographical essay, *Respuesta a Sor Filotea de la Cruz* (1691). In the essay, the Mexican nun tactfully yet sarcastically justifies her scholarly vocation as a natural impulse that God has laid upon her, at the same time admitting that convent life was the most decent path she could follow because she felt total abhorrence toward marriage. In this firsthand account, Sor Juana reveals several aspects of her personality and vehemently defends women's right to receive an education.

14. As quoted in Susan E. Ramírez, "I, the Worst of All," in Stevens, *Based on a True Story*, 47–62.

15. Emilie Bergmann, "Abjection and Ambiguity: Lesbian Desire in Bemberg's *Yo, la peor de todas*," in *Hispanisms and Homosexualities*, ed. Sylvia Molloy and Robert McKee Irwin (Durham, N.C.: Duke University Press, 1998), 229–47.

16. Paz denies the nun's lesbian tendencies by reminding readers that it was only natural for Sor Juana to praise her protectors fervently: "The sensual expressions and amatory images could be accepted and read as metaphors and rhetorical figures of two true sentiments: appreciation and an inferior's devotion to her superior." As quoted in Elena Martínez, *Lesbian Voices from Latin America: Breaking Ground* (New York: Garland Publications, 1996), 201.

17. Ramírez, "I, the Worst of All," 58–59.

18. As quoted in Bergmann, "Abjection and Ambiguity," 234.

19. Ibid., 232.

20. Karla Jay and Joanne Glasgow, as quoted in Suzanne Chávez Silverman, "The Look That Kills: The 'Unacceptable Beauty' of Alejandra Pizarnik's *La condesa sangrienta*," in *¿Entiendes? Queer Readings, Hispanic Writings*, ed. Emilie L. Bergmann and Paul Julian Smith (Durham, N.C.: Duke University Press, 1995). In her outstanding essay on the diversity of the lesbian experience, Martha Vicinus quotes Jackie Stacey's opinion on the lack of a unified collective identity among lesbians: "Lesbian experiences are not only fragmented within lesbian cultures, but also within the culture dominated by heterosexuality in which lesbians are ascribed the contradictory positions of the invisible presence." See Martha Vicinus, "'They Wonder to Which Sex I Belong': The Historical Roots of Modern Lesbian Identity," in Abelove et al., *Lesbian and Gay Studies Reader*, 433.

21. See Josefina Ludmer, "Tretas del débil," in *La sartén por el mango: Encuentro de escritoras latinoamericanas*, ed. Patricia Elena González and Eliana Ortega (Río Piedras: Ediciones Huracán, 1984).

22. Luce Irigaray, *This Sex Which Is Not One*, trans. Catherine Porter and Caroline Burke (Ithaca, N.Y.: Cornell University Press, 1985). See also Diana Fuss, ed., *Inside/Out: Lesbian Theories, Gay Theories* (New York: Routledge, 1991), 3.

23. Lis Whitelaw, "Make of Our Lives a Study: Reading and Writing Lesbian Biography," in *Volcanoes and Pearl Divers: Essays in Lesbian Feminist Studies*, ed. Suzanne Raitt (London: Harrington Press, 1994), 103–22.

24. According to Terry Castle, "the concept of lesbianism, at least in the flagrantly sexualized sense that we usually understand the term today, is by and large a fabrication of late nineteenth and early twentieth-century male sexologists": Terry Castle, *The Apparitional Lesbian: Female Homosexuality and Modern Culture* (New York: Columbia University Press 1993), 8. See also Vicinus, "'They Wonder to Which Sex I Belong.'"

25. Denis Diderot, *The Nun*, trans. Leonard Tancock (Harmondsworth, U.K.: Penguin, 1974). Diderot's pathetic heroine, Suzanne Simonin, forced to become a nun by her selfish and obdurate family, is imprisoned within a series of corrupt convents, each worse than the last, where she is singled out for cruel and incessant persecution by her superiors. See also Castle, *Apparitional Lesbian*, 31.

26. Ros Ballaster, "'The Vices of Old Rome Revived': Representations of Female Same-Sex Desire in Seventeenth- and Eighteenth-Century England," in Raitt, *Volcanoes and Pearl Divers*, 13–37. In 1971, the American director Ken Russell produced the surrealistic drama *The Devils*, an adaptation of Whiting's play and Huxley's book dealing with sex, witchcraft, and politics inside a seventeenth-century French convent.

27. In her popular essay *A Room of One's Own* (New York: Penguin Books, 1945), Virginia Woolf describes women's need to create a liberated space far from the masculine domain in which to explore and articulate their anger, rebellion, and repressed sexuality.

28. Interesting parallels can be drawn if one also evaluates the subtleties behind the dialogues between the viceroy and the misogynous archbishop of Mexico (and the role of the Inquisition). Both men voice, almost literally, the authoritarian discourse of the military junta (1976–83), which promised to eradicate all "subversive" and "tendentious" activities to restore the sacred values of Argentine society: the family, the state, and the Catholic church.

29. Franco, "Sor Juana," 29.

30. Leigh Gilmore, *Autobiographics: A Feminist Theory of Women's Self Representation* (Ithaca, N.Y.: Cornell University Press, 1994), 44.

31. Ibid., 44; Martínez, *Lesbian Voices*, 110.

32. Gilmore, *Autobiographics*, 133.

33. Paul J. Smith, *Representing the Other: "Race," Text, and Gender in Spanish and Spanish American Narrative* (Oxford: Clarendon Press, 1992). Quoting Hélène Cixous, Gilmore writes in *Autobiographics*, 62, that "women are figures of rapture, those wild women, sorceresses, and conjurers who threaten phallogocentrism with their witchy words and ways. Another perspective would argue that women are agents of rapture whose actions in the world, including writing, are appropriated by masculinist institutions that women can nevertheless, resist." See Hélène Cixous, "The Laugh of the Medusa," in *New French Feminisms: An Anthology*, trans. Keith Cohen and Paula Cohen (New York: Schocken Books, 1981), 245–46. See also Amy Hollywood, "Beauvoir, Irigaray, and the Mystical," *Hypathia* 9 (1994).

34. Smith, *Representing the Other*, 105–6.

35. Teresa de Lauretis, *Technologies of Gender: Essays on Theory, Film, and Fiction* (Bloomington: Indiana University Press, 1987), 17. See also de Lauretis's "Rethinking Women's Cinema: Aesthetics and Feminist Theory," in *Multiple Voices in Feminist Film Criticism*, ed. Diane Carson, Linda Dittmar, and Janice R. Welsch (Bloomington: Indiana University Press, 1991). Another perspective is presented in Mary C. Gentile, *Film Feminisms: Theory and Practice* (Westport, Conn.: Greenwood Press, 1985), and Annette Kuhn, *Women's Pictures: Feminism and Cinema* (London: Routledge and Kegan Paul, 1982).

36. Castle, *Apparitional Lesbian*, 2. See Shameen Kabir, "Lesbian Representation in Film," in Raitt, *Volcanoes and Pearl Divers*.

37. Diana Fuss, "Introduction," in Fuss, *Inside/Out*, 4. On ghosting in film, see Patricia White, "Female Spectator, Lesbian Specter: The Haunting," and Judith Butler, "Imitation and Gender Insubordination," both in ibid.

38. White, "Female Spectator," 146. See also Laura Mulvey, "Visual Pleasure and Narrative Cinema," *Screen* 16, no. 3 (1975).

39. As John King has pointed out, "Elements of the Catholic Church in Argentina are among the most reactionary in Latin America and the Catholic hierarchy had kept largely silent during the years of repression, despite the murder of a number of priests and nuns. Social reforms under Alfonsín, such as the final acceptance of divorce, had to proceed extremely cautiously for fear of a right-wing, Church-led revolt": John King, "Assailing the Heights of Macho Pictures: Women Film-makers in Contemporary Argentina," in Basnett, *Knives and Angels,* 162. According to the Argentine sociologist Juan José Sebreli, "Lesbians don't exist—in the eyes of the rules or the police or the church"; Ilse Fuskove, an Argentine lesbian feminist, agrees: "Lesbians are absolutely invisible here." Both remarks are quoted in Chávez Silverman, "The Look That Kills." 282

40. Bergmann, "Abjection and Ambiguity," 231–42.

41. As Elaine Showalter notes in *A Literature of Their Own* (New York: Princeton University Press, 1977), 302: "In trying to deal with this recognition of an ongoing struggle for personal and artistic autonomy, contemporary women writers have reasserted their continuity with the women of the past, through essays and criticism as well as through fiction. They use all the resources of the modern novel, including exploded chronology, dreams, myth, and stream-of-consciousness, but they have been profoundly influenced by nineteenth-century feminine literature."

42. Sylvia Molloy, "Disappearing Acts: Reading Lesbian in Teresa de la Parra," in Bergmann and Smith, *¿Entiendes?* 237.

43. Lorde, "Uses of the Erotic," 340.

44. "Being lesbian and raised Catholic, indoctrinated as straight, I made the choice to be queer. Like writing and being Chicana, queerness means living in the borderlands, a way of balancing, of mitigating duality. All three (being Chicana, writing, and queerness) are vehicles for breaking down dualisms in the production of a third thing, or a hybrid element": Gloria Anzaldúa's self-definition of "queerness," as quoted in Yvonne Yarbo-Bejarano, "The Lesbian Body in Latina Cultural Production," in Bergmann and Smith, *¿Entiendes?* 181–97. Yarbo-Bejarano also believes that Cherríe Moraga takes a more radical positioning, as she "opens up a space in her writing for a subjectivity that is shaped across and through multiplicity of discourses in relation to the unified female subject of much white feminist theory. The mapping of subjectivity and oppression in Moraga's writing is the cartography of lesbian desire, the unspeakable speaking and unrepresentable desire of the lesbian subject of color, the Chicana lesbian": Yvonne Yarbo-Bejarano, "De-Constructioning the Lesbian Body: Cherríe Moraga's *Loving in the War Years,*" in Abelove et al., *Lesbian and Gay Studies Reader,* 595–603.

45. It is worth considering Showalter's explanation of Virginia Woolf's definition of the androgynous vision. "In Woolf's terms, it is a response to the dilemma of a woman writer embarrassed and alarmed by feelings too hot to handle without risking real rejection by her family, her audience, and her class. A room of one's own is the first step toward her solution more than an office with a typewriter, it is a symbol of psychic withdrawal, an escape from the demands of other people": Showalter, *Literature of Their Own,* 286.

46. Before receiving her visitors, the nun puts on a bracelet, splashes on perfume, and adjusts her veil in front of a mirror.

47. Franco, "Sor Juana," 43. Yet the interpretation of the social role must never be dismissed, as Franco points out in her excellent study on Sor Juana's life and work. "There was no private space for women writers since to write was to write within an institution and even when males may represent an entire institution, females were never more than individuals": ibid.

48. This nickname was given to Sor Juana by her contemporaries because of her inner wisdom, her charismatic personality, and her physical beauty.

49. The Jesuit critic Father Tineo de Morales used this term in reference to Sor Juana's work, saying that it "could only have been produced by someone out of the ordinary, an *Ave rara* which would only be found in the New World": Franco, "Sor Juana," 24.

50. For Bergmann, "the gift of the headdress of quetzal feathers serves multiple purposes: it inscribes this discourse in a Mexican content, it recreates a gift Sor Juana commemorated in a poem, it pictures Sor Juana as a rare avis in her cage, and it creates a self-conscious scene of colonial dominance and submission": Bergmann, "Abjection and Ambiguity," 240.

51. Chris Straayer, "The Hypothetical Lesbian Heroine in Narrative Feature Film," in Carson et al., *Multiple Voices*, 338–43.

52. Castle, *Apparitional Lesbian*, 4–5.

53. Lillian Faderman, *Surpassing the Love of Men: Romantic Friendship and Love between Women from the Renaissance to the Present* (New York: William Morrow, 1981), 341.

54. Fuss's perspective may be even more worthy of consideration. "What we need is a theory of sexual borders that will help us come to terms with, and to organize around, the new cultural and sexual arrangements occasioned by the movements and transmutations of pleasure in the social field": Fuss, "Introduction," 5.

55. "Sexual deviation and aberration may be considered positive when they free the character or negative when they are the direct result of the violence that dominated the rest of the social body. Sexuality and gender roles can be sites where struggles and social contracts are negotiated and mediated": Fares, *Argentinean Women Writers*, 11.

56. Bach, "María Luisa Bemberg," 22.

Sara E. Cooper

11

The Lesbian Family in Cristina Peri Rossi's "The Witness": A Study in Utopia and Infiltration

Contrary to popular belief, the "Latin American family" is anything but a homogeneous or biological structure. Rather, the rich and varied cultural heritage of the Americas, which includes countless indigenous clans as well as immigrants from myriad African, Asian, and European countries, has contributed to a complex social definition of family that has always stretched beyond any legal prescription imposed by the Spanish empire.[1] Hence, Latin American cultures have consistently produced "subversive" families, to use Ferdinand Mount's term: families that model officially proscribed behavior and viewpoints and provide alternative value systems.[2] Contemporary narrative, especially that by women, has increasingly called into question the existing stereotypes of the traditional family, thus using the image of the subversive family to upset the dominant literary discourse as well as sociocultural norms.

The short story "The Witness," by the Uruguayan Cristina Peri Rossi (b. 1941) is an example of a more radical reformulation of the concept of Latin American family.[3] In this work, the narrative revolves around the interpersonal dynamic of a lesbian family, and in so doing raises a stream of questions that hold interest for literary and cultural studies. Peri Rossi uses the focus on family, and particularly the gay family, to explore the ideas of exile, utopia, marginalization, patriarchal infiltration, and—naturally—family. It is a revolutionary narrative in that it both questions the validity of existing social structures and presents an alternative that directly opposes traditional gender roles and family composition. Complementing the thematic locus, "The Witness" makes use of various narrative techniques to underline certain points, subtly suggest correlation, or interject implicit contradictions to what may be presented explicitly. In this way, the lesbian family is represented as a complex system that is by no means free of problems or stresses but nevertheless fulfills the basic functions of family. The resulting story, a socially relevant and complex narration, opens the field of contemporary Latin American literature to include a new subgenre: the lesbian and gay family narrative.

Accessing the Lesbian Family

The expansion of Latin American and U.S. Latina literary studies and its concurrent blending with cultural studies—especially queer theory—has created an aperture through which the critical reader can view previously unconsidered material. This opening has been mirrored in the fields of psychology and sociology, where the lesbian and gay family is finally receiving merited and necessary study.

Such a propitious happening is providing ever more inclusive paradigms and terminology, which, in the tradition of psychological and social approaches to literature, may be adapted for use in literary analysis. By the same token, the study of fiction often will add to the body of knowledge in the social sciences; in the case of "The Witness," family systems theories contribute to a multilevel reading of the text, just as the text contributes a fictional case study of a lesbian family.

Before studying Peri Rossi's text, we should pause to consider the lesbian family as both a term and a social system. More than any other type of family, the lesbian family is socially and academically invisible,[4] making the construction of an acceptable definition difficult. First, it must be acknowledged that, outside the field of gay and lesbian (or gender) studies, relatively little scholarly attention has been paid to the impact of sexual orientation on the family experience (and vice versa), much less to the composition or dynamics of families that might be termed gay or lesbian. As Katherine R. Allen and David H. Demo concisely explain:

> Sexist and heterosexist assumptions continue to underlie most of the research on families by focusing analysis on heterosexual partnerships and parenthood. . . . This reflects the society-wide belief that "gayness" and family are mutually exclusive concepts, a belief that prevails because "the same-sex family, more than any other form, challenges fundamental patriarchal notions of family and gender relationships."[5]

Until the 1980s, researchers had assumed a limited and pejorative definition of the lesbian or gay household, using the term "gay family" as a static referent lacking any individual dynamic or diversity. In the words of U. Bronfenbrenner and A. C. Crouter, the expression "gay and lesbian family" has been an "environmental label—with no attention to what the environment is like, what people are living there, what they are doing, or how the activities taking place could affect the child."[6] According to Allen and Demo, what is generally missing from the academic forum is a discussion of family processes, the dynamics of family relationships, and the way these are affected by the gender and sexual orientation of the family's members.[7] The result is that "lesbian and gay families are commonly ignored, poorly understood, stigmatized, and problematized."[8] This in turn creates a distortion that masks the true definition and representation of families overall, excluding an ample number of existing families (not only those that are gay and lesbian).

Kath Weston's *Families We Choose*, a seminal work in the study of gay families, explores the functionality of families of choice created by gays and lesbians.[9] Among other things, Weston underlines the importance of security, adaptability, communication, and economic and emotional support, adding: "In the description of gay families, sentiment and emotion often appeared alongside material aid, conflict resolution, and the narrative encapsulation of a shared past."[10] Again, the element of choice suggests that emotions and feelings are paramount for the founding and maintenance of gay or lesbian families, which is in keeping with the contemporary view of family as the main provider of nurturing and emotional support. In these terms, the gay family is one unrestricted by a procreative or biological prescription and therefore able to be defined—and chosen—as a functional relationship of mutual love, respect, support, and growth.

To appreciate fully the intricacies of a gay family dynamic, it is necessary to have recourse to a methodology that accepts a broader definition of kinship. When speaking of the nuclear family's emotional system, family systems theories generally do not differentiate between blood ties and other family connections.[11]

Salvador Minuchin and Charles Fishman address the point directly, stating, "Our limited clinical experience with homosexual couples with children suggests that family therapy concepts are as valid with them as with heterosexual couples with children."[12] As is consistent with family systems theory in general, the emphasis is not on delimiting or prescribing an ideal family structure. Rather, it is on assessing the level of functioning in the system that exists. The tendency to value what is there and expunge or modify only the parts that severely limit healthy functioning will be extremely helpful in viewing gay families.

Writing and Reading the Lesbian and Gay Family Narrative

Peri Rossi's "The Witness" can be viewed as gay family narrative both for its portrayal of lesbian family dynamics and for its intertwining of the ideas of gay family and narrative. As mentioned earlier, Weston makes clear the correlation between gay families and narrative, both of which are the creative efforts of their authors. Heterosexual families are the subject of countless stories, both fiction and nonfiction; the relative scarcity of lesbian and gay family narratives, by contrast, is daunting. The resultant historical and textual invisibility makes it more difficult for gay and lesbians (and their families) to find the support and validation they need, or even to believe in their own existence. Adrienne Rich explains that "cultural imperialism . . . [is] the decision made by one group of people that another shall be cut off from their past, shall be kept from the power of memory, context, continuity. This is why lesbians, meeting, need to tell and retell stories."[13]

A cultural phenomenon that is documented in much gay film and literature, the "coming-out story" is one of the most self-affirming and revolutionary acts performed in the gay community.[14] Rich maintains that the evolving oral tradition "has sustained us. These stories, which bring us together and which also confirm for each of us the path and meaning of her individual journey, are like the oldest tribal legends: tales of birth and rebirth, of death and rebirth."[15] Similarly, Bonnie Zimmerman notes the relationship between artistic or literary production and coming out:

Lesbian feminists define lesbian oppression primarily as mutilation of self characterized by speechlessness, invisibility, and inauthenticity. Lesbian resistance to this oppression necessarily lies in telling our stories and naming ourselves. Our power, as individuals and as a community, flows from language, imagination, and culture. By controlling and defining images and ideas, lesbians "reconstitute the world." For all these reasons, the lesbian feminist novel often presents the writing of a text or painting of a picture as both means and metaphor for the creation of the lesbian self.[16]

The point is that narrative self-creation is naturally present in the gay experience. The "narrative encapsulation" also contributes to the forming of gay family, as documented by Weston. Lesbian and gay kinship networks are rife with an oral—and increasingly written—tradition that chronicles their own construction, carefully or spontaneously providing the history and mythology that is needed to support a newly emerging social order. This inescapable interweaving of kinship networks and story is apparent in "The Witness" and will be discussed as part of the analysis to follow.

Even under the label of gay family narrative in Latin American literature readers will find relatively few examples of lesbian families. This reflects the fact that Latin American lesbian texts are even less prevalent than those by and about gay men, as are critical works on lesbian-focused fiction. David William Foster speculates why this may be:

Since the very notion of homosexuality derives from patriarchal programs to control the individual body, as the starting point for total social control, part of a feminist rejection of the patriarchy may simply entail ignoring such a "problematization" of erotic expression between women as irrelevant in the face of other concerns.[17]

This is an interesting but incomplete argument. Further explanation is found in Foster's comments on the voluntary invisibility of lesbians in Western society,[18] which, coupled with women's general lack of visibility, economic power, and political or literary voice, makes difficult the emergence of a women-centered canon. For this reason, studies of lesbian works, like those of women's literature in general, often dwell on silence versus the finding of voice as a key concern. A case in point, Suzanne Chávez Silverman's 1995 article on Alejandra Pizarnik's novel *La condesa sangrienta*, begins with the following series of epigraphs:

A lesbian who does not reinvent the word is a lesbian in the process of disappearing. —Nicole Brossard, *The Aerial Letter*

Lesbians don't exist—in the eyes of the rulers or the police or the church. —Juan José Sebreli, Argentine sociologist

Lesbians are absolutely invisible here. —Ilse Fuskova, Argentine lesbian-feminist (age 60)

A dual masquerade—passing straight/passing lesbian enervates and contributes to speechlessness—to speak might be to reveal. —Michelle Cliff, "Notes on Speechlessness"

I don't exist anymore and I know it. . . . I lose my mind if I speak; I lose years if I don't. Sometime, perhaps, we will find refuge in the true reality. —Alejandra Pizarnik, *El deseo de la palabra* (Desire for the word)[19]

As another Southern Cone writer who also has experienced social and political censure for her sexually explicit writing, Pizarnik provides an example that is doubly relevant in a study of Peri Rossi. Chávez Silverman's apt framing of Pizarnik's words makes an unmistakable point: Lesbian silence still exists in the context of homosexual culture and feminist culture in Latin America; lesbians are oppressed and invisible both because they are women and because they are gay. Elizabeth Meese reiterates that writing the lesbian experience is not a simple task:

> Lesbian is a word written in invisible ink, readable when held up to a flame and self-consuming, a disappearing trick before my eyes where the letters appear and fade into the paper on which they are written. . . . An unwriting goes on as quickly as the inscription takes [its] place.[20]

Lesbians are ignored (and by turns harassed) in the larger social context, to be sure, but they are condemned to the same voicelessness in their family system. It will be of no surprise, therefore, to find that lesbian silence or invisibility in the family is a key issue in the texts to be studied here. As suggested earlier, the act of narration is significant for the survival of gay identity, and it seems even more so for the lesbian characters portrayed in gay family narrative.

As the gay/lesbian family begins to emerge as a theme in Latin American literature, it is depicted in different texts as dysfunctional, problematic, fairly normal, or even utopian. In "The Witness" the reader finds a representation—or better said, a questioning—of the gay family as a utopian space. Such a preoccupation is not at all unusual in the context of gay families or gay literature. Weston reports in her study of gay and lesbian families in the Bay area that

> people often presented gay families as a foray into uncharted territory, where the lack of cultural guideposts to mark the journey engendered fear and exhilaration. Indeed, there was a utopian cast to the way many lesbians and gay men talked about the families they were fashioning.[21]

Whether as a result of the expansiveness inherent in creating a new form of kinship or because of the oppression and isolation experienced by those who choose to deviate from the accepted and legal standard of a heterosexual marriage, there is a tendency in the gay community to idealize the gay and lesbian family.

A similar idealization is present in many literary representations of the gay experience. Zimmerman asserts that "lesbian writers create a *mythology* for the lesbian community, one that can be both inspirational and stifling."[22] Lesbian mythmaking, which according to Zimmerman is "a political project aimed at overturning the patriarchal domination of culture and language," has culminated in the writing of the lesbian feminist utopian novel.[23] Zimmerman names a variety of themes and metaphors present in the utopian speculative novel, including: "the quest/journey, exile, islands, the country and the city, and particularly Lesbian Nation."[24] The exile may be forced or chosen, but it is usually the result of some cataclysmic event such as nuclear war, ecological decline, or the revolt of nature herself.[25] Afterward, the all-women haven invokes the safety of separatism, strength, and (sometimes) militancy, as well as virtues assumed to be female, such as nurturing, empathy, and mothering. Zimmerman comments that the strict dualism of feminine and masculine roles or identity— the latter characterized as "aggressive, violent, and domineering"—presented in these novels is ironically similar to that upheld by the patriarchy.[26] In turn, the crisis that emerges in most of the feminist lesbian utopian novels is a threatening intrusion of men into the idyllic female space; if the women must regain their sanctuary using "masculine" traits of violence or aggression, is the possibility of safety worth the risk of change?[27] Although Zimmerman's study does not focus on the depiction of family, she does emphasize that sisterhood and mothers play key roles in these feminist utopias. Peri Rossi's short story incorporates some elements of the utopian novel and to a certain extent presents the lesbian family as a utopian space. Nevertheless, as will become clear, the text questions and subverts the idea of utopia, providing a more complex and interesting narrative than a simple utopian work of fiction.

The Lesbian Family as "I" See It

Peri Rossi, in exile from her native Uruguay since the military coup of 1972, has been described as a political writer as well as one who has developed an innovative and experimental prose. "Peri's political sophistication infuses her stories with a clear understanding of the causes and effects of social ills," Gabriela Mora writes in Diane E. Marting's *Spanish American Women Writers*. "The reader can perceive those causes in spite of the elliptic and indirect fashion with which the stories refer to them."[28] In general, her fiction underlines that political, social, and sexual domination are the main source of society's problems and as such must be recognized and denounced.[29] Mora indicates that the author's denunciation of oppression and domination often centers on the family: "In her attack on social ills, the bourgeois family is one of Peri's favorite targets for parodies and satires in which the status of women occupies a prominent place."[30]

Peri Rossi's pessimistic take on the family is not limited to the bourgeois. Her own family was proletarian yet maintained a strictly conservative view of women and family. In an interview with John F. Deredita, Peri Rossi explains, "What especially shocked me was the bad effect that this activity [writing] had in the heart of my family, not at all open to the idea that one of its members abandon the traditional role of the woman as a producer of children, a good housewife, and a hysterical and repressed person."[31] It is no surprise, then, that her writing should continue to criticize and satirize the institution that wanted to limit both her personal and her professional development. Mora examines one example of the author's devastating criticism of the traditional family in the article "El mito degradado de la familia en *El libro de mis primos* de Cristina Peri Rossi" (The degraded myth of the family in *The Book of My Cousins* by Cristina Peri Rossi).[32] Mora shows that Peri Rossi's use of innovative techniques such as temporal disruptions and sudden changes of point of view, and her imaginative use of typography, is instrumental in her portrayal of the family as weak, pathetic, and abusive. In "The Witness," the traditional bourgeois family is indirectly parodied by its absence and by its similarities to the gay family that Peri Rossi portrays. "The Witness" is the history of a family that consists of a young man, his mother, and the series of female lovers that have been with her. Although the short story at first seems to be a utopic representation of the lesbian family and the serenity, strength, and power of a women-centered environment, it contains many elements that force the reader to question these assumptions. In particular, the use of a male as narrator/protagonist, the narrator's unreliability and ultimate psychological instability, and the intrusion of a violent and oppressive denouement are factors that subvert a utopic reading of the lesbian family. Yet it is not immediately clear whether the story is intended as a defense or rejection of the lesbian family system or whether it consists of a more general (and elliptical) social criticism.

Peri Rossi has not restricted herself to topics easily digested by a conservative and oppressive South American society, but by the same token she does not define herself as dedicated to fighting for gay rights, or even feminism. She describes herself as a commentator on human problems. In an interview with Adriana Bergero, Peri Rossi affirms that she is a writer "of Modernity; and this means cosmopolitan as well; and more than anything else I think I have something to say about the present, about today's world."[33] Nevertheless, Foster argues that "in all of Peri Rossi's writing, both her fiction and her poetry, there is a sustained rejection of the heterosexual as the only form of sexual encounter."[34] In "The Witness," one of the author's more open narrative representations of the homosexual relationship, Peri Rossi sketches the existence of human problems within a lesbian family. Because of this, she lands herself in the middle of a debate when she questions the limitations of a purely sexual definition of homosexuality by presenting a contemporary lesbian family.

As suggested by Weston and Allen and Demo, mainstream society usually perceives a strict separation of the ideas of gay and family. A juxtaposition of the two concepts is necessarily controversial, and Peri Rossi makes the short story even more intense by introducing the elements of sex, violence, and gender identity. What begins as a seemingly utopian configuration of a lesbian family ends in a profound transgression that questions and threatens the family structure and dynamic. The reader could interpret this ending in many ways—for instance, as a critique of the lesbian family as deviant and dysfunctional or, contrastingly, as a condemnation of men as inevitably aggressive. The latter interpretation suggests a correlation with the lesbian utopian novel described by Zimmerman, although many elements of the tale, including the lack of a positive resolution, do not fit in such a reading. In summation, it is difficult to ascertain exactly how the lesbian family is portrayed in the text—that is, whether in a positive or negative light. While the pure intensity of "The Witness" may be a deterrent to seeing the ambiguities of the story, a focus on the lesbian family as system and the narrator as a participant in that system will provide an insightful approach to the topic.

In the introduction to the anthology *El placer de la palabra*, "The Witness" is described as "a fascinating text exploring the masculine reaction to lesbianism and a woman who dares to assume control of her own sexuality."[35] This comment implies that the tale is male-centered—or, at least, that the point of view will be masculine. This idea seems to be substantiated by the masculine first-person narrator, a technique that Peri Rossi often uses and on which I will comment later. In essence, the narrator does give an account of his family, which ends with his confession (or boast) of a violent sexual attack on his part. But viewing the story as the tale of a "masculine reaction to lesbianism" is a simplification that does not take into account the complexities of the communication network that exists in every family. Is it possible that this story makes the simple case of a male individual (both son and narrator) reacting to a concept, the concept of lesbianism? Could his disturbing sexual violation of his mother and her lover be merely the boy's Oedipal attempt to recuperate control and the "name of the father"? Or is this a struggle of gender archetypes and power dynamics between the sexes? Perhaps each of these elements sheds light on the narrative, but a careful reading of the climactic rape (and of that which it follows) also reveals that it is communication, response—or, in other words, personal interaction—that has much to do with a family system uncommon in Latin American literature.

Turning to the text, the reader is immediately struck by the strongly biased view of family held by the adolescent narrator/protagonist. The first thing that he brings up is the tenderness and love inherent in his female-centered family system: "'I really enjoy not having other men around the house,' I told my mother once, thanking her for not having blighted my childhood with the screams of a violent father or a demanding lover. Women are so much sweeter. I get along much better with them."[36] In fact, although he does mention blandly and in passing his strange preference for machines over most people (besides the women of his household), he paints an almost utopic scene of his family's domestic life. This wishful portrait of feminine harmony harks back to the theoretical and poetic notion that lesbian households or lesbian communities would embody a peacefulness and domestic tranquillity ascribed to the female character, which would contrast sharply with the patriarchal, male, and warring nature of our present culture. Such a utopic portrayal is suspect in itself, particularly in light of the story's denouement, and brings to mind literature's *naive* or *unreliable* narrator. According to C. Hugh Holman and William Harmon's *A Handbook to Literature*, the naive narrator is

> an ingenuous character who is the ostensible author (often the oral narrator) of a narrative, the implications of which are much plainer to the reader than they are to the narrator. The naive narrator can be a device for irony, either gentle or savage, or it can be a device for pathos, as it frequently is when a child narrates, with innocence, events with tragic or horrible implications.[37]

Similarly, Holman and Harmon define the *unreliable* narrator as "in error in his or her understanding or report of things and who thus leaves readers without the guides essential for making judgments about the character and the actions with any confidence that their conclusions are those intended by the author." A narrator may be unreliable because of immaturity, lack of sophistication, or "some retardation or derangement that precludes reliability."[38]

Exactly why the narrator's point of view is skewed in "The Witness" remains unclear, although his mother's lover accuses him of being "crazy."[39] In fact, his naive and otherwise unreliable commentary at first seems in opposition to Peri Rossi's frequent use of child narrators to present a wise yet less embittered judgment of the adult world.[40] The narrator/protagonist seems to lack wisdom or perceptiveness throughout the story, and although he does offer judgments of the family (first positive, then negative at the end), one senses that, contrary to Peri Rossi's description of the child narrator, this narrator's interior lucidity has indeed been damaged, and he does not apply "logic and imagination . . . in a fanatical and implacable attempt to demystify [and] project a better reality."[41] One possible explanation is that the narrator has passed the age of childhood proper: Even though his narrative voice often conserves the speech patterns of a young boy, he is in actuality already a young man.

The text holds even more evidence that the reader should be suspicious of the narrator's reliability. From the beginning of the story one notes a use of hyperbole, a denial or ignoring of any contradictory facts, and a certain detachment from the emotional content of his tale. Also, at times during the story his narrative voice becomes simplistic and repetitive, and during the rape scene, his emotions, behavior, and language are increasingly childlike. When he is not able to show his mother and her lover a prize he has just won at school, his excitement is replaced by anguish. The infantile need for instantaneous gratification is frustrated, and he begins to cry, even as he refuses to leave their bedroom. He blushes, he "pounces" on them, and as he holds them down he "let[s] out a grave, dull and anguishing scream."[42] He is petulantly judgmental, noting that "Helena had started to cry. I don't like women who cry. I never saw my mother cry."[43] Of course his negative opinion of Helena's tears is ironic considering his own at the beginning of the scene, but he overlooks this point, as well. His dialogue with the two women is minimal, consisting of his short and pointed sexual directions and their resisting cries. In a strange juxtaposition with the adult sexual act, most of the narrator's utterances contain a maximum of two words, such as "Kiss her!" "Now," "Do it!" "More," and "That's good."[44] At the end of the sequence, the structure of the narrative voice becomes simpler as phrases get shorter. The narrator says, "I burst like a broken flower. I exploded. Then, exhausted, I left the room. I left them quickly."[45] The use of simplistic simile and metaphor combined with the repetition seems consistent with young or backward attempts at conversation and description. It stands in direct opposition to the narrator's self-proclaimed height, strength, and manliness and suggests an ironic meshing of youthful innocence and adult male aggression.

The narrator's perspective becomes even more questionable when contextualized in the rest of his description of his family. He insists that his family has been idyllic and never suggests that he has felt insecure as a result of the various occasions on which his nuclear family has changed in composition. In the words of the narrator, "I don't know how many [lovers] there have been, nor can I claim to remember them all, but I haven't forgotten many of them, and though I may have not seen them again, or though they may visit the house only sporadically, I know who they are and have fond memories of them."[46] In its different manifestations, the small family eats, plays, reads, goes out, and sometimes sleeps together in one bed. He says that he understands his mother's lovers and that they give him affection and keep him company. What he does not acknowledge are the problems that must accompany such a variable family structure. Speaking to this point, Minuchin and Fishman have shown that a family that undergoes many fluctuations can create a situation in which the members—especially children—feel unsure of themselves and experience fear of abandonment.[47] It seems unusual that the only comments the young narrator should make (before the rape scene) are positive ones, not expressing a word of discontent about the constant transitions required of him as a child. Has he truly not felt the instability of his situation, or is this a case of denial, a subtle refusal to live in his (fictional) reality? In that case, could it be a stubborn defense of a lesbian utopic vision assumed in childhood, or might it be the first narrative indication of a latent machismo that is creeping into the young man's being?

Common sense seems to echo psychological theory in that constant or radical changes in the family environment are unsettling, to say the least, particularly for a youngster who must depend on his or her parents for survival on every level. Not surprisingly, and as would be expected in any normative family, this fictional household has employed communicative and behavioral tools that serve to quiet the sense of crisis and maintain the status quo or homeostasis of the family. In this case what maintains stability is a triangulation, or cross-generational coalition, in which mother and son form a dyad that assumes some of the responsibilities and privileges normally (and ideally) reserved for the parents. The family triangulation in "The Witness" is maintained not only for the benefit of the boy; he notes that his mother needs the intense relationship with him, as well. When one of the mother's lovers is too attentive to her son, he sees that she is perturbed, but he reinforces the boundaries of their dyad: "I put my mother's fears to rest, telling her that I certainly preferred her, that she was more beautiful and more intelligent."[48]

As an example of triangulation, the mother–son pair always has helped the mother's "friends" who come to stay with them. In particular, they band together in aid of Helena, who "had an unhappy childhood and now she needed to learn a lot of things before continuing her career: we were going to give her a home and the knowledge she lacked. . . . We had to protect her, that's what my mother told me."[49] The narrator is led to believe that he is more powerful than the other adult, and rather than learning from her or depending on her, he must come to her defense. In speaking about Helena, the narrator assumes the superiority of the adult judging the child, saying that "you could tell right away that she needed protection: even though she was cheerful, amusing and very likable, she was not very consistent and seemed to lack method."[50] Later, he directly labels her "childlike," then "weak" when she cries.[51] This permeability of boundaries is unlike the family dynamics portrayed in other works by Peri Rossi. In *El libro de mis primos* Mora observes "a rigid code, respected and conserved for generations, [that] divides in a strict way the individuals of the family clan with respect to ages and sexes."[52] Mora also notes that when a role inversion takes place, it sparks a desire for revenge in the protagonist.[53] In "The Witness," the lesbian family obviously breaks out of the rigidity that characterizes its heterosexual bourgeois counterpart. At no point is there a strict division of power or a definition of roles by gender or age. Although this seems to be a positive movement in some aspects, providing an alternative non-hierarchical family system that fails to privilege the traditional patriarchal order, at some unspecified moment it becomes problematic.

In an action that encourages a further redrawing of traditional boundaries, the mother decides that Helena should learn to study along with the adolescent boy. In this case he is encouraged to see himself as a peer rather than a protector, which sets up another cross-generational coalition. It is in part this coalition that creates his confused boundaries, because he has brought Helena into his room to see his collection of butterflies, he has fantasized about her sexually, and in general he does not view her as a parental figure at all. This confusion is exacerbated by Helena herself. When the narrator is locked out of Helena and his mother's bedroom while they have sex, he feels angry and vengeful and tries to start a fight with his mother. "But Helena intervened on my behalf," he says. "She winked at me, smiled, and touched my leg with her foot under the table. Her complicity comforted me."[54] It would seem that the narrator's assigned familial roles have been able to bolster his sense of security, but they have also created ambiguities as to his rights within the system. If he is treated as an adult, and if the adults in the system are treated as children, then he will naturally confuse a child's rights with an adult's rights. Although the narrator still views his family as utopic, in reality the situation is becoming even more volatile because of the leveling of mother and son, on the one hand, and the leveling of the son and the mother's lover, on the other. The parental dyad is undermined and corrupted, losing much in terms of responsibility, credibility, and authority; in turn, the child is given emotional power over one "mother," the very one with whom he is encouraged to study as a equal.

Although the cross-generational coalitions alone might not be enough to precipitate a crisis, another factor adds stress to the family dynamic. Chronologically, the family is passing through what Minuchin calls the third transition period (the children's adolescence) in which "a minor imbalance requiring adaptation is characteristic of families throughout. . . . But dissipative conditions are evident at . . . various points of adolescence when sexual needs . . . disrupt the established patterns in the family."[55] The adolescent's rampant sexual energy is a new element that must be integrated into both the individual's psychology and the dynamic of the family system, and this hormonal force is only reinforced by the social expectations of a teenager. In other words, the feelings that surface in adolescence can be powerful enough to change the very fabric of family—hence, the typical view of teenagers as rebellious, disrespectful, and challenging. As young pre-adults in an urban, postmodern society they question the credos previously held as questionable by society in general, by their own family systems, and even by them themselves. By this point in the story, the fable of lesbian utopia previously internalized by the son is unmistakably infiltrated by patriarchal ideology. The climactic and violent rupturing of the family pattern is in actuality merely an exaggeration of the privileges previously given to the boy when his mother made him an "accomplice" in the "raising" of her lovers. Now he completely assumes a distorted mixture of the roles of father, lover, and patriarchal authority, disregarding the tacit agreements with his mother, as he enters her bedroom and forces both her and Helena to submit to his desires.

A family systems reading of this brutal exploit neither assigns singular blame nor offers excuses for what happens. As John Knapp explains in his application of family systems theory to D. H. Lawrence:

> What is crucial for this clinical psychology is examining not who is at fault, but rather the dynamics of a conflict. It focuses not upon *the* guilt, but upon the graduated levels of responsibility in an area where one may conveniently look over one's shoulder at one's parents, they at theirs, and so on, each generation blaming the last for its own malaise. . . . Realistically, very few members of a family are ever totally innocent because each person ultimately swings his or her share of the family dance.[56]

Rather than blame the parents, a popular practice in the talk-show mentality of the 1990s, or single out the young man as pathological and an aberration in an otherwise utopic system, a conscientious critic can perceive the fascinating and complex family interplay unwittingly laid clear by the narrator. All members of the family have contributed in some way to the outcome and have participated in the patterns built over an entire lifetime. Of course, this in no way implies that the women deserve the experience they undergo or that this particular denouement is the only possible one under the circumstances. The outcome is a product of each individual's psychology, the family dynamic up to that moment, and all the social stressors that come to bear upon their situation. The narrator's attack is obviously wrong and inexcusable, but there are reasons that may explain how it comes to pass. Family systems theory underlines that each individual *must be responsible* for his or her own actions even while recognizing that these actions happen in a context.

Some critics might argue that the narrator performs the rapes because he has not been shown how a man should act—in other words, because he does not have a father figure. Therefore, some might say, he cannot be properly socialized or learn how to channel his sexual or aggressive energy appropriately. There are flaws in such a position. First, it contains an essentialist implication that men are basically violent and must be socialized out of it. The short story does seem to play with this assumption, but there is an ironic tone to the piece that points the reader toward a more tongue-in-cheek reading. Then, there is the further supposition that only another man could socialize the son into curbing his behavior, which is not supported by the story or by psychological theory. Neither family systems theory nor contemporary psychology in general would assume that such a reaction was precipitated merely because the parental dyad had no positive male role model. According to Allen and Demo:

> [The same-sex] parent argument, based largely on psychoanalytic and social learning theories, holds that the presence of and identification with the same-sex parent is necessary for the child's healthy emotional adjustment and appropriate gender role development. . . . Importantly, Downey and Powell [1993] found no evidence to support the same-sex argument.[57]

Further, "a thorough and provocative review article (Patterson 1992) identified emerging patterns in the study of children reared in lesbian and gay households, documented the overall well-being of such children."[58] Peri Rossi's short story presents a case in which the child's emotional and gender-role development are ultimately unhealthy but in a way that conforms to the exterior social reality rather than to the internal dynamic of the lesbian family portrayed.

Within the narrative one finds clues to the narrator's confusion, such as the obvious discrepancy between his judgment of men at the beginning and then at the end of the tale. At first he negatively judges men as violent and demanding and states that he is glad the house is free of them; at the end, he perpetrates a violent act and claims finally to be a real man—the real man that the house needed. By the same token, the women's traditional characteristics that he cherishes at the beginning of the story are later scorned. When in the midst of the utopic description of his household the narrator laments, "I regretted many times not having been born a girl, so that my mother could brush my hair with the same fervor and absorption; I regretted being a short-haired boy and thus being excluded from something that afforded them so much pleasure."[59] One has to wonder how he has acquired his negative impression of men, and why he has then assumed the very characteristics he disdained earlier. Throughout the narrative, none of the women are shown to have spoken a single word against men or masculinity, suggesting that his changeover occurs as a result of external influences, as the social system struggles to maintain a heterosexual and patriarchal homeostasis. As a system, Latin American society is intolerant of alternative sexualities and gender roles, and social groups push for conformity in an untold number of ways. This is not to say that other societies—the United States, for instance—are tolerant, accepting, and open to the nonconformist. Nevertheless, the cultural imperative of machismo seems to make Latin American intolerance more overt. It is this social rigidity that bursts through in the young man's rhetoric.

To claim his position in the dominant patriarchal discourse, the narrator must discard his belief in a utopic lesbian space. This he does, and so he is left holding the power of the word as well as the power of the sexual aggressor. His narration is an attempt at self-justification, and he tries to claim and control the story by his telling of it. However, his unreliability as a narrator and obvious emotional instability shine through, marking the tale as a personal perspective rather than the objective relation of factual incidents. This type of narrator is markedly different from the narrators of Peri Rossi's novel *La nave de los locos*.[60] Mary Beth Tierney-Tello remarks that, as exiles, the novel's narrators "view the society from the margins, able therefore to see its flaws," and that they are on a "quest for a lost order and harmony."[61] In contrast, the narrator of "The Witness" is more like the *"ombliguistas"* who are mired within their own selfish and limited existence and cannot see any farther than their own bellybuttons.

The important question is: What does it mean for Peri Rossi to give the narrative voice to the male in this particular story? For one, it is a potent indication of the continued silence and invisibility of lesbians in the social system, which is underlined by the use of the euphemism "friend" to refer to the mother's sexual and romantic partners. Moreover, the masculine voice powerfully speaks of the male's fears, angers, and frustrations over being excluded from the women-centered relationship. In the only complaint offered in the first portion of the text, the narrator shows a clear resentment about not being allowed to participate in every rite and experience belonging to the women. While his feelings are understandable, a family systems perspective reminds the reader that the boundaries that are held are, in fact, adequate and necessary. They are not simply a gender-based oppression or exclusion but are mostly based on a separation of the parental dyad during sex. Nevertheless, the isolation the narrator feels in this exclusion is overshadowed by the reader's realization that the lesbian family is actually what is marginalized.

Amy Kaminsky notes that Peri Rossi's use of male characters to tell stories of exile paradoxically accentuates the similarities between the exile and the woman in male-dominated culture. She remarks, "The male exile is feminized by his displacement into a foreign culture. He experiences there the alienation and disempowerment that women 'at home' have learned to consider normal."[62] In this case, there is a double exile: Not only is the male narrator exiled from his mother's (the female) bedroom during the sexual act, but the lesbian family (including the son) seems to be in exile from the whole of society. The story shows no context of a gay community—or any community, for that matter—and one gets the impression that the family system is closed to the outside only out of sheer self-preservation or because of outside forces. In other words, the lesbian family is a "tangible figure of absence," inhabiting the "null space" of the exile Kaminsky describes. Kept on the outside of a social system, the family is invisible, impotent, and marginalized, just as the boy is. His comfort with machines and discomfort with people, mentioned earlier, is a condition of his alienation as part of an exiled family. It is worth noting that in this text, the mechanisms of exile are all hidden, secret, and implicit. This stands in contrast to other texts by Peri Rossi, including *La nave de los locos*, which, as Tierney-Tello cogently observes, "is a novel with a critical agenda, grappling with the alienation and social discrimination of contemporary society as well as searching for a way to subvert the restrictive binary operations that act violently to exclude so many 'others.'"[63]

Although "The Witness" examines the same issues, the treatment is much more subtle and indirect. Nevertheless, especially when one sets the story in the context of Peri Rossi's overall literary production, it seems clear that an underlying message is that the family's problems stem in part from its forced exile from society rather than being simply a product of its unusual composition. Because of its forced isolation, the family develops diffuse interior boundaries that allow too much flexibility in roles, particularly in the relationship of parent and child. Many of the family functions are fulfilled beyond what may happen in other traditional homes, such as the provision of emotional and intellectual support. However, some of the patterns are so disjunctive with societal expectations that they provoke a reaction in the larger system. The boy's actions, although certainly personal, also represent the outside pressures to conform to patriarchy. Ironically, in his attempt to displace his own "alienation and disempowerment" and to reclaim a masculinity that is denied him by his position as exile, he merely mimics and exacerbates the social oppression that produced the exile of his family. Instead of being merely an indictment of gay or lesbian families as unable to produce emotionally stable personalities, "The Witness" shows both that vicious acts do not occur in a social vacuum and that no family composition is by itself sufficient to prevent violence.

The language used in Peri Rossi's story offers further material for exploration. The communication between the family members is of particular interest here. In "The Witness," the critic should pay particularly close attention to the protagonist's final words, which have implications that far outreach a simple utterance. On vacating the room, the narrator says: "Don't worry about me. Now I am really a man. The one that was lacking in this house."[64] With this *machista* act and affirmation, he effects a chaotic climax in the family system that had prevailed until then. Such a stereotypical and loaded statement recommends a somewhat guarded reception, and one has to question the extent to which even the boy believes in his own position. Although ending the narration with the strong justification of the patriarchal family structure implies finality and authority, a literal reading of his claim simply does not fit with the ambiguity and irony of the rest of the story.

The utopic definition of the lesbian family that the boy had characterized as full of affection, mutual comprehension, and cooperation is contaminated with insecurity, need, and sexual frustration, all of which he attempts to resolve through violence. In a seemingly complete turnaround of attitude, the narrator eschews the lesbian mythology to appropriate with a vengeance a heterosexist perspective that not only allows his horrific behavior but, indeed, necessitates it. One can speculate about how the narrator has altered his position, but it is reasonable for the reader to infer that both personal changes and outside influences have brought about the change. As Allen and Demo explain:

> Heterosexism operates in personal belief systems and institutional practices. Like racism, sexism, and classism, heterosexism is a form of institutional oppression designed to ridicule, limit, or silence alternative discourses about identity and behavior. Societal institutions reinforce heterosexism by shaping and controlling knowledge.[65]

By co-opting (or being co-opted by) the dominant form of bigotry, the young man introduces a new element into the family system that not only produces the story's climax, but, according to family systems theory, would induce further changes in the system to fight against or somehow incorporate it. This last element is what most forcefully calls for a more open reading of the story's ending.

Knowing that any change in a family system will bring about some sort of a response designed to combat the threat to its homeostasis, the reader is left with questions about what will happen next in this fictional lesbian family. The narrative ambiguity is an effective technique that, more than just engaging the reader, begins to erase the line between this fictional representation and the cultural context in which it occurs. Even though the text does not continue, the family in crisis continues to be a topic of discussion. Mora has said that Peri Rossi's work calls for the "necessity of destroying the present family structure" and predicts "the inevitable crumbling of the bourgeois system."[66] In "The Witness," the author presents an alternative to the traditional bourgeois family system, at the beginning portrayed in a decidedly utopic light but at the end involved in major crisis.

Tierney-Tello claims that in Peri Rossi's works the condition of exile "not only enables the adoption of a critical perspective, but can actually open a space for utopian possibilities."[67] So what must one conclude when a utopian family space is constructed, then violated? It is difficult for the reader to tease out the underlying message about the lesbian family offered in the short story—if, indeed, there is one correct message to find. In an attempt to concretize an interpretation, one is tempted to speculate about the fictional future of the protagonist's family. Will the old "utopic" family system be reestablished, with or without the implementation of protective devices against further violence? Will the problems that weakened the system be revealed, with a subsequent restructuring that incorporates new and positive elements? Or could the family revert to a more socially acceptable configuration, in which the women take a subordinate role to the young man?

The only thing that seems sure is that some changes must be instituted, because the patriarchal infiltration of the lesbian utopia has seriously undermined the false picture of perfection and purity that the narrator paints at the beginning. Even so, one senses that Peri Rossi pokes fun at the utopic lesbian narrative without seriously criticizing lesbian families as such. Her tongue-in-cheek treatment of this lesbian family is certainly not as biting as her representation of some other bourgeois, heterosexual families, as shown in Mora's study. Although the text shows a family that enjoys advantages and disadvantages because of its unique composition, the crisis that erupts is directly related to the utopic practice of dichotomizing gender identities and criminalizing the male character. Although "The Witness" shows the paradigm of a lesbian *utopic* family to be unsustainable in practice, it maintains an equally critical stance toward the patriarchal system that makes the very existence of any lesbian family a struggle. In the end, what does emerge is the idea that this family has faced some of the same challenges that other family systems face. While some of the consequences are tragic, they are not unique to the lesbian family system.

In closing, one more question must be asked: If Peri Rossi's short story is an example of a lesbian and gay family narrative in Latin America, how does it fit within such a body of work? One way to pinpoint the significance of the story is to say briefly what it is not. It is not an oblique or obscure portrayal of gay sensibility; nor is it akin to the lesbian pulp fiction or gay male tales of sexual promiscuity. Although it contains elements that suggest the marginalized position of the lesbian family, it is far from a didactic text meant to lament social injustice. Finally, just as "The Witness" problematizes the genre of lesbian utopic fiction, it also provides a significant twist to the coming-out story. For the purposes of this essay, these are the most interesting oppositions. Even as the existence of a male narrator, one who violently subverts the lesbian family system, seemingly precludes the definition of the work as a lesbian coming-out story, this perhaps is not an absolute interpretation. Clearly, the story does not center on a lesbian girl or woman coming to terms with her sexuality. Nevertheless, it is a further incursion into queer narrative by a Latin American writer who initially shocked her society with women-centered erotic poetry. However, what truly eventually "comes out" in this reading is more than the sexuality of a protagonist. As Zimmerman notes:

> Fiction is a particularly useful medium through which to shape a new lesbian consciousness, for fiction, of all literary forms, makes the most complex and detailed use of historical events and social discourse. By incorporating many interacting voices and points of view, novelists give the appearance of reality to a variety of imaginary worlds. Novels can show us as we were, as we are, and as we would like to be. This is a potent combination for a group whose very existence has been either suppressed or distorted.[68]

Peri Rossi's short story bears witness to a phenomenon of which many people are still unaware: an expansion of social constructs that allows much more deviation from what has been called the norm. The author employs the most intimate and adversarial voice to give the appearance of reality to a world that is both imaginary and real, silent and vocal. This is the coming out of the lesbian family.

Notes

1. For a discussion of cultural patterns related to family that focuses on elements from Spanish, indigenous, and African groups, see Guillermo Paez Morales, *Sociología de la familia: Elementos de análisis en Colombia y América Latina* (Bogotá: Universidad Santo Tomás Centro de Enseñanza Desescolarizada, 1984).

2. See Ferdinand Mount, *The Subversive Family: An Alternative History of Love and Marriage* (London: Jonathan Cape, 1982).

3. In the original Spanish, Cristina Peri Rossi's "El testigo" appears in *El placer de la palabra: Literatura erótica femenina de América Latina*, ed. Margarite Fernández Olmos and Lizabeth Paravisini-Gebert (México, D.F.: Planeta, 1991), 93–99. All citations in this chapter, unless noted otherwise, are from Cristina Peri Rossi, "The Witness," trans. Lizabeth Paravisini-Gebert, in *Pleasure in the Word: Erotic Writings by Latin American Women*, ed. Margarite Fernández Olmos and Lizabeth Paravisini-Gebert (New York: White Wine Press, 1993).

4. In contrast with the invisibility of the gay and lesbian family in academic psychological and sociological literature, the estimated numbers of existing families are startlingly high. In *Sexual Orientation and the Law* (Cambridge, Mass.: Harvard University Press, 1990), 119, the editors of the *Harvard Law Review* reported that "approximately three million gay men and lesbians in the United States are parents, and between eight and ten million children are raised in gay or lesbian households."

5. See Katherine R. Allen and David H. Demo, "The Families of Lesbians and Gay Men: A New Frontier in Family Research," *Journal of Marriage and the Family* 57 (February 1995): 112. Allen and Demo are citing J. Laird, "Lesbian and Gay Families," in *Normal Family Processes*, ed. F. Walsh (New York: Guilford, 1993), 295.

6. U. Bronfenbrenner and A. C. Crouter, "The Evolution of Environmental Models in Developmental Research," in *Handbook of Child Psychology*, ed. P. H. Mussen (New York: John Wiley, 1983), 361–62.

7. Allen and Demo, "Families of Lesbians and Gay Men," 112. Nevertheless, Allen and Demo do recognize that the field is opening up for the possibility of such research to be conducted. For instance, according to *Family Relations,* the journal with the highest percentage of coverage of gay and lesbian issues (1 percent explicit content; 4 percent related content), "lesbians and gay men gained modest visibility in applied family studies, but still with definite limits.... This recognition ranges from perfunctory mention of 'homosexual families' in a list of other diverse family types to illustrations and examples involving lesbians and gay men.... Over the past 2 years, articles on relationship quality and domestic partnerships involving lesbian and gay couples appeared for the first time in [*Family Relations*]": as quoted in ibid., 117.

8. Ibid.

9. Kath Weston, *Families We Choose: Lesbians, Gays, Kinship* (New York: Columbia University Press, 1991). For studies of family function, see Murray Bowen, *Family Therapy in Clinical Practice* (New York: Jason Aronson, 1978); Salvador Minuchin, *Families and Family Therapy* (Cambridge, Mass.: Harvard University Press, 1974).

10. Weston, *Families We Choose,* 15.

11. Writings in family systems theory offer different levels of tolerance for gay and lesbian families, and even of homosexuality. For instance, Michael E. Kerr and Murray Bowen refer to homosexuality more than once as an anxiety-related symptom or as social misconduct rather than as a determined lifestyle: Michael E. Kerr and Murray Bowen, *Family Evaluation: An Approach Based on Bowen Theory* (New York: University Press of America, 1987), 119, 241.

12. Salvador Minuchin and Charles Fishman, *Family Therapy Techniques* (Cambridge, Mass.: Harvard University Press, 1981), 16. The Argentine family psychologist and theorist Salvador Minuchin is one of the main proponents of family systems theories. His position as a Latin American educated in the United States allows a particularly culture-sensitive approach to the study of family.

13. Adrienne Rich, "Foreword," in *The Coming-Out Stories,* ed. Julia Penelope Stanley and Susan J. Wolfe (Watertown, Mass: Persephone Press, 1980), xii.

14. In this case, the definition of "coming out" diverges from the simple idea of making other people aware of one's sexual preferences. Whereas public knowledge is the element of coming out that is most evident to the outside community, there are other elements that are equally—if not more—important within the gay community. These include the exploration of one's own identity and the finding of a community.

15. Rich, "Foreword," xii.

16. Bonnie Zimmerman, *The Safe Sea of Women: Lesbian Fiction 1969–1989* (Boston: Beacon Press, 1990), 74.

17. David William Foster, ed., *Gay and Lesbian Themes in Latin American Writing* (Austin: University of Texas Press, 1991), 4.

18. Ibid., 3.

19. Suzanne Chávez Silverman, "The Look That Kills: The 'Unacceptable Beauty' of Alejandra Pizarnik's *La condesa sangrienta,*" in *¿Entiendes? Queer Readings, Hispanic Writings,* ed. Emilie Bergmann and Paul Julian Smith (Durham, N.C.: Duke University Press, 1995), 281.

20. Elizabeth Meese, *(SEM)erotics: Theorizing Lesbian Writing* (New York: New York University Press, 1992), 18.

21. Weston, *Families We Choose,* 110.

22. Zimmerman, *Safe Sea,* 16; emphasis added.

23. Ibid., 21.

24. Ibid., 143.

25. Ibid., 148.

26. Ibid., 143–44.

27. Ibid., 150–52.

28. Gabriela Mora, "Cristina Peri Rossi," in *Spanish American Women Writers,* ed. Diane E. Marting (New York: Greenwood Press, 1990), 439.

29. David William Foster, *Latin American Writers on Gay and Lesbian Themes* (Westport, Conn.: Greenwood Press, 1994), 320.

30. Mora, "Peri Rossi," 439–40.

31. John F. Deredita, "Desde la diáspora: entrevista con Cristina Peri Rossi," in *Texto Crítico* 4, no. 9 (1978): 133.

32. Gabriela Mora, "El mito degradado de la familia en *El libro de mis primos* de Cristina Peri Rossi," in *The Analysis of Literary Texts: Current Trends in Methodology,* ed. Randolph D. Pope (Ypsilanti, Mich.: Bilingual Press, 1980), 66–77.

33. Adriana Bergero, "Yo me percibo como una escritora de la Modernidad," *Mester* 7, no. 1 (Spring 1993): 68.

34. Foster, *Latin American Writers,* 316.

35. Fernández Olmos and Paravisini-Gebert, "Introduction," in Fernández Olmos and Paravisini-Gebert, *El placer de la palabra,* xxii.

36. Peri Rossi, "The Witness," 150.

37. C. Hugh Holman and William Harmon, *A Handbook to Literature: Fifth Edition* (New York: Macmillan, 1986), 319.

38. Ibid., 518–19.

30. Peri Rossi, "The Witness," 156.

40. Deredita, "Desde la diáspora," 142.

41. Ibid.

42. Peri Rossi, "The Witness," 154.

43. Ibid., 155.

44. Ibid., 156.

45. Ibid., 157.

46. Ibid., 150.

47. Minuchin and Fishman, *Family Therapy Techniques,* 55.

48. Peri Rossi, "The Witness," 151.

49. Ibid.

50. Ibid.

51. Ibid., 153, 155.

52. Mora, "Mito, " 68.

53. Ibid., 73.

54. Peri Rossi, "The Witness," 154.

55. Minuchin, *Families,* 25.

56. John V. Knapp, *Striking at the Joints: Contemporary Psychology and Literary Criticism* (New York: University Press of America, 1996), 62.

57. Allen and Demo, "Families of Lesbians and Gay Men," 118, citing D. B. Downey and B. Powell, "Do Children in Single-Parent Households Fare Better Living with Same-Sex Parents?" *Journal of Marriage and the Family* 55 (1993): 55–71.

58. Ibid., 120, citing C. J. Patterson, "Children of Lesbian and Gay Parents," *Child Development* 63: 1025–42.

59. Peri Rossi, "The Witness," 151.

60. Cristina Peri Rossi, *La nave de los locos* (The ship of fools) (Barcelona: Seix Barral, 1984).

61. Mary Beth Tierney-Tello, *Allegories of Transgression and Transformation: Experimental Fiction by Women Writing under Dictatorship* (New York: State University of New York Press, 1996), 181.

62. Amy Kaminsky, "Gender and Exile in Cristina Peri Rossi," in *Continental, Latin-American and Francophone Women Writers,* ed. Eunice Myers and Ginette Adamson (New York: University Press of America, 1987), 152.

63. Tierney-Tello, *Allegories,* 176.

64. Peri Rossi, "The Witness,"157.

65. Allen and Demo, "Families of Lesbians and Gay Men," 122.

66. Mora, "Mito," 75.

67. Ibid., 188–89.

68. Zimmerman, *Safe Sea,* 2.

Elisa A. Garza

---

12   Chicana Lesbianism and
the Multigenre Text

> *My lesbianism first brought me into writing. My first poems were love
> poems. That's the source—el amor, el deseo—that brought me into politics.*
> —Cherríe Moraga

> *Perhaps if we give up loving women, we will be worthy of having some-
> thing to say worth saying.*
> —Gloria Anzaldúa

Cherríe Moraga and Gloria Anzaldúa have been active as writers and editors since
the early 1980s, a decade that saw the publication of their anthology featuring "radical women of color," *This Bridge Called My Back,* as well as groundbreaking books by
each of them featuring what some would call their own "radical" expressions of feminism, cultural critique, and lesbianism.[1] Fifteen years later, these works, *Loving in the
War Years* and *Borderlands/La Frontera,* are studied and written about by Chicano,
Latino, and gay studies scholars; anthologized in freshmen composition textbooks;
and included on the reading lists for literature, women's studies, and gay studies
courses.[2] Much has been written by academics about Moraga's and Anzaldúa's contributions to these areas of study, particularly the articulation of their feminist sensi-
bilities and lesbian identities and the resulting cultural alienation they felt because of
their lesbianism. But these two books have also received attention because of the
increasing interest in diversifying the canon with multicultural literature. In most
cases, these works are classified as autobiography when they are included on reading lists, although nearly half of Anzaldúa's book is poetry, and Moraga's contains a
number of poems and journal excerpts. In fact, the multigenre nature of the works
is worth examining, because it has an impact on the strength and delivery of the
messages—and, hence, the theories—that Moraga and Anzaldúa are proposing. In this
sense, these books share some characteristics with other types of ethnic narratives and
"autobiographies."

In the preface to her book on ethnic women's autobiography, *Take My Word,* Anne Goldman explains how the personal narratives of ethnic women disguised within nonliterary texts such as cookbooks, oral histories, and labor-organization histories both transgress and stretch the boundaries of literature.[3] She suggests that we should resist a definition of ethnic literature that aligns it with contemporary U. S. literature and thus ignores other literary traditions: "In arguing for a wider autobiographical field we describe a wider spectrum of the ways and means by which people in the twentieth century speak themselves into textual existence."[4] As such a move suggests, "the ways and means" of ethnic literature may not always fit into the labels of conventional genres. Although cookbooks may distinguish themselves as a separate genre, the autobiographical essay narratives of Moraga and Anzaldúa challenge the very notion of genre by incorporating poetry, memoir, journal entries, and dreams.

Both Goldman and Sonia Saldívar-Hull have located ethnic women's autobiography in texts and narratives that are often carefully disguised as anything but self-expression or theory: cookbooks, oral histories of midwife practice, cultural artifacts, *cuentos* (stories or tales). Goldman's examination of two New Mexican cookbooks published in the first half of the twentieth century reveals the subtlety of their autobiographical nature and their critical practice: "A cookbook can reproduce the means to more than material nourishment. . . . It may reproduce as well those cultural practices and values that provide a community with a means of self-definition and survival."[5] Goldman reveals that such moves can be considered both political and activist in a climate in which the government and its dominant culture were encouraging assimilation through the promotion of Anglo foods and adoption of modern food-preparation methods. However, the political nature of these cookbooks is subtle: "Presenting a family recipe and figuring its circulation within a community of readers provides a metaphor nonthreatening in its apparent avoidance of overt political discourse."[6] A subtle and non-threatening presentation is also an important characteristic to explore in a discussion of Chicana literature, and of Moraga's and Anzaldúa's writing, in particular.

Indeed, Ramón Saldívar suggests that all Chicano literature originated in another type of disguised political statement. In *Chicano Narrative,* Saldívar maintains that all contemporary Chicano writing rises from a narrative tradition of community resistance to political, cultural, and linguistic domination.[7] He traces the origins of Chicano literature to the *corrido,* a type of ballad or story song that evolved in the U.S.–Mexico border regions during the second half of the nineteenth century to chronicle acts of individual and community resistance to Anglo domination.[8] In the late nineteenth and early twentieth century, opposition to dominance in the form of assemblies and meetings was often violently suppressed by the Texas Rangers, which enhanced the power and presence of the *corrido:* "In the symbolic sphere, the *corrido* became the preeminent form of action and resistance against the ever-increasing political and cultural hegemony of Anglo-American society."[9]

Saldívar maintains that the symbolic power of the *corrido* not only provided a means to articulate resistance, but that this "male performance genre" also initiated a particular type of Chicano literature, a specifically male literature: "Later, when Mexican-American artists turn to other genres of symbolic action, the male-oriented system of values cultivated during the period of open conflict and transmitted through the corrido will be replicated by male authors."[10] The public nature of the *corrido* performance designates its maleness, and if all contemporary Chicano literature derives from this tradition, as Saldívar claims, then contemporary Chicano literature must have a decidedly male slant. Indeed, intentionally or not, this male slant has been maintained. As recently as 1995, Tey Diana Rebolledo commented that "many male critics continue to ignore Chicana writers in favor of the now-canonical male figures of the tradition."[11] The paucity of Chicana critics reported by Rebolledo, and their continued relegation to small and minority presses and to the tail end of studies of Chicano literature, suggests that cultural bias in favor of the male continues to influence the production, dissemination, and reception of Chicana texts.[12]

A combination of ethnocentric literary standards and cultural and sexist domination has therefore produced a literary tradition that promotes male subjectivity (along with sexism and homophobia) and relegates female subjectivity to a disguised role in both literary and "nonliterary" texts. Early attempts at the expression of Chicana subjectivity understandably took as their task the construction of female identities and role models (see Rebolledo and Eliana Rivero's *Infinite Divisions* [1993] for numerous examples), paving the way for the more critical texts of Moraga and Anzaldúa that followed. I have limited my examination of early Chicana subjectivity to poetry for two reasons: Poetry is central to the texts by Moraga and Anzaldúa that I will discuss later in this essay, and in their anthology of Chicana literature, Rebolledo and Rivero claim that "poetry constitutes a primary medium and major literary mode for Chicana authors."[13]

Since the 1970s, Chicana poets have focused their energy on constructing female identities, challenging the sexist nature of Chicano writing published before, during, and after the Civil Rights *Movimiento* of the 1960s by offering identity constructions that are woman-, rather than culturally, centered. These woman-centered descriptions of experience and feeling give the poems distinct Chicana voices and offer potentially, if not outright, feminist interpretations of the lives of Chicanas as women. In her 1985 study "The Maturing of Chicana Poetry," Rebolledo outlines how Chicana poetry of the 1980s develops along seven "trends." Several of them can be considered woman-centered, including self-identity, the female tradition, and the acceptance of the everyday life of woman as being fit material for poetry.[14] Much of the poetry Rebolledo discusses does not, however, offer an example of a feminist Chicana voice that simultaneously constructs identity and critiques the sexist cultural boundaries of that identity. Indeed, Rebolledo suggests that such a complex identity construction is either not possible or not appropriate to poetry, because, in the course of Chicana poetry's maturation, "the themes of woman and independent feminist, perhaps more tolerant and less bitter toward the men in her life, appear in a more subtle way."[15]

This subtlety warrants examination. Take, for example, Miriam Bornstein-Gómez's poem "Toma de nombre/Taking of Name," which quietly challenges the practice of taking the husband's name at marriage and from then on linking the woman's identity to that of wife and mother. Bornstein-Gómez articulates the situation from a woman-centered perspective, but even so the poem does not move far beyond that articulation:

> cargo con el nombre de mujer casada
> soy
> fulana de tal
> esposa de fulano
> madre de zutano
> y algunas veces presiento que solamente soy
> mujer de sola

> I carry my married name
> I am
> so and so
> wife of so and so
> mother of so and so
> and at times I feel that I am only
> a woman alone[16]

The repetitions of "so and so" set up a critical pattern that challenges traditional methods of constructing women's identities. The different Spanish words translated into the English "so and so" also indicate someone of no importance. The generic nature of the references, along with the use of line breaks and the deliberate spacing in the poem that separates each of these expressions from the others, suggests that the labels "wife of" and "mother of" inaccurately represent the speaker's identity, a fine start in establishing a critical stance for the poem. However, the poem ends with the speaker's articulation of solitude, without further articulating a critical source for that solitude. Perhaps the subtlety that Rebolledo comments on prevents criticism from coming to the forefront of this poem. For example, a claim by Bornstein-Gómez's speaker that she is a woman alone in wishing for an identity separate from that of wife and mother would clearly establish a critical stance, but it would also articulate a position interpreted as anti-family, and possibly anti-culture—a position that is problematic and threatening to the male-oriented tenets of Chicano literature.

"Woman-centered" Chicana writing is not always critical and therefore is not always necessarily "feminist," which means that it is not always an articulation of the oppression women face as women. How, then, does a feminist critical stance become possible for Chicana writing? The Personal Narratives Group, an offshoot of the Center for Advanced Feminist Studies at the University of Minnesota, suggests that initial forays into female subjectivity may appear simply to document experience but potentially could do more:

> Some women's narratives can be read as counter-narratives, because they reveal that the narrators do not think, feel, or act as they are "supposed to." . . . Many women's personal

narratives unfold within the framework of an apparent acceptance of social norms and expectations but nevertheless describe strategies and activities that challenge those same norms.[17]

Such characteristics are present in the New Mexican cookbooks discussed by Goldman and in poems anthologized by Rebolledo and Rivero. In the texts of Moraga and Anzaldúa, narrative elements mix with the articulation of theory, thus enabling the narratives to support and clarify the self-defined lesbian feminist positions explained in the theoretical parts. Their critiques are carefully positioned within autobiographical narratives that reflect the larger frameworks of ethnic, women's, and lesbian writing. Moraga's and Anzaldúa's multigenred writing not only grows out of a Chicano tradition that articulates oppression; their efforts also define and therefore rely on the power of their simultaneous identities as Chicanas, as women, and as lesbians. As such, their attempts at self-definition reflect their struggles to reconcile those simultaneous identities, and therefore their texts move beyond autobiography into criticism, theory, poetry, and narratives. This multigenre articulation reflects both multiple identities and multiple modes of expression.

Because this multigenre writing enables a clearer presentation of both sexism and homophobia, it is a richer critique than the attempts discussed earlier. For example, the "acceptance of social norms" is an important tenet of Chicano culture, often seen as a measurement of its strength. Moraga articulates how even tacit "acceptance" can become imperative during the fight against cultural and racial oppression and can therefore counter and suppress the expression of feminism and support homophobia.

In "A Long Line of Vendidas," Moraga calls for a strong feminist position that stays true to the needs of women: "The feminist-oriented material which appeared in the late 70s and early 80s for the most part strains in its attempt to stay safely within the boundaries of Chicano—male-defined and often anti-feminist—values."[18] This early feminist material often took the women's movement to task for excluding Chicana concerns, but it did not take the Chicano *Movimiento* to task for excluding women's concerns: "It is far easier for the Chicana to criticize white women who on the face of things could never be familia, than to take issue with or complain, as it were, to a brother, uncle, father."[19] For many Chicanos and Chicanas, the preservation of sex roles and enforcement of heterosexuality is paramount to cultural survival: "We believe the more severely we protect the sex roles within the family, the stronger we will be as a unit in opposition to the anglo threat."[20] Moraga's struggle to reconcile the culturally incompatible images of lesbian and Chicana push her to suggest that "truly feminist Chicanas" must move beyond the cultural and familial loyalty that constrains female sexuality through the normalization of heterosexuality.[21]

Saldívar acknowledges the special position of feminist narratives, recognizing that by the 1980s some Chicana writers openly articulated critical positions that reflect the multiplicity of their oppressions:

> If Chicano narrative is, as we have claimed throughout this study, a perfect case study of the work of ideologies that are not simply counterhegemonic but truly oppositional and revolutionary, then the literature produced by Chicana authors is counterhegemonic to

the second power, serving as a critique of critiques of oppression that fail to take into account the full range of domination.[22]

From this perspective, it is the very nature of their critical act, one that arises from the consciousness of their multiple identities, that distinguishes writers such as Moraga and Anzaldúa from both Chicano and other Chicana writers. And their identities as lesbians preclude subtlety, enabling them to push their writing beyond woman-centered toward feminist and, ultimately, lesbian expression.

Biddy Martin explains how, in similar ways, Moraga and Anzaldúa also distinguish their writing from other lesbian autobiographical narratives.[23] In her study of lesbian coming-out stories and autobiographical essays, Martin notes that a nearly identical focus and structure connects the act of autobiography with community and individual definition. Lesbian autobiographical writing, she says, "aims to give lesbian identity a coherence and legitimacy that can make both individual and social action possible," and that writing therefore has distinct political intentions.[24] However, writers such as Moraga and Anzaldúa

> attend to the irreducibly complex intersections of race, gender, and sexuality, attempts that both directly and indirectly work against assumptions that there are no differences within the "lesbian self" and that lesbian authors, autobiographical subjects, readers, and critics can be conflated and marginalized as self-identical and separable from questions of race, class, sexuality, and ethnicity.[25]

Clearly, Moraga and Anzaldúa have made a deliberate effort to push their writing beyond a simple articulation of identity based on race, gender, and sexuality.

I suggest, then, that Moraga's and Anzaldúa's intentions to write from and define multiple identities and multiple oppressions create the need to both redefine and critique their culture in the process. This dual purpose of self and community definition results in a multigenred writing that defies categorization and therefore illustrates both the difficulties and the rewards of individual and cultural self-definition. It also makes possible a powerful expression of lesbian experience in a homophobic culture.

Moraga's introduction to *Loving in the War Years* begins with a *sueño*, a dream. From the start, she supplants the convention of genre, writing an introduction that parallels the book as a whole as well as the individual sections: part essay, part dreams, and one journal entry. For practical reasons, I will limit my examination to what Moraga has labeled one of "the two main essays of the book."[26] "A Long Line of Vendidas" is a testament to the sexist and heterosexist elements of Chicano culture revealed in sections of essay, dreams, journal entries, memories, and poems. The essay is more than fifty pages long and presents nearly all of the important themes of the book.

Although "A Long Line of Vendidas" changes genres frequently, moving from essay to memory excerpt to diary entry to dream back to essay is easy: Each switch of genre provides a specific illustration of Moraga's claims. For example, she claims that Chicano mothers are overly dedicated to their sons:

> Sometimes I sense that she feels this way because she wants to believe that through her mothering, she can develop the kind of man she would have liked to have married, or

even have been. That through her son she can get a small taste of male privilege, since without race or class privilege that's all there is to be had. The daughter can never offer the mother such hope, straddled by the same forces that confine the mother.[27]

The words of the journal entry describing her mother's desperate phone call invoke a powerfully sympathetic reaction that renders her claim impossible to deny:

> My mother's pleading "mi'jita, I love you, I hate to feel so far away from you." succeed in opening my heart again to her. . . . Moments later, "It is your brother," she says. My knees lock under me, bracing myself for the fall. Her voice lightens up. "Okay, mi'jita. I love you. I'll talk to you later," cutting off the line in the middle of the connection.[28]

Female subservience to male interests and desires is a cultural imperative: "You are a traitor to your race if you do not put the man first."[29] The impact of Moraga's explanations and claims is strengthened by her incorporation of remembered events written in other genres.

These early sections of "A Long Line of Vendidas" are an introduction to what follows, where Moraga outlines the heterosexist assumptions that pervade early feminist Chicana thinking. After her long treatise on this issue, Moraga reveals her personal stake in wanting to change things: "I am a Chicana lesbian. My own particular relationship to being a sexual person; and a radical stand in direct contradiction to, and in violation of, the woman I was raised to be."[30] She cannot establish her own identity without also explaining, and then critiquing, her culture's constructions of women and lesbians. This dual purpose is accomplished by switching genres, by alternating narrative with critique.

Leslie Bow has examined *Loving in the War Years* for its relationship to "*écriture feminine*, women's writing," based on Hélène Cixous's definition in "The Laugh of the Medusa."[31] Although she ultimately concludes that Moraga does not follow Cixous's suggestions to distinguish women's writing on the level of syntax or stylistics, Bow claims that "Moraga's text is innovative both in its narrative chronology and its multiplicity of form."[32] She finds the multigenred nature of Moraga's writing to be its most important and radical move: "By writing verse, personal narrative, and fiction, Moraga subverts the generic conception of political theory . . . what Moraga ultimately rejects is a unitary method for written expression, while keeping intact the social function of discourse . . . [which] gives *Loving* its power and significance."[33] I agree with Bow that Moraga's writing has a "social function." Her subversion of genres is a means to reveal her very personal concerns as social concerns with large social implications.

In *Interpreting Women's Lives*, the Personal Narrative Group prefers to describe women's autobiographical writings as "narrative forms"; the group also stresses a careful examination of the form of the writing itself rather than the writing's adherence to the strictures of genre: "*Narrative form*, an inclusive term amenable to cross-disciplinary studies, suggests in its more encompassing nature that a narrative might be viewed as fluid rather than fixed in the variety of shapes that it can assume."[34] In this sense, it is important to understand that Moraga's intentions succeed partly because of her use of personal narrative and because of her innovative inclusion of several different types of narrative. As Bow suggests, and the Personal Narrative Group confirms, the very form of Moraga's writing is an important part of her statement: "Finding a form in which to present a life means, in addition to choosing from the available models, adapting those models to suit one's needs and purposes.... By choosing and adapting the form her narrative will take, the narrator interprets and, in a sense, makes or remakes her life."[35] When Moraga says, *"I come from a long line of Vendidas. I am a Chicana lesbian,"* she attempts to come to terms with her individual self and her identity within her community, and this effort is reflected in the form of her narrative.[36]

In her examination of self-construction in Latina autobiographies, Lourdes Torres suggests that a dual goal influences Moraga's narrative form, requiring her to write outside the conventions of genre: "The project of presenting the personal and collective selves takes precedence over conventional stylistics or established structures."[37] Moraga's personal self is multiple: biracial, bilingual, working class, educated, feminist, lesbian, writer. She has therefore chosen to represent her multiple self in multiple genres, constructing and reconstructing her life as the multiplicity it is. As she concludes "My Brother's Sex Was White, Mine Brown"—the first section of "Vendidas"—Moraga uses three genres to represent three different aspects of herself, memories for *la hija: "But my tía had not warned me about the smell, the unmistakable smell of the woman, mi mamá—el olor de aceite y jabón and comfort and home"*; poetry for *la lesbiana:*

it is as if I spent the rest of my years driven by this scent toward la mujer.
when her india makes love
it is with the greatest reverence
to color, texture, smell

by now she knew the scent of the earth
could call it up
even between the cracks
in sidewalks;

and essay for *la chicana:* "If I were to build my womanhood on this self evident truth, it is the love of the Chicana, the love of myself as a Chicana I had to embrace."[38]

When Moraga illustrates how her multiple personal self functions within her cultural community, she constructs a public identity. But that public identity is not distinct and separate from her private identity. Saldívar articulates how Moraga moves beyond the private–public dichotomy in her cultural critique: "Moraga's autobiography disrupts facile conceptions of a private and a public self as she constructs her life story amid the historical conditions, material circumstances, the analytical categories of race, class, and gender that are the crucial mechanisms in the maintenance of power."[39] The power of "Vendidas" as cultural critique is Moraga's disruption of the line between private life and public life; through writing, and writing a multi-genred personal critical narrative in particular, Moraga collapses her search for a personal identity into a public criticism of her culture and her culture's attitudes toward lesbians. She cannot separate one life, personal or public, from the other: "On some level you have to be willing to lose it all to write—to risk telling the truth that no one may want to hear, even you."[40] The truth of her personal experiences and struggles for self-definition will not allow her to keep silent, to keep her personal life out of the public realm.

The disruptive nature of this move is made particularly clear when she concludes "Vendidas": "'I am a lesbian. And I am a Chicana,' I say to the men and women at the conference. I watch their faces twist up on me. 'These are two inseparable facts of my life. I can't talk or write about one without the other.'"[41] The public power of the written word is also confirmed in Moraga's own words, taken from a 1989 interview:

> In 1983, when *Loving in the War Years* came out, I left the country because I was very frightened of bringing up the issue of being lesbian and Chicana together within the covers of a book. It is only now, because there is such a strong movement of women writers, some of whom are lesbians but taking on feminist themes, that there is now a community, in which to make that voice public.[42]

That community came into existence partly because of the space that Moraga forged with her own public voice.

Moraga's notes reveal that Anzaldúa wrote portions of her multigenred cultural critique and manifesto, *Borderlands/La Frontera*, around the same time.[43] Anzaldúa does share similar purposes and intentions. She indicates her intention to define both self and culture in the book's preface:

> I am a border woman. I grew up between two cultures. . . . This book, then, speaks of my existence. My preoccupations with the inner life of the Self, and with the struggle of that Self amidst adversity and violation; with the confluence of primordial images; with the unique positionings consciousness takes at these confluent streams; and with my almost instinctive urge to communicate, to speak, to write about life on the borders, life in the shadows.[44]

Anzaldúa gives no hint of the mixed-genre nature of her essays or of the structure of her book as half-essay, half-poetry, in the preface or table of contents, but her first chapter begins with a mixing of genres: quotes from songs and poems, essay, her own poetry, and memories. This first chapter is also one of four whose main purpose can be seen as anthropological recovery, recounting the history, myths, religion, and lost or buried culture of the Chicano people: "During the original peopling of the Americas, the first inhabitants migrated across the Bering Straits and walked south across the continent."[45] Her attempts at recovery serve two purposes: to reveal cultural facts and icons repressed by the Spaniards and Anglos, and to restore respect and power to the female myths and symbols subverted by sexism.

Torres explains how Anzaldúa's recovery process enables a simultaneous critique:

> Anzaldúa devotes much of the text to recovering the female myths and symbols that are the basis of Chicano mythology and spirituality. She argues that the three dominating figures in Chicana history—the Virgen Guadalupe, La Malinche, and La Llorona—are all

ambiguous symbols that have been subverted and used to oppress women. She reinterprets the myths concerning these female deities and reclaims a woman-centered mythology. This strategy is not an alternative to radical structural change but a means to challenge the misogynist mythology which plays an important part in the cultural history of the Chicano people.[46]

Anzaldúa's reinterpretation from a feminist perspective automatically puts her at odds with some of the central tenets of Chicano culture. Her focus on women, and on the lesbian in particular, disrupts community and cultural order: "Women are at the bottom of the ladder one rung above the deviants. The Chicano, *mexicano*, and some Indian cultures have no tolerance for deviance. Deviance is whatever is condemned by the community. Most societies try to get rid of their deviants."[47] Like Moraga, Anzaldúa is aware that such a public critique has personal consequences: "And if going home is denied me then I will have to stand and claim my space, making a new culture—*una cultura mestiza*—with my own lumber, my own bricks and mortar and my own feminist architecture."[48] The tools of this cultural critique and construction are multigenre writing tools.

Like Moraga, Anzaldúa supplements her recovery/critique with self-definition. Several of the chapters, while retaining an anthropological slant, also detail her search for self-identity within her culture while simultaneously redefining and critiquing that culture's construction of women and lesbians. Also like Moraga, Anzaldúa mixes genres to offer specific illustrations of her claims. When she discusses the ways Chicano culture and the Spanish language encourage women to be silent, she writes a memory and quotes a poem by Irena Klepfisz to prove her point:

The first time I heard two women, a Puerto Rican and a Cuban, say the word *"nosotras,"* I was shocked. I had not known the word existed. Chicanas use *nosotros* whether we're male or female. We are robbed of our female being by the masculine plural. Language is a male discourse.

> And our tongues have become
> dry the wilderness has
> dried out our tongues.[49]

Anzaldúa's combination of and switching among genres reflects her multiple purposes and her multiple identities: mestiza, octolingual, working class, educated, feminist, lesbian, writer. As she concludes the first half of *Borderlands*, Anzaldúa uses four genres to reinforce the need for a new Mestiza Consciousness, and she takes on a different role for each one. She is reporter: "Because the Valley is heavily dependent on agriculture and Mexican retail trade, it has the highest unemployment rates along the entire border region; it is the Valley that has been hardest hit"; daughter: "My father has been dead for 29 years, having worked himself to death. The life span of a Mexican farm laborer is 56—he lived to be 38. It shocks me that I am older than he"; family historian: "Again I see the four of us kids getting off the school bus, changing into our work clothes, walking into the field with Papi and Mami, all six of us bending to the ground"; and poet:

> This land was Mexican once
> was Indian always
> and is.
> And will be again.[50]

Anzaldúa, however, is not as concerned as Moraga about the potential for public betrayal: "So *mamá Raza,* how wonderful, *no tener que rendir cuentas a nadie.* I feel perfectly free to rebel and to rail against my culture. I fear no betrayal on my part."[51] Indeed, Anzaldúa sees her identities as a writer, as a Chicana, and as a lesbian as one in the same: "Writing produces anxiety. Looking inside myself and my experience, looking at my conflicts, engenders anxiety in me. Being a writer feels very much like being a Chicana, or being queer—a lot of squirming, coming up against all sorts of walls."[52] Here she compares writing to her public roles as cultural and sexual minority in a world that suppresses those minority voices. Therefore, Anzaldúa's written search for personal identity, like Moraga's, is already collapsed into a public critique of the cultural forces that shape that identity:

> To write, to be a writer, I have to trust and believe in myself as a speaker, as a voice for the images. I have to believe that I can communicate with images and words and that I can do it well. A lack of belief in my creative self is a lack of belief in my total self and vice versa—I cannot separate my writing from any part of my life. It is all one.[53]

But unlike Moraga, Anzaldúa ultimately defines her own space and her own task: "I am cultureless because, as a feminist, I challenge the collective cultural/religious male-derived beliefs of Indo-Hispanics and Anglos; yet I am cultured because I am participating in the creation of yet another culture, a new story to explain the world and our participation in it."[54] While Moraga focuses on creating a space to discuss Chicana lesbianism, Anzaldúa sets out to revitalize a culture by reincorporating all that has been repressed. And Anzaldúa's conception of the Mestiza Consciousness is also a call to action: "It is imperative that mestizas support each other in changing the sexist elements in the Mexican-Indian culture. As long as woman is put down, the Indian and the Black in all of us is put down. The struggle of the mestiza is above all a feminist one."[55] Both Anzaldúa and Moraga remind us that the struggles to write about identity, cultural definition, women's oppression, and the oppression of women's love for other women are struggles rooted in feminist thinking and theory.

In the context of the essays, the poems in the second half of Anzaldúa's book build on and strengthen the critical stances articulated in other sections. Considered by themselves, the poems in Anzaldúa's text (and in Moraga's) are not as powerfully critical in a feminist or cultural sense as the multigenred "prose." However, the poems evoke meaningful images. In "Cultures," the speaker hoes a garden plot, turning up buried trash meant to represent the intrusion of Anglo culture:

> with my eyes I'd measure out a rectangle
> I'd swing and shove and lift
> my sweat dripping on the swelling mounds

into the hole I'd rake up and pitch
rubber-nippled baby bottles
cans of Spam with twisted umbilicals
I'd overturn the cultures
spawning in Coke bottles
murky and motleyed

my brothers never helped
woman's work and beneath them.[56]

This one-page poem does not have the space to clarify the conflict of cultures engendered by the border and the secondary status of women within Chicano and Indio cultures that the earlier chapters articulate; however, the images do offer further support of Anzaldúa's claims. In her study of American literary biographies, Jeanne Braham agrees that Anzaldúa's poems make less emphatic statements on their own:

> The second half of *Borderlands,* entitled "Echecate, the Wind" is composed of poems that, perhaps even more elliptically than in the first section, render the experience of "living at the crossroads" of culture, class, gender, race, sexuality. Anzaldúa wants her reader to *experience* her way of seeing the world.[57]

These often studied and much anthologized texts by Anzaldúa and Moraga suggest that the power required to move from rendering experience to a feminist and lesbian critique of that experience might best be gained through multigenre work, enabling the separate, but integrated, articulation of multiple experiences and analysis. In fact, Anzaldúa's choice to place the poems in the second half of *Borderlands* suggests that they are meant to supplement and support the more critical claims she makes in the cultural and critical narrative "essays" that come before. Moraga's opposite organization enables the poems that come before "Vendidas" to introduce the conflicts she discusses late in *Loving.*

Torres also hints that single-genre critical attempts can be inadequate to their tasks. She suggests that a new type of discourse is necessary to meet the task of working through the positive and negative elements of one's identity, which "results in the fragmentation of identity, and the inability to speak from a unified, noncontradictory subject position. No existing discourse is satisfactory . . . to incorporate the often contradictory aspects of their gender, ethnicity, class, sexuality, and feminist politics."[58] Anzaldúa confirms that the New Mestiza does not operate as a unity: "She learns to juggle cultures. She has a plural personality, she operates in a pluralistic mode. . . . Not only does she sustain contradictions, she turns the ambivalence into something else."[59] That something else is a powerful multigenred critique of her multiple oppressions, a refusal to submit to limited definitions of the Chicana self. In the course of their struggles, Anzaldúa and Moraga also refuse to stay within the boundaries genre places on women's—and, hence, feminist and lesbian—expression.

In her cultural analysis of Chicana literature, Rebolledo also makes the connection between genre switches and multiple identities and representations:

A mixture of politics, poetry, oral tradition, personal essay, and autobiography, Anzaldúa's *Borderlands* is the epitome of a creative/critical praxis that tries to identify and imbue a purely Chicana–Mestiza–India (and all of the aforementioned complications) theoretical discourse with practice. Here Anzaldúa, in seizing the subject, shifts from the personal to the collective, from the emotional to the political, from the details of her lived personal life to its connections with the mythic. . . . Anzaldúa's theoretic praxis is more baroque, thereby allowing very useful shifting zones of representation and signification.[60]

Writing in multiple genres enables Moraga to speak from both of her races, from both culture and sexuality, and to two different communities, including an academic one: "I have learned analysis as a mode to communicate what I feel the experience itself already speaks for. The combining of poetry and essays in this book is the compromise I make in the effort to be understood."[61]

Rebolledo also claims that representation of such multiple identity perspectives and the internal struggle between them has had an impact on our understanding of borders, physical, gender, and cultural:

The tensions, the conflict, the shiftings were finally articulated. And Anzaldúa . . . recognized the multiplicities we had felt, and the ambivalences we instinctively intuited in going against a unifying tradition. Most important, in many ways she validated the shiftings, seeing them as coming from a position of resistance . . . [and] recognized that the lines drawn for the borders were arbitrary and limiting and did not reflect the real world. It was okay to see the limitations and to cross them.[62]

This statement also speaks to the way Anzaldúa and Moraga have shifted the borders among genres, recognizing that the distinctions among genres were "arbitrary and limiting and did not reflect the real world" of their experiences. Their resistance to multiple oppressions requires an additional resistance to the boundaries of genre, and their ability "to see the limitations" of genre and "to cross them" enabled them to articulate the Chicana feminist positions that "had been in the air for some time," and, in the process, to develop a powerful mode of lesbian expression.[63]

Notes

Epigraphs: Cherríe Moraga, *Loving in the War Years: Lo que nunca pasó por sus labios* (Boston: South End Press, 1983), iv; Gloria Anzaldúa, "Speaking in Tongues: A Letter to Third World Women Writers," in *This Bridge Called My Back: Writings by Radical Women of Color*, ed. Cherríe Moraga and Gloria Anzaldúa (New York: Kitchen Table/Women of Color Press, 1983), 167.

1. Moraga and Anzaldúa, *This Bridge Called My Back*.

2. Moraga, *Loving*; Gloria Anzaldúa, *Borderlands/La Frontera: The New Mestiza* (San Francisco: Aunt Lute Books, 1987).

3. Anne E. Goldman, *Take My Word: Autobiographical Innovations of Ethnic American Working Women* (Berkeley: University of California Press, 1996).

4. Ibid., ix.

5. Ibid., 28.

6. Ibid., 172.

7. Ramón Saldívar, *Chicano Narrative: The Dialectics of Difference* (Madison: University of Wisconsin Press, 1990).

8. Ibid., 27–28.

9. Ibid., 39.

10. Ibid., 38–39.

11. Tey Diana Rebolledo, *Women Singing in the Snow: A Cultural Analysis of Chicana Literature* (Tucson: University of Arizona Press, 1995), 3.

12. Ibid., 1–3.

13. Tey Diana Rebolledo and Eliana Rivero, eds., *Infinite Divisions: An Anthology of Chicana Literature* (Tucson: University of Arizona Press, 1993), 78.

14. Tey Diana Rebolledo, "The Maturing of Chicana Poetry: The Quiet Revolution of the 1980s," in *For Alma Mater: Theory and Practice in Feminist Scholarship,* ed. Paula A. Treichler, Cheris Kramarae, and Beth Stafford (Chicago: University of Illinois Press, 1985).

15. Ibid., 146.

16. Miriam Bornstein-Gómez, "Toma de nombre/Taking of Name," in Rebolledo and Rivero, *Infinite Divisions,* 79–80.

17. Personal Narratives Group, ed., *Interpreting Women's Lives: Feminist Theory and Personal Narratives* (Bloomington: Indiana University Press, 1989), 7.

18. Moraga, *Loving,* 105.

19. Ibid., 106–7.

20. Ibid., 110.

21. Ibid., 105.

22. Saldívar, *Chicano Narrative,* 173.

23. Biddy Martin, "Lesbian Identity and Autobiographical Difference[s]," in *Theorizing Feminism: Parallel Trends in the Humanities and Social Sciences,* ed. Anne C. Herrmann and Abigail J. Stewart (Boulder, Colo.: Westview Press, 1994).

24. Ibid., 320–21.

25. Ibid, 320.

26. Moraga, *Loving,* i.

27. Ibid., 102.

28. Ibid., 102–3.

29. Ibid., 103.

30. Ibid., 117.

31. Leslie Bow, "Hole to Whole: Feminine Subversion and Subversion of the Feminine in Cherríe Moraga's *Loving in the War Years," Dispositio: Revista Americana de Estudios Comparados y Culturales* 16, no. 41 (1991): 6.

32. Ibid., 9.

33. Ibid., 10–11.

34. Personal Narratives Group, *Interpreting Women's Lives,* 99.

35. Ibid., 101.

36. Moraga, *Loving,* 117.

37. Lourdes Torres, "The Construction of the Self in U. S. Latina Autobiographies," in *Third World Women and the Politics of Feminism,* ed. Chandra Talpade Mohanty, Ann Russo, and Lourdes Torres (Bloomington: Indiana University Press, 1991), 273.

38. Moraga, *Loving,* 94.

39. Saldívar, *Chicano Narrative,* 188.

40. Moraga, *Loving,* v.

41. Ibid., 142.

42. Dorothy Allison, Tomás Almaguer, and Jackie Goldsby, "Writing Is the Measure of My Life" (interview with Cherríe Moraga), *OUT/LOOK: National Lesbian and Gay Quarterly* 1, no. 4 (1989): 53–57, as quoted in Saldívar, *Chicano Narrative,* 188.

43. Moraga, *Loving,* 143.

44. Anzaldúa, *Borderlands,* n.p.

45. Ibid., 4.

46. Torres, "Construction of the Self," 281.

47. Anzaldúa, *Borderlands,* 18.

48. Ibid., 22.

49. Ibid., 54.

50. Ibid., 90–91.

51. Ibid., 21.

52. Ibid., 72.

53. Ibid., 73.

54. Ibid., 80–81.

55. Ibid., 84.

56. Ibid., 120.

57. Jeanne Braham, *Crucial Conversations: Interpreting Contemporary American Literary Auto-biographies by Women* (New York: Teachers College Press, 1995), 96; emphasis added.

58. Torres, "Construction of the Self," 275.

59. Anzaldúa, *Borderlands,* 79.

60. Rebolledo, *Women,* 6.

61. Moraga, *Loving,* vi.

62. Rebolledo, *Women,* 103.

63. Ibid., 2.

Part IV

Racialized Lesbianisms

Sherry Velasco

13 Interracial Lesbian Erotics in Early Modern Spain: Catalina de Erauso and Elena/o de Céspedes

Recent studies on same-sex female erotics during the early modern period examine how "women-loving women" were represented (or ignored) in official and popular culture. Frequently these investigations conclude that under certain conditions the expression of desire between women was tolerated, and perhaps even condoned, especially if the erotic encounters were believed to be non-penetrative—if they were interpreted as spiritual or philosophical considerations within the Neoplatonic tradition or perhaps even a means of facilitating restraint from heterosexual relations outside the confines of matrimony. Unlike the consistent prohibition of male homosexuality during the same period, female homoeroticism was occasionally cited as an entertaining and innocent pastime. Pierre de Brantôme (1540–1614), for example, defends "Lesbian women" in his provocative sixteenth-century *Lives of Fair and Gallant Ladies*:

> Still excuse may be made for maids and widows for loving these frivolous and empty pleasures, preferring to devote themselves to these than to go with men and come to dishonour. . . . They do not so much offend God, and are not such great harlots, as if they had to do with the men, maintaining that there is a great difference betwixt throwing water in a vessel and merely watering about it and round the rim.[1]

Sexual activity between women was criminalized, however, if it was seen as imitative of heterosexual intercourse. Charles V's 1532 statute condemns anyone who "commits impurity with a beast, or a man with a man, or a woman with a woman, they have forfeited their lives and shall, after the common custom, be sentenced to death by burning."[2] Likewise, Gregorio López's 1556 recompilation of *Las Siete Partidas* assigns the death penalty not only to male sodomites but also to women who have "unnatural intercourse" with other women.[3] However, according to sixteenth-century legal authorities, female homosexuality without use of an instrument as a penis substitute was not as threatening as male sodomy and therefore should be punished not with death but with a more lenient penalty, such as a lashing and exile.[4]

As early modern scholars explore the distinctions between male homosexuality and female homoeroticism, they grapple with terminology and changing definitions and conceptualizations of sexual identities and behaviors. For example, the term "lesbian" (as an identity category) has been highly contested and critiqued as anachronistic for women who desired other women before the nineteenth century, despite the term's appearance in sixteenth-century texts: "two ladies that be in love with one with the other ... sleeping together in one bed, and doing what is called *donna con donna*, imitating in fact that learned poetess Sappho, of Lesbos, ... such is the character of the Lesbian women."[5] Along similar lines, Erasmo associates Sappho with convent homoeroticism in his colloquy "The Girl with no Interest in Marriage": "Not everything is virginal among these virgins ... [b]ecause there are more who copy Sappho's behavior than share her talent."[6] Other terms for same-sex female eroticism in early modern writings include *"tribades," "fricatrices,"* "rubsters," *"donna con donna," "amiga particular,"* and so forth.[7] Regardless of differing terminology, current thought and study of same-sex female desire during this period point to a complex and often contradictory context that participates in a general history of homosexuality and yet establishes a unique trajectory apart from male homoeroticism.

Two historical cases in particular reveal imperial Spain's cultural anxieties regarding gender, sex identification, desire, race, and nation. Born female in the mid-sixteenth century to an African slave (Francisca de Medina) and a Castilian peasant (Pero Hernández), Elena de Céspedes (named after the mistress of the household) was permanently marked as the *mulata* offspring of a slave through the brand marks on her cheeks.[8] Nevertheless, she transformed herself into a man during her adolescence (because of what she describes as a sudden onset of hermaphroditism while giving birth to her son), and thereafter adopted the name Eleno de Céspedes.

The second case involves another individual born female in the late sixteenth century who also begins to live as a man during her adolescence. Unlike the socially and racially marginalized Céspedes, Catalina de Erauso (also known as the Monja Alférez or the Lieutenant Nun) was an educated Basque aristocrat who enjoyed the privilege and entitlement of her class and ethnicity but chose not to endure the subjugation of her female gender. When she turned fifteen, she escaped from the convent in San Sebastián where she had lived since age four and turned her novice's habit into an outfit appropriate for a young man. Before leaving port for the New World, she adopted the name Francisco de Loyola, but later she was known as Alonso Díaz Ramírez de Guzmán and as Antonio de Erauso. Both historical individuals might be described in today's terms as FTMs (female-to-male transsexuals) who desire women, although during the sixteenth and seventeenth centuries their birth identities were privileged in both official and popular culture.[9] Despite their attempts to escape the conflation of binary gender roles and sex identity based on genitalia, they were identified as women-loving women who impersonated men.[10] However, although both individuals transgressed traditional proscriptions for gender behavior, sex recon-struction, and sexual attraction, the ways in which their cases were processed by the legal, medical, and religious authorities (as well as in the popular imagination) vary significantly and ultimately indicate that early modern conceptions of female homo-eroticism dealt just as much with race, ethnicity, and imperialism as they did with specific sexual behaviors.

When compared, Erauso's and Céspedes's cases reveal the politics of entitlement conferred on representatives of upper-class white patriarchy during the height of Spain's empire-building project. Despite years of violent crimes (including about a dozen alleged murders off the battlefield), Erauso was rewarded for her gender trans-gression in 1626 with a soldier's pension from the Spanish monarch Philip IV (for years of military service in Peru and Chile) and a dispensation from Pope Urban VIII to continue dressing in men's clothing. In 1630, she returned to the New World and lived the last two decades of her life in Mexico working as a mule driver, again dressed in men's attire and using the name Antonio de Erauso until her death in 1650. Cés-pedes, by contrast, was first charged with female sodomy but eventually was con-victed of bigamy and possible demonic collusion, which resulted in a sentence of two hundred public lashes and ten years of confined service in a local hospital. The diver-gent outcomes for these two "lesbian outlaws" clearly demonstrates the parameters within which same-sex female attraction could be sanctioned, the cultural construc-tion of gender and anatomical identity, and finally, the fear of interracial desire in early modern Spanish society.

Erauso's attraction to other women was represented openly after her transgen-derism became public, not only in her autobiography, but also in a letter published in 1618, a play performed in Madrid in 1626, and two of three broadsides (the first published in 1625 in Madrid and Seville and the last in 1653 in Mexico) relating the sensationalist aspects of her life.[11] During one episode in her memoirs, Erauso describes for her readers how she was fired by her boss when he caught her "fooling around" with his sister-in-law: "Tenía en casa a dos doncellas hermanas de su muger, con las quales, i más con una que más se me inclinó, solía yo más jugar i triscar: i un día, estando en el estrado peinándome acostado en sus faldas i andándole en las pier-nas."[12] This instance of explicit same-sex erotic interaction is not isolated: Erauso fre-quently expresses romantic interest in various women in the New World that occa-sionally results in physical petting but apparently never leads to the discovery of her anatomical identity.[13]

Erauso's identity, based on the nature and "condition" of her primary sex charac-teristics, was determined through only one examination, which was conducted in 1617, once she confessed her transgender adventures to the bishop in Guamanga. According to her autobiography, when the bishop was somewhat incredulous of her story, Erauso requested a physical exam to prove both her female sex and her status as a virgin: "'Señor, es así; i si quiere salir de duda Vuestra Señoría Ilustrísima por experiencia de Matronas, yo llana estoi'";[14] "Entraron dos Matronas i me miraron i satisfacieron i declararon después ante el Obispo con juramento, haverme visto i reconocido quanto fue menester para certificarse i haverme hallado virgen intacta, como el día en que nací."[15] Compared with the mistrust that surrounded Céspedes's case, the officials in Peru, as well as in Spain and Italy, were predisposed to believe Erauso's story. The bishop quickly congratulated the transgressive gender-bender "os venero como una de las personas notables de este mundo i os prometo asistiros en quanto pueda."[16] According to her memoirs, as well as the letters, testimonies, and certifications written on her behalf, the exam conducted in Peru was the only confirmation of her female genitalia. Apparently no attempts were made to interview the women with whom she had engaged in romantic activities. In the end, the seeming chastity was based on a heterobiased configuration determined by the presence or lack of penetration, assuming that the primary issue at stake was whether this *mujer varonil* had been the "passive" recipient of any sexual encounters, while no doubt was raised about her possible active role in female sodomy or other genital contact with women, even while remaining a *"virgen intacta."*

Despite the celebrated results of Erauso's physical examination, according to a letter written by Pedro de la Valle in 1626, during a private conversation she admitted to having used an invasive technique to remove permanently the secondary sex characteristic of breasts: "No tiene pechos: que desde mui muchacha me dixo haver hecho no sé qué remedio para secarlos i quedar llanos, como le quedaron: el qual fue un emplasto que le dio un Ytaliano, que quando se lo puso le causó gran dolor; pero después, sin hacerle otro mal, ni mal tratamiento, surtió el efecto."[17] Although there are no accounts of genital reconstructive techniques, or indications of primary sex disconformity (such as an enlarged clitoris, bisexed status, or hermaphroditism), Erauso, by eliminating any external trace of her female identity through the breasts, left little doubt about her serious and enduring preference for the male gender.[18]

The nature of Céspedes's anatomy was much more controversial, not to mention elusive. According to her autobiographical testimony (*discurso de su vida*), she suddenly acquired a penis after giving birth at age sixteen to a son while she was briefly married to Christóval Lombardo. Her husband soon left town, and Céspedes later received word of his death. Because the masculine nature of her/his bisexed condition predominated after childbirth, she/he decided to follow suit and start living as a man. However, medical intervention was necessary to facilitate sexual relations with women, as his/her newly developed phallus was impeded from full erection by a layer of skin, which she/he then had removed surgically. Céspedes eventually married María del Caño after receiving official medical confirmation of his/her male genitalia from the physician Francisco Díaz. In a 1586 deposition, Díaz determined Céspedes's identity as male, and not hermaphrodite: "Verdad que él le ha visto sus miembros genitales, y las manos puso vecinas [y] ha vista de ojos, y tocadole con las manos. Y que declarábase de él así: que él tiene su miembro genital, el cual es bastante y perfecto, con sus testículos formados, como cual quiera hombre. . . . Y ansí dicho y declaró que a su parecer no tiene semejanza de hermafrodita ni cosa dello."[19] Despite previous medical confirmation of Céspedes's exclusively male identity, in 1587, during the preliminary sodomy hearings in Ocaña, she/he was charged with having used an instrument during sexual intercourse ("con un instrumento tieso y liso ... cometió el delito nefando de sodomia"[20]), and midwives testified that the defendant (like Erauso) possessed only female genitalia and that her virginity had not been compromised: "La cual le metió por su natura de mujer la dicha vela, la cual entró premiosa y poco, y esta testigo no se confió y también le metió el dedo ..., y entró premioso, y con esto esta testigo no entiende que haya llegado varón a ella."[21] After the charges were changed to bigamy, and the trial was transferred to the Inquisition courts in Toledo, Díaz changed his testimony, now believing that the defendant's male genitalia had been a deception, "algún arte tan sutil que bastó para engañar a éste así en la vista como en el tacto."[22] Céspedes nevertheless attributed the loss of her/his penis to cancer and insisted that his/her sexual identity as a hermaphrodite could not be monosexed or static, and therefore she/he was not guilty of sodomy, lesbianism, consecration of the sacrament of holy matrimony, or demonic intervention:

> Porque yo con pacto expreso ni tácito del demonio nunca me fingí hombre para casarme con mujer como se me pretende imputar. Y lo que pasa es que como en este mundo muchas veces se han visto personas que son andróginos, que por otro nombre se llaman hermafroditos, que tienen entramos sexos, yo también he sido uno de éstos. Y al tiempo que me pretendí casar incalecía y prevalescía más en el sexo masculino, y naturalmente era hombre y tenía todo lo necesario de hombre para poder casar. Y de que lo era hice información y probanza ocular de médicos y cirujanos peritos en el arte, los cuales me vieron y tentaron y testificaron con juramento que era tal hombre y me podía casar con mujer. Y con la dicha probanza hecha judicialmente me casé por hombre.[23]

An initial review of the cases presented against Céspedes and in support of Erauso reveals a few crucial differences that rerouted interpretations of their same-sex desire toward two separate outcomes. Although Erauso was believed by some to be a eunuch while living as a man, the physical exam in Peru confirmed both female genital regularity and an intact hymen, regardless of her attraction and unspecified sexual adventures with women in the New World.[24] Conversely, if the investigation of Céspedes's anatomy had relied on one specific testimony (as did Erauso's) his/her case might have taken a different turn. However, the multiple and contradictory interpretations appear to follow a fluid trajectory, fluctuating between and outside a binary model of sexual identity. In the end, the medical and legal authorities deemed Céspedes's identity unequivocally female and therefore her desire transgressive (that is, lesbian), given her open sexual relations with other women: "Y ésta quedó con aptitud de poder tener cuenta con mujer y volvió a la dicha Ana de Albánchez, y con ella tuvo muchas veces cuenta y actos como hombre."[25] As a result, confirmation of both active and passive genital penetration (with Céspedes's onetime husband and subsequent female lovers and wife) required punitive legislation of her sexual activity.

At this point, we might return to the question of how race affects an apparent penetration-based model for legislating desire between women during this period. Again, the differences between Erauso's and Céspedes's interracial homoeroticism are striking. While Erauso embodies the white, upper-class colonial subject who evaluates various mestiza women in Chile, Peru, and Mexico as potential lovers, Céspedes is portrayed as the *mulata* lesbian predator, an invader of gender, sexual conformity, and national and racial expectations. Céspedes's self-defense nevertheless attempts to reassign identity from female (lesbian) slave to that of male (and therefore hetero-sexual) hermaphrodite. According to Israel Burshatin, Céspedes's hermaphroditism "stands as a metaphor for race that displaces slavery/femininity. In claiming the sta-tus of hermaphrodite, Eleno transforms the meaning of her brown skin."[26]

It is not by chance, then, that Erauso's entertaining yet "non-threatening" lesbian escapades were conducted far from Spain and, moreover, with New World, non-European women, while Céspedes was "preying" on women close to home. In fact, Erauso's account of how she took advantage of and then abandoned two women in Chile actually invites the early modern reader to excuse her behavior when she describes the women in the New World as opportunistic: "I como parece que apor-tan por allí pocos españoles, parece que me apeteció para su hija."[27] Two concurrent episodes in Chapter 7 of Erauso's autobiography involve efforts to arrange marriages with the Basque nobleman. On more than one occasion, the protagonist willingly accepts the gifts offered by her fiancées, then escapes, leaving the women *"burladas"* (deceived): "A pocos más días me dio a entender que tendría bien que me casase con su hija que allí consigo tenía, la qual era una Negra fea como unos diablos, mui con-traria a mi gusto que fue siempre de buenas caras."[28] Although Erauso has no inten-tion of marrying the girl, perhaps in part because of the potential risk of being dis-covered, she clearly reveals her racist colonial ideology through her preference for light-skinned women.[29] Erauso's extreme repulsion based on race is further empha-sized in the hyperbolic comment included in one of the eighteenth-century manuscript copies of her autobiography deposited in the Archivo Capitular in Seville: "Era mi esposa negra y fea, cosa muy contraria a mi gusto, que fue siempre de buenas caras, *por lo qual se puede creer que los quatro meses que estube con esta señora fueron para mí qua-tro siglos.*"[30]

Although Marjorie Garber downplays the role of desire in this episode, writing that "the resistance to marriage is more strongly marked by aversions of class, race, and nobility than by gender or sexuality,"[31] the intersection of race and desire here cre-ates a significant contrast to other ambiguous representations of the Monja Alférez. Instead of eroticizing the exotic Other (as is frequent in early modern representations of Moorish women in Spain, for example), Erauso enacts a sexual demonization of the mestiza ("black and ugly as the devil himself"). Like Garber, other critics also see race as the more relevant identity marker in the seventeenth century. Referring to Erauso's possible status as a beardless *capón,* or eunuch, Mary Elizabeth Perry notes the predominance of race over sex categories: "The body of this soldier became sexed only in the context of power relations, which assumed that lightness of complexion counted for more than body hair. In the New World outposts at this time the Span-ish soldier had the power not only to subjugate darker-skinned peoples, but to deter-mine the discourse used to describe this experience."[32] For postcolonial critics such as Anne McClintock, racist representations of the unappealing mestiza might be analyzed effectively through the filter of what she terms "porno-tropics," or the portrayal of New World women as imperial boundary markers.[33] Dramatizing the colonialist's responses of desire and repulsion, Erauso presents the women of Chile and Peru as sexual objects available for her consumption, even if only temporary and for economic gain.[34]

At the same time, however—just as Erauso demonized the potential object of her affection—her desire for the "pretty faces" of other light-skinned women is indirectly criminalized in the text through her mistreatment of women in the New World. Even when Erauso seems positively inclined to a potential wife—"Vide a la moza, i pareción bien"—she abandons the girl after collecting the valuables.[35] Despite many critics' assertion that the protagonist's behavior reflects her desire to avoid discovery, in the *relaciones* (news pamphlets) and in the autobiography Erauso's same-sex desire is frequently associated with aggression or criminality.[36] However, what neutralizes this negative image in the minds of the early modern readers is the fact that the objects of Erauso's disdain were considered inferior both socially and racially to the upper-class European suitor. For Garber, the tensions between "Indians and 'Spaniards,' between purebreds and 'half-breeds,' and between the merchant class and the nobility" helped produce a sympathetic audience for Erauso's story.[37]

When considering Erauso's racist comments about the mestiza, Michele Stepto encourages her readers not to compare the protagonist's own victimization as a transvestite spectacle with Erauso's embodiment of aristocratic imperialism: "It would be a misreading to see her as anything other than the perfect colonialist, manipulative, grasping, and at moments out and out bigoted. To align Catalina, as a cross-dressing 'other,' with the victims of colonialism is to miss the truth that the rewards of her transformation were gained almost wholly at their expense."[38] In this way, despite her participation in the history of transgenderism (as well as her perceived lesbianism), Erauso undoubtedly contributed to the assault on the personal and cultural integrity of mestiza women, which was based on sexual, racial, and class relations.[39] Consequently, Erauso's "romantic" episodes with the women of Peru and Chile are just as much about violence and power as they are about desire and fantasy.

If we compare, then, the portrayal of race and desire in Erauso's autobiography with an analogous episode from María de Zayas's 1637 story "El prevenido engañado," we may find different perspectives regarding interracial attraction (and repulsion), but in the end these texts support an unambiguous condemnation of such behavior. In Zayas's story, the narrator performs a textual and sexual demonization of Beatriz's black lover Antonio that is similar to Erauso's racist characterization of the mestiza. Antonio is described as "un negro tan atezado, que parecía hecho de un bocací su rostro ... tan feo y abominable ... el demonio no podía serlo tanto ... un fiero demonio ... del endemoniado negro."[40] Despite this demonization of Antonio, it is the white noble woman who, like Erauso, selfishly uses the dark-skinned lover for her own gain. However, while Erauso and Zayas's narrator, Alonso, seem to share a marked repulsion by the brown skin of the other parties, Beatriz is unambiguous about her physical attraction for Antonio. Moreover, in Zayas's text, Antonio presents himself as the innocent victim of Beatriz's voracious sexual appetite: "¿Qué me quieres, señora? ¡Déxame ya, por Dios! ¿Qué es esto, que aun estando yo acabando la vida me persigues? No basta que tu viciosa condición me tiene como estoy, sino que quieres que cuando ya estoy en el fin de mi vida, acuda a cumplir tus viciosos apetitos. Cásate, señora, cásate, y déxame ya a mí, que ni te quiero ver ni comer lo que me das; morir quiero, pues ya no estoy para otra cosa."[41]

Given that, in Zayas's narrative, the "black stud" (as described by José Piedra) is allowed to voice his own opinion, we are invited to reprove Beatriz for her deviant interracial desire.[42] However, because the focalization in Erauso's autobiography is limited to the narrator–protagonist, we are not able to see directly the mestiza's point of view, although in the conclusion to Chapter 7 the author hints at the consequences of having abandoned her fiancées: "No he sabido cómo se huvieron después la Negra i la Provisora."[43] One might assume, then, that the women deceived by Erauso's false promises of marriage would have their own stories of rage and exploitation, similar to that presented by Antonio in Zayas's story. In Erauso's life narrative (as well as in the testimonies written on her behalf) there is an untold story: the perspective of the women who were not only the objects of the protagonist's desire but also desiring subjects who found themselves attracted to the beardless Basque soldier. It is in these intersections of race, class, gender, and sexuality that the early modern audience is forced to reconcile the inherent conflicts between the orthodox repulsion of the New World mestiza and the deviant (yet celebrated) lesbian imperialist. Ultimately, the dilemma is short-lived, as Erauso's service to the Spanish empire redeems her sexual and gender transgression. Likewise, the combination of the critique of same-sex desire with proof of her abstinence from heterosexual intercourse allows the containment of a potential "Lieutenant Nun epidemic" inspired by the precedent set by her successful case. This in turn allows a hero to emerge who can be invoked by the crown or the church as an example of imperial Catholic ideology.

Despite their efforts to live permanently as men, both Céspedes and Erauso were identified as female and, given the accounts of their sexual desire for other women, were linked to an early modern conception of lesbian erotics. Although medical, legal, royal, and religious authorities undoubtedly considered race, class, and empire when they examined specific sexual and gender transgressions, the same system that rewarded the noble "virgin" war hero but condemned the *mulata* bigamist (who had also fought loyally for Felipe II against the morisco rebels in the Alpujarras War from 1568 to 1570) created popular lesbian celebrities out of both cases. After their private experiences were made public, crowds of curious fans and critics rushed to get a glimpse of the famous transgendered icons. The Lieutenant Nun's first public appearance was a celebration sponsored by the ecclesiastic authorities in Peru: "Salió Su Ilustrísima de casa llevándome a su lado con un concurso tan grande, que no huvo de quedar persona alguna en la ciudad que no viniese."[44] Céspedes, by contrast, was publicly punished in two locations, Toledo and Ciempozuelos (the town where she had married María): "Her case is given a higher profile by the Inquisitors themselves, when they also make her appear in an *auto da fé*, held in Toledo . . . and is forced to parade around the central square wearing the requisite mitre and robes (*sambenito*), with insignias 'appropriate' to her crime of bigamy."[45] Shortly after Céspedes began her obligatory service in Toledo, the hospital administrator complained of the inconvenience of her celebrity status: "The presence of Elena de Céspedes has caused great annoyance and embarrassment from the beginning, since many people come to see and be healed by her."[46] As Burshatin summarizes: "A reputed hermaphrodite, a woman who has lived, loved and married as a man, has become a surgeon, and has even been suspected of possessing magical healing powers, this *mulata* is now a local *cause célèbre*. Of Eleno's many bodies, none is as powerful as this latest incarnation. Thanks to the formidable Toledo Inquisitors, Elena alias Eleno is a pilgrimage site."[47]

Erauso (known after 1620 as the Monja Alférez) likewise becomes a marketable draw for the masses, as well as for the elite in the New World and throughout Spain and Italy ("Corrió la noticia de este suceso por todas las Yndias, i los que antes me vieron, i los que antes i después supieron mis cosas, se maravillaron en todas las Yndias . . . no podíamos valernos de [tanta] gente curiosa que venía a ver a la Monja Alférez"[48]) and later in Spain ("escondiéndome quanto pude, huyendo del concurso que acudía a verme vestida en hábito de hombre"[49]). At the same time, in Rome, "Hízose el caso allí notorio, i fue notable al concurso de que me vide cercado de Personages, Príncipes, Obispos, Cardenales."[50] Both individuals became something like freak-show attractions, but one was compensated and free to continue living as a man, while the other was publicly punished and then confined, forced to repay a perceived debt to society.

Interestingly, their notoriety continued years after the initial scandals filled the public squares and news pamphlets. Céspedes is written into Jerónimo de Huerta's 1599 annotated translation of Pliny's *Natural History* as a transgendered *mulata* criminal lesbian: "con aquella esclava Andaluça, llamada Elena de Céspedes, la qual dexado el habito de muger, fingio muchos años ser hombre, mostrava serlo aunque mal tallado, y sin barba con cierto artificio engañoso, y era tan al natural que despues de auerle mirado algunos cirujanos, y declarado ser hombre, se caso en Cien Poçuelos."[51] Ironically, Céspedes herself had cited Pliny years earlier to document the prevailing medical belief in sexual transmutations, which argued that a humoral change could instigate an insufficiency of moisture and an excess of heat capable of converting women into men. Huerta, however, uses Céspedes's case to show how deceptive reconstructive surgery can create an appearance of genital regularity.[52]

Erauso's gender, sex, and sexuality were likewise held under surveillance for the remainder of her life. A broadside published in Mexico in 1653 (three years after her death) provides a telling interpretation of how the Monja Alférez's icon had persevered even after her case had been decided by church and state. Although the news pamphlet continues the sensationalized adventures where the 1625 *relaciones* had left off, it is the only text to focus the majority of the story on the lesbian identity of the protagonist. With the king's and the pope's blessings, she was by then now living and working in Mexico as Antonio de Erauso. However, she no longer needed to worry about discovery, because those familiar with her history already knew the official version of the genital "truth" beneath the masculine attire. The central plot of the 1653 broadside centers on a tale of frustrated same-sex desire. When Erauso is asked to accompany a young woman on a trip, the former falls in love with the beauty of the latter, "caminando con ella de su hermosura enamorada."[53] However, when a gentleman also falls in love with the woman, Erauso is overcome with jealousy and tries to persuade the woman to enter a convent with her, as the protagonist would pay all the expenses. When the woman rejects the offer and decides to marry the man instead, Erauso cannot contain her envy and becomes physically ill. She eventually recovers her health, deciding that she would rather be jealous than die of separation from her beloved: "teniendo por menor daño tenerla embidia a los ojos, que morir de ausencia de los de su querida."[54] Accordingly, she starts to visit her love interest but becomes so jealous of the other female friends who visit the young woman that the husband decides to prohibit Erauso from coming to the house. Not surprisingly, Erauso becomes irate and challenges the husband to a duel; when the husband refuses, saying that he would not fight a woman, Erauso explodes: "Bolcanes arrojava nuestra Peregrina por los ojos." She later confronts the husband but eventually controls her anger and turns her back on her competitor, while those who witness the scene are impressed by her fearlessness: "sabida la bizarría de su despejo, se celebró mucho de los que la conocían."[55]

Despite (or perhaps because of) the open lesbian characterization of the protagonist, the 1653 news pamphlet ends with a hagiographic description of Erauso's saintly life and death: "falleció con una muerte ejemplar. . . . Tenía todos los días por costumbre rezar lo que es de obligación, a las Religiosas professas, ayunaba toda la Quaresma y los advientos y Vigilias, hazía todas las semanas, Lunes, Miércoles y Viernes tres deciplinas, y oya todos los días missa."[56] Erauso's transgressive desire, then, was neutralized by her military service and the official confirmation that she had not compromised her female chastity while living among men. In Erauso's case, cross-dressing and lesbian flirtation were perhaps believed to facilitate abstinence from heterosexual or a phallus-centered model for sexual activity, while Céspedes's scandal highlighted her efforts to usurp the male sexual role through marriage and penetrative sexual relations.

Despite Erauso's and Céspedes's intention of living as men (with or without changes to primary or secondary sex characteristics), the identity imposed on them by legal and cultural authorities reflected their female sex at birth. As a result, their romantic desire for women was inevitably rendered non-heterosexual. Accordingly, an analysis of these two famous gender-benders reveals some of the rules of the game for interracial lesbian erotics in early modern Spain. First, female same-sex desire must appear to avoid genital contact, especially through penetration. Second, a woman-loving woman is celebrated only when the lesbian suitor is an upper-class European imperialist far from home and involved with women who are considered socially and racially inferior. And third, regardless of class, race, or alleged chastity, tolerance of same-sex attraction is only temporary and, in the end, the early modern lesbian is not allowed to "get the girl" and live with her lover happily ever after.

Notes

1. Pierre Brantôme, *Lives of Fair and Gallant Ladies*, trans. A. R. Allinson (New York: Liveright Publishing, 1933), 133–34.

2. Louis Crompton, "The Myth of Lesbian Impunity Capital Laws from 1270 to 1791," in "Special Issue: Historical Perspectives on Homosexuality," ed. Salvatore J. Licata and Robert P. Peterson, *Journal of Homosexuality* 6, no. 1–2 (1980–81): 18.

3. Judith C. Brown, *Immodest Acts: The Life of a Lesbian Nun in Renaissance Italy* (New York: Oxford University Press, 1986), 14.

4. Javier Pérez Escohotado, *Sexo e inquisición en España* (Madrid: Temas de Hoy, 1992), 181.

5. Brantôme, *Lives*, 128–29; emphasis added. See Adrienne L. Martín, "Desnudo de una travestí, o la 'autobiografía de Catalina de Erauso," in *La mujer y su representación en la literaturas hispánicas. Actas Irvine–1992. Asociación Internacional de Hispanistas* (Irvine: University of California Press, 1994), 34–41, and Patricia Simons, "Lesbian (In)Visibility in Italian Renaissance Culture: Diana and Other Cases of *donna con donna*," *Journal of Homosexuality* 27, no. 1–2 (1994): 81–122.

6. Janice G. Raymond, *A Passion for Friends: Toward a Philosophy of Female Affection* (Boston: Beacon Press, 1986), 95.

7. See Simons, "Lesbian (In)Visibility"; Harriette Andreadis, "The Erotics of Female Friendship in Early Modern England," in *Maids and Mistresses, Cousins and Queens: Women's Alliances in Early Modern England*, ed. Susan Frye and Karen Robertson (New York: Oxford University Press, 1999), 241–58; and Emma Donoghue, *Passions between Women: British Lesbian Culture 1668–1801* (London: Scarlet Press, 1993).

8. Manuscript documents related to Elena de Céspedes's case are housed in the Archivo Histórico Nacional, Madrid (Sección Inquisición, Tribunal de Toledo: Legajo 234, Expediente 24). To facilitate reading in Spanish, I have modernized the spelling and punctuation. All translations in English are from Israel Burshatin, "Elena Alias Eleno: Genders, Sexualities, and 'Race' in the Mirror of Natural History in Sixteenth-Century Spain," in *Gender Reversals and Gender Cultures: Anthropological and Historical Perspectives* (London: Routledge, 1996), 105–22; idem, "Interrogating Hermaphroditism in Sixteenth-Century Spain," in *Hispanisms and Homosexualities*, ed. Sylvia Molloy and Robert McKee Irwin (Durham, N.C.: Duke University Press, 1998), 3–18; and idem, "Written on the Body: Slave or Hermaphrodite in Sixteenth-Century Spain," in *Queer Iberia: Sexualities, Cultures, and Crossings from the Middle Ages to the Renaissance*, ed. Josiah Blackmore and Gregory S. Hutcheson (Durham, N.C. .: Duke University Press, 1999), 420–56.

9. Holly Devor defines female-to-male transsexuals as "persons who have begun to identify themselves as transsexual or are in the process of transforming their genders and sexes": Holly Devor, *FTM: Female-to-Male Transsexuals in Society* (Bloomington: Indiana University Press, 1999), xxv. Devor uses Erauso's case when exploring whether FTMs have always existed. "When considering the possibility that some female crossdressers of previous eras might have qualified as what we today call transsexuals, it is important to remember that even now many female-to-male transsexuals move in and out of marriages as women, in and out of lesbian relationships as women, and in and out of living as men before they finally make a commitment to a permanent transsexual transition. The fact that Catalina de Erauso publicly exploited her notoriety as the 'nun ensign' says more about economic opportunities for women than it does about de Erauso's gender. Once exposed, she made the best of her situation until her star faded and she returned to living as a man": ibid., 15–16.

10. The use of gendered pronoun markers referring to early modern transgenderists is highly variable. Most studies on Erauso use feminine markers, although a few recent essays use masculine pronouns or alternate feminine and masculine markers. See Mary Elizabeth Perry, "From Convent to Battlefield: Cross-Dressing and Gendering the Self in the New World of Imperial Spain," in Blackmore and Hutcheson, *Queer Iberia,* 394–419, and Chloe Rutter, "Transatlantic, Transsexual, Transhistorical: A Reading of the Monja Alférez Catalina de Erauso," typescript, 19 November 1998. Research on Céspedes tends to interchange pronoun markers or use a combination she/he. In this study, I have elected to use feminine pronouns for Erauso to emphasize that, in the seventeenth century, she was perceived as a female celebrity. Moreover, she decided to define her own identity for the royal and religious authorities as a woman. "The truth is this: that I am a woman": see Michele Stepto and Gabriel Stepto, translation and introduction to *Lieutenant Nun: Memoir of a Basque Transvestite in the New World* (Boston: Beacon Press, 1996), 64. I recognize, however, that the use of female markers is inadequate in reflecting an identity based on gender instead of sex at birth. Ironically, it was her successful manipulation of binary gender roles that ultimately allowed her to live the last two decades of her life openly as Antonio de Erauso. Because the official response to Céspedes's case was so contradictory, and his/her own defense was based on a bisexed identity, I use both pronouns to refer to hermaphroditism, and I occasionally employ feminine pronouns to reflect sex at birth and the final official insistence on Céspedes's female identity.

11. For reproductions of the autobiography, broadsides, and supporting documents, see Rima de Vallbona, *Vida i sucesos de la monja alférez. Autobiografía atribuida a Doña Catalina de Erauso* (Tempe: Arizona State University, 1992). For a complete discussion of lesbian desire in these seventeenth-century texts, see Sherry Velasco, *The Lieutenant Nun: Transgenderism, Lesbian Desire, and Catalina de Erauso* (Austin: University of Texas Press, 2000).

12. Vallbona, *Vida,* 51. "There were two young ladies in the house, his wife's sisters, and I had become accustomed to frolicking with them and teasing them—one, in particular, who had taken a fancy to me. And one day, when she and I were in the front parlor, and I had my head in the folds of her skirt and she was combing my hair while I ran my hand up and down between her legs": Stepto and Stepto, *Lieutenant Nun,* 17.

13. There has been much speculation and doubt about the authorship and veracity of the autobiography. Some critics believe that the memoirs were forged by refashioning the 1625 *relaciones,* while others have suggested the opposite—that the pamphlets were sensationalized adaptations of the original *Vida* penned by Erauso. Others scholars suggest that Erauso dictated her life story or, at least, authorized a ghost writer to record her adventures. See Stephanie Merrim, "Catalina de Erauso: From Anomaly to Icon," in *Coded Encounters. Writing, Gender, and Ethnicity in Colonial Latin America,* ed. Francisco Javier Cevallos-Candau, Jeffrey A. Cole, Nina M. Scott, and Nicomedes Suárez-Araúz (Amherst: University of Massachusetts Press, 1994), 177–205; *Early Modern Women's Writing and Sor Juana Inés de la Cruz* (Nashville: Vanderbilt University Press, 1999); Manuel Serrano y Sanz, Apuntes para una biblioteca de escritoras españolas (Madrid: Atlas, 1975); and Vallbona, *Vida.*

14. Vallbona, *Vida,* 111. "Señor—I said, it is the truth, and if it will remove your doubts, let other women examine me—I will submit to such a test": Stepto and Stepto, *Lieutenant Nun,* 65.

15. Vallbona, *Vida,* 112. "Two old women came in and looked me over and satisfied themselves, declaring afterward before the bishop that they had examined me and found me to be a woman, and were ready to swear to it under oath, if necessary—and that what's more they had found me to be an intact virgin": Stepto and Stepto, *Lieutenant Nun,* 66.

16. Vallbona, *Vida,* 112. "I esteem you as one of the more remarkable people in this world, and promise to help you in whatever you do": Stepto and Stepto, *Lieutenant Nun,* 66.

17. Vallbona, *Vida,* 128. "She has no more breasts than a girl. She told me that she had used some sort of remedy to make them disappear. I believe it was a poultice given her by an Italian—it hurt a great deal, but the effect was very much to her liking": Stepto and Stepto, *Lieutenant Nun,* xxxiv.

18. See Kathryn Schwarz, "Missing the Breast," in *The Body in Parts: Fantasies of Corporeality in Early Modern Europe,* ed. David Hillman and Carla Mazzio (London: Routledge, 1997), 147–69.

19. No page numbers are available from the manuscript documents in Céspedes's file. "It is true that he has seen Eleno's genital member, and having touched all around it with his hands and seen it with his eyes, he made the following declaration: That he has his genital member, which is sufficient and perfect, with its testicles formed like any other man. . . . And he thus said and declared that in his opinion Eleno does not bear any resemblance to a hermaphrodite or anything like it": Burshatin, "Written on the Body," 433.

20. Ibid., 423–24. "with a stiff and smooth instrument she committed the unspeakable crime of sodomy": my translation.

21. "She stuck the candle up her female sex, and it entered a bit, with difficulty, and this witness was suspicious, so she also introduced her finger, and it entered with difficulty, and the witness, therefore, does not think that a man has ever been with her": Burshatin "Elena Alias Eleno," 106.

22. "An art so subtle that it sufficed to fool him by sight and by touch": Burshatin, "Written on the Body," 433.

23. "I never made any pact, explicitly or tacit, with the devil, in order to pose as a man to marry a woman, as is attributed to me. What happens is that many times the world has seen androgynous beings or, in other words, hermaphrodites, who have both sexes. I, too, have been one of these, and at the time I arranged to be married the masculine sex was more prevalent in me; and I was naturally a man and had all that was necessary for a man to marry a woman. And I filed information and eyewitness proof by physicians and surgeons, experts in the art, who looked at me and touched me, and swore under oath that I was a man and could marry a woman, and with this judicial proof I married as a man": ibid., 447–48.

24. Vallbona, *Vida,* 126–28.

25. "And she remained with the wherewithal to have relations with women, and she returned to Ana de Albánchez and had sex with her many times as a man": Burshatin "Interrogating," 13.

26. Burshatin, "Elena Alias Eleno," 110.

27. Vallbona, *Vida,* 70. "And it seems that, since Spaniards were scarce in those parts, she began to fancy me as a husband for her daughter": Stepto and Stepto, *Lieutenant Nun,* 28.

28. Vallbona, *Vida,* 70. "And a couple of days later, she let me know it would be fine by her if I married her daughter—a girl as black and ugly as the devil himself, quite the opposite of my taste, which has always run to pretty faces": Stepto and Stepto, *Lieutenant Nun,* 28.

29. Mary Elizabeth Perry also notes that "here Erauso may have made an allusion to racism in the ideal of female beauty held by most Spanish men at this time. However, she did not simply leave the dark-skinned mestiza, but continued to keep her company until she could no longer delay the marriage": Perry, "From Convent to Battlefield," 737.

30. Pedro Rubio Merino, *La Monja Alférez Doña Catalina de Erauso. Dos manuscritos autobiográficos inéditos* (Seville: Cabildo Metropolitano de la Catedral de Sevilla, 1995), 68. "My wife

was black and ugly, quite the opposite of my taste, which has always been for pretty faces; *which is why one can imagine that the four months that I was with this woman, for me, were like four centuries"*: my translation and emphasis.

31. Marjorie Garber, "Foreword: The Marvel of Peru," in Stepto and Stepto, *Lieutenant Nun*, xv.

32. Perry, "From Convent to Battlefield," 402.

33. Anne McClintock, *Imperial Leather: Race, Gender and Sexuality in the Colonial Contest* (New York: Routledge, 1995), 25.

34. Encarnación Juárez, however, argues that, for Erauso's autobiography to participate in the process of writing the male imperial desire on the body of the passive woman in the New World, the transgendered icon must also "colonize" her own female body beneath the masculine disguise: see Encarnación Juárez, "La mujer militar en la América colonial: El caso de la Monja Alférez," *Indiana Journal of Hispanic Literature* 10–11 (1997): 147–64.

35. Vallbona, *Vida*, 70. "I met the girl, and she seemed good enough": Stepto and Stepto, *Lieutenant Nun*, 29.

36. Vallbona argues that the homoerotic episodes did not develop beyond an initial stage of flirtation, hinting that the protagonist's attraction was less than sincere. "Mientras ella esté en las primeras etapas de la caricia y el flirteo, colabora hasta hacer concesiones a las mujeres que la pretenden creyéndola hombre. Sin embargo, en el momento de llegar a un compromiso, se retracta, adopta como en este caso, una actitud de dignidad incorruptible, o escapa y deja a las mujeres burladas": Vallbona, *Vida*, 48.

37. Garber, "Foreword," xvi.

38. Stepto and Stepto, *Lieutenant Nun*, xli.

39. See Irene Silverblatt, "Andean Witches and Virgins: Seventeenth-Century Nativism and Subversive Gender Ideologies," and Verena Stolcke, "Invaded Women: Gender, Race, and Class in the Formation of Colonial Society," both in *Women, "Race," and Writing in the Early Modern Period*, ed. Margo Hendricks and Patricia Parker (London: Routledge, 1994) 259–86. See also McClintock, *Imperial Leather*.

40. María de Zayas, *Novelas amorosas y ejemplares* (Madrid: Cátreda, 2000), 309. "A Negro so black that his face seemed made of black silk . . . his aspect was hideous, abominable . . . the devil himself couldn't have looked more awful . . . a fierce devil . . . the devilish black face: María de Zayas, *The Enchantments of Love: Amourous and Exemplary Novels*, trans. H. Patsy Boyer (Berkeley: University of California Press, 1990), 127.

41. Zayas, *Novelas amorosas*, 310. "What do you want of me, madam? Leave me alone, for the love of God! How can you pursue me even as I lie dying? Isn't it enough that your lasciviousness has brought me to this end? Even now you want me to satisfy your vicious appetites when I am breathing my last? Get yourself a husband, madam, marry, and leave me in peace. I never want to see you again! I won't touch the food you bring me; I want to die, that's all I'm good for now": Zayas, *Enchantments*, 127–28.

42. José Piedra, "In Search of the Black Stud," in *Premodern Sexualities*, ed. Louise Fradenburg and Carla Freccero (New York: Routledge, 1996), 23–43.

43. Vallbona, *Vida*, 71. "And I have never heard exactly what became of the black girl or the little vicaress": Stepto and Stepto, *Lieutenant Nun*, 29.

44. Vallbona, *Vida*, 112. "His Eminence left the palace with me at his side, and we made our way slowly through a crowd so huge, it was hard to believe there was anyone left at home": Stepto and Stepto, *Lieutenant Nun*, 66.

45. Burshatin, "Elena Alias Eleno," 118.

46. Ibid.

47. Ibid.

48. Vallbona, *Vida*, 113. "News of this event had spread far and wide, and it was a source of amazement to the people who had known me before, and to those who had only heard of my exploits in the Indies. . . . There were more people waiting than we knew what to do with, all come out of curiosity, hoping to catch a glimpse of the Lieutenant Nun: Stepto and Stepto, *Lieutenant Nun*, 67–68.

49. Vallbona, *Vida*, 118. "Lying low as much as possible and fleeing from the swarms of people that turned up everywhere, trying to get a glimpse of me in men's clothing": Stepto and Stepto, *Lieutenant Nun*, 73.

50. Vallbona, *Vida*, 123. "My fame had spread abroad, and it was remarkable to see the throng that followed me about—famous people, princes, bishops, cardinals": Stepto and Stepto, *Lieutenant Nun*, 79.

51. "That Andalusian slave, named Elena de Céspedes, who having abandoned female dress, for many years pretended to be a man [and] gave indications of being one, though badly sculpted, and without a beard and with some deceitful artifice; and it was so natural in style that after being examined by several surgeons and declared a man, she was married in Cien Poçuelos": Burshatin, "Elena Alias Eleno, 119.

52. For early modern humoral transmutations that cause immediate sex changes, see Juan Huarte de San Juan, *Examen de ingenios para las ciencias*, ed. Guillermo Serés (Madrid: Cátedra, 1989), and Antonio de Torquemada, *Jardín de flores curiosas*, ed. Giovanni Allegra (Madrid: Castalia, 1982).

53. Vallbona, *Vida*, 172. "traveling with her, enamored by her beauty": my translation.

54. Ibid., 173. "considering it to be less painful to be jealous in person than die of separation from her beloved": my translation.

55. Ibid., 174. "Our traveler exploded volcanos from her eyes" and "The bravery of her retreat was well known and was much celebrated by those who knew her": my translations.

56. Ibid., 174–75. "She died an exemplary death. . . . She had the habit of praying every day, for all the professed nuns, she fasted every Easter, Advent, and on vigils, every week on Mondays, Wednesdays, and Fridays she did three flagellations and she went to mass every day": my translation.

14   Violence, Desire, and
Transformative Remembering in
Emma Pérez's *Gulf Dreams*

*If I could follow the stream down and down to the hidden voice, would
I come at last to the freeing word?*

—Joy Kogawa

*It is in looking to the nightmare that the dream is found. There, the sur-
vivor emerges to insist on a future, a vision.*

—Cherríe Moraga

In *Gulf Dreams*, Emma Pérez presents an intricate novel of memory, desire, and violence that offers a unique site from which to examine interlocking oppressions and
systems of domination.[1] Through an exploration of one woman's memories, Pérez
deconstructs the experiences of violence in a Chicana's life; specifically, she reveals
how the Chicana's position in racial and sexual hierarchies affects the internalization
of those experiences. Pérez's text destabilizes any simplistic notions of nationalism,
lesbianism, or feminism as exclusive sites from which Latinas can articulate a politics of resistance and transformation. *Gulf Dreams* underscores the importance of
"remembering" as an active tool that allows recognition of the connections among
individual and collective oppression, as well as the personal and political responses
necessary to struggle against simultaneous oppressions.

In the United States, Latina, African American, Asian American, and other feminists of color have been developing theory that replaces additive models of oppression with a framework that emphasizes the intersectionality of oppressions.[2] Such a
model foregrounds the necessity of considering not only gender when discussing
women's condition but also its interconnection with discrimination based on race,
ethnicity, sexuality, and class. Rather than isolating particular oppressions as singularly important, viewing these destructive systems as a "matrix of oppression" or an

"overarching" system of domination allows one to examine how they intersect, feed, and reinforce one another.[3] Under such an analysis, power is conceptualized so as to capture the simultaneity of oppressions and how this simultaneity operates at different levels of analysis. This theoretical approach makes clear that the relationships that hold under such systems at individual, community, and institutional levels are enmeshed and complex. Under such an interlocking system of domination, individuals are differently located along an axis of penalty and privilege that depends on context. For example, although a heterosexual woman of color may suffer racist, classist, and sexist oppression, she may also derive benefits from the institution of heterosexuality. A nuanced analysis illustrates how in one situation an individual might be both victim and oppressor. A framework that focuses on intersectionality does not claim that all oppressions are the same; rather, it details the specific and material ways women of color are affected by a matrix of domination. This kind of framework also clarifies why resistance to oppression may lead women of color into conflict with members of the various groups in which they participate, when monocausal explanations for oppression are posited and solutions that privilege one form of oppression over another are enacted.

In *Gulf Dreams,* the experience of violence serves as a site from which to understand how Chicanas experience and resist multiple and simultaneous oppressions. In the novel, an unnamed Chicana narrator undertakes a process of writing in an attempt to set herself free from an obsessive love that has consumed her young life. Her writings recall her relationship with another unnamed Chicana who seems to reciprocate her strong attraction but who denies her feelings. Although the two women are lovers at various points in their lives, they mostly engage in a bitter taunting and tormenting of each other. Their paths cross repeatedly over the years, most dramatically in the rape trial of Ermila, another young Chicana from their small town. The narrator's piecing together of her own history forms the central motif of the novel. Her process of remembering her relationship with her love object leads her to engage in a more all-encompassing process of recovery and discovery.

The process undertaken is active and dynamic and thus is appropriately termed a "transformative remembering." Janice Haaken uses this expression to describe recollections from a previous time that serve as a current form of self-knowledge.[4] Recent and present-day traumatic situations may provide a new vantage point from which to understand recovered or recently unrepressed memories in a new light. Previously unseen patterns and novel meanings can be recognized as memories and analyzed and interpreted. New insight emerges when recovered information is reorganized in a new social and psychological context. In *Gulf Dreams* this journey to transformative understanding is textualized in a series of fragmented passages that fuse the past, the present, dreams, hallucinations, and fantasies. The presentation of the story is a metaphor for the story itself in that the drawing together of fragmented pieces of lost history is an essential component of the healing process that the recovering trauma survivor experiences. This process is both a personal and political reconstitutive act because the narrator is trying to make sense of apparently senseless instances of racial and sexual abuse in order to purge the self. At the same time, by naming and bearing witness to social and personal injustices, the testimony challenges the status quo and provides an indictment against criminal acts.[5]

The quest to exorcise her obsession with another Chicana leads the unnamed narrator, quite unexpectedly, to remember the sexual and racial abuse she suffered as a child and to piece together how these experiences informed her relationships and immobilized her throughout much of her life. Although at first the narrator has no memory of the harms done to her, the experience is locked in her body and is played out in her adult life below a level of awareness and language. As Roberta Culbertson says, "Trapped there, the violation seems to continue in a reverberating present that belies the supposed linearity of time and the possibility of endings."[6] Through a recovery process, the narrator comes to understand the connection between apparently unrelated episodes from her life and the disintegration and fragmentation that she continues to experience as an adult. It is also through the layered unveiling of her lost history that the narrator articulates the relationship between personal and political violence and the limitations offered by any monocausal or singularly focused analysis of sexual and racial violence.

The narrator names not only the violence of her relationship with her reluctant lover, but also the repeated violence that she suffered as a child and adolescent. The two women are similar in having endured repeated episodes of class, sexual, and racial abuse from the time they were children. The narrator remembers that, as a child, she experienced and witnessed degradation in the racist Texan town where she lived. In school, white teachers and classmates taunted her because of her brown skin, Spanish language, and hand-me-down clothing. As an adult contemplating pictures of herself as a child, the narrator observes:

> When I stared into cameras, I didn't laugh or clown as children do, so unfamiliar to me how my cousins giggled with each other. My mother framed photographs that captured the sadness, held it squarely like a package with a time bomb that would not explode for years. Right now, the sadness glared. There was one photograph. Not yet one-year-old and I laughed openly and happily. Evidence of childhood. I wondered, when did the sadness begin?[7]

As this passage suggests, the injuries committed against the narrator are not only felt at the time of their perpetration; they also persist and invade the developing identity of the Latina body and spirit. Like a time bomb, memories of racist and sexual violence lie buried until a crisis forces the survivor to respond. Racist attacks do not come only from the Anglo culture. These attacks are perhaps most insidious when they are internalized by community members and used against themselves and one another. The narrator recalls how racial politics were played out in her community and in her own home:

> In a town where humidity bred hostility I memorized hate. Bronze in the summer with hair and eyes so light I could pass through doors that shut out my sisters and brother. Their color and brown eyes, I envied. I grew up to resent the colors that set me apart from my family. At four, my sisters convinced me that I was adopted. Eyes so green, this was

not my family. At five, I took a butcher knife, sat calmly, sadly, on the pink chenille bed-spread, threatening to slice at tanned skin.[8]

The narrator explores how her light skin gave her access and privilege in the external community at the same time that it served as a source of conflict within the community, and specifically within the family.[9] In her family, her light skin earned her the status of an outsider and led to emotional and physical pain. Despite the disapproval of family and friends, the narrator chooses to date a white boy in high school, because she understands the benefits of white privilege in the outside community. Although this choice means that she suffered rejection from some people in her community, it opens doors that otherwise would have been closed to her. However, the author undercuts any simplistic reading of whiteness as privilege, because in the context of a Chicano family, white skin is clearly both a gift and a curse.

The author further complicates the situation by representing how race intersects with other factors to condition the experience of Anglos. Although the narrator's white boyfriend enjoys race privilege, he is burdened by his working-class status. His white mother is forced to work as a domestic because the family is poor. Once again, under an interlocking system of domination, the benefits of skin privilege are not absolute. Because of her status near the bottom of class and gender hierarchies, the boy's white mother must labor as a cleaning woman. Even as the mother's scornful family—specifically, her husband and her son—look down on her because she is engaged in work that they interpret as the province of women of color, they are dependent on her labor for their survival. Pérez demonstrates how sex, race, and class intersect to condition the lives of all people, regardless of their position of privilege or deprivation in each and all socially constructed hierarchies.

In addition to suffering from racism in the Anglo community and internalized racism at home, both of the Chicana protagonists are sexualized and abused by men from their communities, as well as by Anglos. The narrator is sexually molested by a group of young neighbors when she is three years old. The narrator's beloved has also endured public and private attacks on her body and spirit. Her stepfather molests her; poverty leads her to accept molestation from grocers in exchange for food. As adults, the two Chicana women continue to suffer repercussions from these assaults in the form of self-mutilation, suicide attempts, deep depression, promiscuity, the inability to form satisfying relationships, and a general distancing and fragmentation from their bodies. These are all symptoms of post-traumatic stress, which, according to Judith Herman, are typically found in survivors of sexual violence.[10] And as Mari Matsuda points out, many of these symptoms are also common among victims of racial hatred.[11] As part of the aftermath of these experiences, the two Chicanas engage in psychological, emotional, and physical abuse of themselves and each other. When they reach out to each other, loving caresses lead to rage and violence. Sexual and racial abuse has deadened their capacity to express tenderness and leads them to explore complex, sometimes violent, avenues to achieve intimacy.

Feminists' analysis of violence against women are often critiqued for their "fixation on a rhetoric of victimhood."[12] Throughout the novel, Pérez undermines any facile or partial characterization that leaves women's agency unexamined or simpli-fies women's complex relationship to violence. The narrator of *Gulf Dreams*, although revealed to be someone who has experienced considerable exploitation in her life, is not written as a static victim. Rather, she is presented as an active subject whose desires, imprinted by a history of abuse, also involve violence against others. In *Gulf Dreams*, sexual desire and psychic, emotional, and physical violence merge and are difficult to separate. The novel presents two Chicana women from a coastal Texan town who are erotically drawn to each other but are kept apart by one of the women's fears. Although the narrator's loved one seems to reciprocate her intense feelings, she "chooses" a conventional life over a lesbian relationship. In their small town, gener-ically called "El Pueblo," an open lesbian lifestyle is not an option. There is no con-text for the identification of a lesbian identity in the community to the extent that the two women never name their lesbian desire as such. Rather, intense periods of flirt-ing, repression, and denial between the two women are interspersed with their inflic-tion of emotional and physical violence on each other. In a context of heteropatriarchy, when all avenues of expressing love between women are closed, violence becomes the only means of achieving a type of intimacy. The narrator writes:

> I bit her tongue. Maliciously. I bit again, harder. Her hand, stroking my hair, clenched a fist, and yanked hard. My head jerked back. Blood trickled from her wound to my bot-tom lip. She wiped the blood with her tongue, confused, injured, but not angry. Desper-ate, she followed me, maybe afraid I would leave again.[13]

The merging of pain and pleasure, violence and desire, characterizes the relation-ship between the two women. That they should be intensely attracted to each other yet repeatedly physically harm each other may seem paradoxical. However, accord-ing to psychoanalytic theory, pain can be a means to pleasure when it is associated with submission to someone to whom one is intensely devoted. As Jessica Benjamin explains, "The pain of violation serves to protect the self by substituting physical pain for the psychic pain of loss and abandonment"[14] In fact, the interactions between the woman have many elements of a sadomasochistic relationship.[15] They repeatedly seek each other out, only to entice and then hurt each other. While unwilling to risk a social transgression by acknowledging and living out their lesbian desire, the women do transgress normal emotional and physical boundaries through violent erotic interactions that enable them to achieve connection and break through their iso-lation. Not surprisingly, this type of interaction leads to an "exhaustion of sensation" rather than to a loving intimacy. However, these encounters succeed in allowing the protagonist—at least, momentarily—to escape loneliness. The narrator explores this complex dynamic in the following passage:

> You don't deserve love. Never did only harm. Repeatedly, you do this, invite into your life those who humiliate you. You welcome it. Beseech it. Expect it and nothing else. Not gentleness. Not love. I am accustomed to pain. Pain is the source of my pleasure. The woman from El Pueblo, I craved her insults, begged for punishment to feel something puncture deadened flesh.[16]

In this passage, the sudden change from third person to first person creates ambiguity about the subject. This occurs often in the novel and suggests that subject and object, the narrator and the object of her love, are interchangeable and at times merge. Both women are alternately or concurrently victimizer and victimized, masochist and sadist; the categories of oppressed and oppressor are blurred and complicated. The fact that the women are unnamed in the novel further confirms the interchangeability of each woman's position in the text. By rendering the women anonymous and the town generic, the author suggests several things. First, the women are not individualized; they can be any woman in this specific context—any and every Chicana woman. Second, because names connote a sense of identity and place, the women's namelessness suggests that they lack a defined self from which to negotiate the world. It is interesting that, even at the end of the novel, the narrator remains unnamed. This attests to the fact that we do not arrive at a superficial happy ending with everything resolved. Rather, the self is always in a state of becoming, and the process of discovery and growth continues.

However, it is the act of writing, and of using memory to interrogate the past, that separates the narrator from the novel's other nameless protagonist. The narrator does name her experience, bears witness to painful elements from her history, and then confronts the present. As Kali Tal explains:

> Bearing witness is an aggressive act. It is born out of a refusal to bow to outside pressure to revise or repress experience, a decision to embrace conflict rather than conformity, to endure a lifetime of anger and pain rather than to submit to the seductive pull of revision and repression. Its goal is to change. The battle over the meaning of a traumatic experience is fought in the arena of political discourse, popular culture, and scholarly debate. The outcome of this battle shapes the rhetoric of the dominant culture and influences future political action.[17]

Although much of the text is concerned with bearing witness against men's violence, the author interrupts any essentialist reading that posits men as the enemy. The text further complicates the binary of oppressed and oppressor with the introduction of Inocencio, a Chicano who molests the narrator and instigates the gang rape of Ermila, another Chicana in El Pueblo. Inocencio himself is revealed to have suffered long-term sexual abuse by his uncle, who became a father figure to the boy only to betray him by sexually assaulting him as a young child and teenager. Although Inocencio is presented as a violent and ruthless abuser of women, he is simultaneously portrayed as a weak, insecure Chicano, haunted by years of exploitation as well as denial of his own repressed homosexual desire. From childhood on, Inocencio is often involved in the violation of girls and women. In addition, as an adult he frequents gay bars, apparently to engage in homophobic violent acts, but he also sometimes engages in sex with men he meets at the bars. Simplistic analyses that posit the male as inherently violent are challenged in the text. The naming of this character suggests that although "Inocencio" was born innocent, childhood abuse is in part responsible for the brutal man he has become.[18]

Although the gang rape is instigated by Inocencio, almost the entire community of El Pueblo chooses to stand behind the rapists rather than behind the woman who dares to accuse the men. In a situation that is not uncommon in communities of color that are under constant attack and threat of genocide, the women in this community are compelled to bear sexual assault in silence in the name of cultural loyalty. In *Gulf Dreams,* the Chicano men use nationalism and family cohesion to rally the community against the accuser. Within traditional Latino communities, women are defined in reference to the family, by their roles as wives and mothers. As Jenny Rivera says, "By encouraging definitions of Latinas as interconnected with and dependent upon status within a family structure, the Latino patriarchy denies Latinas individuality on the basis of gender. For Latinas, cultural norms and myths of national origin intersect with these patriarchal notions of a woman's role and identity."[19] Although both the accused and the accuser are Chicano, the Chicano community vilifies the young woman for having forsaken her expected role as self-sacrificing caretaker of men and for exposing the Chicano men to Anglo violence at the hands of the police and the judicial system. Pelón, the Chicano lawyer who defends Inocencio and his accomplices, argues that the Chicano men are being lynched by a racist court, and he presents the rape victim as a promiscuous, fallen woman who is a puppet of Anglo prosecutors. In contrast, the Anglo prosecutor is barely interested in the case, because he is contemptuous of both the rape victim and the accused. Thus, Ermila experiences multiple levels of assault from the Anglo and Chicano community. She is abandoned by her people, who brand her as the aggressor and the betrayer of Chicano unity. Meanwhile, the Anglo legal system is indifferent to her suffering and her rights. The text thus problematizes the options available to Latina women in a context of both sexism and racism. As Cherríe Moraga points out in the essay "A Long Line of Vendidas," when one analyzes the problem of violence against women in terms of the intersectionality of racism and sexism, "the power no longer breaks down into neat little hierarchical categories, but becomes a series of starts and detours. Since the categories are not easy to arrive at, the enemy is not easy to name."[20] The task of speaking out against sexual violence is fraught with danger and risk for all women, but speaking out places women of color in an even more vulnerable and conflicted position.

The stories of the three women in *Gulf Dreams* intersect at the trial. It is interesting that the only Chicana named in the novel is Ermila, a Chicana who is gang-raped but fights back by taking the rapists to court. Perhaps the bold act of naming the rapists— or resisting the rapists' attempts to make her invisible—allows her to be individualized. The nameless protagonists, who do not speak out against their molesters, observe and become part of Ermila's story, albeit from different positions. The narrator joins the few women who support Ermila's struggle, and her beloved enters the trial as the spouse of Pelón, the lawyer who defends the rapists. The commonality of the three women's experience again attests to the fact that this is not one woman's story but the story of a community of Chicana women who have chosen different paths, given their limited options.

Although Ermila's bravery earns her a name in the text, the outcome of her coura-geous act is ambiguous. *Gulf Dreams* does suggest, however, that by facing the rapists and telling her story, Ermila frees herself from the lies the community asks her to suc-cumb to and that she gains some peace of mind in that act of testifying against the violence done to her.

> There can be no happy ending, only in fantasy, what the mind chooses to make up, to hold onto as real. The imagination will dodge cruelty, escaping the crime—how the body has been pillaged, scarred—pretending this never happened, fooling memory with another meaning. She would live her life pretending, lying. If Ermila didn't bargain with it now, the act itself, the rape, the violation, would haunt her waiting to happen again in mem-ory that is so real that when the man behind a checkout stand glares at your breast, you bear the shame all over again.[21]

Despite Ermila's testimony, most of the rapists go free, and Inocencio serves less than a year in jail. Ermila disappears after the trial. When a body washes up on the beach, the townspeople identify the bones as Ermila's, but the narrator refuses to accept this ending to Ermila's story. Rather, she imagines that Ermila has escaped to her grand-mother's village, where she finds love and peace. Ermila and the narrator share sev-eral connections. The same man, Inocencio, instigated the episodes of sexual violence that they endure, and both women find the courage to break the silence around their abuse. Ermila accomplishes this in the courtroom; the narrator accomplishes this through her writing. The trial does not bring Ermila justice, but it does give her the opportunity to accuse her attackers and testify against the violation she endures.

Although Ermilia's speaking out entails more public risks and danger, the narra-tor's process is no less important. By reconstructing history and demonstrating the harm inflicted on her, the narrator questions societal tendencies to accept as normal the violence done to women of color. The narrator bears witness not only to the per-sonal harm done to her but to an entire system that keeps women subjugated and silent. Her reconstructed story serves as a testimonial that threatens the status quo surrounding issues of racial and sexual violence. The woman the narrator loves, how-ever, never deals with her lesbian desire, the sexual and racial abuse she suffered as a child, or the physical and emotional abuse she experiences at the hands of her hus-band, Pelón. She is presented as a static figure whose refusal to interrogate her past and her same-sex desire leads to a stagnant position. At the end of the novel, she is still with Pelón, her abusive husband, and continues to live an empty, unexplored life.

Although Inocencio, the rapist, is found guilty, he serves little time in jail, and shortly after his release from prison he is found murdered, with his testicles stuffed in his mouth. Whether the narrator has committed this murder as an act of vengeance against the man who abused her, raped Ermila, and violated other women is left ambiguous. She often dreams about murdering the rapist. While writing about the crime, the narrator says:

> When it happened doesn't matter. You may not believe me, the hysteric who invokes myth, reinvents truth. My hysteria tells you this part of the story. I sometimes lack the

ability to discern what is real, or unreal, what I imagine to be true, or what I've made up to entertain myself, to pass away dreary hours and days. What is invisible is as alive and true to me as the visible.[22]

It is nevertheless clear that the narrator's obsession with her beloved and her nightmares about Inocencio merge. To exorcise the beloved from her heart, she must also work through the sexual violence she has experienced.

But my hallucinations loomed as if real. Madness could have motive. What I planned came easily. The time had come. I mustered courage to help me execute the loud rapist, the costurera's son, to purge him from my nightmares, the ones that kept me tied to the woman from El Pueblo.[23]

Whether she really murders Inocencio or simply has fantasies and hallucinations about enacting vengeance is not the crucial point. As Judith Halberstam notes, the relationship between "real" and imagined violence is complex, unstable, and unpredictable; they are not in a relationship of binary opposition but, rather, interact in a place of rage and on a ground of resistance. "Imagined violence is the fantasy of unsanctioned eruptions of aggression from the 'wrong people, of the wrong skin, the wrong sexuality, the wrong gender,'" Halberstam argues. "We have to be able to imagine violence and our violence needs to be imaginable because the power of fantasy is not to represent but to destabilize the real."[24] For the narrator of *Gulf Dreams*, the function of the real or imagined violence is catharsis; it connotes resistance to the sexual violence she and other women endure and enables a freeing of her desire. Women's aggression as either fantasy or reality challenges the status quo. Women's violence, says Halberstam, "transforms the symbolic function of the feminine within the popular narratives and it simultaneously challenges the hegemonic insistence upon the linking of might and right under the sign of masculinity."[25]

Although she has been scarred by silence and by various forms of violence, the narrator uses these experiences to construct a new beginning. The narrator is a young woman in process, reactivating memory to understand the past and reclaim the future. She is not merely a victim of what has been done to her; what is crucial is the quality of her response to these experiences. The novel enacts what bell hooks calls "a politicization of memory that distinguishes nostalgia, that longing for something to be as it once was, a kind of useless act, from that remembering that serves to illuminate and transform the present."[26] It is through the writing process that the narrator begins to make sense of her memories, fantasies, and dreams; to establish the connections among them; and to understand the past in order to live in the present. Although time and social messages to forget or accept harm done make the reconstitutive process difficult, a new self does emerge in the writing process. And although what is "true" and what is imagined is not made entirely clear in the text, the crucial point is that a speaking (or writing) subject emerges. As Culbertson argues, narrative makes possible the reconstruction of loss and recovery. While the horror of sexual and racial trauma is often unspeakable, it is nevertheless imprinted in the victim's body, and writing thus serves as a means to translate the body's knowledge into language.[27] Narrative is also a tool that makes possible an adult's understanding of the child's repressed trauma. This self who has been immobilized by repeated episodes of sexual and racial violence emerges to testify about what she has experienced.

While she continues to be "cursed" with memories of racist and sexual cruelty, the narrator of *Gulf Dreams* works through these memories to extricate herself from a damaging relationship. Toward the end of her recorded process, she decides that, although painful recollections will always be with her, she can also remember comforting, positive past experiences. "I choose this past—my mother's strong arms as she bent to pick cotton, my father's fried chicken when we came home from *la pisca*. I remember my sisters dressing and painting their faces, my brother strolling beside me. I remember my *güelita's empanadas*."[28] These good recollections, however, begin to surface only after she has begun to deal with the negative memories.

The narrator reclaims her body through remembering and a reconstitutive writing process. Writing is a linguistic and therefore symbolic process, but through the use of this tool the author is able to release truths that are buried in her flesh. She takes back her body while simultaneously producing a political statement that bears witness to the injustices committed against her and other women. As it has for other trauma survivors, writing for the narrator becomes a way to visualize and concretize memories that lead to confrontation and integration.[29] Although her spirit and her sexuality have been damaged, she contends with this reality, integrates past experiences, and moves on, committed to creating new memories, a new story. As Culbertson writes, "Survival stories are in the classic sense religious stories of death and rebirth, as much as they are often nearly technically such stories at the time of the survival itself. The survivor survives twice: survives the violation; and survives the death that follows it, reborn as a new person, the one who tells the story."[30] Pérez's novel suggests that, through the active use of memory to confront the violence and silences of the past, new stories arise.

In her presentation of three Chicanas' stories, Pérez dramatizes several options that are available to Chicana women and the possible repercussions associated with each of these alternatives. Although she by no means suggests a utopic conclusion, Pérez articulates both the risks and the value of moving toward integrity by refusing to accept the status quo and by disobeying social prohibitions against naming violence. She foregrounds the difficulty and the advantages of facing the truth, of honestly analyzing Latina lives in all their complexity and pain. *Gulf Dreams* suggests that only through undergoing such a process of rediscovery does true understanding and integration emerge. As Andrea Dworkin writes:

> The mind struggling toward integrity will fight for the significance of her own life and will not give up that significance for any reason. Rooted in the reality of her own experience—which includes all that has happened to her faced squarely and all that she has seen, heard, learned, and done—a woman who understands that integrity is the first necessity will find the courage not to defend herself from the pain.[31]

Through these personal and social avenues of reconstituting memory and breaking silence Pérez demonstrates the connection between the personal and the political. Likewise, by linking sexual trauma to other forms of violence, she highlights the intersections between the politics of sexual trauma and the politics of racial and class discrimination. Although Pérez does not provide any easy answers to questions of violence, she does depict the minefield Chicanas must traverse within both Chicano/a and Anglo culture as they work toward personal and political freedom.

Notes

Epigraphs: Joy Kogawa, *Obasan* (New York: Bantam, 1993); Cherríe Moraga, "La Güera," in *This Bridge Called My Back: Writings by Radical Women of Color,* ed. Cherríe Moraga and Gloria Anzaldúa (Watertown, Mass.: Persephone Press, 1981), 34.

1. Emma Pérez, *Gulf Dreams* (Berkeley, Calif.: Third Woman Press, 1996).

2. See Norma Alarcón, "The Theoretical Subject(s) of *This Bridge Called My Back* and Anglo-American Feminism," in *Making Face, Making Soul/Haciendo Caras: Creative and Critical Perspectives,* ed. Gloria Anzaldúa (San Francisco: Aunt Lute Books, 1990); Chela Sandoval, "U.S. Third World Feminism: The Theory and Method of Oppositional Consciousness in a Postmodern World," *Genders* 10 (Spring 1991): 1–24; Yvonne Yarbo-Bejarano, "Gloria Anzaldúa's *Borderlands/La Frontera,* Cultural Studies, 'Difference,' and the Non-Unitary Subject," *Cultural Critique* 28 (Fall 1994): 5–88; bell hooks, "Choosing the Margin as a Space of Radical Openness," in idem, *Yearning: Race, Gender and Cultural Politics* (Boston: South End Press, 1990); Kimberlé Williams Crenshaw, "Beyond Racism and Misogyny," in *Words That Wound: Critical Race Theory, Assaultive Speech, and the First Amendment,* New Perspectives on Law, Culture, and Society, eds. Mari Matsuda, Charles Lawrence III, Richard Delgado, and Kimberlé Williams Crenshaw (Boulder, Colo.: Westview Press, 1983), 11–132; Patricia Collins, *Black Feminist Thought* (New York: Routledge, 1990); and Mari Matsuda, "Public Response to Racist Speech: Considering the Victim's Story," in Matsuda et al., *Words That Wound,* 17–52.

3. See Collins, *Black Feminist Thought.*

4. Janice Haaken, *Pillar of Salt: Gender, Memory, and the Perils of Looking Back* (New Brunswick, N.J.: Rutgers University Press, 1988).

5. See Kali Tal, *Words of Hurt: Reading the Literature of Trauma* (New York: Cambridge University Press, 1996), 223.

6. Roberta Culbertson, "Embodied Memory, Transcendence, and Telling: Recounting Trauma, Re-establishing the Self, " *New Literary History* 26 (1995): 170.

7. Pérez, *Gulf Dreams,* 16.

8. Ibid., 15.

9. The narrator undergoes a process similar to that described by Cherríe Moraga in *Loving in the War Years* (Boston: South End Press, 1983). Moraga says that because her father was white, she could pass as white and enjoy all the privileges white skin affords. However, her ability to pass made her suspect in her Chicana community and often an outsider in her own family.

10. Judith Herman, *Trauma and Recovery* (New York: Basic Books, 1997).

11. Matsuda, "Public Response," 24.

12. bell hooks, *Killing Rage: Ending Racism* (New York: Henry Holt, 1995), 51.

13. Pérez, *Gulf Dreams,* 108.

14. Jessica Benjamin, *The Bonds of Love* (New York: Pantheon Books, 1988), 61.

15. See Benjamin's discussion of sadomasochism in ibid. The relationship between the two women is not strictly a consensual sadomasochistic exchange; I want only to highlight the many similarities between such a relationship and the behavior in which the two protagonists engage.

16. Pérez, *Gulf Dreams,* 150.

17. Tal, *Words of Hurt,* 7.

18. The text suggests that Inocencio's violent sexuality is connected to his uncle's betrayal, but it concurrently leaves open the problematic insinuation that his homosexual desire also stems from his abusive relationship with his uncle. Another possible reading suggested by Inocencio's character is that the basis for homophobic violence is repressed same-sex desire.

19. Jenny Rivera, "Domestic Violence against Latinas by Latino Males," in *The Latino Condition: A Critical Reader,* ed. Richard Delgado and Jean Stefancic (New York: New York University Press, 1988), 502.

20. Moraga, *Loving,* 108.

21. Pérez, *Gulf Dreams,* 92.

22. Ibid, 142.

23. Ibid., 133.

24. Judith Halberstam, "Imagined Violence/Queer Violence: Representation, Rage, and Resistance," *Social Text* 37 (Winter 1993): 199.

25. Ibid., 191.

26. hooks, *Yearning,* 147.

27. Culbertson, "Embodied Memory," 180.

28. Pérez, *Gulf Dreams,* 156.

29. Tal, *Words of Hurt,* 229.

30. Culbertson, "Embodied Memory," 191.

31. Andrea Dworkin, "Look Dick, Look. See Jane Blow It," in *Letters from a War Zone* (London: Secker and Warburg, 1988), 129.

Christina Sharpe

---

15   Learning to Live without
Black Familia: Cherríe Moraga's
Nationalist Articulations

In the January 1997 issue of *Wired* magazine, the Mexicano performance artist Guillermo Gómez-Peña takes up the question of the Internet and the place of Latino/as in technoculture.[1] We are currently "witnessing the creation of nations that are not defined by territory, culture, race, or language," Gómez-Peña says. "They will be defined by the Internet."[2] That they will not be created by what we usually think of as forming nation (territory, race, culture, language, ethnicity, etc.) does not mean that these nations will be borderless, that the Internet and those nations and people from those nations that access and define the Internet are not always already constructed by those very things. Gómez-Peña's concerns complicate popular constructions of the Internet as a potential borderless space. They point to the continual constructions and reconstructions of borders and "the border"; they point to how borders are always both virtual and "real." The Internet's rhetoric of unlimited access to information and resources (at least, in the context of U.S. discussions about the Net) collides with the logic, for example, of California's anti-affirmative action legislation and legislation that delimits rights of entry and educational access. One can further complicate enunciations of the Internet by setting the various print and television ads that feature people of diverse races, ages, and abilities who all find equal access on the Internet against the actual number of people of color who have access to the Net.

This chapter does not focus on technoculture, but I am interested in the persistent construction of the Internet as a space without borders and how this affects discussions of national borders and nationalist movements. Specifically, I am interested in Cherríe Moraga's recent re-formations of Chicana/o nationalism and her apparent rejection of the metaphorical border as a place of contradictions that is in "a constant state of transition."[3] In much theoretical writing by Chicanos and Mexicans, the metaphorical border is conceived as a place where contradictory impulses and practices coexist and force one another in and out of primacy. For Gloria Anzaldúa, co-editor with Moraga of *This Bridge Called My Back*, editor of *Making Face, Making Soul*, and author of *Borderlands/La Frontera*, the border is not only geopolitical. It is present "whenever two or more cultures edge each other, where people of different races occupy the same territory, where upper and middle classes touch, where the space between two individuals shrinks with intimacy."[4]

For Anzaldúa, life in the borderlands is uncomfortable: "Tension grips the inhabitants of the borderlands like a virus."[5] For Moraga, borders are most often places where differences are simultaneously explored, enforced, and erased.[6] Gómez-Peña, another border theorist, talks in *Wired* about playing with racist naming and the language of the Internet.[7] He labels himself a trespasser, a "webback" in cyberspace; he also fashions himself "a *coyote*, a smuggler of ideas" (a coyote is one who smuggles "illegals" looking for work into the United States).[8] Yet in terms of the Internet, how does one smuggle something into a "free" space? Gómez-Peña writes that on the Internet, "we do encounter the linguistic border patrol. . . . We often send techno-placas, which are basically just humorous Spanglish texts questioning matters of access, privilege, and power relative to the Net. We often receive responses such as, 'go back to your cyber barrio.'"[9] The "virtual society" and "virtual citizens" of the Web often reproduce the very inclusions and exclusions of our in-person social encounters and alienations.

Nationalist struggles also always entail the "policing of borders." In other words, it is important to police borders in struggles for dominance as well as in counter-hegemonic struggles. In her writings, Moraga undertakes some of her own "policing of borders." Moraga writes in opposition to, and yet reproduces some of, the structures that inform repressive legislation such as California's Propositions 187 and 209 (without, of course, reproducing the same legislative effects). Moraga is explicitly involved with the political climate and the political struggles within which she is writing. For example, the plays collected as *Heroes and Saints* focus on migrant workers and working-class and indigenous population movements.[10] In this essay, I map out some of Moraga's political shifts from the late 1970s and early 1980s, when she edited *This Bridge Called My Back* and published *Loving in the War Years*, to the 1993 publication of *The Last Generation* to illustrate how Moraga's exorcism of black familia repeats some of the logic of other kinds of racial inclusions and exclusions.[11]

Ethnic Productions

The foreword to the second edition of *This Bridge Called My Back*, published in 1983, reveals a discouraged Moraga. Although there "are many issues that divide us, she writes, "the need for a broad-based U.S. women of color movement capable of spanning borders of nation and ethnicity has never been so strong." She continues, "If we are interested in building a movement that will not constantly be subverted by internal differences, then we must build from the inside out, not the other way around."[12]

Loving in the War Years, which was also published in 1983, is a further articulation of this building from the inside out. *Loving* calls for a "theory in the flesh," a theorizing that takes into account the experiences of women of color and is a "politic born out of necessity."[13] As part of this theorizing in the flesh, Moraga battles the fears that inform one's sense of self and others, and she writes that it is this deep struggling with what is within as well as with what is outside our bodies and our experiences that will inform Third World feminist movements. This articulation of feminism, she says, was "first voiced by U.S. Black women, [and it] promised to deal with the oppression that occurred under the skin as well, and by virtue of the fact that the skin was female and colored."[14]

In her shift from coalitionist to nationalist politics, Moraga seems trapped by her very insistence on the signifying power of flesh, the knowledge that flesh carries. Her *"la güera"* flesh in particular is one that produces suspect meaning and knowledge. As Alicia Arrizón notes, Moraga envisions Queer Aztlán as a place

> where the male-centered, nationalistic specter of the mythical Chicano homeland is ide-alistically transformed into the land of the Chicana–mestiza. This transformation "gen-ders" the territory as a female brown body, one that will become a place for all raza, het-erosexuals and queers.[15]

The burden of the production of "ethnic identity" and "citizenship" is internal as well as external to Moraga's work and is often performed through her uses of "black-ness." Blackness, the very thing that she evokes as sustaining, must now be exorcised as a source of further alienation from *la raza*—in the same way that her previously unquestioning use of white-skin privilege is marked as she works out a feminist- and lesbian-of-color consciousness. Central to Moraga's project is the queer configuration of Aztlán, the Chicano homeland. I am uncomfortable with Moraga's nationalist dis-course and with how she sometimes works out questions of inside and outside on the bodies of black and "mulatto" people. In *Loving* and *Last Generation*, Moraga enacts and reenacts her complicated relationship to blackness, as well as to the "ori-gin" stories (La Malinche, La Llorona, Quetzalcóatl) that function as one set of bor-ders within and against which Chicana identities are constructed. As she says, "Even if a Chicana knew no Mexican history, the concept of betraying one's race through sex and sexual politics is as common as corn."[16]

It is from this history that Moraga initially removes herself in order to stage a return to her Chicano family. In "'When Something Goes Queer': Familiarity, Formalism, and Minority Intellectuals in the 1980s," Lora Romero writes that Moraga removes her-self in *Loving* from both her biological family and from Chicanos, and that Moraga consistently imagines herself as outsider, a particular construction of 1980s minority intellectuals. Moraga "uses familia to refer to both her family and the Chicano com-munity," Romero says.[17] Moraga then constructs her "racial family," ignoring the fact that, "despite its appeals to family, the Chicano movement damaged some forms of familial harmony in the process of creating a new platform for ethnic solidarity."[18] This oppositional narrativization leads Moraga to conclude: "It seemed I had to step outside my familia to see what we as a people were doing suffering. This is my politics. This is my writing."[19]

This is a rhetorical strategy for Moraga: Once she returns to family, she can better critique it. In *Last Generation,* once she qualifies her community, she can resist particular kinds of textual (and bodily) incorporation. The enforcing and editing of difference foregrounded in Moraga's work becomes even more complicated when her writings (and the writings of other women of color) are taken up for academic consumption. In scholarly readings, the inclusions and exclusions are repeated yet again. Romero argues that, under the "peculiar political and professional pressures of the 1980s . . . and in trying to escape the *barrio*-ization imposed by underfunding and underrecognition of the ethnic studies departments during those years," minority scholars constructed themselves in opposition to populations that were non-intellectual.[20] They removed themselves from "family" to better critique family. In their writing, both Moraga and Norma Alarcón address the fact that the attention to difference and its deployment increases the pressure on the texts and on the bodies of the women who occupy various borderlands by intensifying the ways in which the limits of their identities are scrutinized—that is, where and when they are included or excluded. Acknowledging the *mestizaje* of Chicanos ("Indian, Spanish and Africano"), Moraga's early works attempt to intervene in a privileged, yet still marginalized, academic *mestizaje.* As Alarcón writes, the place of the Chicana critic in academia, on both sides of the border, is such that "they'd be happy to take her text but not her, except as a seasonal worker," and that "racism (or the particular historical constructions of Mexicanness) makes [the Chicana academic] subject to a constant demand for production (proof) of 'ethnic' identity and citizenship in both Mexico and the United States."[21]

The rhetoric and public performance surrounding "illegal aliens" obscure the fact that one cannot apprehend a person's documentation status simply by looking at her, and that whether someone "looks" like an alien also depends on the situation—on who is being looked at and on who is doing the looking. The law (in this case, Proposition 187) attempts to render people of color visible by setting people's gazes against one another, locating others as potential candidates for expulsion or holding them as the invisible labor on which California is dependent. It calls on "citizens" to police themselves as well as one another. Interactions on the Internet often rely on self-disclosed "facts," and Gómez-Peña's articulation of himself as a wetback reveals both the limits of "self-construction" and the sort of revelations about the fantasies of others that inform what we allow ourselves to say and who we imagine ourselves to be. "People reveal a lot even by choosing a fictional identity or creating a fictitious literary narrative," Gómez-Peña says.[22]

Looking at Moraga is not enough to locate her. She is the chameleon whose skin color changes meaning according to who is looking at her and whom she is with. In *Loving,* she writes: "To write as a Chicana feminist lesbian, I am afraid of being mistaken, of being made an outsider again—having to fight the kids at school to get them to believe that Teresita and I were cousins. You don't *look* like cousins."[23] In *The Last Generation,* she says: "My lovers have always been the environment that defined my color. With a Black lover in apartheid Boston I was seen as a white girl. When we moved to Brooklyn we were both Ricans. . . . I got to be choosy 'bout who I hang with. Everybody so contagious, I pick up their gesture, their joke, their jive."[24] As the chameleon, Moraga polices her own body's borders, her proximity to the ethnically and racially inflected gestures and bodies of the others by whom she is defined. As productions of these positionings of visibility, which communities will police which other communities as the fight continues for "opportunities" that exist largely, if not solely, in the American imaginary? Which communities will be defined by which other communities, and which communities will be the barrios of other communities?

Sue-Ellen Case explicitly addresses the links between legislation and "transgressive" acts.[25] She considers, among other things, the "intimate relationship between the US and Mexico" and "Mexican-hating"—which are both always about desiring the other—in convergence with the increasing power of the religious right and its "concern" with the "supremacy" of the English language. About the reactions of non–Spanish-speakers to the Spanish-language text that he disseminates, Gómez-Peña says: "Many of these online confessions are more outrageous, and more performative. . . . Someone may confess to a crime, such as having killed a migrant worker. Even if that confession is false, the desire is real and culturally significant."[26] When Case writes about her obsession with fighting (which becomes an obsession with touching) Gloria Valenzuela, and the complex desires that compelled her to spend time figuring out where and how to grab the body of her (presumably) Spanish-speaking "Mexican" rival, she enacts (makes visible) the very things that English-only laws and Proposition 187s seek to repress. Case writes:

> Raised as poor white (white trash) in Southern California, I grew up in the neighborhood of what we then called "Mexicans," derogatorily, "cholos." From the ages of eleven to thirteen I was the head of a white girls' gang that fought the "Mexican" girls' gang over issues of "territory" and "honor." Spanish was the enemy language, though we all knew the "bad" words. In fact, Spanish served as my original profane language, marking it with racism, sexuality, and transgression. In this way, its taboo status later became associated with my own repressed homosexuality.[27]

Just as Case links the complicated taboo status of Spanish with the taboo of lesbianism (and Moraga comes to writing through lesbianism and through entering into the life of her mother), so are English-only laws attempts to repress the significance of the increasing presence of Latinos in the United States. (And, by extension, repressing Spanish represses other practices that are coded as transgressive.) Case writes that she and her "rival," Gloria, were consumed with the "breaches of honor and territorial incursion that set up our fights. Only much later did I realize . . . I was obsessed with Gloria's body."[28] Case's confessions that her family's "racist hatred served as the amulet with which we held the promise of upward mobility"; that "on the privilege of my whiteness, I left the gangs and the 'Mexicans' just in time to get through high school"; and that "I worked at losing my working-class accent, my tomboyish gestures and my white trash sense of fashion"[29] re-articulate, with an emphasis on differences in class, race, and motivation, Moraga's anxiety about her (forced and enforced) Anglicization in high school.

Moraga's "Anglicization," in some ways similar to Case's class–race–sex transformation as she enters college, also occurs around educational opportunities; she becomes white in response to an educational system that tracks "Mexicans" to lower levels and whites to higher levels and in response to her mother's desire to "protect her from poverty and illiteracy."[30] Moraga writes:

> Rocky Hernandez was brilliant and tough.... "Antagonistic" the nuns would say.... When it came time for the Catholic high school entrance exams, we learned in May what track we would be in for the coming freshman year. To my amazement I got into the "A" group—college prep. To my equal amazement Rocky and her cousin were tracked into the "C" group—business and general education where they teach home economics and typing. Rocky could talk and write and compute circles around me, which didn't seem to compute on our entrance exams.
>
> After we got into high school the Irish and Italian girls became my friends. And Rocky and I seldom, if ever, spoke.[31]

Writing about growing up in California and about current political crises, Case says that "supremacy was the narrative....The 'Mexicans' (actually an apt name for these people since California was, at one time, part of Mexico) just had to lose. This is an obsession currently at the forefront of California politics since, demographically, it seems they are 'winning.'"[32] Case writes that that supremacy was "physical for her," and it would seem that, from the perspective of various groups that I collectively identify as the right, it remains so. This fear necessitates that U.S. borders be redrawn, that exclusionary practices be re-formed and reimplemented. The unspoken component of statements such as this for these lawmakers is that if one does not look like an "American" (like one who belongs) there is no becoming American. Of course, this represses the obvious: that those of "Mexican" descent are more indigenously "American" than those who are making the charges of "illegality." However, as Moraga, Alarcón, and others have already established, "looking" is not enough to determine citizenship status or group affiliation. In Moraga's words, one becomes American not through a change in legal status but "by virtue of the collective voice [one] assumes in staking [one's] claim to this land and its resources."[33] Potentially then, "a new generation of future Chicanos arrives everyday with every Mexican immigrant."[34]

Consider, then, that Moraga's texts enact a "becoming chicananess," a politicization that is most symbolically evident in her name change from Cecilia Lawrence to Cherríe Moraga; in an increased attention to the use of Caló, Chicana Spanish, and other "border" languages in her works; and in her increasing attention to the lives of working-class Chicanas and Mexicanas. "Moraga presents an interesting case because she did not participate in the Chicano movement but has been at the forefront of the Chicana feminist response to both Chicano cultural nationalism and Anglo-American feminism," Moya notes.[35] During what she refers to as the "classic period" of the

Chicano movement, Moraga writes that, regretfully, she "was unable to act publicly."[36] However, she now knows that "what was right about Chicano / a nationalism was its commitment to preserving the integrity of the Chicano people," and what was wrong with it was its heterosexism and "inbred machismo."[37] In (re)turning to a nationalist space, Moraga wants simultaneously to recast nationalism as always already more feminist and more queer than publicly acknowledged and to rearticulate a more feminist, more queer nationalism.

I will turn now, however, to what is worked out in the naming of nationalism in Moraga's writing on the spaces occupied by non-white racial others. In other words, in the name of a potentially transformative nationalism, what is, perhaps necessarily, performed in and exorcised from Moraga's work, and at what cost to Third World feminist movements?

Family Matters

The short story "Pesadilla" in *Loving in the War Years* is one of Moraga's most interesting and sustained engagements with the problematic of blackness as it appears in her work. In the italicized epigraph that frames the story we read that one day "Cecilia began to think about color," and that her acknowledgment of skin color and the concomitant ways of seeing make "all the difference in the world."[38] It is not only the bodies around Cecilia that change with this new way of seeing, but also her own body as she begins to re-vision it and its relationship to the world. Cecilia "felt her skin, like a casing, a beige bag into which the guts of her life were poured. And inside it, she swam through her day.... Always, the shell of this skin, leading her around."[39] Cecilia's skin is, in this instance, a boundary that establishes separation. However, as Yvonne Yarbro-Bejarano writes, it is "also a boundary in Gloria Anzaldúa's sense of a place where two edges meet and mingle."[40] The meanings that attach to skin color are contested border zones, and once Cecilia begins to take note of skin color, "nothing seems fair to her anymore."[41] Color has moved in with Cecilia in the form of Deborah (her black woman partner), in her relationship to Deborah, and in relationship to her own body and her ways of seeing and being in the world. Through these changes, Cecilia struggles with simultaneously sustaining and dismantling the belief that whiteness is unmarked, that white-skin privilege is unproblematically assumed or self-consciously invoked, and that blackness is self-evident. Although she is not black, Cecilia (Cherríe) is defined by those who are black.

Cecilia and Deborah's apartment functions as a space that assumes their mutual identity as lovers, familia. Within the apartment Cecilia imagines an impenetrable interior of their relationship, the space within which they can come together away from the reflections of the world. In this space within both the relationship and the apartment, Cecilia believes that she and Deborah can be removed from further inscriptions of the outside world. "*This* was the apartment they had wanted—the one they believed their love could rescue from its previous incarnation."[42] Within this space,

Cecilia wants to remove the couple from the violence of words, which are "a war to me. / They threaten my family."[43] We learn that the previous incarnation of the apartment was one of unrelenting poverty. In the poem "It's the Poverty," Moraga writes: "I am poorer than you. / In my experience. fictions / are for hearing about, / not living."[44] In "Pesadilla," however, it is Cecilia (a coming-into-consciousness Cherríe?) who reproduces and maintains fictions about La Loca (the previous tenant), about Deborah, and about herself. That is, she maintains and reproduces the myths that obscure the complexity of real people's lives. Despite Cecilia's stated belief that their love could rescue the apartment, the rage of La Loca (who shared the one-bedroom apartment with five children and five dogs) haunts her. Rage becomes a "bad omen" captured in her memory of dog food "red and raw" stuffed "in its anger" into the mouth of the drain.[45] La Loca is La Llorona, the mythical Mexican woman who wails from rage and pain for her drowned children.[46] Like the disembodied echo of La Llorona's wailing, La Loca's rage cannot "be washed out of the apartment walls."[47] La Loca is La Llorona, who is often collapsed into La Malinche—the traitor, the fucked one, the one Cecilia refuses to be—in the same way that Chicana lesbians are cast as traitors to the nation.

After a day spent cleaning the apartment in an attempt to erase the traces of rage and poverty, Cecilia and Deborah venture out into the world. They return to find their apartment door open and a light shining in the bedroom. Cecilia wonders whether, in her carelessness as the last to leave, she has left the door open for this intrusion. As they proceed down the hallway, it transforms into "a dark labyrinth to the pesadilla that awaited them."[48] At the hallway's end, written on the bedroom wall, are the words:

SUCK MY DICK YOU HOLE
I'M BLACK YOU MOTHERFUCKER BITCH
YOU BUTCH

The women turn their backs and collapse into the writing on the wall. Cecilia misrecognizes—and, indeed, forecloses—the possibility of the intruder's discourse also being addressed to her. When she says, "Everybody, it seemed, had *something* to say about Deborah's place on the planet,"[49] she refuses both to include herself as one of the people who has something to say about Deborah's place and to allow that the writing is also about her. With that displacement, Cecilia's analysis of the intruder's writing becomes an intraracial dialogue between a black man and a black woman (family: a woman who could have been a sister or a lover or a mother).

In this section, Moraga shifts the focus (and the critique) from La Loca/La Llorona as traitor to Chicano family to Deborah as traitor to black family. With the narrative insistence on Deborah as marked, the site of cultural betrayal shifts from the already marked (and now erased) site of supposed Chicana lesbian betrayal to the men of the nation to black lesbian desire as betrayal to black family. This is a move that once again connects and disconnects, a moment of traumatic repetition for which Cecilia literally leaves the door open. Becoming a lesbian through proximity with whiteness and safety necessitates a refusal to be marked as family with Deborah—this despite the fact that Moraga notes that behind that supposed safety was the danger of the man.

So, despite the fact that *together* she and Deborah "fall against the wall, crying. The animal's scrawl disappearing behind them,"[50] Cecilia disallows the possibility that she is located on the inside of this discourse, just as the intruder does not allow the possibility that Cecilia and Deborah constitute family. Cecilia's misreading leads her to place herself outside the reach of these words, and "these feelings of outsiderhood became . . . a thin film between [her] and the people [she] longed to touch, to reach to for help."[51] The writing reveals to Cecilia the dangers of being with Deborah; this is another instance in which her white skin, like the apartment wall, is insistently marked by forces beyond her control.

Simultaneously within and outside of this discourse, Cecilia locates herself on the inside in relation to the contest for meaning and possession in which both she and the intruder engage over Deborah. Both he and Cecilia "wanted Cecilia's lover,"[52] and everybody wants to define Deborah. Cecilia and the intruder are doing battle on the field of representation that in this instance is the space occupied by Deborah's body. Thus, the "intruder" can label Deborah or Cecilia a "butch" in his writing, and Cecilia can read this writing and determine that it is specifically addressed to Deborah—that it is Deborah who occupies the space of butch.[53] While Cecilia insists on remaining unmarked, Deborah bears the burden of being marked by class, race, and sex. Cecilia refuses to admit that this intruder, this black man, has the ability to script her and read her. The intruder scratches his words and pictures of his genitalia on the wall for the women to "see and suck."[54] He "scrawls," which marks the writing as illegible to Cecilia, except that she can read this writing and knows that this "scrawl" is about Deborah. Not only is this scrawl "about" Deborah, but it labels her butch (a role that black lesbians have played, and have been placed in the position of playing, with their non-black partners).

Cecilia refuses to allow this writing to be about her. Donna Haraway, however, contends that in *Loving*, "writing marks Moraga's body, affirms it as the body of a woman of color against the possibility of passing into the unmarked category of the Anglo father."[55] "Pesadilla" reveals Cecilia's refusal to account for the ways that she is marked—repressing the ways that the intruder writes her. As both Romero and Moya note, for Haraway, women of color—particularly Chicanas—become the paradigmatic cyborgs, the cyborgs par excellence. As such, Chicanas' identities are " 'fully political' (in other words, not merely familial)."[56] Haraway's reading insists that Moraga's use of spliced language "prevents [her] from 'basing identity on . . . a fall from innocence and right to natural names, mother's or father's'."[57] Haraway misreads Moraga's textual body, overlooking the textual nuances and complications in order to recuperate Moraga's body within her own work as *the* "privileged" body of a woman of color. This recuperation runs contrary, on several levels, to much of the work of the text. Moraga's writing is intent on marking whiteness. She marks the body of her father and her former white lovers; she tries to account for the "whiteness" and "privilege" that are part of her brother's experience ("My brother's sex was white.

Mine, brown") and that mark her entrance into lesbianism ("It was whiteness and safety. . . . It was whiteness and money. In this way she had learned to be a lesbian").[58] Within "Pesadilla," Deborah (not Cecilia/Cherríe) is the site on which issues of color, sex, and gender are worked out, covered over, and worked out again.

Despite Cecilia's and Deborah's efforts to cover the signs of filth with fresh *white* coats of plaster and paint, "The signs of filth, yes, still remained. But *that* Cecilia and Deborah believed they could remove."[59] The whiteness, the illusion of safety, insistently attracts dirt; it simultaneously insists on recognition and erasure. The outside has encroached; the borders are porous. Cecilia has been included in this writing that she wants to determine as being "about" black familia. Cecilia's disavowal of inclusion and her insistence that it is Deborah who occupies the position of the marked function in ways similar to Proposition 187's attempts to make people of color visible by setting people's gazes against one another, locating others as potential candidates for expulsion or holding them as an invisible and necessary force.

In "Pesadilla," and throughout *Loving*, the recurrent challenge for Cecilia is to open up definitions of familia to recognize the possibility of a continued alliance with Deborah across relations of consanguinity yet in accord with another kind of familial "pull and tug of blood." The challenge is to find herself in the complexity of desire, coalition, and blood relations and to begin to work through her multiple relations to queerness and race, class, and skin-color privilege. When brought face to face with this challenge in the form of Deborah, Cecilia "closes up the thought," "shrinks back," and begins to wonder whether she is "up to the task of such loving."[60] Among other things, the intruder's writing on the wall reveals to Cecilia the dangers of being with Deborah, for this is one instance in which her white skin, like the wall, is insistently marked. She has been included in this writing that she determines is "about" black familia. Indeed, as Moraga writes, the meanings that attach to her skin shift in relation to the women that she is with. Again, I quote:

> We light-skinned breeds are like chameleons, those lagartijas with the capacity to change the color of their skins. . . . My lovers have always been the environment that defined my color. With a Black lover in apartheid Boston I was seen as a white girl. When we moved to Brooklyn we were both Ricans. . . . Whitegirls change my shade to a paler version. . . . *No body* notices me. For that reason, I got to be choosy 'bout who I hang with. Everybody so contagious, I pick up their gesture, their joke, their jive.[61]

The problem, in fact, becomes that *every* body notices, reflects, and determines her body.

Moraga writes in *The Last Generation*, "There was a time when I truly believed I could never live without black women in my life. And then I learned how—how to forget uptown city buses, her fedora-feathered dreads, her femme-fatality sliding up next to me. . . . What happened to all those women I laid and made history with?"[62] Moraga learns to forget those things—"uptown city buses," "fedora-feathered dreads"—that she codes as synecdochically black. In transcribing this memory, dreads become linked with dread, and those things affiliated with blackness hark back to the "intruder" in "Pesadilla" as that which must be expelled. What did happen to the women of other races with whom Moraga laid and with whom she made family, and what happened to their shared feminist visions? In the ten years between the publication of *Loving in the War Years* and *The Last Generation*, Moraga shifted from a complicated and often contradictory coalitionist politics rooted in a less articulated form of cultural nationalism to a more articulated, sexually inclusive cultural nationalism shown by her commitment to "Raza" and the fact that she had "tasted assimilation and it is bitter on [her] tongue."[63]

As Cecilia attends to Deborah, she feels "her heart like a steel clamp inside her chest, twisting what was only moments ago a living beating fear into a slow cool numbing between her breasts. *Her loving couldn't change a thing.*"[64] Cecilia's body and the bodies of those with whom she is in contact continue to metamorphose with her increased ways of seeing, being seen, and refusing to see. While looking for Deborah's pills, Cecilia remembers that the first time she felt this particular coldness in her chest was in relation to her mother. Cecilia remembers her mother, "elbows dug into the kitchen table . . . tears streaming down her cheeks," telling her, "You're just like the rest of 'em. You don't know how to love."[65] The tears of Cecilia and her mother mingle "like communion."[66] The tears signify the pull and tug of blood; the pull of culture, race, class, religion/faith, and sex: familia. "Again. A river return. / A river whose pull always before that moment had swept Cecilia off her chair into her mother's arms."[67]

In this instance, Deborah's tears seem to function as a reminder of the heaviness of family, the "inescapability" of a certain kind of desire; the "inescapability" of raced, classed, gendered history; the "inescapability" of betrayal. One possible reading of Deborah's vision of the broad and black hand raised in violence is as the embodiment of both Deborah's and Cecilia's nightmares (one of the nightmares embedded within the narrative titled "Nightmare"). The night of the break-in, Cecilia for the first time witnesses Deborah's nightmare. She describes Deborah's experience of the seizure, or "fit," as she relates that Deborah calls it "mimicking some 1930's sci-fi version of epileptics or schizophrenics."[68] Her "fit" arises at the moment of the intruder's insistence on compulsory heterosexuality as it combines with race and class. This is the only time that Deborah speaks within this piece, and what she says is, "Blahblahblah-blahblah-blahblah! Po' lil cullud girl, me."[69] Her speech is as unintelligible as the "animal's" writing is illegible. Cecilia, however, is capable of translating both. Moraga writes that for the man (and for Cecilia), "Blood is blood." And, "standing on her knees in bed, [Deborah] would go through the motions once again of the man coming down on her with the back of his hand"—the hand broader and blacker than she has ever seen it.[70]

The hand that Cecilia says Deborah sees belongs to the "second and last man [Deborah's] mother kicked out." It is interesting that Cecilia reads the hand that is threatening Deborah as broader and *blacker* than Deborah had ever seen it. It is Cecilia who is struck by the blackness of the hand. If Deborah were a reader in this text, would she read her nightmare this way? Remember Romero's assertion that, in her writing, Moraga "assumes that community inhibits intellectual mastery."[71] Within the narrative structure of "Pesadilla," Deborah exists to be read. Mired in her community, she is unable to communicate the meanings attached to the writing on the wall or her own experience of terror. After Cecilia has located herself on the outside as reader—because in Moraga's formulation, one removes oneself from the family in order to read it—we learn that it is the *shared* maternal history of "the dark definite women of their childhoods" that purportedly brings Cecilia and Deborah together.[72]

In "The Breakdown of the Bicultural Mind" (in the section of *The Last Generation* titled "La Fuerza Femenina"), Moraga tells a fascinating and revealing story about a little black girl at an amusement park whom "she wanted to see as different." (I read this "different" as different from her.) The section begins with an epigraph from "Pesadilla" that is about Deborah, *"the dark woman looking in through the glass is as frightened as I am. She is weeping. I will not let her in."*[73] Recalling the little black girl whom she sees in line while they wait to get on the "Wild Car" ride, Moraga remembers her "darkness, her difference, her nappy hair corralled into three perfectly plaited pigtails," and the memory reminds her of how her mother fixed her own "buster-brown straight" hair in two braids as a girl. The remembered similarity and dissimilarity of the braids leads to another remembrance, to a connection between the little black girl's hair and the hair of a former black lover, the "soft density" of which "support[ed] my chin as we two slept."[74] In this remembering, a material difference between the young Moraga and the little black girl is made manifest in the third braid. "I didn't understand the third one. Why was it there?"[75] This tactile memory performs a typical inclusionary, exclusionary gesture in Moraga's writing. In one beat, sight, smell, and memory connect, and in the next beat the distance—and, more important, the need for distance—reappears. Moraga continues, writing that, after a particularly rough rollercoaster ride, the little black girl throws up "a puddle of stink and sickness one person away." Cecilia is nauseated, but she fights "desperately to keep down the cheap spaghetti dinner rolling around in [her] stomach," because she "didn't want to be that human, that exposed, that dark."[76]

This story enacts the possibility of exposure and marking that, in memory (reading back to a time when she was Cecilia Lawrence), Moraga once again wants to remain unmarked; she wants to remain stripped of her own "darkness." Following the story of the little girl, Moraga remembers "that biography [of black womanhood] denied [her]" and she concludes that she is no longer part of the black family that she once belonged to and imagined that she could not live without.[77] She has, however, reached this point before. This passage is consistent with other moments in other texts by Moraga: She typically needs to separate from family in order to come to her self.[78] This separation from black family and from "Puerto Rican dreams, Mexican childhood and white forgetfulness" allows Moraga to focus on the specificity of claiming a Chicana, cultural nationalist, feminist, lesbian, activist identity.

These articulations of color and desire are compelled by a conscious and unconscious working out in Moraga's writing of her complicated relationships to biraciality and blackness—as in the story with which she opens "The Breakdown of the Bicultural Mind." In that story, "Quetzalcóatl the man (not the god) [is] destined to relive the primal act which brought his soul into the world . . . compulsively re-enact[ing] that history."[79] Moraga's writing enacts and reenacts those oppressions that are "under the skin." She repeatedly and alternately performs, transgresses, and reproduces the cultural myths and stories that are in circulation. She performs these things not only in relation to blackness—the black male intruder and Deborah in "Pesadilla"; the mulatto in *The Last Generation*—but she also refigures La Malinche and the Indian woman as the center of the Chicano/a nation.

Moraga's rewriting of cultural myths enacts and passes on a particular racial memory. These "stories," regardless of whether they are "our" particular cultural myths (that is, regardless of whether we produce them), are reproduced, inherited, and passed on. When asked in an interview with Alarcón about intertextuality with other Chicano writers, Moraga said: "I do believe in racial memory. I do believe in the collective unconscious, this kind of thing. As a writer you're calling forth your unconscious, that is, if you are writing well."[80] She attempts to make visible, in herself and in her writing, that which is unconscious in her relationships to other "racial/ethnic/national" groups. In the following story, Moraga explores the burden of the mestizo and the pain of biraciality, ultimately locating this story on a black/mulatto man. Before she does this, however, Moraga constructs an alternative prophetic genealogy. She reads Moses and Malcom for a clue, for some "sense of how [her] mixed blood identity has driven [her] to politics, protest and poetry."[81] She constructs a writerly genealogy that cannot necessarily be collapsed into her life story. She comes to realize that her "writer's journey is not strictly wedded to [her] individual story."[82] In *The Last Generation*, Moraga also enacts a re-membering (remaking and recalling) of Chicana feminism and Chicana/o nationalism as distinct from black feminist and black nationalist movements. A link that she makes in *Loving in the War Years* is expurgated in *The Last Generation*. In *Loving in the War Years,* she writes: "Contrary to popular belief among Chicanos, Chicana Feminism did not borrow from white feminists to create a movement. If any borrowing was done, it was from Black feminists."[83] In *The Last Generation,* Moraga rejects black familia and the links between black and Chicano/a movements in order to re-member her family in different terms.

The secret of racial memory that becomes known and lived allows Moraga to work through to another experience of racial memory and her claim that "I am of that endangered culture and that murderous race, but I am loyal only to one. My mother culture, my mother land, my mother tongue, further back than even (her mother) can remember."[84] The place she reaches is more original than that of her biological mother. She writes:

> I read and I remember. At nineteen, I first heard the story of the "mulatto," as my friend called him. A musician she knew who was born a black smudge into an otherwise lily-white family. No one ever spoke about it. He was never told he was Black, but figured it out in a life in and out of prison, drugs and jazz clubs. And then one night, alone in his apartment and thrashing so bad inside, he went, without thinking, into the bathroom and filled the tub with scalding hot water. At the moment he submerged his body, long legs, then back, then face into the water, he remembered. He remembered being no bigger than

the length of his mother's arm as she dropped him suffocating into the liquid flame. *Sometimes one lifetime is not enough to repair the damage. That is what we fear, isn't it?*[85]

In this story, the "mulatto" performs his unconscious desire to reenact that of which, until the moment of submergence, he was unaware. In the trajectory of Moraga's writing, this story functions as an exorcism of what she has, in other writings, identified as the secrets that people are compelled to repeat and the fear that walls people off from one another. In the context of this work, the "mulatto" is unconsciously repeating a racial memory. Moraga says that, for the mulatta, the notion of "choice" is the "curse": "There is no denying this güera-face has often secured my safe passage through the minefields of Amerikan racism."[86] A friend challenges Moraga in *Loving in the War Years*—saying that he does not trust *güeros;* that they have to "prove" themselves—and she tells him, "You call this a choice? To constantly push up against a wall of resistance from your own people or to fall away nameless into the mainstream of this country?"[87]

When Moraga writes that the "mulatto" was never *told* that he was black but "figured it out in a life in and out of prison, drugs and jazz clubs," the reader is called on to witness how "secrets kill," to question how one becomes "black" in an "all white family," and to wonder how one learns to be black by moving "in and out of prison."[88] Choice seems not to be functioning for the "mulatto"; he seems to be reliving trauma through a return of the repressed. Locating oneself in the "borderland" of biraciality and bisexuality is a refusal to take a political stand. For Moraga, they are "passive terms without political bite" and "say nothing about where one really stands."[89] Moraga seems to fear that biracial and bisexual bodies and texts are too easily co-opted, and that cultural nationalist bodies, or bodies firmly located in a revised nationalist aesthetic, are not. It is perhaps for these reasons that *The Last Generation* will not be as readily absorbed into women's studies curricula as *This Bridge Called My Back* and *Loving in the War Years.*

Moraga acknowledges the mestizo (and acknowledges that this *mestizaje* fuels her activism), yet she wants to displace the mestizo with the indigenous. Just as one lifetime is not enough to repair the damage of a particular life, Moraga in her writing continually works through the internalized pain of racist, classist, and heterosexist relationships and the extent to which one may go to exorcise or perform that pain. She acknowledges the pitfalls of nationalism, saying, "We are all horrified by the concentration and rape camps in Bosnia. . . . Over and over again we are reminded that sex and race do not define a person's politics. . . . But it is historically evident that the female body, like the Chicano people, has been colonized. And any movement to decolonize . . . must be culturally and sexually specific."[90] We, she writes, are "all horrified by ethnic cleansing" and the maintenance of borders implicit in such acts. Despite this, *The Last Generation* contains perhaps Moraga's strongest push for an internationalist politics that is also culturally specific. She writes:

> We must learn to see ourselves less as U.S. citizens and more as members of a larger world community composed of many nations of people and no longer give credence to

the geopolitical borders that have divided us, Chicano from Mexicano, Filipino-American from Pacific Islander, African-American from Haitian. Call it racial memory. Call it shared economic discrimination. Chicano's call it "Raza,"—be it Quichua, Cubano or Colombiano—an identity that dissolves borders. As a Chicana writer that's the context in which I want to create.[91]

Moraga is concerned with breaking down the borders that divide colonized groups— "Chicano from Mexicano"—and less obviously concerned with those that divide, say, Chicanos from Haitians. Unfortunately, this is similar to what occurs around Proposition 187: Similarities and differences are located and made to appear in a move that reveals by obscuring.

As Moraga works to decolonize her Chicana lesbian body (and by extension, all Chicano people), it is the racial "mulatto" (inside and outside of herself), the sexual mulatto, and the political mulatto that must be exorcised. "*No body* notices me," she writes, but the very problem is that *every* body reflects and determines the meanings that attach to her skin. Moraga is caught within representation—made visible at every turn. The only bodies that will reflect back to her what she wants reflected are the bodies of other Chicano/as. Therefore, with "others" what she most wants reflected is difference—not to be unreadable on her own, collapsed into another racial or ethnic group, or misread. "*Call me breed. Call me trash. Call me spic greaser beaner dyke jota bulldagger. Call me something meant to set me apart from you and I will know who I am. Do not call me 'sister.' I am not yours.*"[92] This list of epithets marks Moraga as belonging to a particular embattled space of Queer Aztlán, but who would she be if she could no longer claim all of that otherness? As Peggy Phelan writes:

> Identity cannot, then, reside in the name you can say or the body you can see—your own or your mother's. Identity emerges in the failure of the body to express being fully and the failure of the signifier to convey meaning exactly. Identity is perceptible only through a relation to an other—which is to say, it is a form of both resisting and claiming the other, declaring the boundary where the self diverges from and merges with the other. In that declaration of identity and identification, there is always loss, the loss of not-being the other and yet remaining dependent on that other for self-seeing, self-being.[93]

Moraga can occupy only a particular space as her definitions of who constitutes politically viable community become more circumscribed. Within her writing, Moraga simultaneously constructs a Chicano space within which she is not different, a queer space within which she is not other, and an other space within which she wants to claim all difference.

Notes

1. Interview with Evantheia Schibsted, "Confessions of a Wetback," *Wired*, vol. 5, no. 1 (January 1997), 142.
2. Ibid.

3. Gloria Anzaldúa, *Borderlands/La Frontera: The New Mestiza* (San Francisco: Aunt Lute Books, 1987), 3.

4. Cherríe Moraga and Gloria Anzaldúa, eds., *This Bridge Called My Back: Writings by Radical Women of Color* (New York: Kitchen Table Press, 1983); Anzaldúa, *Borderlands*, 3.

5. Anzaldúa, *Borderlands*, 3.

6. In Moraga's writing, borders are places where different races or different bodies come together or resist coming together. Borders are the zones that exist between people; to cross them, one needs to examine internalized racism, classism, sexism, and heterosexism.

7. In response to the question, "What is the border?" Gómez-Peña says: "What does the border mean? The border for us is an elastic metaphor that we can reposition in order to talk about many issues. For example, for the Mexican, the U.S.–Mexican border is an absolutely necessary border to defend itself from the United States. The border is a wall. The border is an abyss. The Mexican who crosses traditionally falls into this abyss and becomes a traitor. For the Chicano, the border has multiple mythical connotations. The border is the umbilical cord with Mexico: the place to return to, to regenerate.

"For the North American, the border becomes a mythical notion of national security. The border is where the Third World begins. The U.S. media conceives of the border as a kind of war zone—a place of conflict, of threat, of invasion": Coco Fusco, "Bilingualism, Biculturalism and Borders," in *English Is Broken Here* (New York: New Press, 1995), 148–49.

8. Schibsted, "Confessions," 142.

9. Ibid.

10. Cherríe Moraga, *Heroes and Saints and Other Plays* (Albuquerque: West End Press, 1994).

11. Moraga and Anzaldúa, *This Bridge Called My Back*; Cherríe Moraga, *Loving in the War Years: Lo que nunca pasó por sus labios* (Boston: South End Press, 1983); idem, *The Last Generation* (Boston: South End Press, 1993).

12. Cherríe Moraga, "Foreword: Refugees of a World on Fire," in Moraga and Anzaldúa, *This Bridge Called My Back*.

13. Paula M. L. Moya, "Postmodernism, 'Realism,' and the Politics of Identity: Cherríe Moraga and Chicana Feminism," in *Feminist Genealogies, Colonial Legacies, Democratic Futures*, ed. M. Jacqui Alexander and Chandra Talpade Mohanty (New York: Routledge, 1996).

14. Moraga, *Loving*, 133.

15. Alicia Arrizón, "Mythical Performativity: Relocating Aztlán in Chicana Feminist Cultural Productions," *Theatre Journal* 52, no. 1 (2000): 23–49.

16. Moraga, *Loving*, 103.

17. Lora Romero, "'When Something Goes Queer': Familiarity, Formalism, and Minority Intellectuals in the 1980s," *Yale Journal of Criticism* 6, no. 1 (1993): 121.

18. Ibid., 127.

19. Moraga, *Loving*, ii.

20. Romero, "'When Something Goes Queer,'" 136–37.

21. Norma Alarcón, "Cognitive Desires: An Allegory of/for Chicana Critics," in *Listening to Silences: New Essays in Feminist Criticism*, ed. Elaine Hedges and Shelley Fisher Fishkin (New York: Oxford University Press, 1994), 263–64.

22. Schibsted, "Confessions," 42.

23. Moraga, *Loving*, 95.

24. Idem, *Last Generation*, 116–17.

25. Sue-Ellen Case, "Seduced and Abandoned: Chicanas and Lesbians in Representation," in *Negotiating Performances: Gender, Sexuality, and Theatricality in Latin/o America*, ed. Diana Taylor and Juan Villegas Morales (Durham, N.C.: Duke University Press, 1994).

26. Schibsted, "Confessions," 142.

27. Case, "Seduced," 96.

28. Ibid.

29. Ibid., 97.

30. Moraga, *Loving*, 51.

31. Moraga, *Loving*, 96.

32. Case, "Seduced," 96.

33. Moraga, *Last Generation*, 156.

34. Ibid., 155. Of course, this functions much differently "in the world." Propositions 187 and 209 restrict this becoming American.

35. Moya, "Postmodernism," 143.

36. Moraga, *Last Generation*, 148.

37. Ibid.

38. Moraga, *Loving*, 36.

39. Ibid.

40. Yarbro-Bejarano writes that, in "Pesadilla," "by representing skin color as something she has or becomes rather than as an essence, by detaching 'skin' and 'face' from the body or by calling it a scar or an accident . . . [Moraga] displays the constructedness of 'race'": Yvonne Yarbro-Bejarano, "Cherríe Moraga's 'Shadow of a Man,'" in *Acting Out: Feminist Performances*, ed. Linda Hart and Peggy Phelan (Ann Arbor: University of Michigan Press, 1993), 85–104.

41. Moraga, *Loving*, 36.

42. Ibid., 37.

43. Ibid., 63.

44. Ibid., 64.

45. Ibid., 37.

46. La Llorona is both the bad mother and the mother who cries because of the subjugation of her children to the colonizer. "The image of La Llorona, or weeping woman, at one point became conflated with the image of La Malinche because they share a sadness relating to lost children": Sandra Messinger Cypess, *La Malinche in Mexican Literature from History to Myth* (Austin: University of Texas Press, 1991), 7.

47. Moraga, *Loving*, 37.

48. Ibid., 37.

49. Ibid., 38.

50. Ibid.

51. Ibid., 123.

52. Ibid., 38.

53. This is not an argument about butch-ness or femme-ness. But for Cecilia's assessment that the writing is about Deborah to be correct, there must still be some evidence of another woman in the apartment. Cecilia tells us that there are pictures of Deborah in the apartment, but she absents herself from both a visual and a verbal representation.

54. Moraga, *Loving*, 38.

55. Donna Haraway, "A Cyborg Manifesto: Science, Technology, and Socialist-Feminism in the Late Twentieth Century," in *Simians, Cyborgs and Women: The Reinvention of Nature* (New York: Routledge, 1991), 176.

56. Romero, "'When Something Goes Queer,'" 129.

57. Ibid., 129–30.

58. Moraga, *Loving*, 39.

59. Ibid., 37.

60. Ibid., 38.

61. Moraga, *Last Generation*, 116–17; emphasis added.

62. Ibid., 118.

63. Ibid., 127.

64. Moraga, *Loving*, 41.

65. Ibid., 41–42.

66. Ibid., 41.

67. Ibid.

68. Ibid., 40.

69. Ibid.

70. Ibid.

71. Romero, "'When Something Goes Queer,'" 126.

72. Moraga, *Loving*, 38.

73. Moraga, *Last Generation*, 117.

74. Ibid.

75. Ibid.

76. Ibid.

77. Ibid., 118.

78. Romero writes, "Moraga invokes this trope [of defamiliarization] in her preface, in which she interprets the growing estrangement from la familia chicana that she felt as young adult as precisely what gives her the authority to write about Chicano culture," and "Moraga assumes that community inhibits intellectual mastery": Romero, "'When Something Goes Queer,'" 125, 126.

79. Moraga, *Last Generation*, 113.

80. Norma Alarcón, "Interview with Cherríe Moraga," *Third Woman: Texas and More*, vol. 3, nos. 1 and 2 (1986), 134.

81. Moraga, *Last Generation*, 112.

82. Ibid.

83. Moraga, *Loving*, 132.

84. Moraga, *Last Generation*, 129.

85. Ibid., 113.

86. Ibid., 126.

87. Moraga, *Loving*, 97.

88. Moraga, *Last Generation*, 113.

89. Ibid., 126.

90. Ibid., 149.

91. Ibid., 62.

92. Ibid., 126.

93. Peggy Phelan, *Unmarked: The Politics of Performance* (New York: Routledge, 1993), 146.

Catrióna Rueda Esquibel

16 Shameless Histories:
Chicana Lesbian Fictions
Talking Race/Talking Sex

*How will we choose to describe our past, now, at this moment, as an
enunciation in the present?*

—*Emma Pérez*

Over the past decade, I have been researching a group of texts that I describe collectively as Chicana lesbian fictions.[1] Written by both Chicanos and Chicanas, gay and straight, these short stories and dramas feature Chicana characters who either claim lesbian identity or express homoerotic feelings. The goal of my research is to put the texts in conversation with one another—or, in many cases, to make visible the different conversations in which the stories and their authors participate—in order to explore commonalities and differences. One theme that emerges from these texts is a pressing concern with queer Chicana histories. Stories that address this theme create such histories, situating characters within a long line of women who were proud of their sexuality and their Mexican heritage.

To understand this literary engagement with queer Chicana history, I have found it extremely valuable to examine the research of Chicana feminist historians. For example, in her study of Spanish/Mexican women in Santa Fe from 1848 to 1898, Deena González articulates how feminism informs her study of these women:

Widows are frequently described as wives without husbands. I instead view them as unmarried women, women unpartnered with men; and I place them in the context of generally being unmarried, which was a far more important condition in frontier New Mexico than we have been led to believe. Most adult women spent their lives in a state of unmarriedness.... If we focus on their relationship primarily to [men] ... we miss some crucial elements of their existence. Women were indeed bound in marriage.... Women also managed to disavow marriages, to obtain annulments, and, in many cases, to outlive husbands and never remarry.[2]

González argues that historical means of evaluating women—in relation to men—obscure "crucial elements of their existence," including their work, their class status, and their relationships to other women. By showing that many women "managed to disavow marriages ... obtain annulments ... outlive husbands" González seems to argue that the women themselves refused to be defined solely by their marital status.

Like González, the authors of Chicana lesbian fiction create Chicanas of the past who live their lives independent of men. In so doing, they are both claiming and creating a history of Chicana lesbianism. Their work confronts the erasure of Chicanos from the history of the "American West," the erasure of Chicanas from Chicano history, and the erasure of Chicana lesbians from gay and lesbian histories.

While the body of Chicana lesbian writing is quite extensive, I will focus on three short stories published during the 1980s: Jo Carrillo's "María Littlebear" (1982), Gloria Anzaldúa's "La historia de una marimacho" (1989), and Rocky Gámez's "A Baby for Adela" (1988).[3] Without claiming these authors as "representative" of Chicana lesbians writing in the 1980s, I argue that the stories reveal a search for and creation of legitimating histories of lesbians in Chicana communities. These are not the only stories in which this theme can be found; nor is history the only theme in Chicana lesbian fiction.[4] I remain suspicious of grand narratives, which inevitably erase or subsume whole categories of people and their work. My goal is to introduce the reader to a particular group of texts to demonstrate how they take up and remake history for Chicana lesbians. Their stories, whether passed on, reprinted, or lost in the archives, tell "histories" through short fiction. At the same time, I wish to make clear that Carrillo, Anzaldúa, and Gámez were only a few of the Chicana lesbians active in lesbian, Chicana, and feminist publishing circles in the 1980s.

These three stories employ three different popular forms: Carrillo's "María Littlebear" draws from oral histories; Anzaldúa's "La historia de una marimacho" employs the Mexican *corrido;* and Gámez's "A Baby for Adela" uses pulp fiction. Carrillo's story deploys oral history, which has emerged as the optimal methodology to document the lived history of working-class people. Progressive programs such as women's studies and Chicano studies employ oral history in their pedagogy: Undergraduate students become researchers, taking down the histories of parents and grandparents, community elders, migrants, and immigrants.

In "La historia de una marimacho," Anzaldúa creates her own version of the *corrido,* a narrative produced by a community, specifically the border cultures of south Texas. The *corrido,* or Mexican border ballad, has been an oppositional form of history since the eighteenth century. Widely recognized as a forerunner of Chicano literature and Chicano history, the *corrido* praised male heroes such as Gregorio Cortez, who stood up against the racial violence of the Texas Rangers.

In contrast to the narrative forms that emerge from the community, which are engaged by Carrillo and Anzaldúa, Gámez references pulp fiction—mass-produced paperback books of the 1950s and '60s. Although they were lurid, sensationalist, and sexy, these books were available at every corner drugstore and told stories of "wayward girls and wicked women," shameless lesbians and their deviant lifestyle.

Catering to male readers and often written by male authors using feminine pseudonyms, this genre of fiction nevertheless made public the image (or specter) of the lesbian in a way that affected the sexual identity of hundreds of women. All of these popular forms represent groups who are often left out of officials histories. Thus, they offer authors productive ground for producing fictional accounts of queer Chicana histories—histories that are no less "real" for being fictional.

"My History, Not Yours": The Fictional Autobiography of María Littlebear

In 1993, the historian Genaro Padilla published his research on autobiographies of Californios, Tejanos, and Nuevomejicanos during the period that immediately followed the U.S. annexation of northern Mexico under the title *My History, Not Yours*.[5] Padilla argues that, through their narratives, Mexican Americans "gave utterance to the threat of social erasure . . . opened a terrain of discursive necessity in which fear and resentment found language . . . [and] made los americanos the subject of ironic humor, linguistic derogation, and social villainy."[6] Padilla is involved in the archaeological project to "recover the nineteenth-century formations of Chicano autobiography . . . digging through the archives—layer by textual layer—gleaning those personal narratives with which we may construct an autobiographical tradition."[7]

Padilla takes his title from a statement by Mariano Guadalupe Vallejo, who in 1875 sold his library and allowed his own history to be transcribed for the collection of H. H. Bancroft. Vallejo articulates a resistance to being archived, recorded, and confined by the Anglo ethnographer: "I am willing to relate all I can remember, but I wish it clearly understood that it must be in my own way, and at my own time. I will not be hurried or dictated to. It is my history and not yours I propose to tell."[8] Vallejo clearly differentiates "my history"—a Mexican American history—from "yours," or that of Anglo Americans.

Feminist historians and literary critics participating in the Recovering the U.S. Hispanic Literary Heritage project, including Rosaura Sánchez, Tey Diana Rebolledo, Antonia Castañeda, and Clara Lomas, have focused their research on fiction, nonfiction, and autobiographical writings by the women of northern Mexico following annexation.[9] To date, no Chicana lesbian autobiographies have been recovered.[10] For representation of their lives, Chicana lesbians must look to fiction, it seems, for it is only in fictional writings by contemporary authors that Chicana lesbians become subjects of history. At the time of this writing, Chicana scholars have drawn on historical research to fictionalize queer Chicana histories. Graciela Limón, Alicia Gaspar de Alba, Amelia Montes, and Emma Pérez have all written or are completing historical novels about queer Chicanas.[11]

In short stories, however, Chicana lesbians began creating histories much earlier. In 1981, Jo Carrillo's "María Littlebear" was published in *Lesbian Fiction*, an anthology edited by Elly Bulkin. The book was produced by Persephone Press, a "white women's press of Watertown, Massachusetts [that] ceased production in the spring of 1983."[12] Carrillo's short story thus had a very limited circulation. During the early 1980s, Carrillo was active in women-of-color publishing circles and is perhaps best known for her poem in *This Bridge Called My Back*, which issues a challenge to white women who would exoticize women of color: "And when you leave, take your pictures with you."[13]

"María Littlebear" takes place in northern New Mexico. Set in the middle of the twentieth century, the story shows New Mexico several generations after annexation. While Anglo Americans control the state apparatus, Chicana and Chicano characters such as María Littlebear also "give utterance against a threat of social erasure," to resist the dominant discourse, to mark their families' long histories in the area before "the West was won," and make los americanos "the subject of ironic humor, linguistic derogation, and social villainy."[14] Carrillo skillfully weaves this first-person narrative into a tale of Chicana lesbian history.

In "María Littlebear," the eponymous character narrates her relationship with her lover, Elisa Alvarado, by situating their lives in the racial context of New Mexico in the middle of the twentieth century. Carrillo begins her story with María describing the apparition of God on the chapel wall in Holman, New Mexico, in 1939 or 1940. Nuevomejicanos came from all over the state to view this miraculous sight and to learn their fate, "to know if you were damned or saved."

> Everyone who saw God or the Virgin was safe, if you saw a saint you still had a chance, but if you saw the Devil you were damned. . . . The gringos thought we were all nuts. They wrote an article about us in the Journal. Something like "there were Mexicans standing around just looking at the Holman wall. They claimed to see God but they say that this is only possible when the moon is full." It was in the back by the obituaries. Can you *believe* they put God by the dead people?[15]

María adds that the Anglos attempted to stop the Mexicans' pilgrimage by painting over the chapel wall. Thus, the opening of this story sets up an oppositional relationship between Nuevomejicanos' popular history (the apparition of God in Holman) and official Anglo history (the *Albuquerque Journal*'s report about superstitious Mexicans). Further, the facts that the story is hidden "back by the obituaries" and that the Anglos whitewash the chapel wall indicate an erasure of Nuevomejicanos' history made literal by whitewash.

This is an example of how Carrillo's narrator, María Littlebear, contextualizes her place: not merely as a Chicana lesbian, but as a Nuevomejicana living in a racialized state. María uses this instance of popular history to establish the year that Elisa Alvarado was born. I like to imagine this story as an oral history in which an interviewer asks María, "What was it like for lesbians during that time?" María responds with stories describing the racial context of New Mexico, because for her there is no way to separate being a lesbian from being Nuevomejicana.

María describes the first time she met Elisa, admitting that she fell in love with Elisa immediately. Yet María downplays the romantic aspect to illustrate how Elisa, as a waitress at a truck stop and as a Mexican woman, was perceived as "for sale" by Anglo truckers:

> The day I first ate there, this one guy was yelling at Elisa, calling her "senorida" and saying things like he'd give her ten big ones if she'd go with him. . . . He slapped her real hard, right on the ass. . . . Elisa was just standing there, her face was all twisted and she looked like she was going to start crying any minute.[16]

Implicit throughout María's telling is a critique of racialized power in New Mexico—the Anglo truckers who "thought they owned the place and everything in it," including the women. Not only does this trucker attempt to buy Elisa, he hits her hard enough that everyone in the place knows she has been hit. It is a sexual gauntlet thrown down, daring anyone to tell him he cannot take her and inviting others to appreciate his mastery over her.

The response he elicits surely could not have been anticipated. María Littlebear admits she "just couldn't take it . . . because I hate to see a woman treated like meat."[17] The way she tells it, María had not yet spoken a word to Elisa, yet she feels compelled to rise to her defense and to this racialized sexual challenge:

> Me being who I am, I got up, stuck my thumbs in my pockets and walked over there real cool like. I was shaking, but I would never have let him know it. And I told that guy in Spanish that he was a cabrón, who didn't even know how to shit let alone how to treat a woman. He died! Mostly because Elisa was standing behind me sort of laughing and he didn't know what I was saying. When he left, there was a fifty cent piece—that was a big tip back then—still, he should have left the ten big ones he was bragging about.[18]

Rather than, say, punching him in the nose (something she admits she would be more inclined to do "nowadays, since I'm a lot stronger"), María changes the terms of the exchange by cursing him and criticizing him in a language he does not understand, the language of New Mexico. María thus destabilizes the trucker's ability to control the terms of the exchange, both verbal and sexual.

Together, Elisa and María mean something different from what they mean separately, in part because—at least, in this instance—they are coded as femme and butch. When Elisa is alone, the truck driver reads her as heterosexually available to his desire. Situated in alliance with María, and laughing at her "reading" of him, Elisa's position is quite different: She becomes a Mexican woman who is neither single (unprotected) nor necessarily heterosexual, and thus is doubly unavailable. Although the story makes it clear that Elisa is "already" a lesbian, that she has loved women since age five, in this scene Elisa "becomes" lesbian symbolically and physically in relation to the butch María.

María is performing both for the truck driver and for Elisa. For the former, she answers a challenge; for the latter, she issues an invitation. In a sense, María's action is the beginning of the two women's lifelong relationship. In her representation of that moment, however, Carrillo shows how inextricably love between the two women was intertwined with their gender, racial, and class positions.

"María Littlebear" also emphasizes that Chicana lesbians exist not in isolation but as members of families and of communities.[19] María remembers:

> Her grandma could have died the day she found out about Elisa's . . . feelings, you know, about women and all? . . . The day she found out about Elisa and me, she cried and cried. . . . After at least a week of crying and a month of penance she calmed down. Like nothing ever happened. Ay! She just came into our kitchen—we were living together then—plopped down a bag of flour and started to make tortillas. All she ever said about our being together from then until the morning she died was "you think you're so great? You're not the first two people to fall in love."[20]

The grandmother's initial reaction—shame, mourning, penance—gives way to a defiant acceptance, a challenge to her *two* granddaughters not to think themselves so special. The fact that the grandmother starts making tortillas signifies her acceptance of their relationship through the preparation of food, but it is also likely that Carrillo is punning: The grandmother is making tortillas in the house of las tortilleras.[21]

At the same time that Carrillo emphasizes the significance of one's family of origin, she also shows how lesbian couples, while silently acknowledged, may be erased. María tries to avoid discussing how she, as a lesbian and thus as Elisa's illegitimate partner, was erased from the discourse of family following Elisa's death. "At her funeral, everyone was crying except me. They brought lots of food and flowers, the kind she hated, the kind she always said looked too sad—like little kids who can't even run around without getting in trouble." Almost as an afterthought, María adds, "Oh, and I didn't get to ride in the limo with the 'immediate family' either—that's what González, the funeral man, called her brothers and her papa. Didn't bother me none. I was the one who loved her and I was proud of it."[22] In a sense, María is refusing to accept the official discourse: Elisa Alvarado, *soltera,* was survived by her father and brothers.[23] As María's narrative so eloquently demonstrates, the official discourse tells as much about Elisa Alvarado's life as the *Albuquerque Journal* tells about the apparition of God.

This story consistently marks out Chicana lesbian history in relation to the erasure of Mexican history by Anglo American political and social structures and in relation to the erasure of lesbians through the Mexican discourse of "legitimate" family. Carrillo emphasizes the raced and gendered position of her lesbian characters, thus pointing out how the two discourses that assign them subordinate positions have combined to erase Chicana lesbians from history.

With Her Machete in Her Hand

Gloria Anzaldúa's "La historia de una marimacho" (The *marimacha*'s tale) was first published in a special issue of the journal *Third Woman*.[24] Edited by Norma Alarcón, Ana Castillo, and Cherríe Moraga, the special issue was initially intended to focus on Chicana lesbians but was later broadened to the sexualities of all Latinas. *Third Woman,* published from 1981 to 1989, promoted critical and creative writing by Chicanas, Latinas, and other women of color. In 1989, the journal announced its transition to a book series before ceasing production entirely.[25] In 1993, the special volume was re-issued as an anthology entitled *The Sexuality of Latinas*. Of the more than one hundred short stories, plays, and novels by or about Chicana lesbians that I have studied in my research, "La historia de una marimacho" is one of only two texts written entirely in Spanish—in Anzaldúa's case, the regional Spanish of south Texas.[26]

Marimacha is a slang term for lesbian that is roughly equivalent to "bull-dagger." As Angela García suggests, the term unites two words that are intended to be mutually exclusive: María (woman) and macho (masculine).[27] Although it is usually written as *marimacha*, with a feminine ending, Anzaldúa uses *marimacho* in the title only, perhaps to emphasize the heroine's masculine identification or to contrast the feminine article *una* with a masculine noun.

In spite of the singular *marimacha* referred to in the title, this is a story of two women, because, as Teresa de Lauretis argues, "it takes two women, not one, to make a lesbian."[28] Neither of the two female protagonists is given a name: They are "I" and "she," the butch and the femme, *la marimacha* and *la chaparrita*, the subject and the object of desire. *La marimacha* pursues *la chaparrita* through the streets and woos her earnestly. They are subject to the gossip of the neighbors. When an old woman spies them kissing in the dark, she runs off crying, "*Ave María Purísima*," as if she had seen the devil himself.

In the course of the story, the father of *la chaparrita* learns that she has been seen with *la marimacha* and confines her to the house. The two women run off to the north, with *la marimacha* passing as a man. Although they make several stops, they are always driven farther when the townspeople begin to look at them funny. At long last, they find a place they can call their own. One day, when *la marimacha* arrives home, she finds *la chaparrita*'s father in the kitchen. He has struck *la chaparrita* in the face, and she is on the floor, tears and blood streaming down her cheeks. The daughter tells her father that he must accept the relationship. With her machete, *la marimacha* cuts off the fingers of the hand that struck *la chaparrita* and the ear that would not listen to her cries. The father repents and comes to live with the two women. The story ends with what appears to be the final verses of a *corrido*, telling of the valor of the *marimacha* and the lesson she has taught the local machos:

> La mujermacho alzó su machete
> Allá en San Juan Puñacuato.
> Los dedos de don Rafo saltaron
> Y se le escurrió su coraje.
> De la gente se oye decir
> Que ya un hombre no vale nada
> y hasta los huevos le estorban
> a los machos de San Juan Puñacuato.[29]

When the father ultimately joins the two women in their life, there is no sense that he has left his country behind. *La chaparrita*, expressing her initial fears about running away with *la marimacha*, asks, "¿Qué vamos hacer dos mujeres, sin dinero, sin amigos, sin tierra?"[30] Yet Anzaldúa is not implying that lesbians are "women without a country."[31]

I read Anzaldúa as deliberately refuting that notion that lesbians share a "more profound nationality of their lesbianism"—a notion that Bertha Harris develops in her article on lesbian society of Paris's Left Bank in the 1920s, drawing from Virginia Woolf's statement, "As a woman I have no country."[32] Harris recalls her twenty-one-year-old self following Djuna Barnes through the streets of New York, cherishing the fantasy that Barnes "would stop and take my hand . . . and then tell me how it was to be a dyke in Paris, in the Twenties," a world into which the young Harris believed she ought to have been born.[33] She read Colette and Gertrude Stein as "the books of my ancestors," even as she recognized the disparities between her life and theirs:

> But I was poor and grubby; naive, emotional, sweaty with lower-class need. I was short and peasantmade—and my ancestors, I learned, as I read my censored history, were rich or nearly rich; sophisticated, cool; longlimbed; and our family bloodline, the common identity among us, would always be nothing more, nothing less, than our common need for the world of consequence: will always be my acknowledgment of these women, despite all material difference between us, as my first ancestors, the women my father stole me from.[34]

For Harris, the disjuncture between her self as lesbian and her self as "poor and grubby . . . lower-class . . . peasantmade" are competing identities between the name of the lesbian (Djuna Barnes) and the name of the father. The choice between the two is quite clear. "They were," says Harris, "American and English and French but mostly American but with the father's nationality in effect wiped out by the more profound nationality of their lesbianism."[35] Their lesbianism was like their aristocracy and their expatriate circle: All three represented beauty and distance from the mundane world.

I believe that Anzaldúa is writing a very different kind of lesbian history, one that challenges the idea that "to be lesbian was at its finest to be also upperclass."[36] "La historia de una marimacho" is in fact a "peasantmade" history, with sweat and manual labor. Anzaldúa creates a tradition in which lesbianism is not separate from race, class, and location, a tradition in which the young Harris might have found both her working-class self and her lesbian self represented.

For Anzaldúa, land represents not merely *la tierra patria*, the father's land and the father's name, but the actual means by which to earn a living. At the same time, the emphasis on "*sin tierra*" resonates with Chicana/o history of not possessing their "lost land." In the words of the poet Jimmy Santiago Baca, Chicanas and Chicanos are "Immigrants in Our Own Land."[37] As Chicana/o historians (and, indeed, the Chicano Movement) have consistently argued, "We didn't cross the border. The border crossed us."

This is a border story in the sense that it is situated in "the greater border region": a geographical region to both the north and the south of what is now the Mexico–U.S. border. Anzaldúa's story, however, might more accurately be considered a story of the Mexican frontier—alluding to a historical past, before Mexicans felt the northern encroachment of Anglo settlers. When *la chaparrita* and *la marimacha* are met with *"malas caras"* (dirty looks) from the people they encounter, they simply continue to head farther north—not to the United States but to an area less settled. In fact, in this story there is a sense that the two woman can continue north through unsettled lands until they find some place they can call their own.[38]

Thus, Anzaldúa establishes a popular history of Queer Tejanas. It is precisely for this reason that the story ends with a *corrido:* The *corrido* is a popular form of history that contests the official Anglo account of Texas. Anzaldúa deliberately links lesbian history to a butch–femme economy of desire. In spite of the *marimacha's* assumption of masculine power within the tale, the *chaparrita* is imbued with her own subjectivity. While the narrator suggests that the father repents either because of her chastisement or because he does not want to lose his daughter, I would argue that it is actually the *chaparrita* character who persuades him to accept the relationship. She declares: "No cambiaré por oro o plata ni un segundo de mi vida con ella."[39] Her final argument is that "nuestro cariño es tan fuerte, papi, como el tuyo pa' mamá. Ningún amor es corriente, ni el de una mujer pa' otra."[40] This is the appeal that the father is unable to refuse.

Indeed, the text highlights the subject position of *la chaparrita*, the femme, showing her fears and her courage. Initially, *la chaparrita* is afraid to leave home. She says to her lover, "Pa' ti la vida es tu lucha. . . . Pero . . . yo soy miedosa."[41] When her partner asks whether she wishes to return home, because "nuestra vida no va ser fácil,"[42] *la chaparrita* is offended and responds, "La vida amenaza a todos, rico o pobre, hombre o mujer."[43] When *la marimacha* persists, "pero amenaza más a la mujer, y más todavía a las mujeres como nosotras,"[44] *la chaparrita* ends the conversation and continues the journey upriver.

To some extent, the *corrido* ending shifts from the first person to the third person and minimizes the complexity of the two women's relationship. Instead, like the *corrido* form itself, the ending valorizes the "masculinist" exploits of the *marimacha* in taming the father and shaming the machos. In one sense, Anzaldúa's *corrido* constitutes a meta-critique of Américo Paredes, whose 1959 study, *With His Pistol in His Hand,* similarly minimizes the complexity of Texas–Mexican border culture in favor of the masculine hero while elevating the *corrido,* a narrative form that renders women not as participants in Mexican–American history but as its audience.[45]

The time period of "La historia de una marimacho" is unclear. According to Paredes, the *corrido* was popular from roughly 1830 to 1920, especially during and after the Mexican revolution. The fact that the women do not cross a border indicates that the story takes place before 1920, but the absence of references to Anglo settlers in the region suggests a much earlier setting. The story could take place in 1820, 1720, or 1620—in any of a variety of periods in the history of what is now northern Mexico and the Southwestern United States.

Tey Diana Rebolledo describes the story as "Anzaldúa's creation of a lesbian Chicana mythos."[46] Although Rebolledo does not explain the sense in which she is using "mythos," it appears that she is arguing that the story becomes part of the mythology of Chicana lesbians—who we are, where we come from. I would argue further that the story creates a history. Indeed, I believe that Anzaldúa writes this story in Spanish precisely so that it may serve the reader as a "historical" text, as an artifact of Chicana lesbians who went before us. "La historia de una marimacho" functions like Paredes's study to produce a history of Chicanos—or, in this case, Chicana lesbians—in the greater border region. The reader can imagine that this is a long-lost document, recently discovered, precisely because Spanish was the language of the Mexican frontier. By writing in Spanish, Anzaldúa creates new "ancestors" for contemporary Chicana lesbians, a new "tradition" in this story and *corrido* that can be claimed as Chicana lesbian heritage.

Odd Girls of the Rio Grande Valley

Since 1981, Rocky Gámez has written three short stories detailing the adventures of Gloria, a working-class Tejana butch from the greater border region. They are "From *The Gloria Stories*" (1981), "A Baby for Adela" (1988), and "A Matter of Fact" (1991). The first story in the series has been reprinted no fewer than four times since its original publication in the now defunct journal *Conditions*.[48] Its popularity and success is due to Gámez's humorous characterization of Gloria as a Chicana butch from the lower Rio Grande valley of Texas, and of her narrator, Rocky, who represents Gloria without being seduced by her. Like "María Littlebear," the Gloria stories depict the lives of working-class Chicanas within Chicano communities, claiming a queer Chicana heritage.

Although I focus my discussion on the second of the tales, "A Baby for Adela," I will place it context by giving a brief description of the first story, titled simply "From *The Gloria Stories*." It is set in the fall of 1969, and the narrator, Rocky, has gone away to college. Through letters, she receives news from home, including accounts of the scandalous behavior of her friend Gloria, who has been going around dressed as a man and accompanied by loose women. While Rocky recovers from an automobile accident, she receives a letter from Gloria herself, announcing that she has finally met a nice girl, Rosita, and they have shared wedding vows in a church (albeit silently during a heterosexual wedding ceremony). When Rocky returns home to the valley, she is greeted by a strutting Gloria, who announces that she has successfully impregnated her girlfriend, because "every time I do you-know-what, I come just like a man."[48] With the aid of her college biology text, Rocky explains to Gloria that this just is not possible, and Gloria makes the obvious connection that Rosita has been unfaithful. Gloria, who has attempted to be a good husband and father, has instead ended up the *cabrón*, the cuckold, betrayed by her woman. The story ends abruptly, with a devastated Gloria leaving Rocky on the curb as she drives home to settle things with Rosita.

This is the background for "A Baby for Adela." Set in December 1970, it is the tale of Gloria's second attempt at marriage and fatherhood. Gloria has once again found herself a "real nice" woman, Adela, and they are making a home together. Visiting the happy couple in Gloria's little house, Rocky notes:

> There were bookshelves lining the walls, with real books on them . . . my entire collection of lesbian literature that I had not wanted my family to know I read: *Odd Girl Out, Shadow Of A Woman, Beebo Brinker, Journey To A Woman, The Price Of Salt, The Well Of Loneliness, Carol In A Thousand Cities, We, Too, Must Love,* all of them![49]

This is the first time in any of the stories that Rocky is marked as queer. The books are mainly lesbian pulp fiction of the late 1950s and early 1960s.

The message of the lesbian books is somewhat deflected by the new book on the shelves: *How to Bring Up Your Baby.* Once again, it seems, Gloria is looking forward to "the pattering of tiny feet on the brand new rug. . . . I'm going to get Adela pregnant. . . . This time, I'm really going to get her pregnant. I have the ammunition all ready to go."[50] She has contracted with a local gay Chicano to pay him for his sperm, which she plans to introduce to Adela's ready womb. Rocky constantly challenges Gloria on what she sees as Gloria's sick obsession with getting her women pregnant. Gloria replies that she is merely expressing the natural human urge to procreate. She knows it is possible because one of the lesbian novels depicts artificial insemination, and, of course, Rocky's own father has artificially inseminated his cows. Rocky argues that the process is bound to be much more difficult than Gloria has assumed. And so, in fact, it proves, though for reasons neither woman can foresee.

Gloria drives to a nearby town to introduce Rocky to her selected sperm donor. Moctezuma is a gay Chicano who works as a waiter at his aunt's restaurant. The aunt caters to gays and lesbians as long as they are not too overt, so Gloria dons purple lipstick before entering the establishment. Indeed, her style has changed noticeably in the past six months:

> She even looked a little more feminine than her usual butchy self. She was wearing a brown wool cardigan sweater, women's chino pants, and penny loafers. Her hair was a little longer over the ears. Did I like her new look?
>
> "Oh yes, Gloria," I replied. "but you don't look like Sal Mineo anymore. You look like Toña la Negra."
>
> "Helps me sell more brooms though," she chuckled. "At least the housewives won't bolt their doors on me when they see me stomping up their driveway with my load of brooms."[51]

On the arranged evening—Christmas Eve—Rocky and Gloria go driving in Gloria's old truck on the bumpy back roads of south Texas. Moctezuma does not meet them at the appointed time. After a great deal of pressure, his aunt tells them how to get to his house in El Granjeno. Rocky and Gloria arrive to find a repentant Moctezuma regretting his bargain, trying to reconcile his sexuality and his religion and tapping out a suicide note on his typewriter. Gloria, however, has neither time nor patience for Moctezuma's crisis. While Rocky waits outside, Gloria threatens the young man with physical violence. When Gloria emerges from the house, she has a spoonful of semen, which, she mutters to Rocky, was all she could scrape off the sheets.

And yet their delivery to Adela is destined never to occur. Gloria drives too fast on the pothole-ridden roads, attempting to get Rocky home in time to take her mother to midnight mass. They are signaled by a police car to slow down, and when Gloria attempts to outrun it, she drives the truck off the road. Rocky loses her grip on the spoon, and the "ammunition" drips from the dash to the floorboard. A very glum Gloria drops Rocky at the church door and goes home to her Adela.

Gámez raises a great many issues in this story, but I am most interested in the relationships among history, identity, and literature. Rocky's reference to "real books on the shelves" is significant, because it implies that Gloria is no great reader of books. Her usual reading materials consist of magazines such as *True Confessions*, and perhaps *fotonovelas*. The books that Rocky describes are all lesbian pulp fiction. Although Radclyffe Hall's *The Well of Loneliness* and Claire Morgan's *The Price of Salt* were both published earlier as literary books, they were reissued in pulp editions during the heyday of pulp fiction.[52] Aldrich's books *Carol in a Thousand Cities* and *We, Too, Must Love* were sensational nonfiction, journalistic pulp,[53] an insider's look at the lurid lives of lesbians. The majority of the other titles are Ann Bannon novels focusing on white women in New York City.

In "Pulp Passions," Yvonne Keller discusses the significance of lesbian pulp fiction in terms of representations of lesbians for a mainstream audience but, more important, in the ways that lesbian readers were "hungry for their own lives in literature."[54] She describes the books listed earlier as the most "lesbian-positive" of the genre, written mainly by women and lesbians rather than—as was more often the case—by men using feminine pseudonyms. If we examine Gámez's Gloria stories as a response to this pulp fiction, we see the disparity between Greenwich Village and the Rio Grande valley. In the former, as depicted in *Women in the Shadows*, the lesbian Laura is inseminated by her wealthy gay male friend Jack, while in the latter, where farmers routinely inseminate cattle, Gloria's attempts to inseminate Adela are foiled by church and state.

Gámez also parodies the powerful and benevolent white gay man of Bannon's novels in the character of Moctezuma, a gay Chicano albino who performs Ravel's Bolero on the clarinet at his aunt's restaurant, The Magic Cocina. Moctezuma is clearly not a player in the patriarchy, but a pawn. His "male privilege" is negligible. A drunk patron derides him as "*¡Maricón! ¡Pinche joto!*" while his priest convinces him that suicide would be less sinful than a homosexual life.

Keller argues that pulp fiction was expected to depict a racist and homophobic viewpoint. In a variety of complicated ways, lesbians read these books against the grain to find positive representations of lesbians. Gámez is very clearly marking the racism and exclusion practiced both in the representation of the lesbian pulps and in the public spaces of queer life.[55] Duffy's bar in McAllen, Texas, is "a redneck bar but catered to jotos if they weren't too overtly nelly. A few old gringa dykes that passed as rodeo cowgirls went in to play pool regularly, but they were too prejudiced to talk to Mexicans, so it was best to ignore them."[56]

Further, Gloria, who has left her job at the slaughterhouse for a new profession selling brooms door-to-door, is herself constructing community. Although there are no bars or support groups specifically for Chicana/o queers, Gloria is meeting *jotos* and tortilleras "from Rio Grande City to Brownsville" in Falfurriás, San Juan, and El Granjeno, and is able to "represent" those people to Rocky: "There were thousands like [Moctezuma] all over the Valley, but they were all closeted because of the shitty attitude of the people of the area. Anglos and Mexicans were alike in their intolerance of gays. But she had met zillions of them on her broom-selling route."[57] This is an awakening for Rocky, because, "In the Valley, overt homosexuals were as rare as wings on donkeys," and she has never known any other queers besides Gloria.[58]

Although Rocky is able to find her queerness reflected in the lesbian pulps, they are clearly inadequate to represent the lives of queer Chicanas in the valley. The character Rocky is not able to find either herself or Gloria in these books, but the author Gámez succeeds in writing Chicana lesbian history in true pulp-fiction style.

Together, these three stories speak to a variety of popular traditions in creating Chicana lesbian history. Carrillo contrasts Nuevomejicano memory with official history as represented through the *Albuquerque Journal,* then similarly contrasts the "official" (patriarchal) family with lesbian familia. Anzaldúa uses regional Spanish, high drama, humor, and the *corrido* to tell "la historia de una marimacha." Gámez, in her picaresque adventures of Gloria, uses pulp fiction as a signifier of lesbianism while critiquing the racial exclusivity of the books and of lesbian communities. At the same time, Gloria, as the traveling salesman, herself makes a community, discovering the other queers all over the south valley and representing them to Rocky, while the author represents them to her readers.

Through their portrayal of Chicana lesbians, these authors provide a revisionary reading of Ramón Saldívar's argument that, "in Chicano narrative, ... history ... is the subtext which must be recovered from the oblivion to which American social and literary history have consigned it. Our literary texts will show how aesthetic and cultural productions often turn out to be the ideological rewriting of that banished history."[59] We now see that the banished history that is being rewritten is not merely that of the Mexican in the American West, but also that of the Chicana lesbian in Chicano communities.

In the 1980s, the first wave of Chicana lesbian writers used fiction to write histories of the unnamable: lesbians in Chicano communities. Just as many other Chicana/o writers have used their fiction to show the ways in which the history of Mexicans in the United States have been systematically erased from the "history of the American West," Chicana lesbian writers used the *corrido,* oral history, and pulp fiction to represent Chicano history *as* queer, and to attempt to show Chicana lesbians in their sexed and raced positions in the U.S. Southwest. These tales, which on the surface appear quite simple, are actually playing on the notion of *lo popular,* to create popular histories, histories of the people, to argue that *marimachas, maricones,* and tortilleras are part of Chicana culture and history.

Notes

Author's note: My title situates my work within the genealogies of Chicana and Latina Lesbian writing. I call these histories "shameless"—regardless of whether they deal with explicit sexuality—because telling these stories is not only a political act but one that marks the writer as *una sinvergüenza,* a woman who knows no shame. "Shameless" is also inspired by the editorial work of tatiana de la tierra, whose most recent project, an anthology of Latina lesbian erotica, is entitled *Las Sinvergüenzas.* De la tierra has played an important role in the publication and circulation of Latina lesbian writing. From 1991 to 1994 she was on the editorial board of *Esto no tiene nombre,* a Latina lesbian magazine out of Miami. On her own, de la tierra edited *conMoción* from 1995 to 1996. Both of these *revistas* published new writings by Latina lesbians, many of whom had never before appeared in print. At the same time, they included essays by, interviews with, and reviews of the works of more established writers, such as Cherríe Moraga, Gloria Anzaldúa, Luz María Umpierre, Achy Obejas, and Terri de la Peña.

"Talking Race, Talking Sex" syntactically invokes Gloria Anzaldúa's 1990 anthology *Haciendo Caras: Making Face, Making Soul.* More specifically, however, it marks the ways in which Chicana lesbian fictions that choose a historical setting simultaneously depict the race and class positions of Chicanas/os in the Southwest and articulate lesbian subjectivities.

Epigraph: Emma Pérez, *The Decolonial Imaginary: Writing Chicanas into History,* ed. Teresa de Lauretis (Bloomington: Indiana University Press, 1999), 27.

1. For an extended bibliography of these works, see Catrióna Rueda Esquibel, "A Bibliography of Queer Chicana Fictions," available online at <http://womens-studies.ohio-state.edu/jotas/index.html> (2002).

2. Deena González, *Refusing the Favor: The Spanish–Mexican Women of Santa Fe, 1820–1880* (Oxford: Oxford University Press, 2000), 7.

3. Jo Carrillo, "María Littlebear," in *Lesbian Fiction,* ed. Elly Bulkin (Watertown, Mass.: Persephone Press, 1982); Gloria Anzaldúa, "La historia de una marimacho," *Third Woman* 4 (1989): 64–68; Rocky Gámez, "A Baby for Adela," in *Politics of the Heart: A Lesbian Parenting Anthology,* ed. Sandra Pollack and Jeanne Vaughn (Ithaca, N.Y.: Firebrand Books, 1988), 100–110.

4. See Esquibel, "Memories of Girlhood: Chicana Lesbian Fictions," *Signs* 23, no. 3 (1998): 644–81, for discussion of the theme of girlhood friendships.

5. Genaro M. Padilla, *My History, Not Yours: The Formation of Mexican American Autobiography,* Wisconsin Studies in American Autobiography (Madison: University of Wisconsin Press, 1993).

6. Ibid., 4.

7. Ibid., 5.

8. Ibid., 3.

9. Antonia Castañeda, "Memory, Language and Voice of Mestiza Women on the Northern Frontier," Clara Lomas, "The Articulation of Gender in the Mexican Borderlands," and Rosaura Sánchez, "Nineteenth-Century Californio Narratives," all in *Recovering the U.S. Hispanic Literary Heritage,* ed. Ramon Gutierrez and Genaro Padilla (Houston: Arte Público Press, 1993), 265–78, 293–308, 279–92, respectively.

10. Alicia Gaspar de Alba and Aurora Levins Morales have made convincing arguments to recognize Sor Juana Inés de la Cruz and La Monja Alférez (the lieutenant nun) Catalina de Erauso as Chicana lesbians. See Alicia Gaspar de Alba, "The Politics of Location of the Tenth Muse of America: Interview with Sor Juana Inés de la Cruz," in *Living Chicana Theory,* ed. Carla Trujillo (Berkeley, Calif.: Third Woman Press, 1988), 136–65, and idem, *Sor Juana's Second Dream* (Albuquerque: University of New Mexico Press, 1999). See also Aurora Levins Morales, *Remedios: Stories of Earth and Iron from the History of Puertorriqueñas* (Boston: Beacon Press, 1988).

11. Or perhaps queer novels about historical Chicanas. See Graciela Limón, *The Day of the Moon* (Houston: Arte Público, 1999); and Gaspar de Alba, *Sor Juana's Second Dream.* The novels

by Amelia Montes and Emma Pérez are still in progress. Montes's "As If in a Photographic Instance" moves back and forth in time between a contemporary Chicana scholar and object of her study, a nineteenth-century Californiana; Pérez's "Forgetting the Alamo, or Blood Memory" includes the "discovery" of letters, diaries, and other ephemera documenting Chicana lesbian life in post-annexation Texas in 1848.

12. Persephone Press was the original publisher of *This Bridge Called My Back: Writings by Radical Women of Color.* According to Moraga and Anzaldúa, the first edition of *This Bridge* "had already gone out of print" when the press when out of business. It would be safe to assume that Bulkin's anthology likewise was out of print even before 1983. See Cherríe Moraga and Gloria Anzaldúa, "Publishing Note to the Second Edition," *This Bridge Called My Back: Writings by Radical Women of Color* (New York: Kitchen Table/Women of Color Press, 1983), unnumbered page between iii and viii.

13. Jo Carrillo, "And When You Leave, Take Your Pictures with You," in ibid., 63–64.

14. Padilla, *My History,* 28.

15. Carrillo, "María Littlebear," 17. The implication in "Standing around just looking at the Holman wall," of course, is that they were not working.

16. Ibid., 19–20.

17. Ibid., 20.

18. Ibid.

19. In "The Widowed Women of Santa Fe," González argues that Hispanic cultures have a larger percentage of single women than do Anglo societies, and that such women are more likely to be incorporated into family groups: Deena González, "The Widowed Women of Santa Fe: Assessments on the Lives of an Unmarried Population, 1850–80," in *Unequal Sisters,* ed. E. C. DuBois and V. L. Ruíz (New York: Routledge, 1990), 34–50.

20. Carrillo, "María Littlebear," 19.

21. "Tortillera" (tortilla maker) is a slang term for lesbian. (When you make tortillas, you slap your hands together back and forth. This can be read as a representation of tribadism.)

22. Carrillo, "María Littlebear," 22.

23. Elsewhere, I have demonstrated how the "official discourse" of an obituary can erase a lesbian relationship: See Esquibel, "Memories of Girlhood." Similarly, the pseudonymous GVR's short story "Se le murió" (*Esto no tiene nombre* 2, no. 1 [1992]: 18) demonstrates that lesbian relationships are glossed over at the death of one partner, precisely when the other partner is most in need of support.

24. Anzaldúa uses "*marimacho*" in the title. Current usage is "*marimacha,*" which I use when referring to the butch character.

25. Norma Alarcón's Third Woman Press now publishes a Mujer Latina series, the latest volume of which is Trujillo's anthology *Living Chicana Theory.*

26. See Gloria Anzaldúa, "La historia de una marimacho," in *The Sexuality of Latinas,* ed. Norma Alarcón, Ana Castillo, and Cherríe Moraga (Berkeley, Calif.: Third Woman Press, 1989). The other is Adela Alonso's short story "Virgencita, danos chance," *Third Woman* 4 (1989): 43–46.

27. In García's short story "Yo Yo," the narrator chooses an outfit to visit her grandmother. "I've picked through [the clothes]a dozen times, dressing and undressing, studying myself in the mirror. With each try I see her, Marimacha. That's what I was called growing up. Marimacha: Macho María": Angela García, "Yo Yo," in *Beyond Definition: New Writing from Gay and Lesbian San Francisco,* ed. M. Blackman and T. Healey (San Francisco: Manic D Press, 1994), 39–41.

28. Teresa de Lauretis, *The Practice of Love* (Bloomington: Indiana University Press, 1994), 235n.

29. Anzaldúa, "La historia de una marimacho," 68.

> The macha raised up her machete
> That day in San Juan Puñacuato.
> Don Rafo's fingers fell to the ground
> And his courage ran to the hills.
>
> Today you can still hear it said
> By the people of San Juan Puñacuato
> That a man is not worth a damn
> And huevos do not make the macho.

30. "What can we do, two women, without money, without friends, without land?": Anzaldúa, "La historia de una marimacho," 65. The translations are mine.

31. My argument here is limited to "La historia de una marimacho." In another context, Anzaldúa asserts, "As a mestiza I have no country, my homeland cast me out; yet all countries are mine because I am every woman's sister or potential lover. As a lesbian I have no race, my own people disclaim me; but I am all races because there is the queer of me in all races": see Gloria Anzaldúa, *Borderlands/La Frontera: The New Mestiza*, 2nd ed. (San Francisco: Aunt Lute Books, 1999), 102.

32. Virginia Woolf, *Three Guineas* (London: Hogarth Press, 1938), 197.

33. Bertha Harris, "The More Profound Nationality of Their Lesbianism: Lesbian Society in Paris in the 1920s," in *Amazon Expedition,* ed. P. Birkby, B. Harris, J. Johnston, E. Newton, and J. O'Wyatt (Albion, Calif.: Times Change Press, 1973), 77–88.

34. Ibid., 78–79.

35. Ibid., 79.

36. Ibid.

37. See John R. Chávez, *The Lost Land: The Chicano Image of the Southwest* (Albuquerque: University of New Mexico Press, 1984); Jimmy Santiago Baca, *Immigrants in Our Own Land and Selected Early Poems* (New York: New Directions, 1990), 12.

38. This has colonialist implications, as well. For instance, describing the father after he is maimed, the *marimacha* says, "Parecía indio con su paño doblado alrededor de la cabeza tapando el agüjero que más antes fue su oreja" (The father, like the Indian men, is emasculated): Anzaldúa, "La historia de una marimacho," 67.

39. "I would not trade one second of my life with her, not for gold or silver": ibid., 67.

40. "Our love is strong, papi, just like yours for mama. No love is cheap, not even the love of one woman for another": ibid.

41. "For you life is a struggle.... But ... I am fearful": ibid., 65.

42. "Our life is not going to be easy": ibid., 66.

43. "Life is dangerous to all, rich or poor, man or woman.] Ibid.

44. "Yes, but it's more of a danger for women, and most of all to women like us": ibid.

45. Américo Paredes, *"With His Pistol in His Hand": A Border Ballad and Its Hero* (Austin: University of Texas Press, 1958).

46. Tey Diana Rebolledo, *Women Singing in the Snow: A Cultural Analysis of Chicana Literature* (Tucson: University of Arizona Press, 1995), 201.

47. See Alma Gómez, Cherríe Moraga, and Mariana Romo-Carmona, eds., *Cuentos: Stories by Latinas* (New York: Kitchen Table/Women of Color Press, 1983); Angela Carter, ed., *Wayward Girls and Wicked Women: An Anthology of Stories* (New York: Penguin, 1989) (first published by Virago); Naomi Holoch and Joan Nestle, eds., *Women on Women: An Anthology of American Lesbian Short Fiction* (New York: Plume Holoch and Nestle, 1990); and Joan Nestle, ed., *The Persistent Desire: A Femme–Butch Reader* (Boston: Alyson, 1992).

48. Rocky Gámez, "From *The Gloria Stories,*" *Conditions* 7 (1981): 139–40.

49. Gámez, "A Baby for Adela," 102. Neither Yvonne Keller nor the librarians at the lesbian pulp-fiction archives at Duke University have been able to identify the title *Shadow of a Woman*. It may be a transposition of Bannon's *Women in the Shadows* (1959; repr. Tallahassee, Fla.: Naiad Press 1983), or, as Keller has suggested, it may refer to a different pulp novel that we are unable to identify precisely because lesbian pulp fiction, in spite of its immense popularity, was an illegitimate form of discourse. The other texts include Radclyffe Hall's classic *The Well of Loneliness* (1928; repr. New York: Avon, 1981). The rest are lesbian pulp-fiction texts from the 1950s and '60s: Ann Bannon, *Odd Girl Out* (1957; repr. Tallahassee, Fla.: Naiad Press, 1983); idem, *Journey to Woman* (1960; repr. Tallahassee, Fla.: Naiad Press, 1983); idem, *Beebo Brinker* (1962; repr. Tallahassee, Fla.: Naiad Press, 1983); Claire Morgan (Patricia Highsmith), *The Price of Salt* (1952; repr. Tallahassee, Fla.: Naiad Press, 1984); Ann Aldrich (Marijane Meaker), *We, Too, Must Love* (Greenwich, Conn.: Fawcett Gold Medal, 1960); and idem, *Carol in a Thousand Cities* (Greenwich, Conn.: Fawcett Gold Medal, 1962).

50. Gámez, "A Baby for Adela," 102.

51. Ibid., 101. For a discussion of the trend in the late 1960s and early '70s to make butch lesbians more assimilable, see Sue-Ellen Case, "Towards a Butch–Femme Aesthetic," in *Making a Spectacle: Feminist Essays on Contemporary Women's Theatre*, ed. Linda Hart (Ann Arbor: University of Michigan Press, 1989). In particular, Case argues that the lesbian organization Daughters of Bilitis actively discouraged butch identity. In their history of the Daughters of Bilitis, Del Martin and Philips Lyon give a decidedly ageist and classist dismissal of butch–femme roles. "The minority of Lesbians who still cling to the traditional male–female or husband–wife pattern in their partnerships are more than likely old-timers, gay bar habituées or working class women. The old order changeth, however, and . . . the number of Lesbians involved in butch–femme roles diminishes": See Del Martin, and Phyllis Lyon, *Lesbian/Woman* (1972; repr. Volcano, Calif.: Volcano Press, 1991), 77.

52. Keller describes these reprints as "Re-vamped Pulps": Yvonne C. Keller, "Pulp Passions: Lesbian Popular Fiction, 1950–1965" (Ph.D. diss., History of Consciousness, University of California, Santa Cruz, 1997), 44.

53. I rely here on the classification in Keller, "Pulp Passions," 46.

54. "I read every one of these mass-market paperbacks I could get my hands on, always hungry for my life in literature": Lee Lynch, "Cruising the Libraries," in *Lesbian Texts and Contexts*, ed. Karla Jay and Joanne Glasgow (New York: New York University Press, 1990), 39–48, as quoted in Keller, "Pulp Passions," 1.

55. Carla F. Scott discusses the portrayal of racism in Greenwich Village in Audre Lorde's *Zami*. Scott examines the ways in which the character Audre recognizes and names the manifestations of racism and exclusion in carding practices at the girl bars, which her white friends simply do not see. When Audre persists, the other women attempt to erase the specificity of racism toward blacks by invoking a narrative of "all lesbians are discriminated against": Carla F. Scott, "The Hottentot Effect: The Crisis of Black Lesbian Representation" (Ph.D. qualifying essay, History of Consciousness, University of California, Santa Cruz, 1993).

56. Gámez, "A Baby for Adela," 102

57. Ibid., 101, 105.

58. Ibid., 105, 102. Rocky does not include Rosita Vargas—or, for that matter, Adela—in her reckoning.

59. Ramon Saldívar, *Chicano Narrative: The Dialectics of Difference* (Madison: University of Wisconsin Press, 1990), 19.

About the Contributors

MARÍA CLAUDIA ANDRÉ is Associate Professor of Hispanic American Literature and Latin American Studies at Hope College, Holland, Michigan. She holds a Ph.D. in Latin American and Spanish literature from the State University of New York, Albany. She is the editor of *Chicanas and Latin American Women Writers: Exploring the Realm of the Kitchen as a Self-Empowering Site* (2001). She is now completing a book titled *Antología de escritoras argentinas contemporáneas* and co-editing *De musas, amigas y amantes: Relaciones e influencias en el discurso femenino/feminista latinoamericano.*

JANIS BRECKENRIDGE is Spanish Lecturer and a Ph.D. candidate in Spanish Literature at the University of Chicago. She has presented papers at national and international conferences. Her articles, interviews, and reviews have been published in *Revista monográfica/Monographic Review, Romance Languages Annual, Letras femeninas, Ciudad gótica,* and *Feministas unidas.* Her current research focuses on fictionalized accounts of human-rights abuses during Argentina's "dirty war."

REGINA M. BUCCOLA is Assistant Professor in the School of Liberal Studies at Roosevelt University, Chicago. She teaches early modern and contemporary feminist drama and courses in women's studies. She also writes and performs poetry and performance pieces. She holds a Ph.D. in English Literature from the University of Illinois at Chicago.

KARINA LISSETTE CESPEDES is a graduate student in Ethnic Studies at the University of California, Berkeley. Her research and teaching interests include women-of-color feminisms, the work of queer performers of color in the United States, and the sex industry in the Caribbean.

SARA E. COOPER is Assistant Professor of Spanish at California State University, Chico, where she focuses on feminist and queer analysis of contemporary Latin American women and their cultural production. Her current projects include a critical analysis of the queer family and women in Latin American literature; she is also editing *The Ties That Bind: Questioning Family Dynamics and Family Discourse in Hispanic Literature and Film* and a collection of translated short stories by the Cuban writer Mirta Yañez.

CATRIÓNA RUEDA ESQUIBEL is Assistant Professor of Women's Studies at Ohio State University, Columbus. She holds a Ph.D. from the University of California at Santa Cruz. She is completing a book titled *With Her Machete in Her Hand: Reading Chicana Lesbians.* She maintains the Queer Chicana Fictions bibliography at <http://womens-studies.ohio-state.edu/jotas/index.html>; is editing an anthology of late-twentieth-century Chicana lesbian fiction; and is developing the concentration in women of color for the new women's studies Ph.D. at Ohio State University.

SALVADOR C. FERNÁNDEZ is Chair of the Department of Spanish and French Literary Studies at Occidental College, Los Angeles. His areas of scholarship are Mexican and Chicano/a literature. He is the author of *Gustavo Sainz: Postmodernism in the Mexican Novel* (1999). He is working on a book tentatively titled *The Masking of History and Politics in Contemporary Mexican Narrative.*

ELISA A. GARZA lives, writes, and works in Houston, where she also volunteers with and teaches for Nuestra Palabra: Latino Writers Having Our Say. Her poetry has been published in *Bilingual Review/Revista bilingüe, Southwestern American Literature, Thirteenth Moon,* and other journals. Her bilingual chapbook, *Familia,* won the 2001 Portlandia Chapbook Contest; she is also the recipient of a 2002 Literature Fellowship from the Texas Commission on the Arts.

WILFREDO HERNÁNDEZ is Assistant Professor of Spanish at Allegheny College, Meadville, Pennsylvania. His articles have been published in *Chasqui, Dispositio/n, Romance Notes, Revista de Estudios Hispánicos, Inti, Monographic Review/Revista Monográfica,* and other journals. He is working on the book *Cartography of Desire: Representations of Male Homosexuality in Spanish American Literature (1800–2000).*

LAWRENCE LA FOUNTAIN-STOKES is Assistant Professor of Puerto Rican and Hispanic Caribbean Studies and of Spanish and Portuguese at Rutgers, The State University of New Jersey, New Brunswick. He holds a Ph.D. in Latin American literature from Columbia University, and his dissertation, "Culture, Representation, and the Puerto Rican Queer Diaspora," has been accepted for publication. He has served on the board of the City University of New York's Center for Lesbian and Gay Studies.

GEMA PÉREZ-SÁNCHEZ is Assistant Professor of Spanish at the University of Miami. She holds a Ph.D. in romance studies (Spanish literature) from Cornell University. Her research focuses on contemporary Spanish narrative, cultural studies, and queer theory. Her work has appeared in the *University of Michigan Journal of Law Reform, Michigan Journal of Race and Law, Hispamérica, Arizona Journal of Hispanic Cultural Studies,* and *Letras femeninas.* She is working on a book titled *Queer Transitions in Contemporary Spanish Novels and Mass Cultures.*

INMACULADA PERTUSA is Associate Professor of Spanish at the University of Kentucky, Lexington. She holds a Ph.D. from Colorado University, Boulder, and received her licenciatura in journalism from the Universidad Complutense de Madrid. She has published articles on contemporary Hispanic women writers, focusing on issues of gender and the representation of the lesbian experience in this literature.

CHRISTINA SHARPE is Associate Professor of English at Tufts University, Medford, Massachusetts. She has published articles on race and cyberspace in *Signs: Journal of Women and Culture* and on Gayl Jones's *Corregidora* in *African American Performance and Theatre History: A Critical Reader* (2001). She is working on a book-length study titled *Anxious Transmissions: Reading Race, Reading Desire.*

LOURDES TORRES is Director of Latin American and Latino Studies and Associate Professor of Modern Languages at DePaul University, Chicago. She is the author of *Puerto Rican Discourse: A Sociolinguistic Study of a Puerto Rican Suburb* (1997) and the co-editor of *Third World Women and the Politics of Feminism* (1991). She has published articles on Latino/a language and literature in the United States.

SHERRY VELASCO is Associate Professor of Spanish at the University of Kentucky, Lexington. She specializes in early modern Spanish literature, women writers, and feminist cultural theory. Her books include *Demons, Nausea, and Resistance in the Autobiography of Isabel de Jesús (1611–1682)* (1996) and *The Lieutenant Nun: Transgenderism, Lesbian Desire, and Catalina de Erauso* (2000). Her recent articles focus on gender and sexuality in early modern Spain.

NANCY VOSBURG is Professor of Modern Languages and Literatures at Stetson University, DeLand, Florida. She is the author of several articles on twentieth-century Castillian and Catalan women writers and co-editor of *The Garden across the Border: Merce Rodoreda's Fiction* (1994).